For

Cornelia Barber

Who knows how to shop, and why shopping isn't enough

ALSO BY BENJAMIN R. BARBER

Fear's Empire (2003)

The Truth of Power (2001)

A Place for Us (1998)

A Passion for Democracy: American Essays (1998)

Jihad vs. McWorld (1995)

An Aristocracy of Everyone (1992)

The Conquest of Politics (1988)

Strong Democracy (1984)

Marriage Voices (A Novel) (1981)

Liberating Feminism (1975)

The Death of Communal Liberty (1974)

Superman and Common Men (1971)

IN COLLABORATION

The Struggle for Democracy
with Patrick Watson (1989)

The Artist and Political Vision
edited with M. McGrath (1982)

Totalitarianism in Perspective
with C. J. Friedrich and M. Curtis (1969)

Further praise for
Consumed

"In this powerful and disturbing critique, Benjamin Barber takes dead aim at a fundamental fallacy of our time: the equation of capitalism and democracy. No one who cares about the future of our public life can afford to ignore this book."

—Jackson Lears, author of *Fables of Abundance* and
Board of Governors Professor of History, Rutgers University

"Barber, the prophetic author of *Jihad vs. McWorld* (1995), delivers a frightening analysis of the way consumerism is vitiating shoppers in the United States and around the world. Significant work."

—*Kirkus Reviews*, starred review

"As Ben Barber took scholarly pot shots at the relentless efforts of marketers to manipulate the needs and wants of gullible consumers, I applauded. This book is not merely a lament. It is a guide to help us make our way from where we are to where we need to be."

—Bob Kerrey, president, The New School

"An alarming study of the ways in which our child-centric culture is changing media. . . . [Barber's] observations on the dumbing down of the broader culture are quite troubling."   —*Connecticut Post*

"*Consumed* should be required reading for college students and all Americans who are concerned about the corruption of our values. Benjamin R. Barber turns his powerful analytical and research skills toward the infantilization of Americans citizens by the unrestricted market. His message simply must not be ignored if we hope to have a peaceful and sustainable future for our children."   —John de Graaf, coauthor of *Affluenza*

"[Barber's] hypothesis that consumer culture has turned adult citizens into children by catering only to the lowest common denominator rings only too true. . . . This lifelong study of the effects of capitalism and privatization reveals a pervasiveness of branding and homogenization from which there is no turning back." —*Booklist*

"[Barber's] thoughtful, intelligent commentary reveals the tiny, mean-spirited truth behind the facades of seemingly untouchable institutions. . . . It's almost guaranteed that at least one of your preconceived notions . . . will be exploded by the truths in this book, but Barber is never satisfied by laying waste to cultural mores: he always plants newer, stronger ideas in their wake." —*Conscious Choice*

"Barber is at his best when he bluntly defends capitalism for what it is— a profit-dependent construct. . . . The wealth of information included here, juxtaposed with Barber's thoughtful analysis, [is] an enriching experience." —*Tribune* (UK)

"Every page demonstrates how widely Mr. Barber has read and how deeply he has thought things through. He succeeds in getting you to use your head." —*National Post* (Ontario)

"Powerful. . . . In this well-documented book, the author explores how capitalism has evolved from production and its related values of hard work, responsibility, democracy, and citizenship to consumerism (or hyper-consumerism) characterized by inequalities, immaturity, indulgence, and childishness focused on faux needs. . . . [*Consumed* gives] hope for achieving the common good." —*Journal of Family & Consumer Sciences*

"Lucid and readable. . . . Barber offers a comprehensive look at what's wrong with modern capitalism, who's to blame, how we got here and (tentatively) how to fix it. . . . Chapter One, 'Capitalism Triumphant,' should be required reading for anyone with disposable income. . . . Barber's analysis is clear, forceful and spot-on . . . an urgent book about a topic that affects all of us." —*Berkshire Eagle* (Mass.)

CON $UMED

How Markets Corrupt Children,
Infantilize Adults, and Swallow
Citizens Whole

BENJAMIN R. BARBER

W. W. NORTON & COMPANY
NEW YORK · LONDON

For information about permission to reproduce selections from
this book, write to Permissions, W. W. Norton & Company, Inc.
500 Fifth Avenue, New York, NY 10110

Manufacturing by Quebecor Fairfield
Book design by Chris Welch
Production manager: Julia Druskin

Library of Congress Cataloging-in-Publication Data

Barber, Benjamin R., 1939–
Con$umed : how markets corrupt children, infantilize adults,
and swallow citizens whole
Benjamin R. Barber. — 1st ed.
p. cm.
Includes bibliographical references and index.
ISBN-13: 978-0-393-04961-9 (hardcover)
ISBN-10: 0-393-04961-2 (hardcover)
1. Consumption (Economics)—United States. 2. Consumer behavior—United States.
3. Child consumers—United States. 4. Capitalism—United States. 5. Materialism—United
States. 6. Mass society. 7. United States—Social conditions—1980–
I. Title. II. Title: Consumed. III. Title: How markets corrupt children,
infantilize adults, and swallow citizens whole.
HC110.C6B324 2007
339.4'60973—dc22
2006039751

ISBN 978-0-393-33089-2 pbk.

W. W. Norton & Company, Inc., 500 Fifth Avenue, New York, N.Y. 10110
www.wwnorton.com

W. W. Norton & Company Ltd., Castle House, 75/76 Wells Street, London W1T 3QT

3 4 5 6 7 8 9 0

CONTENTS

ACKNOWLEDGMENTS

Consumed has consumed not only a great deal of my time, but the time and energy of a number of hardworking research assistants. I am grateful to Gary Smith and the American Academy of Berlin for the Berlin Prize Fellowship in 2001–2002 that enabled me to inaugurate research on the book. At various times during the four years I have been at work, significant research contributions were made by Josh Goldstein, Tom Ellington, and Rene Paddags at the University of Maryland. Josh Karant, a brilliant young scholar who worked with me at Rutgers University and the University of Maryland, made substantial research contributions, and my intellectual interactions with him sharpened my own scholarly insights. My niece Kate Barber, who works in the magazine industry, has been a constant source of pertinent leads on marketing and advertising stories that strengthened the sections on children's marketing. Kate's father, my brother Willson Barber, did a final proofread even as he assessed the book's arguments with his sharp critical eye.

In the final two years of work, when the book was actually written,

Patrick Inglis acted not only as my primary research assistant, copyeditor, and fact-checker, but as a sounding board for ideas and as a thoughtful critic of my arguments in ways that significantly improved the book. That he did this even as he was conceiving his own doctoral dissertation and also contributing to my Interdependence Day project attests to his discipline and scholarly focus as well as his infinite good will.

My editor at Norton, Alane Mason, with whom I have now worked on three books, offered sound editorial judgments about the architecture and substance of my arguments. She cannot be blamed for remaining flaws, but deserves much credit for the coherence and continuity of the manuscript.

Finally, my youngest daughter, Cornelia, fifteen at the time I completed the book, contributed research, as well as critical judgments about materials I was drawing on, from her own reservoir of experiential knowledge. Her age and her shopping know-how make her a primary target of the marketing industry. Much more importantly, however, it gives me hope for the future: for Cornelia knows how to shop and takes pleasure in it, but she also knows the limits of shopping, and has the will and insight that allow her along with many others in her generation to mount a resistance to a hyperconsumerist society from within. Among her qualities is a thorough understanding of how she is being marketed to and why that marketing is often a violation of rather than a tribute to the freedom and dignity she seeks. For this reason, and because she harbors a beautiful soul that can only delight her parents and everyone else who knows her, I dedicate this book to her—our "Nellie."

—Benjamin R. Barber
New York, January 2007

PART 1

THE BIRTH OF CONSUMERS

Capitalism Triumphant and the Infantilist Ethos

Last of all, that ends [man's] eventful history,
Is second childishness. . . .
——Shakespeare, *As You Like It*, II, vii

When I was a child I spake as a child,
I understood as a child, I thought as a child,
but when I became a man I put away childish things.
——St. Paul in 1 Corinthians 13:11, the New Testament

IN THESE PALTRY times of capitalism's triumph, as we slide into consumer narcissism, Shakespeare's seven ages of man are in danger of being washed away by lifelong puerility. Pop-cultural journalists have used many terms to depict a new species of perennial adolescent: *kidults*, *rejuveniles*, *twixters*, and *adultescents*;[1] around the world Germans speak of "Nesthocker," Italians of "Mammone," Japanese of "Freeter," Indians of "Zippies," and the French of a "Tanguy" syndrome and "puériculture." What they are discerning with their pop neologisms is the consequence of a powerful new cultural ethos, felt more than recognized. It is an ethos of induced childishness: an infantilization that is closely tied to the demands of consumer capitalism in a global market economy.

This infantilist ethos is as potent in shaping the ideology and behaviors of our radical consumerist society today as what Max Weber called the "Protestant ethic" was in shaping the entrepreneurial culture of what was then a productivist early capitalist society. Affiliated with an ideology of privatization, the marketing of brands, and a homogenization of taste, this ethos of infantilization has worked to sustain consumer capitalism, but at the expense of both civility and civilization and at a growing risk to capitalism itself. Although we use the term *democratic capitalism* in a manner that suggests a certain redundancy, the reality is that the two words describe different systems often in tension with one another. Consumerism has set the two entirely asunder.

How much should we care? In an epoch when terrorism stalks the planet, when fear of Jihad is as prevalent as the infringement of liberties to which fear gives rise, when AIDS and tsunamis and war and genocide put democracy at risk in both the developing and the developed world, it may seem self-indulgent to fret about the dangers of hyperconsumerism. When poor children in the developing world are being exploited, starved, prostituted, and impressed into military service, anxiety about the prosperous young in the developed world who may be growing up into consumers too fast, or about adult consumers being dumbed down too easily, can seem parochial, even solipsistic.

Yet as James Madison said long ago, the pathologies of liberty can be as perilous as the pathologies of tyranny; and far more difficult to discern or remedy. Although forces of Jihad continue to struggle violently against the successes of McWorld, and the abuse of children living under poverty remains a far greater problem than the infantilization of adults living under prosperity, modernization appears to be irreversible over the long term. But the fate of citizens under capitalism triumphant is another matter. The victory of consumers is not synonymous with the victory of citizens. McWorld can prevail and liberty can still lose. The diseases of prosperity which are the afflictions of capitalism do not kill outright. They violate no explicit laws of justice. Yet capitalism's success breeds new and dangerous challenges.

Capitalism per se is not the issue. The question is not whether there is an alternative to markets but whether markets can be made to meet the real needs capitalism is designed to serve, whether capitalism can adapt to the sovereignty of democratic authority that alone will allow it to survive.

ONCE UPON A time, capitalism was allied with virtues that also contributed at least marginally to democracy, responsibility, and citizenship.

Today it is allied with vices which—although they serve consumerism—undermine democracy, responsibility, and citizenship. The question then is whether not just democracy but capitalism itself can survive the infantilist ethos upon which it has come to depend. This book, after it diagnoses liberty's market pathologies, offers a qualified yes. What is clear is that either capitalism will replace the infantilist ethos with a democratic ethos, and regain its capacity to promote equality as well as profit, diversity as well as consumption, or infantilization will undo not only democracy but capitalism itself. Much will depend on our capacity to make sense out of infantilization and relate it to the not-so-creative destruction of consumerism's survival logic.

The idea of an "infantilist ethos" is as provocative and controversial as the idea of what Weber called the "Protestant ethic." *Infantilization* is at once both an elusive *and* a confrontational term, a potent metaphor that points on the one hand to the dumbing down of goods and shoppers in a postmodern global economy that seems to produce more goods than people need; and that points, on the other hand, to the targeting of children as consumers in a market where there are never enough shoppers. Once a staple of Freudian psychology focused on the psychopathology of regression, the term *infantilization* has in the last several years become a favorite of worrywart journalists: David Ansen fretting about the "widespread infantilization of pop culture";[2] Leon Wieseltier charging that "Hollywood is significantly responsible for the infantilization of America";[3] Philip Hensher of Britain's *The Independent* sure that the "signs that adult culture is being infantilized are everywhere."[4]

On the potency of adolescent culture, liberals and conservatives agree. Writes Robert J. Samuelson, a moderate liberal: "We live in an age when people increasingly refuse to act their age. The young (or many of them) yearn to be older, while the older (or many of them) yearn to be younger. We have progressively demolished the life cycle's traditional stages, shortening childhood and following it with a few murky passages. Adolescence . . . begins before puberty and, for some, lasts forever. . . . age denial is everywhere."[5] Samuelson is echoed by Joseph Epstein, a moderate conservative: "The whole sweep of advertising, which is to say of market, culture since soon after World War II has been continuously to lower the criteria of youthfulness while extending the possibility for seeming youthful to older and older people."[6] Even conservatives who reject the charge of consumer infantilization recognize its potency. George F. Will thus charges progressive thinkers with advancing the thesis of the "infantilism of the American public" as one more "we are all victims of manipulation" explanation for Bush's victory in the 2004 presidential campaign.[7] Little surprise then that popular magazines such as *Time* ("They Just Won't Grow Up") and *New York Magazine* ("Forever Youngish: Why Nobody Wants to Be an Adult Anymore") worry in major cover articles about America's Peter Pan tendencies.[8]

There is anecdotal evidence everywhere: airport police handing out lollipops to placate irate passengers at inspection points;[9] television news divisions turned over to entertainment executives, *Vanity Fair*–style pop-cultural chatter about "enfantrepreneurs," and the *New York Times Magazine* enthusing about "what kids want in fashion, right from the filly's mouth" on the way to urging thongs on seven-year-olds;[10] the professionalization of high-school sports that turns teen basketball courts into NBA recruiting turf and basketball-player bodies into advertising billboards; adult fiction readers flocking to *Harry Potter* and *The Lord of the Rings* (when they are not abandoning reading altogether); fast-food franchises girdling the world to exploit (among other things) children's restless aversion to grown-up sit-down dining; teen guy games such as World of Warcraft, Grand Theft Auto, and Narc and comic-book films such as *Terminator, Spider-Man, Catwoman,* and *Shrek* dominating the entertainment market; new "educational" television channels such as BabyFirstTV and videos such as "Baby Einstein"; cosmetic surgery and Botox injections promising a fountain of youth to female baby boomers who envy their daughters;[11] sexual performance drugs such as Levitra, Cialis, and Viagra (2002 sales of over $1 billion) becoming staples of equally uncomfortable male boomers trying to smuggle atavistic youth into the age of social security; and businessmen in baseball caps, jeans, and untucked shirts mimicking the studied sloppiness of their unformed kids. Beyond pop culture, the infantilist ethos also dominates: dogmatic judgments of black and white in politics and religion come to displace the nuanced complexities of adult morality, while the marks of perpetual childishness are grafted onto adults who indulge in puerility without pleasure, and indolence without innocence. Hence, the new consumer penchant for age without dignity, dress without formality, sex without reproduction, work without discipline, play without spontaneity, acquisition without purpose, certainty without doubt, life without responsibility, and narcissism into old age and unto death without a hint of wisdom or humility. In the epoch in which we now live, civilization is not an ideal or an aspiration, it is a video game.[12]

These myriad anecdotes tell a story, but infantilization—not second childhood but enduring childishness—is much more than just a mesmeric metaphor. A new cultural ethos is being forged that is intimately associated with global consumerism. Those responsible for manufacturing and merchandizing goods for the global marketplace, those who are actually researching, teaching, and practicing marketing and advertising today, are aiming both to sell to a younger demographic and to imbue older consumers with the tastes of the young.

Marketers and merchandisers are self-consciously chasing a youthful commercial constituency sufficiently padded in its pocketbook to be a very attractive market, yet sufficiently unformed in its tastes as to be vulnerable to conscious corporate manipulation via advertising, marketing, and branding. At the same time, these avatars of consumer capitalism are seeking to encourage adult regression, hoping to rekindle in grown-ups the tastes and habits of children so that they can sell globally the relatively useless cornucopia of games, gadgets, and myriad consumer goods for which there is no discernible "need market" other than the one created by capitalism's own frantic imperative to sell. As child-development scholar Susan Linn puts it in her critical study of what she calls "the hostile takeover of childhood," corporations are vying "more and more aggressively for young consumers" while popular culture "is being smothered by commercial culture relentlessly sold to children who [are valued] for their consumption."[13]

As the population in the developed world ages—the irony of infantilization—the definition of youth simply moves up, with baby boomers in the

United States smuggling it into their senior years. Meanwhile, the young are big spenders way before they are even modest earners: in 2000, there were 31 million American kids between twelve and nineteen already controlling 155 billion consumer dollars.[14] Just four years later, there were 33.5 million kids controlling $169 billion, or roughly $91 per week per kid.[15] The potential youth market is even more impressive elsewhere in the world, where a far greater proportion of the population is under twenty-five, and where new prosperity in nations such as India and China promises a youth market of hundreds of millions in the coming years.

The Economist summed it up a few years ago in its millennium special report: "Once, when you grew up you put away childish things. Today, the 35-year-old Wall Street analyst who zips to work on his push-scooter, listening to Moby on his headphones and carrying annual reports in his backpack, has far more in common with a 20-year-old than he would have done a generation ago."[16] John Tierney notes in the New York Times that Americans are marrying older (since 1970 the median age for marriage has moved up four years, to twenty-five for women and twenty-seven for men), and that thirty is the new twenty, and forty is the new thirty.[17] In Hollywood, where aspiring to stay young is as old as movies and everything is hyperbole, "40 is the new 30 and 50 the new 40, but only, it seems, when that new 40 and 50 have been surgically enhanced. . . . These days, when a 40-plus-year-old actress lands a starring part opposite a 60-plus-year-old actor, such age-appropriate casting seems meaningless because the actress has a face as unlined as a teenage girl's."[18]

As many as four million not-so-young adults between twenty-five and thirty-four still live with their parents in the United States, many of them middle-class. In Britain, the Office for National Statistics revealed the same trend, noting that "57 per cent of men and 38 per cent of women aged 20–24 are now living with their parents." According to the 2005 report, "by their late 20s more than one in five men still live at their parents' homes, twice the rate of women."[19] "Unencumbered by rent—or mortgages or children," these stay-at-homes have "lots of disposable income, which is why marketers have happily focused on adultescents since at least 1996."[20] A physicians' organization called the Society for Adolescent Medicine reports on its website that it is concerned with people ten to twenty-six years old, while the MacArthur Foundation's "Transitions to Adulthood" project puts the transition's end at thirty-four years old.

The irony of infantilization is, of course, that Americans are actually getting older, the median age having moved from twenty-five in the baby-boomer high-water year of 1960 to thirty-five in 2000; by 2050 there will be more in their seventies than in their teens.[21] The same is true with a vengeance for Europe, and for the indigenous populations (immigrants excluded) of the developed world generally. Only in the Third World and in the Third World immigrant communities of the First World is the majority constituted by the young—although they often lack the means to express their puerility in consumption. Likewise, in the United States, more than a third of those who live below the poverty line are children, who like their cousins in the developing world are relatively insulated by their poverty from the consequences, if not the temptations, of consumer marketing.

Once upon a time, in capitalism's more creative and successful period, a *productivist* capitalism prospered by meeting the real needs of real people. Creating a synergy between making money and helping others (the Puritan Protestant formula for entrepreneurial virtue), producers profited by making commodities for the workers they employed—a circle of virtue that, while it involved elements of risk-taking for producers and exploitation of workers, benefited both classes and society at large. Today, however, consumerist capitalism profits only when it can address those whose essential needs have already been satisfied but who have the means to assuage "new" and invented needs—Marx's "imaginary needs." The global majority still has extensive and real natural needs mirroring what psychologists T. Berry Brazelton and Stanley I. Greenspan have called "the irreducible needs of children."[22] But it is without the means to address them, being cut off by the global market's inequality (the "north/south divide") from the investment in capital and jobs that would allow them to become consumers. This is true not just for the global Third World but for the growing Third World within the First World, the poor who live among the wealthy, exposed to the seductions of the consumer marketplace but without the means to participate in it.

Denizens of the developed world from North America and Europe to

Korea and Japan grow older chronologically but younger in their behavior, style, and controlling ethos, with children dominating consumer markets and the taste cultures that support them in ways that subvert adult culture. Elsewhere in the developing world, though the demographic grows younger (recall the familiar fact that more than half of the population of the Middle East is under sixteen), children remain marginalized and in poverty, irrelevant as consumers despite their overwhelming needs and forced to grow up prematurely, becoming little soldiers, little prostitutes, and little garment-factory workers, giving some to the global market economy but gaining little from it. They are wholly disempowered even where they are used and abused. And they are always the first to pay the cost of global economic inequalities. Their needs are ignored by global capitalism since they have no disposable income to pay for them. Even the World Bank and the International Monetary Fund, the institutions charged with responding to their needs, impose "conditionality" on the aid and loans with which they purport to alleviate their problems. "Corrupt" and "inefficient" Third World governments are punished; the kids starve, fall ill, and die. In war and poverty, in natural disaster and man-made genocide, they are most often the first victims and the last to benefit from capitalism's otherwise voracious appetite for consumers.

In this new epoch in which the needy are without income and the well-heeled are without needs, radical inequality is simply assumed. The United States and Canada, for example, with just over 5 percent of the world's population, control almost one-third (31.5 percent) of the world's private consumption expenditures. Western Europe, with 6.4 percent of the population, controls almost 29 percent of expenditures—that means 11.5 percent of the world's population controls 60 percent of the world's consumer spending. On the other hand, sub-Saharan Africa, with nearly 11 percent of the population, controls only 1.2 percent of consumer expenditures.[23]

Inequality leaves capitalism with a dilemma: the overproducing capitalist market must either grow or expire. If the poor cannot be enriched enough to become consumers, then grown-ups in the First World who are currently responsible for 60 percent of the world's consumption, and with vast disposable income but few needs, will have to be enticed into shopping. Inducing them to remain childish and impetuous in their taste helps ensure that they will buy the global market goods designed for indolent and prosperous youth. When translated into figures for comparative spending on advertising versus spending on foreign aid, these grim inequalities yield a remarkable contrast: while the United States spent about $16 billion in foreign aid in 2003, the projected American expenditure for advertising for 2005 was $276 billion (about one-half of the world's projected advertising expenditure for 2005).[24] If manufacturing needs rather than goods is a primary task of consumer capitalism, however, the massive advertising and marketing budgets are understandable.

Marx himself had remarked in the *Communist Manifesto* of 1848 on the dislodging of old-fashioned industries by new industries in which "in place of old wants, we find new wants." Calvin Coolidge had presciently depicted advertising as "the method by which the desire is created for better things," anticipating by nearly forty years Guy Debord's more radical claim in the 1960s that "the satisfaction of primary human needs, [is] now met in the most summary manner, by a ceaseless manufacture of pseudo-needs."[25] Many of the needs of children that can be regarded as "irreducible," on the other hand, cannot be met by the market at all, but depend on kinship relations, parenting, self-image, learning, and limit-setting.[26] Because so many needs are beyond what capitalism produces and sells, capitalism demands what Keynes called a certain "pumping up" of purchasing power. The founder of Filene's department store, on a visit to Paris back in 1935, grasped even then that (in Victoria de Grazia's description) "the chief economic problem facing the industrial world was to distribute goods in accordance with the now patently inexhaustible capacity to produce them. Not the overproduction of merchandise, but its nondistribution was the problem."[27] From the point of view of businesspeople, they were not producing too much, consumers were buying too little.

This was a theme that coursed through consumerist capitalism from the start. By our own times, it was a theme picked up by marketers for whom the fabricating of needs seemed the better part of wisdom. We no longer have to reference Vance Packard's warning about hidden persuaders: the persuaders have come out of the closet and are teaching corporate managers the arts of marketing to teens at national conferences and are articulating toddler marketing techniques in textbooks and business-school marketing courses. Nor do we need Herbert Marcuse's subtle argument about the one-dimensionality of modern men: clever marketing consultants are openly subverting pluralistic human identity in pursuit not simply of brand loyalty but of lifelong brand identity.

In other words, I am not reading the notion of infantilization into what the market is doing in order to illuminate its practices in an era of mandatory selling; I am extrapolating out of the actual practices of the consumer marketplace the idea of pumping up purchasing power, manufacturing needs, and encouraging infantilization. I am not suggesting in the passive voice that there "is a process of infantilization under way." I am arguing that many of our primary business, educational, and governmental institutions are consciously and purposefully engaged in infantilization and as a consequence that we are vulnerable to such associated practices as privatization and branding. For this is how we maintain a system of consumerist capitalism no longer supported by the traditional market forces of supply and demand.

The argument here then rests on and gives systematic expression to the message of such merchandizing advocates as Gene Del Vecchio. Del Vecchio tells clients that capitalism is under siege and that to sell in the global marketplace where "the demand for adult goods and services has proven not to be endless,"[28] and where there is little profit in selling to those who are in need, manufacturers must not only create homogenous global products aimed at the wealthy young, but must embark on what another marketer calls a veritable "consumerization of the child."[29] The new capitalism must spark a "kidquake of kid-directed goods and services" aimed at children old enough "to articulate their preferences—hence, children ages four and older."[30] At such conferences on marketing to children as Youth Power 2005 in New York (February 24–25, 2005) and the Youth Marketing Mega Event held most recently in Huntington, California (April 10–13, 2005), panel topics have included "Reaching Kids

Through Causes—An In-Depth Tutorial in How to Market with a Heart" and "Youth Observatory Ethnography Fieldtrip," which promise to help companies continually refresh "their knowledge about Toddlers, Teens and Tweens or run the risk of being 'so yesterday.'"

Such conferences have spread globally to places like Paris (Youth Market Conference, April 7–8, 2005, with a panel called "How to acquire and retain customers in the 0–25 [sic] age group"), Singapore (Marketing to Youth Conference: Customizing Conventional Marketing Strategies to Target Specifically at Youths, May 18–19, 2005), Sydney (Youth Marketing, May 20–June 2, 2005), and Shanghai (Youth Marketing Forum China: Targeted Marketing Strategies for Reaching Young Consumers Across China, May 2–26, 2005). These strategies are more than a matter of advertising—though it is certainly a matter of advertising, given that the advertising industry in the United States alone spent over $230 billion in 2001, with as much as $40 billion aimed at children (up from $2.2 billion in 1968 and $4.2 billion in 1984).[31]

The phenomenon is global, with world advertising expected to increase by 5 percent a year over the next few years, with commensurate amounts to be spent on children. Europe is already approaching $100 billion per annum, Latin American advertising is growing 5 percent per annum and is already over $16 billion a year. China is beginning to see the profits that can be earned from the eight- to twenty-one-year-old youth market, whose members have an aggregate annual income totaling perhaps $40 billion. While it is only $9 billion today, China is projected to grow to $12 billion by 2006 and to $18 billion by 2011, when it will become the third largest advertising market in the world.[32]

What observers say about China now is little different from what they say about France or Mexico: "Chinese kids, teens and young adults play an important role in the Chinese consumer retail markets . . . (as) direct spenders" but also, as in the West, in their capacity to "influence their parents' purchasing decisions" and in their growing online spending.[33] In a nation where the one-child policy has created hundreds of millions of families with six adults (two parents, four grandparents) focused on the needs and wants of one child, the climate for infantilizing the market (never mind spoiling the kids) seems extraordinarily promising—if that is the word—while its impact on China's coming global role seems more than disconcerting.

In the United States, no one has identified what is happening with greater lucidity than Boston College cultural critic Juliet B. Schor: "The United States," she writes, "is the most consumer-oriented society in the world . . . [and] the architects of this culture . . . have now set their sights on children. . . . Kids and teens are now the epicenter of American consumer culture. They command the attention, creativity, and dollars of advertisers. Their tastes drive market trends. Their opinions shape brand strategies."[34] Thus, consumerism urges us to retrieve the childish things the Bible told us we had to put away, and to enter into the new world of electronic toys, games, and gadgets that constitute a modern digital playground for adults who, the market seems to have concluded, no longer need to grow up. Rather than employ schools to help children grow out of their toys, we import toys into the schools—video games and computers as "edutainment" teaching aids, as well as ad-sponsored TV in the classroom.[35] Game developer Marc Prensky makes the stakes clear: "The commercial world is promising and delivering," he says. Jenn Shreve adds: "[T]raditional teaching methods simply can't compete with the appeal of a commercial world of games that makes children heroes or puts the fate of Harry Potter in their hands."[36]

In high-school classrooms across America, this commercialization is supported by outfits like Channel One Network that offer in-school soft "news" television complete with hard advertisements that sell at rates which rival such prime-time specials as the American football Super Bowl.[37] In higher education, colleges and universities that once acted as a counterpoint to commercial culture today have gone prostrate before corporate sponsors of research that academic administrators have neither the will nor the independent funding to oppose. Higher education has always been prone to the forces of vocationalism (Thorstein Veblen wrote an angry critique in 1918). Its decline into the multiversity "knowledge factory" Clark Kerr wrote about in the 1960s only marked the beginning of its modern corporatization—about which Stanley Aronowitz on the left and Allan Bloom on the right have in their own ways vociferously complained, and about which I will comment below in my discussion of privatization.[38]

Today's new higher-ed corruption comes from treating students themselves not as autonomous learners but as free consumers and not yet committed brand-shoppers—clients of educational services. Vendors see a $200-billion-a-year market made up of "a particularly attractive subset of American youth" who are still shopping for brands and who control extraordinary disposable income and market influence over their parents and other adults.[39] Cash-strapped colleges and universities see "cobranding" opportunities (an exclusive contract with Coke or Pepsi, a stadium naming opportunity) as a "free" source of replenishment for budgets starved by state funding reductions.

But corporate marketers do not limit themselves to turning education into merchandizing, they turn merchandizing into education, making each moment of the child's day into a merchandizing opportunity—pop-up ads on the internet where students now do their homework instead of in ad-free libraries, holidays which were formerly "holy days" (Thanksgiving, Christmas, Ramadan, Hanukkah, Easter, and Kwanza) turned into selling marathons along with secular holidays like Valentine's Day, Presidents' Day, Mother's Day, Father's Day, Labor Day, all given their own unique commercial inflections, each offering, in Richard Woodward's phrase, "a testament to the bottomless ingenuity of capitalism."[40]

In higher education and elsewhere, the commercializing ethos of infantilization encourages and is encouraged by a political ideology of privatization that delegitimizes adult public goods such as critical thinking and public citizenship (once the primary objectives of higher education) in favor of self-involved private choice and narcissistic personal gain. A college marketing specialist thus sees students first of all as "voracious consumers who use self-gratification to offset the rigors of academics and the stress of an uncertain future."[41] The ethos catalyzes a novel identity politics in which consumer branding rather than race, religion, and other forms of ascriptive identity along with voluntary civic and political identity comes to define who we are. Deliberation and common ground have largely vanished in political debate; reductive talk-radio programming encourages callers to behave like spoiled children; scream-television cable shows pretend to be news programming but are strictly for entertainment. More and more people ascribe to simplistic religious ideologies rooted in dogma and absolutism rather than common faith and universal morals.[42]

More and more adults, according to conservative critic Joseph Epstein, are "locked in a high school of the mind, eating dry cereal, watching a vast quantity of television, hoping to make sexual scores" and generally enjoying "perpetual adolescence, cut loose, free of responsibility, without the real pressures that life, that messy business, always exerts."[43] Juliet Schor on the left agrees that "we have become a nation that places a lower priority on teaching its children how to thrive socially, intellectually, even spiritually, than it does on training them to consume."[44] Norma Pecora argues that "with the consumerization of the child comes the ideological shaping of the adult. That is not to say we will all demand our Lion King as adults, though several recent commercials play on the child within, but we will come to expect life to play out in particular ways."[45] It is our expectations about how life plays out that the infantilist ethos conditions.

The celebration of youth is more than merely a lifestyle choice. Some people are seeking to change biology as well. The Academy of Anti-Aging Medicine denies that aging is "natural and inevitable,"[46] an attitude that gives rise to a celebration of the unnatural and perverse—of surgical and pharmaceutical fountains of perpetual youth and cryonic engines of eternal life.[47] Youth is where the money is, whether consumers are old or young.

In the emerging world of total commerce, there is also advertising on parking meters, advertising on public buildings, advertising on so-called public noncommercial television, ubiquitous blimp- and airplane-borne (smoke generated) signage, naming opportunities on public buildings such as sports stadiums once associated with public figures, and advertising possibilities in outer space—once it is militarized, why not commercialize it as well? The last frontier, now crossed, is not, however, outer space but the human body. The selling of the body, which with the passing of actual slavery became a metaphor for coercive exchanges that were largely invisible (Marx and Foucault), has today become a toxic but remarkably well tolerated exemplar of the subordination of identity to commerce, and includes the selling of the constituent elements of the human genome. Roughly 20 percent of the genome has now been patented for private commercial use, and the trend is accelerating. As with so many other elements in the global race to the bottom, it is globalization that drives privatization: the quest for genetic patents is a function of the globalization of research. If "we" don't do it, the Koreans or the French or the Chinese will. And since consumables along with the "need" for them must in any case be marketed globally for capitalism in its late consumer phase to flourish, bioengineering, cloning, and other advanced forms of genetic research are bound to be put into corporate hands.

Globalization stimulates selling to the young in another important way as well. The global market turns out to be defined by the relatively common tastes of the young. Adult cultures are plural and distinctive, but youth culture is remarkably universal. In the apt description of Chip Walker, "despite different cultures, middle-class youth all over the world seem to live their lives as if in a parallel universe. They get up in the morning, put on their Levi's and Nikes, grab their caps, backpacks, and Sony personal CD players, and head for school."[48] There are French *citoyens* and Ibo tribesmen and Iraqi Sunnis and Brazilian patriots, but kids are kids are kids. If their countries and tribes and religions can be made to appear as secondary to their global market tastes and youth-branded appetites as children, capitalism need not be impeded by pluralism. A *global* consumer economy in a world of differentiated cultures depends on the ability to sell uniform goods. According to Naomi Klein, the question is quite precisely: "What is the best way to sell identical products across multiple borders? What voice should advertisers use to address the whole world at once? How can one company accommodate cultural difference while still remaining internally coherent?"[49] The business guru James U. McNeal, who has written what admirers call the "bible for all children's marketers,"[50] has a compelling answer:

In general, it appears that before there is a geographic culture, there
is a children's culture; that children are very much alike around the
industrialized world. They love to play . . . they love to snack . . . and
they love being children with other children (in contrast to assuming
most adult roles). The result is that they very much want the same
things, that they generally translate their needs into similar wants
that tend to transcend culture. Therefore, it appears that fairly stan-
dardized multinational marketing strategies to children around the
globe are viable.[51]

The starting point for McNeal's logic, as well as Klein's, a logic which
turns out to be the spirit of modern consumer capitalism, is William Greider's global market world of surplus production:[52] too many goods chasing too few consumers in an era of growing inequality and diminishing
consumer wants, at least among those with disposable income, and in a
global economy where customers with the means to buy are too diverse
to desire the same goods (if they desire any at all). Quite simply, in a world
of too many commodities and too few shoppers, "children become valuable as consumers."[53]

Market to kids and secure a single planetary market. That is the blunt
strategy embraced by marketing advocate Arundhati Parmar, who writes
enticingly about "global youth united" as a "homogenous group" that can
be a "prime target for U.S. marketers."[54] And as a bonus, the client constituency grows as the children grow. As Dr. David Jones and Doris Klein
wrote over thirty-five years ago, "the child wants what it wants when it
wants it, without consideration of the needs of others, and man-child does
not outgrow this pattern."[55]

Frozen in time, aging adults remain youth consumers throughout their
lives, the "men-children" of Jones and Klein's title, while toddlers and
preteen "tweens" are converted into "adult" consumers as they come "on
line" at an ever younger age. Thus capitalism in its late consumerist phase
postpones its rendezvous with destiny and survives at least another generation or two. The economic bottom line holds even as other values people
care about are thrust aside. We sow as individuals what we would not nec-

essarily choose to reap as a community. We are trapped in an individualistic consumer culture in which the public goods that belong to us as citizens are not part of the accounting. The fate of capitalism and the fate of citizens no longer converge.

The trouble faced by democratic society is not simply that it is deprived of the responsible grown-up citizens who are its only legitimate custodians, but that the ethic of infantilization perverts childhood as well, prompting us to treat children instrumentally—not as little beings to be serviced by big capitalism but as themselves little servants of big capitalism. J. M. Barrie's fantasy of Peter Pan is neatly inverted. For Barrie, the dream was for kids never to grow up so that they might be spared the burdens of responsible adulthood: jobs, families, mortgages, and political and moral responsibilities. "I don't want to grow up," exclaimed Peter, fleeing to Neverland. "I don't want to be a man, I want always to be a little boy and to have fun."

Modern merchandisers don't want Peter to grow up either: not to preserve his innocence, however, not to keep him safe from the world of commerce, but to make him their loyal customer, to exploit his separation from mother and family to make him theirs, to prompt him to *buy* the fun for which his youth once offered him costless access. Fly to Neverland, Peter, where we await you with everything the little boy in you ever wanted—except you have to buy it with grown-up dollars. Or buy it, in that perversion of Neverland fabricated by the Michael Jackson brand, by selling out both the family and innocence. Leave your parents behind, but be sure to bring *your* wallets and corrupted eroticism with you.

To the professional keepers of the infantilist ethos, whose task is nicely euphemized by Gene Del Vecchio as "creating ever-cool," waging the war for the soul of Peter Pan means engaging in a great "battle," a struggle to achieve "the conquest of cool."[56] It is a battle like Peter's with Captain Hook that is "most fierce" in an arena where "children are both increasingly influential and increasingly selective [and] competition is keen." This battle "will be won by the company that best understands kids, their emotional needs, their fantasies, their dreams, their desires. Such knowledge is the mightiest weapon in a marketer's arsenal to win a child's heart."[57] Exit

Peter Pan. Exit sensitive writers like Barrie and Lewis Carroll who capture children in literature to free the imagination of the young everywhere. Enter those whose aim it is to capture children's imagination in order to indenture them to the marketplace: enter Michael Jackson, *Shrek*, Super Mario Bros., Steven Spielberg, Britney Spears, Grand Theft Auto, Kobe Bryant, *American Idol*, and Disney World—kiddie consumerism all dressed up as consumer cool. Peter Pan incarcerated in what Mike Davis once called the "panoptican mall" in the "carceral city."[58] Wendy watching the Home Shopping Network.

The battle is not limited to marketing and markets. Del Vecchio's words manifest not merely an ethos of marketing, but the language of politics made contentious, argumentative, and simplistic; the language of ideology focused on privatization, narcissism, and interest; and the language of tele-religion and commercialized revivalism, construed more and more as a tele-commodity offering shallow solutions to deep problems; all deployed on behalf of the interests of a declining global consumer economy unable to sell the poor what they need (it doesn't pay) but trying desperately to sell the prosperous what they don't need. Infantilization in this instrumentalist form signals the abandonment of Western civilization's understanding (not necessarily shared by earlier cultures) of childhood as a precious legacy, and children—not yet capable of autonomy or self-defense—as ends in themselves whose happiness and well-being are the ultimate object of the public good. Thus, our democracy is little by little corrupted, our republican realm of public goods and public citizens is gradually privatized, and the capitalist economy, once intended to serve democracy and the republican commonweal alike, is bent and soon likely to be broken.

To the disorderly rulers of ancient Athens, the philosopher Socrates once said for justice to prevail you must make kings philosophers or philosophers kings. Today's sophists of marketing offer an analogous if less noble formula: for consumer capitalism to prevail you must make kids consumers or make consumers kids. That is to say, smarten up the kids—"empower" them as spenders; and dumb down the grown-ups, disempower them as citizens. As McNeal puts it, this requires that we understand that "children are a future market that can be cultivated now so that when children reach market age they can more easily be converted into customers."[59]

In the fashion industry, for example, sellers target "the mother who tries to look 15" at the same time that the kindergartner is "gussied up to look 40"—"an idea makers of children's clothes have creepily endorsed." Says Valerie Steele, director of the Museum at the Fashion Institute of Technology, "At the same time that you're seeing grown-ups in overalls, you're seeing eight-year-old girls essentially wearing push-up bras."[60] Then there is the burgeoning "retro" market that pushes nostalgia apparel, films, and other commodities both to aging adults who want to recapture their youth, and to young people and teens who think adopting the styles of earlier generations is a really cool way to be young. Retro in effect allows being young to grow old and still stay young.

Google search results over the past several years suggest how successful pop-cultural dumbing down has been. What inquiring minds need to know, according to Google's own figures, which rank Google's most common searches from 2001 to 2005 (see table on pages 22–23), focus on Eminem, Britney Spears, Pamela Anderson, Harry Potter, Janet Jackson, and Paris Hilton. Among what are otherwise exclusively teen celebrity, pop-culture, and sports queries in the top ten set of results (with ninety possible slots), only four speak to a wider world (Nostradamus, Hurricane Katrina, tsunami, and Iraq).

In the movies, the impact of infantilization is even more pronounced (although there are elements of change and even resistance explored below in the final chapter). As the sale of movie tickets declines (as it has over the past several years), Hollywood is ever more dominated by blockbuster films aimed at the elongated thirteen- to thirty-year-old "teen market." As Peter Biskind suggests in his history of Hollywood in the 1970s (paraphrased here by Louis Menand), "around 1967 American filmmaking caught fire and grew up, and then Spielberg and Lucas came along and put out the flames with great deluges of cash generated by junk food for fourteen-year-olds."[61] To take but a single year, of the biggest films of 2004 in terms of ticket sales, four of the top five were aimed at kids: *Shrek 2* at

GOOGLE 2001-2005 TOP QUERIES

Year	Category	1	2	3	4	5
2001	Men	Nostradamus	Osama bin Laden	Eminem	Michael Jackson	Howard Stern
	Women	Britney Spears	Pamela Anderson	Jennifer Lopez	Madonna	Aaliyah
	Overall*					
2002	Men	Eminem	Brad Pitt	Nelly	2Pac	Vin Diesel
	Women	Jennifer Lopez	Britney Spears	Shakira	Halle Berry	Jennifer Love Hewitt
	Overall*					
2003	Men*					
	Women*					
	Overall	Britney Spears	Harry Potter	Matrix	Shakira	David Beckham
2004	Men	Orlando Bloom	Eminem	Usher	Johnny Depp	Brad Pitt
	Women	Britney Spears	Paris Hilton	Christina Aguilera	Pamela Anderson	Carmen Electra
	Overall	Britney Spears	Paris Hilton	Christina Aguilera	Pamela Anderson	Chat
2005	Men*					
	Women*					
	Overall	Janet Jackson	Hurricane Katrina	Tsunami	Xbox 360	Brad Pitt

* Data unavailable.
Source: Google Zeitgeist Archive, available at www.google.com/intl/en/press/zeitgeist/archive.html.

number one, *Spider-Man 2* at number two, *Harry Potter and the Prisoner of Azkaban* at number four, and *The Incredibles* at number five. As the following list shows, of the twenty largest-grossing films, at least half are directed at the youth market, and all but Mel Gibson's *The Passion of the Christ* and Michael Moore's *Fahrenheit 9/11*—both special cases of grown-ups struggling against the norm from the religious right and the secular left—belong either to the cartoon market (four of the top twelve), the adventure-action-picture youth market, or the girls' market. Three films (including numbers one and two) are sequels to earlier formula hits. Most belong to the category of "event" films which, like *Star Wars* or *Harry Pot-*

6	7	8	9	10
George Harrison	Josh Hartnett	Dale Earnhardt	Bob Marley	Michael Jordan
Kylie Minogue	Shakira	Anna Kournikova	Andrea Thompson	Mariah Carey
Josh Hartnett	Ben Affleck	David Beckham	Ronaldo	Ja Rule
Heidi Klum	Pamela Anderson	Sarah Michelle Gellar	Carmen Electra	Anna Kournikova
50 Cent	Iraq	Lord of the Rings	Kobe Bryant	Tour de France
David Beckham	50 Cent	Bob Marley	Justin Timberlake	Michael Jackson
Jennifer Lopez	Angelina Jolie	Avril Lavigne	Beyoncé	Hilary Duff
Games	Carmen Electra	Orlando Bloom	Harry Potter	mp3
Michael Jackson	American Idol	Britney Spears	Angelina Jolie	Harry Potter

ter or *The Matrix*, are designed to reach the largest possible global audience where selling to youth is a prime consideration.

THE BIGGEST FILMS OF 2004[62]

1. Shrek 2 (DreamWorks) $441 million in ticket sales
2. *Spider-Man 2* (Sony) $374
3. *The Passion of the Christ* (Newmarket) $370
4. *Harry Potter and the Prisoner of Azkaban* (Warner) $250
5. *The Incredibles** (Disney Pixar) $237
6. *The Day After Tomorrow* (Fox) $187
7. *The Bourne Supremacy* (Universal) $176

8. *Shark Tale** (DreamWorks) $159

9. *I, Robot** (Fox) $145

10. *Troy* (Warner) $133

11. *National Treasure** (Disney) $133

12. *The Polar Express** (Warner) $124

13. *50 First Dates* (Sony) $121

14. *Van Helsing* (Universal) $121

15. *Fahrenheit 9/11* (Lions Gate) $119

16. *Dodgeball* (Fox) $114

17. *The Village* (Buena Vista) $114

18. *The Grudge** (Sony) $110

19. *Collateral* (DreamWorks) $101

20. *Princess Diaries 2** (Disney) $95

The year 2004 is not an anomaly: comparing figures for the top-grossing films from 2001 to 2005, the tendencies are the same.[63]

2001

Harry Potter and the Sorcerer's Stone $349.5

The Lord of the Rings: The Fellowship of the Ring $344.9

Shrek $294.6

Monster, Inc. $281.6

Rush Hour 2 $248.9

The Mummy Returns $222.2

Pearl Harbor $218.4

Ocean's Eleven $201.8

2002

Spider-Man $438.5

The Lord of the Rings: The Two Towers $368

Star Wars, Episode II: Attack of the Clones $327.3

Harry Potter and the Chamber of Secrets $283.8

My Big Fat Greek Wedding $261.6

Signs $247

Austin Powers in Goldmember	$230.9
Men in Black II	$207.4

2003

The Lord of the Rings: The Return of the King	$399.4
Finding Nemo	$359.9
Pirates of the Caribbean: The Curse of the Black Pearl	$323.5
The Matrix Reloaded	$298.2
Bruce Almighty	$257
X2: X-Men United	$227.7

2004

Shrek 2	$450.4
Spider-Man 2	$385.3
The Passion of the Christ	$382.1
Meet the Fockers	$288
The Incredibles	$269.8
Harry Potter and the Prisoner of Azkaban	$257.3

2005 (THROUGH DECEMBER 4)

Star Wars, Episode III: Revenge of the Sith	$380.3
War of the Worlds	$234.3
Harry Potter and the Goblet of Fire	$229.3
Wedding Crashers	$209.1
Charlie and the Chocolate Factory	$206.4
Batman Begins	$205.3

The global film scene mimics the American picture. In 2003, the top-grossing film in Argentina, Germany, Mexico, Switzerland, and the United Kingdom was the animated cartoon *Finding Nemo*. Along with *Finding Nemo*, kiddie blockbusters and youth-marketed movies such as *The Matrix Reloaded*, *Pirates of the Caribbean*, and *Bruce Almighty* prevailed throughout the global marketplace.

Sequels also proliferated. Like children, we increasingly ask of movies and theater "Tell me the story again, please? Now please tell me again!"

This makes for safe marketing, but it also satisfies an unadventurous puerile taste that wishes to be neither surprised nor discomfited. In the winter of 2005, as it learned successfully to track Hollywood's marketing strategies, Broadway offered its public not only the usual menu of musical revivals such as *Chicago*, *La Cage aux Folles*, *Sweet Charity*, and *Fiddler on the Roof*, but a host of dramatic plays that in their time were risk taking, even taboo smashing, but are today drawn from the safe haven of familiarity and past success. (Enjoy the nostalgia of taboos once broken, without risking newly breaking them!) These included *A Streetcar Named Desire* (1947), *Glengarry Glen Ross* (1984), *On Golden Pond* (1979), *Steel Magnolias* (1987), *The Glass Menagerie* (1944), *Who's Afraid of Virginia Woolf?* (1962), and *Hurlyburly* (1984). Were this a tribute to the enduring influence of American dramatic classics, it would be heartening, but in fact it represents the collective cowardice of a commercialized theater sector playing it safe even in the theater zone where you're supposed to play it dangerous.[64]

The movies are a marker not just for theater but for the entire economy. As journalist and critic Lynn Hirschberg has written, "while other countries have interpreted globalism as a chance to reveal their national psyches and circumstances through film, America is more interested in attracting the biggest possible international audience. At Cannes [in 2004], war-torn Croatia was shown through the eye of the director Emir Kusturica, the French elite was exposed in *Look At Me*, the fear of female genital mutilation was depicted in Senegal's *Moolaadé*." Meanwhile, Hollywood gave the world a (yes, charming) green fantasy creature called Shrek who returned for another record-breaking appearance later in *Shrek 2*.[65]

The dumbing down of films and the blockbuster approach to filmmaking are not accidental features of an irrational Hollywood storyline, but a conscious decision by studio executives and film producers who understand that to make money their products have to sell worldwide. Back in 1946, a hundred million Americans went to the movies every week (of a population of 160 million), whereas today, only twenty-five million a week go. The number of big screens in America has been contracting for decades. As the domestic market for films shifted to television, rentals, and video-on-demand, the foreign big-screen market became ever more important. Around 1993, foreign box-office revenue overtook domestic revenue for Hollywood films, and today more than 60 percent of exhibition revenue is from overseas markets.

Hollywood thus needs exportable blockbusters whose primary target "is people with an underdeveloped capacity for deferred gratification; that is, kids."[66] Since increasingly Hollywood has come to depend on customers who see films three or four times or more, these kids—the "tell me the story again" kids referenced above—are ideal customers, along with the new class of re-juveniled adults. Much the same can be said of the Mexican-made soap operas aimed at the American Latino market, "Bollywood" musicals from India's prospering film market looking for an export market (Indian action-adventure tough-guy Salman Kahn has been introduced into the United States along with a couple of Bollywood leading ladies), or Madrid's new appetite for global musicals, all of which suggest that the trends in Hollywood and New York have their global counterparts. The fourteen- to thirty-year-old market dominates. It will surprise no one that the hit television show *American Idol* now has its counterpart in the hit show *Indian Idol*.

Infantilization has been Hollywood's adaptive strategy, with the new blockbuster films featuring universal kid features like comic-book action, branded characters, numberless sequels, extensive product placements, and commercial tie-ins with fast food and other global enterprises, minimal plots, and still more minimal dialogue. What is perhaps surprising is that serious films get made at all—like the ones screened in 2005 when mature fare and politically relevant films such as *Brokeback Mountain*, *Capote*, *The Constant Gardener*, *Syriana*, and *Good Night, and Good Luck* dominated the Academy Awards (see chapter 8).

THUS DO GLOBAL marketers around the world, when not explicitly infantilizing adults, engage in the delicate task of empowering children as adult consumers without allowing them to forgo their childish tastes. To do this requires not simply the shaping of fresh advertising and merchandizing strategies, but the reshaping of cultural, educational, and civic institutions to help sustain an ethos favorable to infantilization—the condition for the selling of uniform commodities the world over. It was once rather common for conservatives to pillory welfare statism for creating childlike dependency in its clients (see Charles Murray for example). Totalitarian states historically were thought to act as overweening authorities which infantilized their subjects to keep them in line. Traditionally, critics have argued that "philanthropists and liberals tend to place themselves in the role of a parent supplying the needs of a helpless child. In doing so they foster the infantilization of the recipients."[67] This was David Jones and Doris Klein's view in their *Man-Child*, where they complained about the "world-wide trend toward the socialization of all services [as] a further indication that man is placing government in the role of Mother."[68]

Yet if paternalistic states create top-down forms of infantilization, markets today are creating bottom-up forms of infantilization—the less visible because they arise from below out of supposedly pluralistic and competitive markets that turn out to be coercive in intractable ways as they seek to inspire childlike dependency in consumers. Now even democratic models of citizenship are subordinated to parent-child paradigms. The scholarly linguist George Lakoff has recently strayed off the academic reservation to beguile the Democratic Party with a reductive, even demeaning, paradigm of politics that sees in Republican leaders a model of the "strict father" and in Democratic leaders a model of the "nurturant parent" (a politically correct version of the "empathetic mother").[69] This paradigm treats citizens as consumers of government services—needy children in search of parental care.

Even grown-ups who avoid having children or interacting with them seem animated by childish desires. A paradoxical example of the infantilist ethos in action in the marketplace is the movement for "childfree" environments that bar kids from grown-up settings in order to allow adults to "be themselves" and hence to be free. But to be free from what? "Free from brats," ardent advocates say. Actually, free to be brats, it would seem—to conduct themselves without the usual grown-up concerns for and responsibilities toward children, hence to be just like children. Not having children (or being like children?) is not "some cute stage" to be grown out of, exclaims a childfree zealot, but is rather "a legitimate life choice."[70] Some such people—10 percent of voters are childless, though obviously only a few of them belong to the antichild zealots—seek the sanctuary of "Minimum Breeder Quotient neighborhoods" and refer to kids as "anklebiters" and "crib lizards" and to couples as "breeder-yuppie-scum" busy "squirting out spawn."

This is silly stuff, and issues from a tiny "kid backlash" minority. Yet it reveals a telling irony that illuminates trends in the larger society. For the autonomy these people seek from the world of children is marked above all by a narcissistic quest for their own freedom from grown-up responsibility in favor of self-obsessed acquisitiveness.[71] "I'm spending my grandchildren's inheritance!" boasts the popular bumper sticker that can be seen peeling from gas-guzzling recreational vehicles prowling the sunbelt, whose inhabitants happily call themselves "SKIers" (Spending the Kids' Inheritance). Nor is it very hard to find signs of narcissistic kid-baiting in wildly popular American television shows like *Desperate Housewives*. As teen movies often ridicule parents, teachers, and other "adult" authority figures, young-adult fare ridicules and reviles kids—the better to displace them in the hierarchy of narcissism that defines infantilism.[72]

The logic carries all the way down to toddlers and perhaps even fetuses who, once they are deemed alive and human, can be treated as shoppers in potentia as well. Del Vecchio takes the age of four as the cutoff, but others see preverbal children as appropriate targets. There is now a 24/7 cable television channel called BabyFirstTV expressly aimed at six-month-to two-year-olds. There is room enough for Barney babies and Teletubby toddlers in the children's market. As Norma Pecora observes (unlike many of the others, she is a critic), "as we move into the 21st century, children are well-trained consumers able to associate Ronald McDonald with good things before they have learned the language."[73] Indeed, according to the Center for a New American Dream, "babies as young as six months of age can form mental images of corporate logos and mascots," which means "brand loyalties can be established as early as age two." It follows that "by the time children head off to school most can recognize hundreds of brand logos."[74] Kids' marketer James McNeal splits the difference, identifying the ideal "kid customer" as "a confident little 9 year old with a cute little nose and arms full of shopping bags, emerging from a department store . . . confident, a big spender, able to cope in the market place."[75] No wonder that spending on advertising to children increased from less than $100 million in 1990 to more than $2 billion in 2000. After all, "kids are the most unsophisticated of all consumers. They have the least and therefore want the most. Consequently, they are in a perfect position to be taken."[76]

Peter Zollo, one of those children's market researchers who seems to salivate as he surveys his research, writes with mocking disdain about the stereotype of today's teen as "a brand-obsessed, label-driven, mall-congregating, free-spending, compulsive shopper." But with a wink and a grin he quickly adds that "there is often some truth to stereotypes." After all (now he is serious), "teen spending is on the rise, and few teens are saddled with payments that inhibit adult spending, like rent, utilities, and groceries. Teens' considerable income is almost exclusively discretionary. They are consumers with a mission: they want to spend on whatever happens to please them. What a compelling target."[77]

It takes more than mere marketing to score a hit on targeted children, however. It requires that the target be separated from its protective environment: that it be uprooted from the homes and habits that initially protect it from predatory marketers and commercial exploitation. Wendy and her brothers, seduced by Peter Pan, flew from home (literally) to escape the overbearing grown-ups who were fixed on seeing them all grow up. Merchandisers entice them from their homes to bring them into an adult consumerist world where their innocence makes them especially vulnerable to commercial blandishments. Liberation here means establishing children's boutiques and Disney and Warner Brothers stores as adult-free zones. It means arranging mall space so that teen and youth shops are on different shopping floors (or wings) so that the young will shop separately from their parents.

Children in earlier totalitarian societies were stripped of familial loyalties and made to serve the party in the name of liberty from "untrustworthy" and "unpatriotic" parents—"Turn your parents in if they are disloyal to the Party!" Today, for trivial economic reasons, children's "gatekeepers" are also confronted and where possible pushed out of the way in the name of "empowerment"—the need to make children "autonomous" consumers.

Again, these are not philosophical abstractions drawn from the old left cultural critique of capitalism that must be read into the marketplace. It is what marketplace vendors acknowledge, even boast, they are doing. A favorite phrase of the kid marketers is "kid empowerment."[78] Youth marketing conferences favor the term.[79] Although actually enabling only irresponsibility and impulse, marketers offer kiddies a flag of a faux "autonomy" that uses the language of liberation and empowerment to justify making the young more vulnerable to the seductions of commercial predators. In a similar rhetorical gesture, a recently defunct teen catalog company, Blu Sphere, wove a rhetoric of "betterment" around its hustling of teen commodities that included clothes, electronics, sports items, and magazine style bibles.

This focus on personal betterment, private liberty, and individual empowerment fosters a potent affiliation between teen marketing and privatization that has been brilliantly exploited by the wildly successful television show *American Idol*, which draws as many as thirty million mostly young viewers to the program by allowing them to vote for winners and losers competing for their support. In a news report that reads like a promotion, *New York Times* reporter Alessandra Stanley writes: "'Idol,' which is watched by parents and children together, gives people a heady but safe sense of empowerment—choice without consequences."[80] Choice without consequences is of course a synonym for disempowerment, but in the new marketing this conflation of consumer games and democratic empowerment is nonetheless everywhere embraced (see chapter 4).

In business lingo, this individuation of choice is "market segmentation" which is portrayed as "consistent with a shift in general consumer patterns from family needs and wants to individual consumption."[81] The child embedded in a family community makes a poor shopper—a disempowered consumer forced to bow to "gatekeepers" like Mom and Dad. But the child liberated through marketing to become a four-year-old "individual" becomes an apt consumer capable even of being an "influencer" over income dispensed by subordinate parents. The child here is autonomous in a technical sense inasmuch as—with respect to the zone of kids' shopping—it is on its own and free from parental guidance. But in truth its autonomy leaves it vulnerable, unprotected, and susceptible to outside manipulation.

As one might imagine, like the producers of BabyFirstTV and "Baby Einstein," those who prey on the very young and write books with titles like *What Kids Buy and Why* parade their academic and expert credentials. Dan Acuff's Ph.D. degree is on the cover of his book to help legitimize his anything but academic mission. Most marketing firms boast sociologists, anthropologists, and psychologists on their staffs to give their marketing research the appearance of pure science. Like Dan Acuff, they prattle on about how they are "not just interested in what sells . . . in the bottom line," but are "four-square against" anything that "can be shown in any significant way to be bad for kids."[82] How can empowering and liberating children be bad? BabyFirstTV issued a guidebook "full of approving pediatricians, psychologists and educators" aimed at immunizing its programming against critics; the guidebook itself says television can "enlighten your baby's experience by opening up a world of imagination and images."[83]

Since kid empowerment is a legitimate aim, why not toddler empowerment? In fact, were it not that younger children are more embedded in families and less autonomous in their spending than older children, their impulsiveness and kid qualities would make them even better targets for consumerism than teens, who are already on the way to becoming dissidents and rebels if not yet adults and may have already begun to put away childish things. The young minds of toddlers are less formed, their tastes more vulnerable to manipulation, their wants more easily played with. "Empowering" them (and thereby disempowering their parents and teachers and pastors) is easier to achieve (if harder to justify). A recent Kaiser Family Foundation survey found that half of all four- to six-year-olds have played video games, while the *New York Times* reported 14 percent of toddlers under three had done so. Meanwhile, old-fashioned toys that engage the active imaginations of children are being displaced by computers, electronic games, cell-phones, and iPods.[84] Unsurprisingly, the trend is rationalized by free-market video-game enthusiasts such as Steven Johnson who proposes that "everything bad is actually good for" us, but his empirical evidence is paltry (limited mostly to video games).[85]

The World Wide Web in fact targets the very young worldwide, offering four-year-olds easy access and designing many of its game and chat sites for preschoolers. There are to be sure some responsible sites for children. Or sites that offer parents reassuring signs of pedagogical relevance. Road Runner's early 2000's "Kid Stuff" homepage included such features as "Build Your Vocabulary," a "Brain Pop" facts column, and links to videos but also to books and audio tapes of classics such as *Charlotte's Web* and *A Great and Terrible Beauty*. But younger children cannot distinguish advertising from storytelling, or fantasy from fact. And until the federal government finally drew a line in the sandbox (in the spring of 2000) on polling and surveying little children, websites often queried tykes as young as three or four about their family's spending habits and their own buying preferences (that's empowerment!) as a condition of logging on. Unlike in Europe, where government protection of children on the web and elsewhere is commonplace, American market ideology prefers self-policing and other market mechanisms to deal with what only some people think are abuses in the first place.

The misuse of normative terms like *autonomy* and *empowerment* to rationalize selling to children far too young to possess either liberty or judgment (the two key components of real choice or self-determining power) is typical of an infantilist ethos that reinforces consumer market ideology by providing corporate predators with an altruistic ethic to rationalize selfish and patently immoral ends. Even Dan Acuff, the happy Ph.D. warrior of marketing cited above, feels constrained to problematize empowerment. He acknowledges that it is not so easy to tell "just what is empowering and what is disempowering" for kids. Having raised the crucial question, however, he quickly eludes it by means of a mindless truism: empowerment is whatever nurtures "positive development" and "disempowerment," whatever furthers "negative development"—keeping in mind that "it's not black and white."[86] Genuine empowerment always treats the person as an end in herself, and is defined by the domain of education, not advertising. It is measured by increased capacity to resist manipulation, not increased vulnerability to it. Hence, infantilization is empowerment's antonym.

IN SPEAKING ABOUT infantilization, I have in mind a relationship between infantilism understood in classical developmental psychology as a pathologically arrested stage of emotional development and infantilism understood in cultural psychology as a pathologically regressive stage of consumer market development—the two together comprising what Freud spoke of as "a pathology of cultural communities" on the study of which he hoped one day to embark.[87]

The cultural pathology of late consumer capitalism effectively prioritizes consumerism at the expense of capitalism's traditional balance between production and consumption, work and leisure, and investment and spending. As described in the classical Freudian and neo-Freudian literature, infantile behavior is a consequence of a regressive process that offers itself as a defense against intimidating adult dilemmas with which a disordered ego is unable to contend. Peter Pan's charming narcissism represents the seductive side of regression, while Wendy turns out to be one of those healthy youngsters who is good at growing up, who "grew up of her own free will a day quicker than other girls."[88]

The infantilism toward which an unhealthy psyche regresses is marked by an inability to distinguish self and world. As Freud concretizes it, "an infant at the breast does not as yet distinguish his ego from the external world as the source of the sensations flowing in upon him."[89] This confusion of "ego and object" initially leads to a bold but ultimately futile attempt either wholly to master the world (ego triumphant), or to merge wholly with that world (object triumphant). Either way, the self tries to erase the as yet unrecognized boundaries between the emerging ego and the object world and remain in that womb-tomb of preindividuated collective identity that offers blanket security immediately before and after birth. What is a passing stage in early child development becomes a pathology when it persists into the period when normal children acknowledge boundaries and direct their psychological and behavioral efforts toward accommodating themselves to them and coming to terms with what it means to grow up—subordinating id to superego in Freud's language; that is to say, becoming civilized.[90]

In the pathological culture of consumer economics, consumer behavior turns out to be remarkably unaccommodating to civilizing tendencies. It mimics infantile aggressiveness in striking ways. The consumer at once both imbibes the world of products, goods, and things being impressed upon her and so conquers it, and yet is defined via brands, trademarks, and consumer identity by that world. She essays to make the market her own even as it makes her its prisoner. She trumpets her freedom even as she is locked up in the cage of private desire and unrestrained libido. She announces a faux consumer power even as she renounces her real citizen power. The dollars or euros or yen with which she imagines she is mastering the world of material things turn her into a thing defined by the material—from self-defined person into market-defined brand; from autonomous public citizen to heteronomous private shopper (this is the subject of chapter 6). The boundary separating her from what she buys vanishes: she ceases to buy goods as instruments of other ends and instead becomes the goods she buys—a Calvin Klein torrid teen or an Anita Roddick Body Shop urbanite or a politically conscious Benetton rebel or a Crate & Barrel urban homesteader or a plasma television Nike spectator "athlete."[91]

The branding game targets consumers, but it also helps erase the boundaries between consumer and what is consumed. In thinking he has conquered the world of things, the consumer is in fact consumed by them. In trying to enlarge himself, he vanishes. His so-called freedom evaporates even as it is named. For it is private rather than public and so seals off the real public consequences of private choices. The gloating Hummer owner may preen with macho pride, unaware or simply uncaring of the fact that he drives an ecological behemoth that squanders fossil fuel resources, pollutes the environment, and makes the United States more dependent than ever on foreign oil resources—contributing quite inadvertently to the justification for Middle East military interventions he otherwise vehemently opposes. *American Idol* "voters" mistake a popularity contest for empowerment. The public consequences of private choices are masked by brand-identity consumerism in which only the private preference and its subjective entailments are visible.

The hidden social costs of consumer preferences are in fact notated neither in the consciousness of consumers nor the statistical indices of the U.S. Treasury Department; or for that matter in the records of the World Trade Organization or the International Monetary Fund. The consumer here is radically individuated rather than socially embedded, and less rather than more free as a consequence. She is permitted to choose from a menu of options offered by the world but not to alter or improve the menu or the world. In this, the dynamics of consumption actually render the individual more rather than less vulnerable to control, much in the way that the infant, for all its sense of power, is actually powerless in a world from which it cannot distinguish itself. In short, in almost every way, the full-time consumer as imagined by the aggressive marketing executive ideally acts regressively, more like an impulsive child than an adult.

The citizen, on the other hand, is an adult, a public chooser empowered by social freedom to effect the environment of choice and the agendas by which choices are determined and portrayed; the infantilized consumer is the private chooser, whose power to participate in communities or effect changes is diminished and whose public judgment is attenuated. The infantilist ethos, then, does the necessary work of consumer capitalism, but at the expense of the civilization that productivist capitalism helped create.

CAPITALISM ITSELF HAS come full circle. Originating in an extraordinary synergy between selfishness and altruism, between profit and productivity, it once upon a time allowed energetic and entrepreneurial risk takers to prosper by serving the growth and welfare of emerging nations. It did so with the succor of a Protestant ethos that lent moral weight to hard work, far-sighted investment, and ascetic self-denial—the very qualities productivist capitalism needed to thrive. Today, its productive capacity has outrun the needs it once served even as its distributive capacity has been stymied by the growing global inequalities it has catalyzed. Depending for its success on consumerism rather than productivity, it has generated an ethos of infantilization that prizes the very attributes the Protestant ethos condemned. It seems quite literally to be consuming itself, leaving democracy in peril and the fate of citizens uncertain. Although it affects to prize and enhance liberty, it leaves liberty's meaning ambiguous in an epoch where shopping seems to have become a more persuasive marker of freedom than voting, and where what we do alone in the mall counts more importantly in shaping our destiny than what we do together in the public square.

2

From Protestantism to Puerility

> The question of the motive forces in the expansion of modern capitalism is not in the first instance a question of the origin of . . . capital sums . . . but, above all, of the development of the spirit of capitalism.
>
> —Max Weber[1]

THE IDEA OF an infantilist ethos is a new twist on an old concept: that capitalism as an economic system demands certain reinforcing cultural attitudes and social behaviors in each of its stages of development, and that such attitudes and behaviors can be inculcated in a society through a value system that takes the form of a society-wide moral or religious ethos. Max Weber gave substance to the idea a century ago with his perceptive account of the ties between early capitalism and what he called the Protestant ethic. The story he told is worth recalling for the light it sheds on the workings of the infantilist ethos today—the peculiar way in which a cultural ethos, without being deterministic, can both reflect and condition a dominant economic system.

The Protestant Ethic and the Spirit of Capitalism

At the beginning of the sixteenth century, carried on a late Renaissance tide of civic individualism, technical innovation, and popular restlessness, two great waves of change swept across Europe. The first was Protestantism: resurgent Christianity on the move in the name of the Word of God, propelled by a cleansing spirit of asceticism in the face of a corrupt and worldly Catholic Church. The second was capitalism, a market economy on the move in the name of a new gospel of entrepreneurship and prosperity in the face of a stagnating feudal economy and a rigid mercantile ideology that left little room for the flexibility and liberty of markets. The two shared a deep cultural ethos that at once expressed Protestantism's new ascetic spirit and entrepreneurial capitalism's new preoccupation with hard work, selfless investment, and common bounty.

When at the beginning of the seventeenth century the Puritans sailed for America, they took with them this powerful cultural ideology manifesting the new ethos—this fresh and vibrant ethic capable of assuaging the yearning soul even as it succored the striving body. Planted on a bounteous new continent and combining the burgeoning new free economy's core values of work, investment, and saving with an energetic and enlightened selfishness on behalf of the common good, the ethos was fortified by a spiritual catechism celebrating altruistic toil, ascetic self-denial, deferred gratification, and a devotion to good works and to charity—all laced with an egalitarianism in which work and faith, virtues available to all, generated both worldly and otherworldly rewards. This new miracle of Protestant theology found a road to the eternal soul's redemption that passed through self-denial yet nonetheless yielded prosperity for the mortal body. It was as perfect a model of dialectical synergy as can be conceived: ascetic renunciation yielded material bounty, while worldly prosperity became a sign of certain spiritual salvation.

This extraordinary cultural synergy was what the great German lawyer and scholar Max Weber specified and critically annotated three hundred years later (a century ago) in *The Protestant Ethic and the Spirit of Capitalism*, a work in which Weber made the intimacy between religion and economics fully apparent. Weber set out to trace "the influence of certain religious ideas on the development of an economic spirit, or the ethos of an economic system . . . the connection of the spirit of modern economic life with the rational ethics of ascetic Protestantism."[2] In a profound paradox, Weber uncovered an ethic that captured both the Protestant ethos and the spirit of capitalism, an ethic that made a "religious valuation of restless, continuous, systematic work in a worldly calling, as the highest means to asceticism, and at the same time the surest and most evident proof of rebirth and genuine faith." This ethic, he wrote, "must have been the most powerful conceivable lever for the expansion of that attitude towards life which we have here called the spirit of capitalism."[3]

In the new world, with its natural abundance and pristine insularity from the rest of the world, the spirit of capitalism was to become typically American and characteristically democratic—the ethos of a free Christian commonwealth where work was truly a calling, and investment a mark of prudent altruism and democratic nation-building rather than mere self-ishness. This sacred mark has been imprinted on the profane face of American capitalism ever since, right up until recent times, when it was supplanted by a new and distinctive ethos more appropriate to American capitalism in its late consumerist phase—what I have called the infantilist ethos.

Although it was deeply contested, provoking an "academic Hundred Years' War,"[4] Weber's insight into the original capitalist ethos—Protestant asceticism as an economic driver for entrepreneurial capitalism—was part of a larger project Weber had conceived of examining the social psychology of the world's great religions.[5] The larger project suggested a number of more general propositions: that capitalism and culture in their many different variations are always more closely allied than the sharp academic boundaries between the disciplines of economics and sociology or psychology might suggest. That our current capitalist dilemma is not, as Daniel Bell portrayed it several years ago, that the passing of the Protestant ethic has left capitalism "with no moral or transcendental ethic,"[6] but that it has acquired a new and different ethic which has both secular and religious overtones and which legitimates the tendencies that consumer capitalism today requires in order to survive—tendencies, as Thomas L. Friedman has described them, "to extol consumption over hard work, investment, and long-term thinking."[7] That if capitalism's productivist rise was attended and fortified by a Protestant ethic, there is today also another ethic to be uncovered—by no means Protestant—attending and fortifying capitalism's incipient decline into hyperconsumerism. Though greed and puerility are natural features of human psychology, they have been given a prominence in modern materialist man reflecting the artificial ambitions of an infantilist ethos trying to ensure capitalism's survival.

Bell may have proclaimed the wholesale "abandonment of Puritanism and the Protestant ethic,"[8] yet there are still true believers to be found who persist in advocating it, still a few romantic capitalists who continue to find in supply-side economics and the marketplace a model of old Christian virtue, albeit transformed by the great American economic experiment. The perduring American myth that associates worldly success and wealth with godliness and that led Andrew Carnegie to write in his *Gospel of Wealth* that "not evil, but good, has come to the race from the accumulation of wealth by those who have the ability and energy to produce it"[9] also continues to be visible in American pop religion, pop therapy, and pop culture—televangelism, twelve-step therapy programs, and many of the more meretricious (and hence successful) get-rich-quick schemes.

Much of the pop-cultural literature apes Puritanism's mood even as it debases its currency. It preaches sobriety (twelve-step programs) while encouraging indulgence (advertising and marketing), calls for temperance of character (conservative cultural critics), even as it molds behavior into a consumerist mold (conservative support for market capitalism). It demands leisure for consumerism (shopping malls as surrogates for town centers) but turns leisure into a kind of work (the imperative to shop) since the ascetic ethos is conserved not in an obligation to produce, but in a new obligation to shop and consume. Greed becomes a form of altruism, indulged not out of love of self but out of love of capitalist productivity. When President Bush wanted to find a metaphor for normalcy in helping Americans find their way back from the nightmare of 9/11, he seized on shopping—imploring Americans to show Al Qaeda its patriotic backbone by going to the mall and getting on with the business of consuming.

The New Gospel of Consumption and
the Infantilist Ethos

In the new gospel of consumption, spending is holy, as saving was holy in the traditional gospel of investment. Work is still cherished, and Americans, the world's most ardent consumers, are also the world's most industrious workers. Yet, as I will argue below, the work of production has also become the work of consumption, with childish playfulness gradually transformed into disciplined leisure and purposive play. So that if Americans still work harder (and longer hours) than anyone else in the Western world, they also play harder, shop harder, and spend more. Though shopping may bring home the value-corroding material culture against which cultural conservatives rant, these same conservatives remain as wedded to consumerism as liberal secularists and thus remain largely incapable of attacking its foundations in corporate culture. This may explain how President Bush was able to win the vote of Christian conservatives in the 2004 election without surrendering his support (tax breaks and deregulation) for the market firms whose profitability depends on a materialist consumerism that necessarily undermines conservative values. In this spirit, conservative pop-cultural commentator David Brooks has found a way to sacralize shopping, becoming a champion of shopping as a vocation imbued "with sacred intent." In a witty but at least half-serious tribute to the "transcendent significance" of spending in the modern marketplace, Brooks portrays the way in which spiritual desire becomes physical desire in what he calls a literal "transubstantiation of goods."[10] Thomas Frank skewers this very same ambivalence in his *What's the Matter with Kansas*, where he asserts that the right fails to discern "the connection between mass culture, most of which conservatives hate, and laissez-faire capitalism, which they adore without reservation." This leads Kansas conservatives to gloat "when celebrities say stupid things" and to "cheer when movie stars go to jail" and in general to scream "for the heads of the liberal elite," but then come election time "vote to cut all those rock stars' taxes."[11]

There are a few neo-Puritan romantics who go Brooks one better and actually try to keep alive the direct connection between Protestant virtue and the superannuated capitalism of yesteryear. There is perhaps no more touching, certainly no more atavistically compelling figure in recent times than George Gilder, who between stints in the 1960s as a critic of feminism and today as a champion of futuristic digital technology, managed in the early 1980s to seize on and romanticize the radical supply-side fervor of neoliberals such as David Stockman and Jack Kemp. Just as their libertarian doctrines were being put into grandiose rhetoric if not actual practice by President Ronald Reagan and Prime Minister Margaret Thatcher, Gilder wrote a book aimed at capturing what he was pleased to call "the high adventure and redemptive morality of capitalism."[12]

In his *Wealth and Poverty*, far from abjuring Weber's thesis, he ups the ante, gilding Weber's dispassionate language of capitalist rationality with an ardent rhetoric of creativity, risk taking, and entrepreneurial epiphany. He does not simply describe a residual Protestant ethos of asceticism, and he is certainly not willing to follow the path later taken by Brooks and embrace and rationalize consumerism. Rather he wishes to rekindle a fresh ethic of spiritual altruism for which religion is the source. He insists that "economists who distrust religion will always fail to comprehend the modes of worship by which progress is achieved."[13] He wants to celebrate "the heroic creativity of entrepreneurs." Like Weber, he thinks of them as more selfless than acquisitive, much as modern consumers may see the "greed" attributed to them as instrumental to higher purposes.[14] He will not be shamed in the face of inequality because, like the English political philosopher John Locke (who was a powerful influence on the New England Puritan preachers of the eighteenth century), he reckons that the poor are motivated as much by laziness, envy, and contentiousness as by ill fortune or injustice—an absence of zeal rather than an absence of opportunity.[15] He sees in capital accumulation not the work of exploiters and expropriators of the labor of others but the achievement of creative risk takers, altruists, and even martyrs: "A successful economy depends on the proliferation of the rich, on creating a large class of risk-taking men who are willing to shun the easy channels of a comfortable life in order to create new enterprise, win huge profit, and invest them again." Gilder insists that "most successful entrepreneurs contribute far more to society than they ever recover."[16]

Gilder was not wrong about the moralizing spirit of supply-side economics and its political champions like Ronald Reagan who, like Gilder, thought of poverty as "less a state of income than a state of mind" and celebrated themselves as altruists martyring their immediate pleasures to the productive risks of entrepreneurial creativity. Indeed, Gilder seems quite prescient inasmuch as his moralization of private profit and corporate self-interest captures perfectly not only televangelism's compromise with materialism, but the spirit of President Bush's successful campaign strategy in 2004 when he managed to keep piety and profits in the same fold, convincing evangelicals that big-time global capitalism was their best friend and persuading capitalists that they had nothing to fear from anti-materialist Christian fundamentalism. In Canada, the *Vancouver Sun* newspaper—Vancouver's largest, most popular daily—published an op-ed on the ethics of shopping titled "Shop till you drop: It's a moral imperative."[17]

Nonetheless, Gilder did not realize that the capitalism he beatified had changed. He confounded late consumer capitalism and what he saw as its celebration of altruistic avarice (greed is good!) with early entrepreneurial capitalism and its celebration of altruistic asceticism (work is holy!). Gilder was singing hymns to saving and investing, while Christians were busy spending and consuming. He applauded the virtue of inventiveness and capital creation, while it was the virtue of product-less mergers and acquisitions and need-generating marketing and branding that were defining the new spirit of consumerism.

By the 1980s, whose Reaganism Gilder foreshadowed, capitalism had moved decisively from a hard to a soft economy, from the manufacture of goods to the manufacture of needs, from an entrepreneurial to a managerial marketplace, from the founding of companies aimed at creating capital to the leveraging of mergers and acquisitions aimed at expropriating and liquidating capital, from financial investment to currency speculation, and from saving to spending. These trends were catalyzed by a successful neoliberal campaign against government regulation—against the very idea of a public sphere—that did more to destroy entrepreneurial innovation and investment in production than venture capital creativity and technological innovation (Gilder's focus) did to create new wealth.

What Gilder failed to grasp was the relationship in the modern economy between the manufacture of goods to meet real needs, which was in decline, and the manufacture of needs to address and absorb the commodity and service surpluses of overproduction, which was growing. What he failed to recognize was how capitalist contradictions were creating great wealth but only by creating great inequality in the same measure; how the traditional productivity of an ethos of ascetic-minded work and investment had over time generated surplus wealth destructive to the ascetic ethos ("the paradox of all rational asceticism . . . is that rational asceticism itself has created the very wealth it rejected," wrote Weber);[18] how overproduction in the world of the haves was paired with underdevelopment in the world of the have-nots such that those with the cash had little need or intrinsic desire to consume while those with true need had little cash with which to address their desperation. These were circumstances designed to accelerate growth but which also spurred inequality both within and among societies.

Capitalism is left in crisis on both sides of the North/South frontier. In the North, in a dynamic compellingly described by William Greider, too many unprofitable products chase too few consumers, too many of whom must be prodded, pushed, and cajoled into consumption;[19] while in the South, too many urgent but unprofitable needs chase too little available capital, held by owners who remain disinterested in those without discretionary income—the impoverished, disease-ridden, deeply needy inhabitants of sub-Saharan Africa, for example.

Consumerism and the Iron Cage

The new consumerism that has become modern capitalism's survival strategy today more closely approximates Weber's somber predictions than it does Gilder's sweet dreams. "In the field of its highest development, in the United States," Weber had warned, "the pursuit of wealth, stripped of its religious and ethical meaning, tends to become associated with purely mundane passions, which often actually give it the character of sport."[20] Gilder hoped to restore the idea of work as a spiritual calling, but though Weber had acknowledged the modern tendency (he wrote at the beginning of the twentieth century) to regard work as a dimension of an obsessive asceticism, he recognized a simple truth: that whereas "the Puritan wanted to work in [what was for him] a calling; we are forced to do so," whether we want to or not. Whereas capitalism once wore a cloak of materialism, of a caring for external goods, that could "be thrown aside at any moment . . . fate decreed that the cloak should become an iron cage."[21]

Gilder wants out of the cage on behalf of his new entrepreneurs, and who is to blame him? But Weber seemed closer to the mark than post-modern neoliberal enthusiasts of the market when he wrote "no one knows who will live in this cage in the future, or whether at the end of this tremendous development entirely new prophets will arise, or there will be a great rebirth of old ideas and ideals."[22] A rebirth of the old ideals is Gilder's fervent wish. But Weber's alternative prophecy about modern capitalism as likely to grow into "mechanized petrification, embellished with a sort of convulsive self-importance" seems more accurate.[23] Weber's shortcoming was that he failed to foresee (or thought it presumptuous and unscientific to pretend to be able to foresee) that modern capitalism, in its "convulsive self-importance," although it initially allowed itself to be stripped of its religious and ethical importance, would in time generate a new ethos. This ethos would be made up in equal parts of an ethic of infantilized consumers and a theology of infantilized true believers.

We need only revisit the rash of television entrepreneurs and business-school gurus over the last decade or two to find a tribe of preachers who, far from abandoning the language of ethics, imitate George Gilder and David Brooks and reinvent it. They draw absurdist parodies of self-rationalizing solipsism and turn them into a new capitalist ethic. Ayn Rand's great libertarian egoist Howard Roark, who in *The Fountainhead* famously declared "I came here today to say that I do not recognize any-one's right to one minute of my life . . . that I am a man who does not exist

for others,"[24] is a rather mild solipsist compared with the moralizing ego-
tists of the new capitalism. A towering example is Oliver Stone's character
Gordon Gekko (played by Michael Douglas in Stone's 1987 film *Wall
Street*) preaching lustily to a choir of stockholders: "The point, ladies and
gentlemen, is that greed, for lack of a better word, is good. Greed is right.
Greed works. Greed clarifies, cuts through, and captures the essence of
the evolutionary spirit." Selfishness no longer cloaks itself in religion: it
has become religion. Greed is not merely good for *me*. The new ethos
wants us to believe it *is* good in itself.

   This postmodern consumer-capitalist gospel is precisely the one found
in the proliferating "how-to" texts of today's consumerist canon where
being rich is defined by spending heartily, and conspicuous consumption is
no longer a vice but a virtue. Jonathan Hoenig's book *Greed Is Good*, whose
title is borrowed from Stone's film, is an example, carrying the whimsical
but telling subtitle *The Capitalist Pig Guide to Investing*. Hoenig counsels
investors to accept that while "greed has been much maligned in our culture . . . [i]n the game called life, the object is to make yourself happy."
Where Weber's early capitalism was a mechanism that gave others what
they wanted and needed, Hoenig understands that "greed is the mechanism to get what you want."[25] Yet Hoenig, as cynical and self-mocking a
guru as you will find, proposes a "Capitalist Pig Credo" whose "capitalist
pig philosophy is not simply about getting rich. More than anything, it's
about the desire to establish lives in which we are in control of our future."
It is about "planning," about "thinking," about "sensitive choices" and "life
goals."[26] Hoenig's real aim is to moralize greed and encourage those who
may have qualms to embrace it—a definition of the new ethos.

   Then there is Suze Orman, the wildly successful television investment
advisor, packaging her advice on money and finance in a book whose
title—*The Courage to Be Rich: Creating a Life of Material and Spiritual Abundance*—might have been crafted in a New England Puritan Sunday school.
Orman does not bother to talk about investment at all; the idea is to jump
right to the getting rich part. The opening pages of her book thus tell
readers "it takes courage to live honestly, wisely, true to yourself—and true
to your desire for more."[27] Orman's prose resonates with the high moral

rhetoric of Benjamin Franklin's *Poor Richard's Almanack* or Bunyan's *The Pilgrim's Progress*: "Our journey started with the act of forgiveness," she writes, "an act that was the first step toward unifying thoughts, words, and action. Through forgiveness, I hoped you would find the clarity and strength to look ahead, with courage and hope. . . . [T]he sum total of your actions makes up your character, and your character determines your destiny."[28] To Orman, those who wring profits from the system are less grasping narcissists than pious pilgrims on their way to salvation. After all, she writes, in a kind of ironic twist on the Calvinist conviction that the saved are known by their good works, "money is attracted to people who are strong and powerful."[29]

Puritanism may then have relaxed its once powerful ethical hold on capitalism, but new believers have replaced it with a trivialized patina of faux spiritualism and instrumental ethics to rationalize the solipsistic psychology of the new relationship between consumers and commodities required for consumer capitalism to succeed. Some time ago, Karl Marx assailed capitalism's (then) new "cash nexus"—a nexus that would drown out "the most heavenly ecstasies of religious fervor . . . in the icy water of egotistical calculation." Worst of all, Marx and Engels explained, it would substitute "for exploitation, veiled by religious and political illusions . . . naked, shameless, direct, brutal exploitation."[30] Modern consumerism, however, reclothes capitalism's nakedness by substituting consumer commodities for the cash nexus. Marx himself had suggested that the triumph of the cash nexus meant that the conventional natural "need for things" would be replaced by what he called "new needs."

The new religion of shopping with its induction of children into the cathedral of commerce sacralizes these new needs. Consumer spending at the turn of the millennium was estimated at 6 trillion a year in the United States, or more than $21,000 per person; super-malls like the Mall of America outside Minneapolis, Potomac Mills in Virginia, or the projected upstate New York DestiNY [sic] Mall do indeed seem to be the American destiny made manifest.[31] Another super-mall in Washington State offers millions of annual visitors over a million square feet of shopping space whose goods target impulse shoppers (only a quarter of visitors come with a specific product in mind) and tourists for whom such malls are "destination" venues and who readily admit they are driven by something other than need—"I didn't need anything," says a typical shopper. "I just went to shop; whatever I like I buy."[32] In the frank words of a 2006 Porsche advertisement introducing the Cayman S, "suddenly the line between want and need seems so arbitrary." Such an impediment, that is to say, to producers who sell products consumers want but are likely to buy only if they can be persuaded they "need" them—in the way that, to take but one example, men now "need" not one or two or three blades, but the Gillette five-blade Fusion razor to secure a clean shave.[33]

Weber imagined a capitalist world in which the cash nexus triumphed over investment, anticipating that late capitalism's managerial overseers were likely to be more interested in liquidating than in creating and investing capital and more concerned to sell unneeded goods to those who could afford them than to produce needed goods for those without the means to purchase them. Hence he envisioned a world where capitalists were transformed into "specialists without spirit, sensualists without heart," women and men singing their own praises yet constituting in truth "this nullity" which "imagines that it has attained a level of civilization never before achieved."[34]

Not everyone who admires capitalism welcomes its decline into the nullity of compulsory consumerism or spiritualizes its coercive kiddie culture. Nor does everyone who appreciates its capacity to create wealth imagine this is the same thing as creating happiness—let alone justice. The somewhat hysterical self-promotion of the 1990s, which allowed investors to persuade themselves capitalism was once again riding a boom fueled by the new digital technology, has given way in some quarters to renewed pessimism. Even as consumer capitalism wins significant electoral victories in the United States as well as in ever more prosperous G-8 nations (including Europe and Japan) or even the G-20 nations (encompassing emerging economies such as India, Brazil, Argentina, Indonesia, South Korea, and South Africa), its mood today is as frequently elegiac as it is celebratory. Already in the 1950s, during the postwar economic boom, there were many voices raised against commercialism and the debasing of the spirit that consumerism could occasion. Erich Fromm, Theodor Adorno, Ernest van den Haag, John Kenneth Galbraith, and Wilhelm Röpke were among the many (conservatives as well as liberals) who rued the costs of an affluence they also admired. Röpke was a typical critic, asking whether there was "any more certain way of desiccating the soul of man than the habit of constantly thinking about money and what it can buy? Is there a more potent poison than our economics system's all-pervasive commercialism?"[35]

There are few Gilder-style enthusiasts in the new millennium, and the optimists must find ways to celebrate consumerism. Often they associate it with the conservative culture and spiritual independence, the very culture and independence critics like Röpke and van den Haag thought commercialism subverted. Few can even muster the cautious mood of semi-affirmation Irving Kristol summoned nearly forty years ago in his *Two Cheers for Capitalism*—a somber tome that was already worried about the "amiable philistinism . . . inherent in bourgeois society" and the "call it what you will, I think I'll call it decadence" against which Kristol recognized the youthful rebels he despised were reacting.[36]

The tone today is more dismal still in some quarters, better conveyed by Robert E. Lane's scholarly but dour (and very aptly titled) study *The Loss of Happiness in Market Democracies*. Lane makes no pretence of enthusiasm: his no-cheers-for-capitalism mood is one of despondency and regret, perhaps because unlike in Kristol's day, today's culture shows little willingness to rebel against the consumer cage in which it is trapped. Lane's pessimism is borne out by survey data: the Worldwatch Institute's *State of the World 2004* reported that within sixty-five surveyed countries, the potential of income and consumption to buy happiness declined as people earned and consumed more than $13,000 a year (a global average whose initial attainment did bring happiness).[37]

In Lane's revealing analysis, one that (predictably) got little commercial attention, he detects "amidst the satisfaction people feel with their material progress" a kind of "shadow on the land." Well before the terrorist catastrophes and economic stagnation that have attended the start of the new millennium, Lane mordantly tracked "the spirit of unhappiness and depression haunting advanced market democracies throughout the world, a spirit that mocks the idea that markets maximize well-being and the eighteenth-century promise of a right to the pursuit of happiness."[38] In this, he was of course only echoing those who have written about alienation in capitalist society going back to Nietzsche (who portrayed bourgeois society's denizens as "last men" little better than small "hopping insects") and Rousseau (who noticed that the more power modern men acquired, the more miserable they became since the power they possessed to assuage their wants merely multiplied those wants).

Then there was Karl Marx who presciently explained how "the expansion of production and of needs becomes an ingenious and always calculating subservience to inhuman, depraved, unnatural and imaginary appetites."[39] And most recently, think of Christopher Lasch's dour predictions about the "culture of narcissism" offered in his book of that title in 1979. Lasch observed how in modern society, "the egomaniacal, experience-devouring, imperial self regresses into a grandiose, narcissistic, infantile, empty self."[40] Lasch's account of narcissism resonates with much of what I will portray as the new capitalist ethos of infantilism. The ethos animating postmodern consumer capitalism is one of joyless compulsiveness. The modern consumer is no free-willed sybarite, but a compulsory shopper driven to consumption because the future of capitalism depends on it. He is less the happy sensualist than the compulsive masturbator, a reluctant addict working at himself with little pleasure, encouraged in his labor by an ethic of infantilization that releases him to a self-indulgence he cannot altogether welcome.

Modern capitalism has in fact been occupied for some time in inventing an ethos that does for consumption what Weber's ascetic ethos once did for production. This has entailed constructing what we have already identified as a difficult and unstable political alliance between prudent Christian conservatism and imprudent consumer materialism, a project originally taken on by the Scottish moralists of the eighteenth century Enlightenment when capitalism still seemed to be addressing real human needs (see for example Adam Smith's *The Theory of Moral Sentiments* of 1759). Today the task is far more difficult. It remains unclear whether a consumerist society can endure the contradiction inherent in a cultural conservatism that upholds values of family cohesion, spiritual growth, and civic responsibility, and a consumerist capitalism that necessarily undermines and destroys such values.

Shopping today is not merely work but has actually become a job for those who act as buyers for rich professionals; just as marketing has become a vocation for those thousands of teens hired by companies to create "buzz" for their products and "influence" leaders for their brands.[41] A kind of choice is preserved, but as I will show, it is only private choice, the prisoner's choice of where to stand or sit inside the consumerist cage: In the mall? At the multiplex? On the internet? In front of the television? eBay? Wal-Mart? Disneyland? Or FedExField?

There is a fiendishly simple method of trapping monkeys in Africa that suggests the paradoxes that confront "choice" in our era of global consumerism. A small box containing a large nut is affixed to a well-anchored post. The nut can be accessed only through a single, small hole in the box designed to accommodate an outstretched monkey's grasping paw. Easy enough for the monkey to reach into, but when it makes a fist to clasp the nut, impossible for the monkey to withdraw. Of course it is immediately evident to everyone (except the monkey) that all the creature need do to free itself is let go of its prize. Clever hunters have discovered, however, that they can secure their prey hours or even days later, because the monkey—driven by desire—will not relinquish the nut. It will die first (and often does).

Consumers are capitalism's one-trick monkeys, free in theory to shop or not; but with the infantilist ethos stoking their desires, once inside the infantilist monkey trap they find themselves unable to let go. The malls and virtual markets are not prisons; but nor can they be said to offer human beings anything resembling public or civic or moral freedom. This is not an argument about "false consciousness" but about "limited consciousness": how consumers are persuaded to embrace a notion of freedom that allows them real personal choice but at the price of subverting their civic liberty (see chapter 4).

Capitalism did not of course make the disheartening journey from noble Puritan commonwealth to joyless consumerist cage overnight. Nor did its ethos evolve from one mandating hard work, productivity for the good of others, investment in the future, and asceticism in daily life to one mandating useless expenditure and backbreaking leisure in the twinkle of a shopper's eye. The economic system changed slowly, and the ethical notions deployed on its behalf evolved with equal deliberateness as capitalism itself was transformed. Between the lost world of Protestantism's productivist winners and today's newfound land of consumerist losers driven as much by an ethos of infantilism as by authentic economic need, lie several complex stages of economic development, each with its own evolving ethos, each connected to the one before it and the one succeeding it. There are slow changes too in the very identity of the beings who were once the market's willing producers and in time have become its ambivalent consumers—or in the case of the poor, disenfranchised and disempowered, its permanent outsiders.

IN THE MANY stages of capitalism, there is a moment that precedes the one Weber identifies, and establishes a context for its success rooted in the very forces Weber's capitalist moment suppresses. That stage of capitalist prelude may be understood as "Creative Capitalism" accompanying and accompanied by an ethic of creative anarchy; it defines the ideal capitalist protagonist as the swashbuckling adventurer. Weber's pivotal stage of bourgeois capitalism is defined by "Investment Capitalism" accompanying and accompanied by an ethic of asceticism (Weber's "Protestant ethic"). It defines the ideal capitalist protagonist as the prudent book-keeper: the calculating investor who is capable of hard work and long-term rational planning as well as sustained saving. The several stages that then interpose themselves between Weber's ideal moment of capitalist takeoff can be called "Liberal Capitalism," accompanied by an ethic of radical individualism and defined by the protagonist as free chooser (the individual defined by autonomy and rights); then "Managerial Capitalism," accompanying and accompanied by an ethic of organization and conservation defined by the ideal protagonist as manager. I will not address these important intermediate phases specifically other than to make clear that the journey from the Protestant to the infantilist ethos was not simple or uninterrupted. The last stage is the one that draws my attention here: "Consumer Capitalism," accompanying and accompanied by an ethic of infantilization and holding as its ideal protagonist the compulsory consumer. As with all such dialectical stages, while these types succeed each other, traces of each are present in each of the others, and none wholly vanish even as they succeed one another. The earlier archetypes of the adventurous entrepreneur, the prudent bookkeeper, the free-choosing individual, and the managerial capitalist all continue to people the world of late consumer capitalism, though it is now dominated by the ethic of infantilism and has as its chief protagonists juvenile consumers unable to achieve the liberty of citizens.

Our abbreviated capitalist story will conclude—although there is nothing absolutely necessary about this progression, and the argument here is not a version of historical determinism[42]—with an emerging phase of opposition to consumerist capitalism, a phase defined by *resistance*. It is however, one of the more daunting features of the ethos of infantilization that it is intractable. Late consumer capitalism is hard either to resist or to change because it creates an illusion of private liberty that renders informal coercion invisible and makes the exercise of public liberty more difficult. Moreover, new marketing strategies aimed particularly at children pick on those least capable of real autonomy or self-conscious resistance. Nevertheless, resistance is possible (see chapters 7 and 8): it depends on a democratizing strategy whose protagonist is the reenergized citizen and whose objective is to address the challenges presented by capitalism's decline into materialist consumerism.

The Stages of Capitalism and the Evolving Power of Ethos

Weber begins his investigation of the link between capitalism and Protestantism not at the beginning but in media res—in the very middle of things, with capitalism already socially formed and politically engaged. The Protestant ethic Weber associates with early capitalism actually defines the values of a capitalism which, if not fully actualized, is well launched, already emerging from spontaneous entrepreneurial creativity into established bourgeois culture. Weber is adamant in noting that his focus is not on acquisition or acquisitiveness per se, features he discerns in every society and that belong to no one economic model. It is rather on capital formation. He is at pains to note that the capitalism whose ethic he is examining is already beyond the stage of "dare-devil and unscrupulous speculators" and those "economic adventurers such as we meet at all periods of economic history." His entrepreneurs are men who, though they have "grown up in the hard school of life" and may be "calculating and daring at the same time," are "above all temperate and reliable, shrewd and completely devoted to their business, with strictly bourgeois opinions and principles."[43] Most critically, Weber believes that the character of the men these capitalists have become is produced in large part by capitalism itself as it achieves rationalization and consolidation.

This is a significant point, because Weber's bourgeois capitalism is well beyond that capitalist prelude that first inaugurates capital accumulation—a protocapitalist stage wholly at odds in its anarchistic wild tendencies with the Puritan ethic of asceticism, yet a phase clearly necessary to capitalism's eventual emergence. During this prelude, the men Weber disdained as daredevils, speculators, and adventurers necessarily predominate. Weber believes such characters may exist in every epoch (and I will suggest they exist in our own as well), but they are prized in the capitalist prelude where their otherwise disruptive personalities appear briefly as quite nearly virtuous, if hardly in the Puritan mold.

THE CAPITALIST PRELUDE:
SWASHBUCKLERS AND WILDCATTERS

The men of the capitalist prelude—exuding virile recklessness, they are rarely women[44]—shape a not-yet-rationalized form of capitalism in which invention and discovery are driven by new and often cockamamie ideas and undisciplined energy. As swashbuckling risk takers, cocky gamblers, and fortune-hunting buccaneers, these precapitalist renegades engender an ethos that rationalizes irresponsibility and gambling and legitimizes an otherwise untrustworthy impulsiveness. They may be called hypocrites by those who come after them since they are men who appear to "teach sin the carriage of a holy saint" (Shakespeare in *The Comedy of Errors*), yet they rarely pretend to be other than they are. And though they are snake-oil salesmen—self-confessed crooks and confidence men—their creative vitality and radical iconoclasm place a halo of virtue over maverick mores that just a short time later will be condemned by the prudent ethos of Protestantism.

Their goal is not yet to accumulate capital. Only to get rich quick (or have a hell of a good time failing to get rich) by breaking with the past, smashing feudal conservatism, stirring imagination, and provoking inventiveness; only to dream dreams and embark on enlivening journeys, even if they lead as often to disaster as to discovery; only to fashion machines and uncover resources which, although they themselves too often squander them, in time become the basis for future capital accumulation and the building of a rational edifice of prosperity. It is protocapitalist men of this sort that George Gilder seems to be celebrating when he prefers risk-taking modern entrepreneurs to Weber's prudent accountants, whose risk taking is always filtered by calculation.

The conservative English philosopher Michael Oakeshott once described this fascinating and trustless tribe who brokered the transition from feudalism to commercial society as "younger sons making their own way in a world which had little place for them . . . footloose adventurers who left the land to take to trade . . . town-dwellers who emancipated themselves from the communal ties of the countryside . . . vagabond scholars."[45] These ragged explorers, uprooted from hearth, home, and comfortable country manse, breaking with the mores of a conservative landed society, were not capitalists, not even traders; but without them, prudent investment and rational management and hence capitalist accumulation and market exchange would not have been possible. There would have been neither the materiel to manage nor the wealth to accumulate: no gold or silver to facilitate trade, no navigational tools to enable exploration, no coal or oil to fuel the economy and build the great monopolies, no machines to gin the cotton, no looms to weave the textiles, no uprooted agrarian laborers to form a restless urban proletariat.

The credo of these explorers and adventurers was imprudence. They refused to calculate and displayed a foolish and destructive indifference to money and its management. Who makes the decision to leave home for the far country based on prudent risk-assessment? The conservative temper is risk averse. Only fools surrender what they have to seek fortunes that may not even exist. These adventurers were clearly fools, bolder than they were wise. The ethos that explained and rationalized their often destructive conduct was deeply American—Whitmanesque—singing the song of the open road, singing the body electric, singing songs of unfettered selves. Whitman's dedication to the spontaneous energy of the solitary self could not comprehend the sort of calculation in which costs are tabulated against benefits. In his "Song of Myself" he captured an America on the creative capitalist threshold as it emerged from the Civil War:

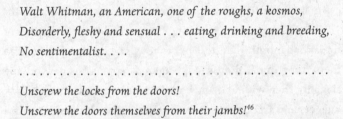

Walt Whitman, an American, one of the roughs, a kosmos,
Disorderly, fleshy and sensual . . . eating, drinking and breeding,
No sentimentalist. . . .
. . . .
Unscrew the locks from the doors!
Unscrew the doors themselves from their jambs![16]

Time and again in each society's early capitalist history, roguish rebels emerge, boasting the size of their own appetites: "I inhale great draughts of space; / The east and the west are mine, and the north and the south are mine," Whitman had exclaimed in his "Song of the Open Road." Time and again, in the manner of American exceptionalism, they have conceived their mission as holy—"I am larger, better than I thought; / I did not know I held so much goodness," Whitman exalted, adding the assurance that "Whoever accepts me, he or she shall be blessed, and shall bless me."[47] It was Whitmanesque adventurers who helped open the trade routes, made the contacts that led to exchange, prepared the roadbeds and laid the rails, mined for the gold and silver and drilled for the oil on which others would found prudent fortunes. Without the brash rogues who came before them, Weber's calculating actuaries who founded the trading firms and investment banks and in time the cartels and monopolies that made nations such as England, Germany, and the United States both prosperous and great would not have been possible. The first generation created first wealth or at least the conditions for creating first wealth; but they were not the accountants who accumulated it, counted it, and gave value to it and who thus gave it its meaning, converting it into collective prosperity.

These precapitalists were Continental explorers like Lewis and Clark, and their seafaring predecessors, who showed not just there was a great wide world beyond the safety of the hearth, but showed how to tie it together through knowledge, communication, and trade. They were wildcatters and miners who became small-town founders, building saloons and general stores around Colorado silver mines and surrounding Pennsylvania oil rigs with opera houses and brothels. The towns sometimes came and went in the flash of a pyrite nugget in a prospector's pan and survived only as long as the oil kept pumping from a shallow field that might dry up in a year or a month. The little boom towns mirrored the men who founded them: they came, flourished, acquired reputations beyond any substantial reality, then withered and vanished in the twenty years it took for the managers and accountants to bring the new wealth under control and rationalize it into a system of accumulation, distribution, and consumption that helped whole societies prosper for centuries to come, but which no longer needed the anarchic new towns and the outlaw adventurers who built them.

In the modern America era they were men like Howard Hughes who multiplied, spent, lost, and regained the fortune represented by his prudent father's Hughes Tool Company on a series of romantic escapades and entrepreneurial adventures involving aircraft, movies, women, real estate, Las Vegas hotels and casinos, and the commercial aviation giant TWA. In all these fields he was a pioneer and speculator who led the way for more prudent followers like Pan American Airways and the great Hollywood studios. Like his love life that touched most of the fabled names of Hollywood glory days (Ginger Rogers, Katharine Hepburn, Bar-

bara Hutton, Susan Hayward, Jane Russell, Linda Darnell, Zizi Jeanmaire, Jean Simmons, Elizabeth Taylor, Rita Hayworth, Ava Gardner, Joan Fontaine, Gene Tierney, and his wives, Jean Peters and Terry Moore), his business career was a bizarre concoction of daring and foolhardiness, invention and corruption, vision and insanity, that left him and the companies he founded deeply distressed.[48] His 1930 $4-million blockbuster film Hell's Angels paved the way for all the excessive Hollywood megahits to come, just as his Spruce Goose flying ship that flew but once, Hughes at the controls, became an icon of the aviation imagination that pushed America toward global leadership in the military and commercial aviation field.

Still more recently, they were the pioneers of the electronic and digital revolution, Silicon Valley cowboys who made the imaginative leaps and took the risks in the 1960s and 1970s that allowed the consolidators and businessmen who established the monopolies and made the fortunes in the 1980s and 1990s to flourish. These were not the Bill Gateses of the cyberworld, but people like novelist William Gibson, John Perry Barlow (who wrote lyrics for the Grateful Dead), and the great cyber-pioneer Norbert Wiener.

There is perhaps no better American model of this precapitalist swashbuckler archetype than John D. Rockefeller's father. On his way to depicting the life of John D., biographer Ron Chernow offers a sidebar portrait of William Rockefeller that captures America's precapitalist prelude right after the Civil War and immediately before the great capitalist breakout that would be called the Gilded Age. Chernow describes this period as "the most fertile in American history for schemers and dreamers, sharp-elbowed men and fast-talking swindlers. A perfect mania for patents and inventions swept America, as everybody tinkered with some new contrivance. It was a time of bombastic rhetoric and outsize dreams."[49] The schemers and dreamers deserve their due, however, which neither Weber nor the prudent capitalists he celebrated ever gave them. We need only look at John D. Rockefeller's disdain for his father's irresponsible ways as well as for the dream-dazed adventurers and self-destructing risk takers he met, used, and overcame on his way up fortune's ladder to understand how valuable the precapitalist miscreants were, both as founders and as instructive counterexamples of what mature, moralizing bourgeois capitalism would require to sustain itself.

John D. Rockefeller's father was one of these maddening mavericks. Chernow calls him "the flimflam man," a charming bigamist raising two families, counties apart, a character also known as "devil Bill" gossiped about as a "gambler, a horse thief, a desperado."[50] William Rockefeller was quite literally a snake-oil salesman, and had crafted schemes as numerous as they were apparently futile on the way to making and losing several minifortunes. He was a father who made early loans to his titan-to-be son but never once grasped how much closer to the truths of mature capitalism his son was than he would ever be.

Walt Whitman was not simply a literary alter ego to William Rockefeller but his actual contemporary. Bill Rockefeller was Whitman's unthinking proxy living out the character Whitman gave to himself when he wrote about what Chernow called those "roughs . . . / Disorderly, fleshy and sensual . . . eating, drinking and breeding." But William's prudent son knew well enough that "the weak immoral man was also destined to be a poor businessman." That as the frontiersman was but a moment in America's journey to maturation, the flimflam man was but a passing stage in the early life of capitalism, a man who created the conditions for capital accumulation but quickly came to stand between capitalism and its destiny.

Throughout his life, John D. encountered and overcame men of the kind his father had been. He had despised an early wildcatter partner, Jim Clark, as "an immoral man . . . [who] gambles in oil," and bought him out with a bluff that was an early example of Rockefeller's own calculating risk-taking in the name of prudent management.[51] And he had disdained swaggering show-offs like his first partner, George W. Gardner, who spent all he earned on fancy clothes and large watches to announce his wealth to an envious world he should have been diligently and quietly serving. John D. carried a like contempt for the kinds of boom towns that must have fired his father's imagination. Towns like Pithole Creek, where the first Pennsylvania oil wells had come in, represented to John D. the noisome souls of men like his father writ large. They were "a cautionary fable of blasted hopes and counterfeit dreams," a fable that renewed "fears of the [oil] industry's short life span."

Yet without William, there would have been no John D.—no child of fortune but no fortune-founding capitalist either. For John D.'s own success was dependent on the boundary-breaking creativity and narcissistic spontaneity of foolhardy swaggerers like his father, those willing to forfeit their own lives and fortunes to generate the energy that—once captured and contained—would allow capitalism to grow up and become a mighty engine of productivity. Bourgeois capitalism was able to root itself in firm soil only because of the deracination of those who came before. What was true for America after the Civil War had been true for Weber's Europe earlier. Europe's new riverside trading towns that had catalyzed early European capitalism in the Renaissance were possible only because of the bold young men who fled the safety of medieval manses in the late Middle Ages to seek their fortune on the road. The homey family values of America's bourgeois Protestantism (Methodism for example) that would in time secure and underwrite mature capitalism depended likewise on the homeless mobility of an earlier generation willing to turn its back on its own roots.

The creative precapitalist was not concerned with creating wealth by addressing long-term needs; adventurers were short-term narcissists after all. But they prepared the ground for the machines and mechanisms by which needs would in time be addressed and met. Oil wildcatters were drilling with mindless excitement for a commodity that had no obvious early purpose other than supplementing whale oil supplies, and it was not until the internal combustion engine that oil would come to serve the vast needs of a fully industrialized mobile society. Gold and silver addressed no human needs absent a complex and mature system of trade, capital production, and exchange, but those who mined for or traded them set the stage for the families of Fuggers and Rothschilds and Rockefellers who later figured out how to turn them into sustainable economic and political power. Many early inventions were forged from curiosity and pure science and gained their value as capital only when put to use instrumentally by prudent capitalist middlemen. Copernicus and Galileo were driven by scientific curiosity and drawn in by the starry night; but they made discoveries that would facilitate navigation and lead in time to global exploration, which in turn would open the world to trade and exchange of goods and labor. Yet astronomers had no more interest in the mundane but world-altering applications their science would occasion than explorers had in the financial bounty their magical journeys would eventually precipitate. Marco Polo was no prudent capitalist playing out a Puritan asceticism; nor was Christopher Columbus (unlike his sponsors) a cautious actuary concerned with accumulating wealth. But without them one cannot imagine free trade or capitalism—or the modern world *tout court*.

To put it in contemporary terms, early capitalism was not yet a demand or a "pull" economy based on need; it was still a "push" economy based on finding things and then seeking a use and a market for them. In this sense, early capitalist economies resemble the digital economy of the 1990s where technological ingenuity and invention outran by far the potential need for what was being engineered, leading to a boom-bust cycle still being played out. If (see below) Bill Gates plays Rockefeller to information capitalism's golden age, crazies, prophets, and adventurers like William Gibson and John Perry Barlow are, as I have already suggested, its digital wildcatters and electronic swashbucklers.

If each epoch in capitalism's evolving story is represented by a civic prototype, the period of prelude can be said to feature an anticivic prototype—the outlaw innocent, the romantic anarchist. His values are radical individualist, often anarchistic, displaying an obliviousness to if not a disdain for conventions and mores. His headstrong behavior is antisocial and iconoclastic, but his motives are innocent and childlike. He may be utterly disreputable, but he seems lovable. He belongs to the family of charming bad boys, winked at even as they are being criticized, appreciated for their groundbreaking spirit even as they are condemned for their rule-breaking boisterousness. These first-stage capitalist forbearers share with last-stage obsessive consumers a penchant for impulsive, childish behavior. To call them infantile would distort their nature, but there is ironically a streak of the childish in them that—as will become apparent—brings capitalism full circle in its late global consumerist phase.

WEBER'S RATIONAL CAPITALISM:
CALCULATING INVESTORS AND PRUDENT BOOKKEEPERS

When Max Weber drew his portrait of the spirit of capitalism on the rise, he depicted an ethic and an era. A sociologist rather than a storyteller, he did not deign to identify actual capitalists from the Reformation era (and beyond) who might have illustrated and dramatized his sociological account. But he might in fact have been describing the powerful Family Fugger, a Catholic merchant family that spread out from the German Renaissance city of Augsburg in the age of Luther and Calvin to encompass much of Renaissance Europe in a network of mining, trading, and banking interests that controlled emperors and popes alike. Or portraying the Northern Baptist American Rockefeller family turning a nascent and anarchic oil industry and emergent systems of transportation into a national fortune that helped create a capitalist American nation after the Civil War. Or even depicting the secular Gates family taking the new technology of our own age and recasting it as a vast monopoly of software platforms and digital paradigms signaling the passing of the Industrial Age and the coming of the Information Age. These capitalists embody the abstract ethic of Protestantism in ways that illustrate the powerful effect a cultural ethos can have on economic and political behavior. While other religious cultures have proven compatible with trade and banking, notably Judaism, only Protestantism has offered so dramatic a cultural foundation to the growth of industrial capitalism in its entrenched and rationalized modern form.

Ron Chernow offers a compelling account of this second more rational stage of capitalist development when the colorful daredevils and pioneering speculators give way, as Max Weber wrote, to the "men who had grown up in the hard school of life, calculating and daring at the same time.[52] Chernow is writing about John D. Rockefeller (to whom we will turn our attention presently), but he might have been describing the Fuggers.

Jacob "The Rich" Fugger: At the very moment in 1517 when Martin Luther was pinning his ninety-five theses on the doors of Wittenberg Cathedral, Jacob Fugger ("Jakob der Reich," or Jacob the Rich) was deploying a family fortune that came to rival and then surpass that of the Medicis (who controlled the Renaissance supercity Florence) on the way to dominating Europe from Rome and Madrid to London and Vienna, casting its shadow across the widening world as far as Chile, Peru, and the Orient. As Luther was preaching (Thesis 43) that "Christians are to be taught that he who gives to the poor or lends to the needy does a better work than buying pardons," Jacob Fugger was using his fortune to help the Papacy sell pardons yet also to found in Augsburg the first settlement house for the poor in Europe—the Fuggerei, an institution conceived by Jacob in 1505 that survives into the modern day as both the oldest continuing settlement house in the world, and a landmark in the development of the idea of charitable activity as a responsibility of great wealth. "Gain, save, and give," which was to become John Wesley's Methodist gospel, seemed already to be permeating Jacob Fugger's Catholic soul.

The Latin inscription that stands to this day over the entrance to the Fuggerei commemorates Jacob and his two brothers, who describe themselves as inspired by "piety" and "born for the good of the city." They acknowledge that "for their great property they have to thank chiefly an all-powerful and benevolent God."[53] When assailed by his many enemies as an ambitious and evil cartelist, Fugger reproached them in language later piety-struck American millionaires would emulate. To Duke George of Saxony, Fugger would write: "They say I am rich. I am rich by God's grace, without injury to any man."[54] Like Rockefeller in a later century, Fugger disciplined his risk taking with piety and justified his wealth accumulation through service. His innovations were calculated rather than risk taking, wholly in the Weberian mold. Prudent competence was his hallmark. His "talent for organization not only broke new paths in the development of trade, but exploited for the benefit of his enterprises the whole new machinery for the communication of news."[55]

He was in fact a uniquely protomodern capitalist, perhaps because he was an ardent cartelist who saw in monopoly a prudent business practice. In the words of a popular biography, though "actually still a person of the Middle Ages," Jacob Fugger was "simply a manager of modern style. He was a stranger to sentimentality . . . excluding incompetent and female members of the family from business matters in order to keep capital tied up in the firm." He turned to monopoly practices, much as Rockefeller would do later, "to ensure that capital [received] . . . a high return, and one as regular as possible, in order to compensate for the risk involved. Monopoly alone provides such a return."[56] This would not be the last time monopoly was justified as a blunt instrument that might impose regularity and order on the chaos of competitive markets. Fugger appealed to more than his own risk: to be sure, monopoly would assure him profits, but it would also redound "to the benefit of the whole German economic system."[57]

Jacob Fugger was a Catholic, but so too was Luther before his rebellion; and as Luther discovered in his interaction with the Catholic Church and the peasant communities of Germany the source for a new religious ethos that became Protestantism, so the Fuggers discovered in their business activities and intellectual practices a moral outlook that would in its own way contribute to Protestantism as well. For by the measure of his enterprise and his managerial and monopolistic inclinations, he was a Catholic possessed of an ethos that seemed both modern and in that sense Protestant. He not only breathed in but helped generate the Protestant spirit of his age. His financial empire served (and to a degree controlled) both Emperors Maximilian I and Charles V of Hapsburg *and* the Papacy, paying in 1505 for the establishment of the Swiss Guard and minting coins from the output of his mines in the Austrian Tyrol and Hungary for Popes Julius II and Leo X. While the Fugger family played some role in the sale of papal indulgences—call it investment, if not quite in the Puritan mode—it also set a pattern for later Protestant capitalism by founding many of Europe's first charities (including the aforementioned Fuggerei).

For all of this, the Fuggers remained faithful Catholics, and Jacob Fugger actually drew the ire of Martin Luther (if also a certain grudging admiration).[58] But Fugger's business practices and experience as "a manager of modern character" whose "advanced knowledge and innovations, forbidden transactions involving interest and monopolies and the giving and taking between himself and the great powers of his time" suggested what Weber would see as a Protestant mentality that both absorbed and helped generate the new ethos Weber would later celebrate—an ethos that made it possible for the Fuggers to capture, control, and deploy the fantastic new energy of monopoly capital.[59]

The secret weapons of the Fuggers, along with cartelism, were double entry bookkeeping and Giro credit transfers that allowed commodities to be converted into cash and cash into the cashless moving and accumulation of wealth. The Fuggers had learned their bookkeeping secrets in the great Renaissance trading port of Venice and then, propelled by their mining and trading interests, put them into practice in Germany and the rest of Europe with consequences that were to impact profoundly European capitalism. As Weber had grasped, it was accounting that turned capitalism from an adventurer's dream into a prudent man's empire.

The Fuggers' economic power, it is crucial to see, came however not merely from the control of cash flow. Later banking empires like the one established by the Rothschilds from their base in France exercised a kind of financial hegemony over extended sectors of worldly power—the Rothschilds rescued Denmark from bankruptcy and bankrolled Napoleon. But as Frederick Morton notes in his short biography of the family, "from 1810 on, and to this very hour the family [Rothschild] would buy and sell money only."[60] Not the Fuggers. This talented family trafficked in a wide variety of commodities, engaged in trade, and used the banking business associated with their properties to build monopolies and influence political power—acting the part of Weberian capitalists by investing wealth as well as creating it, deploying it as well as saving it, in the name of both worldly and spiritual ends.

They began as merchants and their fortune originated in the spice trade and in woven goods in whose manufacture they were directly involved. In time, the business grew to encompass the mining industry (above all copper, but also silver, gold, and zinc), where Jacob the Rich eventually established near monopolies of a kind rare in the sixteenth century, though a model of cartelism for later centuries. This was perhaps Jacob Fugger's greatest achievement. It was this model that defined investment capitalism in its Weberian productivist phase, and this model that was eventually to define the work of John D. Rockefeller, the prudent bookkeeper who helped catalyze the great capitalist "takeoff" after the Civil War in the United States.

John D. Rockefeller: Indeed, in this later epoch during which the United States was embarking on its own storied capitalist journey, John D. Rockefeller introduced many of the entrepreneurial and bookkeeping techniques that Jacob Fugger had used centuries earlier and that Weber had portrayed in the abstract into the practical business of constructing America's first great corporate colossus. Rockefeller's rise defined and was defined by the emergence of an unprecedented monopoly in oil production, refinement, and distribution (Standard Oil) as well as in the national transportation systems they required (rail and waterways). As Ron Chernow discerns, Rockefeller's business career was deeply embedded in his religious convictions. His devotion to work, to rationality, to thriftiness, and to saving spoke eloquently to the piety instilled in him by his evangelical Northern Baptist mother. When, for example, he introduced rational bookkeeping into large-scale businesses, he not only tamed the wild capitalist adventure that was the Pennsylvania oil boom but managed to sacralize accounting and ennoble the most quotidian moments in his mundane commercial life. The day on which he got his first appointment as an assistant bookkeeper to the firm of Hewitt and Tuttle (September 26, 1855) he commemorated as "job day." The double entry bookkeeping ledgers that enabled him to impose rational control over the chaos of early capitalist oil and commodity markets became "sacred books that guided decisions and saved one from fallible emotions." His first ledger in time took on the aspect of a "sacred relic."[61]

We do not then need to read Protestantism into Rockefeller's life. What Chernow calls "the close mesh of Christianity and capitalism in his early career" is already apparent in the leadership role he played at the Erie Street Baptist Mission Church in Cleveland, in his commitment to charity work even before he became enormously wealthy, as well as in the way in which he read his capitalist successes as a part of a providential design: "These vast stores of wealth were," he was certain, ". . . the bountiful gifts of the great Creator."[62] His creed was simple: "I believe the power to make money is a gift from God . . . to be developed to the best of our ability for the good of mankind. Having been endowed with the gift I possess, I believe it is my duty to make money and still more money, and to use the money I make for the good of my fellow man according to the dictates of my conscience."[63]

Weber conceived capitalism's ethic as Protestant. The great Puritan preacher John Wesley regarded Christianity itself as an "essentially social religion." What Wesley understood as the obligation to gain all the wealth you can, save all the wealth you can, and give away all the wealth you can became the shared legacy of Methodists and Northern Baptists as well as the obligation of America's Gilded Age capitalists[64]—a gospel which, in historian Gertrude Himmelfarb's phrase, united frugality and industry.[65] Hence, even as Rockefeller devoted himself to "preparing and distributing this valuable product [oil] to supply the wants of the world,"[66] using methods some likened to thuggery, he could thus think of himself as embracing Wesley's "new trinity" calling for gain, saving, and giving. During this period, this social gospel had become the shared legacy of Methodism and Northern Baptism. The "robber barons" might be conniving monopolists prepared to smother the capitalist competition that had afforded them their successes, but they were also self-described noble philanthropists heeding the words of 1 Timothy (6:17–18) in the Bible: "Charge them that are rich in this world. . . . That they do good, that they be rich in good works, ready to distribute, willing to communicate."

Rockefeller in fact set himself to proving Weber wrong on one score: that industry and frugality were incompatible in the long run. Along with Wesley, Weber had worried that the greatest achievement of the Protestant ethos—the common devotion of the best of men to both industry and frugality—could not long endure since, in Wesley's words, "whenever riches have increased, the essence of religion has decreased in the same proportion." Why? Because "as riches increase, so will pride, anger, and love of the world in all its branches."[67] But Rockefeller committed himself to both industry and frugality, gaining and giving, capitalism and piety, the twin pillars of a life in which creating wealth brought with it the responsibility of being wealth's prudent steward. In an age entirely before capitalism, America had been founded on high-minded principles of the sort

espoused by Benjamin Franklin declaring that a man diligent in his business would surely stand before kings. Rockefeller stood Franklin on his
head, believing not only that being good at business entailed a life of
moral probity and charitable activity but that being an undisciplined and
immoral person destined one "to be a poor businessman."[68]

This is not the place to compare Rockefeller's pious scruples with his
capitalist behavior. Even Chernow, whom some might regard as a little too
sympathetic with Rockefeller's rationalizations, is clear that in the name of
imposing a "hypertrophied craving for order" on the "lawless, godless
business" that was oil, Rockefeller was displaying "lust for domination . . .
messianic self-righteousness, and contempt for those shortsighted mortals
who made the mistake of standing in his way,"[69] along with "competitive
cruelty," "knavery," and "grand-scale collusion" that were "unparalleled in
industry."[70] But this was precisely the power of the Protestant ethos—not
just a theology that in Rousseau's words could "spread garlands of flowers
over [our] chains,"[71] but a living philosophy that allowed selfishness to
serve altruism and acquisitiveness to fuel philanthropy. In taking over
competitors he had helped to break, Rockefeller thus "liked to make Standard Oil sound like a philanthropic agency or angel of mercy, come to succor downtrodden refiners," offering himself not as their liquidator but
their savior. As he would say, "we will take your burdens."[72]

What was perhaps most innovative in Rockefeller's deployment of a
religious ethos to explain and animate his economic behavior was that,
echoing Weber's equation of modernity and rationality, he argued that the
creating of cartels and monopolies was actually rationality incarnate—a
way to tame disorder and permit monopoly to serve the interests of society at large. Weber's Protestantism had served capitalism by liberating the
individual and putting a moral premium on both work and investment.
Rockefeller's Northern Baptist rationalism allowed him to justify monopoly as a way of bringing orderliness and beneficent profitability to society
by eliminating the competition that had once defined capitalism's essence.
As once Weber had argued that the medieval guild served to unite and
thus to "limit" competitors,[73] Rockefeller could argue modern cartelism
limited competition among the anarchic forces that had created wealth,

enabling a society (and its cartel owners) to maximize the rationality and orderliness of a prosperous and growing industrial economy.

Bill Gates, Jr.:[74] To the extent archetypes of capitalist development, early, middle, and late, coexist in every period of capitalism, we should be able to identify more contemporary exemplars of Weber's capitalist accountant, people who like John D. Rockefeller forge monopoly to secure control over the "rational growth" of capitalism. Bill Gates, Jr., is an apt candidate, if obviously far too modern and postindustrial to fully incarnate the ethos Weber celebrated. Exploiting the work done by earlier inventors and engineers, Gates adapted software to different hardware platforms, especially BASIC, that was to become the foundation for his business at Microsoft. But much more importantly, Gates created a new business model.[75] For the Microsoft DOS and Microsoft BASIC platforms became the industry standards through methods that were aimed at creating domination rather than competition. The operating-system platform on which the software would run would be tied to IBM personal computers—"bundled" with them, as this questionable arrangement became known. At the same time, Microsoft would retain the rights to license the software and operating system to other hardware manufacturers.[76] This allowed Microsoft to become the most sought after supplier rather than just another hardware manufacturer. It also led the federal government eventually to challenge Microsoft for illegal and monopolistic practices, charging that "Microsoft maintained its monopoly power by anticompetitive means and attempted to monopolize the Web browser market . . . by unlawfully tying its Web browser to its operating system."[77]

Gates's success was then not simply the result of a good product whose intrinsic virtues trumped those of the competition. There were many firms like Apple, Netscape, or Novell offering attractive (some would claim superior) alternative platforms, while open source software (Linux for example) was promising a more or less "free" alternative option. Rather, as the federal government's legal case against Gates made clear, "the company behaved anti-competitively . . . [and] these actions contributed to the maintenance of its monopoly power," which led the government to "affirm the court's finding of liability for monopolization."[78]

Gates had created his working monopoly via bundling—trust-style tie-ins with hardware—as well as other techniques that not only went well beyond the virtues of his product, but made competition around the real virtues of competing software impossible.

Gates's Microsoft did for software what Rockefeller had done for oil. It embraced a commodity whose initial value in terms of market demand was less than clear, one produced by risk-taking adventurers with a frontier mentality. It tamed this frontier spirit by eliminating much of the competition that was capitalism's great virtue, rationalizing the distribution system and creating a monopoly over the product. Gates was what all the great institution-builders of industry were, a brilliant opportunist. He preferred the de facto to high principles: "Many of the most successful standards, however," he observes, "are 'de facto': ones the market discovers. . . . But because de facto standards are supported by the marketplace rather than by law, they are chosen for the right reasons and to get replaced when something truly better shows up."[79] In his boosterist paean to new technologies called *The World Is Flat*, Thomas L. Friedman rightly extols the pioneering work of Marc Andreessen in developing the Mosaic web browser, which set an industry standard and turned the internet into a usable technology.[80] What he fails to notice is that it was not Andreessen the pioneer but Gates the rational consolidator who fashions the consumer monopoly and makes the fortune off of pioneers who came first. Let others test the market: then jump when the results are in. Let someone else invent: then buy the fruits of their invention.

It was a field with pioneers aplenty, a plethora of brilliant people with ingenious ideas going all the way back to the father of modern cybernetics, Norbert Wiener of MIT. There were mathematicians like John Kemeny and Thomas Kurtz, who invented BASIC but never managed to commercialize their work, as well as other visionaries who either lacked the technical expertise (William Gibson or John Perry Barlow, for example), or creators like Ed Roberts, the inventor of the Altair 8800, whose careers floundered as their fledgling companies were bought up before the big money was made. The creator of the Cray Supercomputers, Seymour Cray, built what many people regarded as the best computers in the world, only to see his company go under and his own personal fortune vanish. The mass consumer market in electronics, like the petroleum products market, had to be created before the great profits it promised could be reaped. Others focused on the products, but Bill Gates created the market and in the end fashioned a market monopoly for his company.

The difficulty everyone in the computer industry had to overcome was the challenge of platform compatibility. Initially, many viable platforms and programming languages existed which could be used by programmers to expand consumer possibilities. But which platform would consumers be induced to choose? How much genuine choice would there be? Was it to be a genuine demand market in which the pull of consumers determined the corporate winners? Or a supply-side market in which a monopolist pushed its product on a public deprived of real competition (the model we will examine in the balance of the book)? The company controlling the chosen platform would in fact dominate the market. Bill Gates recognized this feature of the new digital economy early on. In a speech at the Rosen Forum in 1981, he observed in his characteristically modest fashion (again not unlike John D. Rockefeller), "I really shouldn't say this, but in some ways it leads, in an individual product category, to a natural monopoly: where somebody properly documents, properly trains, properly promotes a particular package and through momentum, user loyalty, reputation, sales force, and prices builds a very strong position within that product."[81]

The computer market was of course extremely mutable: platforms could change, software would evolve. Even as Gates established a strong, near-monopoly position in the personal computer market, he knew he would face new competition inspired by what he had achieved—what David Bank has called the "monopolist's dilemma."[82] As expected, when a new graphic user interface was developed by Apple which allowed the iconic representation of a desktop on the computer screen, Microsoft was centrally challenged. But Bill Gates quickly outfoxed competitors like Steve Jobs of Apple, Phillipe Kahn of Borland, and Bruce Bastian and Alan Ashton of WordPerfect. These companies had provided what many users regarded as superior products, sometimes even gaining an initial market

position that looked dominating, only to see Microsoft buy up other competitors, or develop its own imitative products, or—most successfully—by
combining or "bundling" products which were previously kept discrete
(the move to bundle office applications into "suites," for example), forging
an effective market monopoly that prevented competitors from selling
rival products, however superior. This was particularly important in the
early 1990s as Bill Gates expanded Microsoft's business from the operating
system into applications. Technology was changing rapidly, often under
the leadership of others, but over the decades Microsoft showed a remarkable ability to keep up or at least keep close through bundling, buyins,
buyouts, or new products of its own. When computer networks first
emerged, powerful competitors like Raymond Noorda of Novell or 3Com
seemed poised for leadership, but Bill Gates again relied on the initial platform of the operating system to forestall competitors seeking to get
around it. Each time Microsoft made fundamental changes to its operating system, switching from MS-DOS to NT or from 16-bit to 32-bit technology, competitors thought they had a chance to overtake it; but
Microsoft always managed to use the downward compatibility of its products to close the window of opportunity.[83] Microsoft was quite simply
what came with most of the hardware on the market; not much choice
there. Some even claimed Microsoft systems were built to be incompatible with other platforms so that, despite the putative presence of a choice
to switch, such change really wasn't viable. All of this suggests a business
model in which real consumer choice is no longer the driving force in
making a company profitable—our subject below.

Even in the brash new business associated with the internet, where
Microsoft initially seemed to stumble badly, Bill Gates managed to recover.
When Netscape's cofounders Andreessen and Jim Clark, together with
other internet service providers (ISPs), radically altered the shape of the
digital market, Microsoft seemed stymied. It had nearly missed what was
happening and almost failed to enter the market. Yet in time Gates developed his MSN service provider and myriad associated services in email
and instant messaging. More recently still he has entered the hot search-
engine market, showing a willingness to take on industry favorite Google.

Successful as Google has been (the "new Microsoft"), only a romantic would bet against Microsoft as it once again moves aggressively into a market pioneered by others.

Chernow tells us that Rockefeller "was almost certain to feel distressed by this unstable economy, which forced him to steer his orderly business through a maelstrom of incessant change."[84] Gates too must have felt that his own success depended on controlling the maddening fluctuations of the marketplace that might look like freedom to others but appeared as chaos to him. Struggling against the "maelstrom of incessant change" led capitalists like Rockefeller and Gates to seek monopoly control of the marketplace. Rockefeller had once created a cartel controlling not just 90 percent of the petroleum refined in the United States along with the refineries themselves, but also barrel making and the factories that made them, warehouses, shipping facilities, a fleet of tank cars, and—well beyond the energy sector—interest in or control over railways, waterways, and pipeways—every industry implicated in the vast business network through which oil was extracted from the ground, moved around the world, and converted into saleable consumer products. Bill Gates, Jr., had to do exactly the same in the new anarchic information society economy. He needed to control not just a single programming language, but also operating systems, networking, hardware development, consumer applications, business applications, internet browsers, communication and search applications, and everything else in the information economy on which a profit was to be made.

Gates was seeking his own systematic solution to the chaos of early market relations in the digital software industry. As Chernow observes, Rockefeller had gotten hold of "a momentous insight, pregnant with consequences. Instead of just tending to his own business, he began to conceive of the industry as a gigantic, interrelated mechanism" that had to be managed through "strategic alliances and long-term planning . . . [replacing] competition with cooperation in the industry."[85] The new telecommunications industry of the 1990s needed the same remedy: "cooperation" as a euphemism for the suppression of competition, the elimination of choice, in a phrase, total domination.[86]

What Rockefeller in effect achieved then was not merely the deploying of the Protestant ethos to rationalize and explain the need for work, saving, investment, and giving as features of both world gain and spiritual salvation. He achieved something even more remarkable: the deploying of the Protestant ethos to rationalize and explain the need for monopoly. When he was charged with outlawry by the competitors in the refinery industry he crushed, Rockefeller would simply claim that Standard Oil was "the Moses who delivered [the refiners] from their folly which had wrought such havoc in their fortunes." He would boast that his efforts were "heroic, well meant—and I would say reverently, Godlike—to pull this broken-down industry out of the Slough of Despond."[87] What passes for competitive capitalism is actually "a vulgar materialism" replete with "rapacious business practices that dissolved the bonds of human brotherhood," whereas Rockefeller's strategy of cartels could end this "egoism and materialism abhorrent to Christian values." His rivals were "blackmailers, sharpsters and crooks," so many "selfish people forever stirring up trouble or creating annoyances, like so many mischievous children who need a good stiff spanking from father."[88]

Thus did Rockefeller try to use the Protestant ethos to overcome a fundamental contradiction of capitalism—that on the way to consolidating the inventions, products, and commodities that emerge from the early capitalist competition that is the market economy's greatest virtue, monopolies are created which not only breed inequality and unfair competition practices, but that destroy the very freedom upon which capitalism builds its success.

Gates may have been less direct in rationalizing monopoly, but he did respond as the great monopolists of the Gilded Age once had to charges of selfishness and abuse by seeking to become a philanthropist on a scale no less grand than the scale of his business career. As the Fuggers established their social welfare settlement in Augsburg and Rockefeller his foundations and religious charities in Cleveland and New York, Gates made Redmond, Washington, the home not merely of his corporate ambitions but of the philanthropic efforts that, in scale and ambition, became Microsoft's good angel twin. The Bill and Melinda Gates Foundation, run by his father, almost immediately became one of the world's largest and most generous foundations—taking on not merely challenges of the digital divide (where philanthropic efforts might be said to help Microsoft's own business) but working in areas like HIV education, providing vaccinations and medications in developing countries, and nurturing secondary education. Worth roughly $46 billion, Gates has pledged to give away up to 95 percent of his wealth to his foundation. In 2006, Warren Buffett, second-richest man on earth after Gates, pledged the greater part of his $30-billion fortune to the Gates Foundation, making it larger than the next seven largest foundations in the world combined.

Like earlier giants of capitalism, Gates brings to his philanthropy the same hearty optimism that characterizes his business career. The upbeat prose of his foundation website mirrors the upbeat marketing language of Microsoft: "While the world around us fuels our sense of urgency, it also fuels our optimism. We believe that by increasing equity and opportunity, the world will become a better place for generations to come. We see positive changes every day in the work of dedicated partners who are helping millions of people transform their lives and communities. As the years ahead bring more advances in health and learning, we share the global responsibility to ensure that they reach the people who need them most."[89]

Gates himself, although not exactly a self-rationalizing and grandiloquent moralist on the model of such predecessors as Andrew Carnegie or John D. Rockefeller, has used the language of what is "good" and "right." He has said, "In the US there's always talk about equity—racial inequity and gender inequity. And if you think, boy, inequity as the world is getting richer—improving these inequities is something that it's right that we do."[90] On December 26, 2005, appearing above the title "The Good Samaritans," Bill and Melinda Gates, flanking the U2 band rock star activist Bono on the cover of *Time*, were with Bono named *Time*'s "Persons of the Year." In rhetoric that could have been used for Andrew Carnegie, *Time* set up Gates: "Billionaires are . . . removed [from reality]," it pontificated, "nestled atop fantastic wealth where they never again have to place their own calls or defrost dinner or fly commercial." But not Gates: "For being shrewd about doing good, for rewiring politics and re-engineering justice, for making mercy smarter and hope strategic and then daring the rest of us to follow," Bill Gates (and Melinda and Bono too) was a *Time* Person of the Year.[91]

The Protestant way: doing well by doing good. And you don't have to be Christian anymore to grasp it. It is a residual of a vanishing system, still evident in big-time philanthropy, even as we plunge into an era of rank infantilization and bottom-line consumer capitalism. We can be glad Carnegie built libraries, glad that the Gateses are battling AIDS, but inequality will not end because billionaires give back some of the spoils of monopoly.

THE TRANSITION TO INFANTILISM

There is no instant transition from the great era of capitalist consolidation reinforced by the Protestant ethos to this new era of capitalist consumerism shored up by an infantilist ethos, no fast road from corporate altruism in which capitalism serves society to our own era of capitalist narcissism where business mandates profligate spending on faux wants while ignoring real human needs. A full history of the evolution of ideological rationalizations would pause between the ethos of asceticism and ethos of infantilization to ponder transitional stages that include both a phase of radical individualism and a phase of managerial capitalism—phases evident not just historically, but as moments within the dominant consumerist epoch we see today.

Capitalism is defined by entrepreneurship and competition, and even in its days of cartelist consolidation (the Fuggers, Rockefellers, and Gateses), freedom remained its most advertised public virtue. Hence, as productivist capitalism evolved, the tensions between monopoly and competition remained fierce. The balance between the two was from time to time restored, both through liberal market ideology and government intervention on behalf of competition (Theodore Roosevelt or Bismarck, for example). Capitalism's liberal individualist phase is closely associated with the marriage of capitalism and liberal democracy—defined more by freedom and personal choice than by participation or equality. Nonetheless, in response to the market's natural contradictions, stark during capitalism's liberal phase, the emerging democratic state played a balancing role that kept markets in check. As capitalism's rapid growth created wealth faster than jobs, and promoted prosperity without redistributing it justly, the democratic state legalized unions and authorized safety nets and a progressive income tax that balanced market accounts. As entrepreneurial competition was overtaken by cartels and monopoly, democratic antitrust legislation saved capitalism from itself. Egoism found itself up against a civic community willing to enforce the rights of the public. Ayn Rand in a face-off with John Dewey. Hoover versus FDR. John D. Rockefeller's capitalism in check.

Liberal capitalism was accompanied and to some degree succeeded by a phase of managerial capitalism, best exemplified by the 1950s and 1960s in the United States when management of capital became more important than ownership, and the deployment of resources more valuable than the creation of resources. Corporate managers grew conservative, seeing their task as maintaining wealth and perhaps expanding it on paper rather than in reality. Mergers and acquisitions took precedence over the creation of new wealth. James Burnham, John Kenneth Galbraith, and other theorists of managerial capitalism have described the new protagonists effectively.

In the hundred years that separated the Gilded Age from the consumer revolution in the United States, then, productivism gave way to consumerism, and the fate of citizens, so promising under liberal democracy, grew dim. A truly distinctive new ethos did not emerge, however, until consumerism found itself staggering under the burdens of overproduction, without enough customers for the myriad products its triumph made possible. The virtues of the old capitalism began to calcify. Which brings us to our own era and the dilemmas of the infantilist ethos, which has put capitalism at risk and citizenship in danger.

PART 2

THE ECLIPSE
OF CITIZENS

3

Infantilizing Consumers:
The Coming of Kidults

Childhood makes capitalism hum over the long haul.
—Dan Cook[1]

THE INFANTILIST ETHOS generates a set of habits, preferences, and attitudes that encourage and legitimate childishness. As with Protestant asceticism in its time, infantilism reflects broad attitudes and general behavior that mirror the age, beyond the specific concerns of capitalism. But it also serves capitalist consumerism directly by nurturing a culture of impetuous consumption necessary to selling puerile goods in a developed world that has few genuine needs. As the earlier ethos helped explain and shape the leadership of capitalist producers such as Jacob Fugger and John D. Rockefeller, but also Bill Gates in our own period, the infantilist ethos helps explain and shape the behavior of capitalism's marketing executives and ardent consumers in our era.

A cultural ethos, whether Protestant or infantilist, cannot be said to have a particular "author," and the linkage between it and the requirements of capitalism is always oblique and informal, although no less efficacious for that. This is to say, it does not result from a silent conspiracy of corporate meddlers and marketing propagandists. Yet it serves capitalism—in the case of the infantilist ethos, it serves consumerism—in ways that can be quite concretely elucidated. For the ethos is impressively efficient in creating market demand by encouraging the manufacture of faux needs in the affluent world, thereby assuring the sale of all the goods and services capitalism is zealously overproducing. I have depicted the impact of infantilization on our society and on the character of consumer capitalism in general. But what exactly is it? How do its dynamics work to support radical consumerism?

Infantilization aims at inducing puerility in adults and preserving what is childish in children trying to grow up, even as children are "empowered" to consume. What counts as childish is of course measured by norms embodied in the construct of childhood itself, which is less a biological fact than a contrivance of human imagination, "invented" for social, economic, and political purposes. The modern idea of childhood was introduced only in the Renaissance around the time of the rise of Protestantism, and like Protestantism was conditioned to some degree by the printing press and the growth of literacy.[2] It gained ground in the Enlightenment with the work of writers such as John Locke and Jean-Jacques Rousseau who insisted on the idea of human development (and its defining rationality) as a series of stages in which the young and very young were to be understood not merely as little adults in waiting but as a distinctive genus with distinctive developmental and educational needs. In his study positing the vanishing of childhood, social critic Neil Postman observed that it was the idea of childhood that permitted a portrait of the modern idea of adulthood, distinguished by "the characteristics . . . of a fully literate culture: the capacity for self-restraint, a tolerance for delayed gratification, a sophisticated ability to think conceptually and sequentially, a preoccupation with both historical continuity and the future, a high valuation of reason and hierarchical order."[3]

Postman is typical of modern psychological and sociological views of child development, which to some degree track the Protestant ethos (self-restraint, delayed gratification, rationality, and order). Playing on child/adult dualisms, this perspective suggests that childishness, in contrast to adulthood, privileges:

IMPULSE over DELIBERATION;

FEELING over REASON;

CERTAINTY over UNCERTAINTY;

DOGMATISM over DOUBT;

PLAY over WORK;

PICTURES over WORDS;

IMAGES over IDEAS;

PLEASURE over HAPPINESS;

INSTANT GRATIFICATION over LONG-TERM SATISFACTION;

EGOISM over ALTRUISM;

PRIVATE over PUBLIC;

NARCISSISM over SOCIABILITY;

ENTITLEMENT (RIGHT) over OBLIGATION (RESPONSIBILITY);

THE TIMELESS PRESENT over TEMPORALITY (NOW over PAST and FUTURE);

THE NEAR over THE REMOTE (INSTANTANEOUS over ENDURING);

PHYSICAL SEXUALITY over EROTIC LOVE;

INDIVIDUALISM over COMMUNITY;

IGNORANCE over KNOWLEDGE.

Such an ungainly set of dyads offers a telling psychological landscape, but one more expansive than we can traverse in this spare portrait of the infantilist ethos. That landscape's contours are reduced here to three archetypical dualisms that capture infantilization: EASY over HARD, SIMPLE over COMPLEX, and FAST over SLOW.[4] As with the stages of capitalist development charted earlier, such stages of psychological development as manifested by these dualisms often tend to intersect and overlap with one another in ways that are more dialectical than dyadic, ways that can conserve what is virtuous and attractive in children while superseding what is merely puerile or (in adults) retarded. In elaborating the child/adult dualism, it is in fact more useful to think about a process, about the triadic rather than the dyadic. To do so is to conceive of plural stages of maturation in which the move from (say) easy to hard or simple to complex or fast to slow takes the form of an evolution in which something of the child (the easy, the simple, and the fast) is retained and elaborated in the fully evolved adult. Since, as Erik Erikson wisely observed, "every adult . . . was once a child," society has to learn how to "take care of the unavoidable remnants of infantilism in its adults."[5]

Hence, for example, while one might generalize that children prefer the easy way to do things while adults accept and even cultivate the hard and disciplined way, it is more judicious to suggest that truly mature adults supercede easy/hard altogether, and instead achieve something like *fluency*, the seeming ease that comes with extensive learning, effort, and discipline, that consummate skill that makes art and achievement appear effortless. Fluency manifests some of that unself-conscious youthful ease which we prize in children but which in its raw form can morph into sloppiness, laziness, or complaisance, whereas when reproduced by virtue of hard work and purposeful discipline it may reappear in a mature and productive form that moves beyond the obsessive authoritarianism sometimes associated with being grown up. Deploying the language of William Blake, Erik Erikson thus suggests that "the child's toys and the old man's reasons are the fruits of the two seasons." By this he means "the child's play is the infantile form of the human ability to deal with experience by creating model situations and to master reality by experiment and planning."[6] Adults invent and create by transforming child's play into a grownup tool, which is an aspect of what artists do, for example.

In the same vein, while it is inviting to suppose that children often prefer fast, while adults appreciate the virtues of slow, it is probably more accurate to attribute maturity neither to the rabbit nor the hare but to the owl who is deliberate when necessary but can also pounce like the hawk. Deliberateness is not ponderousness but a prudent pace of the kind captured by the phrase "proceed with all deliberate speed." The same is true for many of the other dualisms referenced here: where children are characterized by a kind of anarchic spirit of liberation which is not at all the same as adult autonomy (think of Peter Pan), the absence of such anarchic liberty need not be what Peter Pan feared would turn out to be adult servitude or what the philosophers call heteronomy (being morally ruled by others), but can be moral autonomy—the use of freedom to choose the purposeful and the good. This is the kind of disciplined liberty Kant and Rousseau associate with free moral willing. Unlike childish license, adult moral autonomy is neither anarchic nor authoritarian but both purposive and common, a foundation J. M. Barrie's Wendy (in *Peter Pan*) seemed to appreciate was associated with growing up and having her own family. It was this foundation that Rousseau suggested created the conditions for democratic self-rule.

In this more dialectical spirit, children may be said to be playful (playfulness without purpose), young adults earnest (purposefulness without play), while fully mature adults can achieve that disciplining of playfulness by purpose that we associate with artistry—as Erikson has argued, using play as adults to help "master reality." Children are innocent by virtue of their ignorance, young adults knowledgeable and informed without necessarily being wise (and so beyond innocence without yet being good), while fully mature adults are wise in that they can use knowledge and experience to become capable of informed ethical judgment. Childhood tends to treat "truth" absolutely, even dogmatically, while doubt and uncertainty characterize skeptical young-adult understandings of the world. Yet the doubt that follows dogmatism in a maturing intelligence can in time issue in a renewed and tolerant belief, but one which, more universal and acknowledging (sometimes even encompassing) of other belief systems, espouses faith anew without reembracing dogmatism. This is perhaps one difference between the kind of dogmatic, fundamentalist faith that can be characterized as infantilizing, and mature faith that has weathered self-reflection and critical doubt.

This more dialectical approach helps explain how certain features of childhood impact on adult culture, not by being conserved in their original form, but by being transformed and reintegrated into mature behavior in a fashion that retains the virtues of the childlike in a mature adult setting. Such dialectical complexity needs to stand in the background of our analysis here.

Nonetheless, because my aim here is to understand the nature, causes, and consequences of infantilization—of puerility and childishness—in catalyzing and reinforcing consumerist behavior, rather than to offer a full-blown, dialectical account of developmental psychology, I will focus on the trio of closely associated pairs introduced above: the easy over the hard, the simple over the complex, and the fast over the slow. In doing so, I will treat civilization a little simplistically, even reductively, as the culture of grown-ups in general; and I will identify the ethos of consumer capitalism in decline with the cultivation of childishness in the broadest sense.

EASY over HARD

To say the infantilist ethos prefers easy over hard is actually also to say the young are naturally drawn to what is simple rather than what is complex and what is fast rather than what is slow. Easy versus hard acts as a template for much of what distinguishes the childish from the adult. Phrases such as "easy listening," "shopping made easy," "easy (appropriate for ages 2–8) games," and a person of "easy morals" push and promote commercial products tailored to the attention span and tastes of the young. Easy in the realm of happiness supposes simple pleasures trump complex ones, whereas spiritual and moral leaders have generally made the opposite case.

The preference for easy plays off of modern utilitarian ideas. Traditional ethics (in Aristotle, Augustine, or Kant, for example) distinguished higher and lower forms of pleasure and presumed that what gave pleasure might not always be identical with what was good. But modern ethical utilitarianism of the kind found in philosophers like David Hume and Jeremy Bentham tried to subordinate "the good" to what was merely pleasurable and then to simplify and reduce pleasure to elementary physical stimulation. It made no distinctions between kinds of pleasure (or pain), assuming that happiness depended merely on maximizing elementary pleasure and minimizing elementary pain for the greatest number of people. This permitted Bentham at the beginning of the nineteenth century to offer a useful if simplistic "felicific calculus" that associated all human behavior and all human ethics with simple, easy-to-measure indicators of elementary pleasure and pain. The good was what *felt* good. What felt good was pleasure's presence and the absence of pain as measured by the lowest common denominator of sense experience. Happiness was quantifiable. How intense was it? How long did it last? How soon would it come? How certain was its realization? But this meant the child's easy pleasure (to take a Freudian example) in playing with his own excrement was simply another (largely indistinguishable) example of the kind of reductive pleasure an adult might find in playing the flute in an Afro-Caribbean rock band.

Jeremy Bentham's own student John Stuart Mill rebelled against such simplifications and insisted that pleasures had to be qualified, that there were *kinds* of pleasure, some worth more than others, some easy, others harder, some simple, others more complex, some childish, one might say, and some more grown-up. Not all pleasures were immediately commensurable with one another: like apples and oranges, or feces and flutes, they were distinguished by quality as well as quantity. Some were to be preferred to others because they offered "higher" pleasures won at the cost of harder work and more disciplined effort and yielding more complex and satisfying kinds of happiness. On Mill's scale, like Aristotle's, the pleasures of the hard and complex trump the pleasures of the easy and the simple. In his celebrated aphorism, poetry was preferable to pushpin, because happiness required embracing the Epicurean mandate to "exchange easier for more difficult pleasure" since "difficult pleasures are more rewarding."[7]

These features of modern utilitarianism with its roots in psychological "pleasure-pain" hedonism are worth noting because they suggest that infantilism has assimilated the utilitarian and instrumentalist inclinations of the age and used them to rationalize supposed "virtues" of puerility. The tensions between easy and hard have challenged every society, but ours is perhaps the first in which the adult institutions of a civilization seem to be on the side of easy. Ours rewards the easy and penalizes the hard. It promises profits for life to those who cut corners and simplify the complex at every turn. Weight loss without exercise, marriage without commitment, painting or piano by the numbers without practice or discipline, internet "college degrees" without course work or learning, athletic success through steroids and showboating. In the realm of foreign policy, President Bush's high-minded global strategy of liberty shares in the ethos of easy, comprised by words without consequences: war without conscription, idealism without taxation, morality without sacrifice, and virtue without effort. The very opposite of a Protestant ethos: not "no pain, no gain," but "all gain, no pain." An infantile dream-view of the world in which saying "I want it to be so" is enough to make it so; in which, critic Slavoj Žižek has pointedly remarked, the consumer market offers products that make choice easy—"products deprived of their malignant property: coffee without caffeine, cream without fat, beer without alcohol . . . virtual sex as sex without sex, the Colin Powell doctrine of war with no casualties (on our side, of course) as war without war, the redefinition of politics as expert administration as politics without politics."[8]

Lying, cheating, and deception (especially self-deception) are features of the human condition, but they become more acceptable today in part because they are seen as a justifiable form of taking the easy way. How much easier to set sports records and achieve athletic celebrity with steroids than without. The widespread use of performance-enhancing drugs has been disclosed by the media, and addressed by Congress, but though the new rules for baseball mandating a fifty-game suspension for proven use are stiffer than the old (along the lines of a ten-day suspension for first offense, up to a sixty-day suspension for the third, and so on), the record books have not been modified to reflect earlier drug use. How much easier to lie about drug use when asked than confess the truth. Even athletes caught in flagrante delicto have persisted in lying. Baseball player Rafael Palmeiro addressed congressional hearings on steroid use with the flat denial "I have never used steroids, period,"[9] just months before he tested positive for steroid use.

Students too find it easy and wholly defensible to cheat on tests and plagiarize term papers. "On most campuses, 70% of students admit to some cheating."[10] With plagiarism, the issue is no longer that it is common, or that numerous websites offer term papers for sale, but that many students are unable to see what is wrong with it. Among the dozens of websites offering fully written and ready-to-submit essays, term papers, theses, and (!) "doctoral dissertations" is the company Best Custom Term Papers, whose web ad carries the remarkable header "100% Non-Plagiarized Custom Term Papers." By which the company presumably means *it* has not plagiarized *its* offering, so that the student purchasing it can be sure that there is only *one* plagiarist involved![11]

With producers intent on rationalizing intellectual theft on behalf of their customers, and grown-up writers and scholars fuzzy about the meaning of intellectual property (especially in an age of postmodern literary criticism where texts are commodities supposedly belonging as much to those who consume them as those who produce them), it is little wonder that students find plagiarism so easy to indulge in—hardly even of sufficient importance by the loose standards of larceny to warrant forgiveness. After all, borrowing language or forgetting to reference other scholars' work has not significantly damaged a number of well-known historians' reputations any more than contriving facts and experience in a drug and prison memoir did major damage to the sales of James Frey's *A Million Little Pieces*, not at least until Frey received a crushing on-the-air rebuke from celebrity "critic" Oprah (who when Frey's malfeasance was first exposed, initially supported him). Journalists at *The New Republic* and the *New York Times* made large reputations on the basis of wholly fabricated "news" stories, where they seemed (without success) to have to work harder at getting caught than they did at composing their entertaining fictions.

Unlike more traditional societies, ours makes many things that ought to be hard, easy, such as acquiring a gun or a spouse. It is easier to get a marriage license than a driver's license and about as easy to get divorced as to get married. That half of all marriages end in divorce has at least something to do with the narcissistically puerile and irresponsible attitudes that people bring to marriage and to divorce, and of course to the children their marriages produce. Prudent ideas such as covenant marriage, which makes it harder to get married in the hope that people will find it less easy to get divorced, have had strong advocates but few followers outside the mostly Christian communities where the idea has been endorsed.[12]

It is also easier in a generic sense to watch than to do, easier to watch television, where the imagination is more passive, than to read books, where the imagination must be activated, easier to masturbate than establish relationships within which reciprocal sexuality and interpersonal sensuality are a healthy part, easier to maintain a sexual relationship that is discretionary and capricious than one involving commitment. In sum it's easier to be a kid than a grown-up, easier to play than to work, easier to push aside than to assume responsibility. This is not a fustian conservative point (although conservatives have perhaps understood it better than others). Call it Aristotelian or even utilitarian in John Stuart Mill's version. For what is being argued is that on every count, what is easy may also turn out to be less gratifying, hampering rather than furthering human happiness. But this is a lesson that only adults learn—after they have been helped by parents, schools, church, and society to grow up. Under the cultural sway of infantilization this lesson is made to seem rigid and Puritanical, the preserve of people who are hostile to happiness.

SIMPLE over COMPLEX

As an entailment of its preference for easy over hard, then, the infantilist ethos also prefers the simple over the complex. Simplicity has a sweetness all its own, but adult civilizations are generally defined by their capacity to embrace nuance and complexity in their thinking and behavior, even where decision making may ultimately require reaching a conclusion that puts aside nuance.[13] Complexity avoids simplistic dualisms, and looks for shades of gray. Scales of moral complexity such as the one postulated by the late Harvard experimental psychologist Lawrence Kohlberg rank complexity of thinking and the ability to shade as features of a more developed moral sense. Carol Gilligan has shown that the moral voice of women may be defined by a still greater complexity and sensitivity to context, one that moves beyond Kohlberg's own perhaps too gendered dualisms.[14]

Philosophers and scientists often explain and elaborate the meaning of life itself, along with the consciousness in which life issues, in terms of a widening and deepening spiral of complexity: subatomic particles and force fields constitute atomic particles like electrons and protons which in turn constitute atoms and molecules which constitute the complex atomic elements that constitute molecular matter; matter is made more complex yet as it becomes organic matter; organic matter assumes still greater complexity on its way to becoming life; and life at its most complex yields consciousness, reflection, and then self-consciousness and self-reflection. We are beings defined by the very complexity by which we understand ourselves as being complex. Yet this very complexity contains a defining simplicity that speaks to the dialectics of these dualisms. Complexity entails "the spontaneous self-organizing dynamics of the world," writes science commentator M. Mitchell Waldrop. Summing up the science literature, he notes that "complexity, adaptation, upheavals at the edge of chaos [are themes] . . . so striking that a growing number of scientists are convinced . . . [they point to] an underlying unity, a common theoretical framework for complexity that would illuminate nature and humankind alike."[15]

Complexity defies the reductive principles by which we might insist our essence is defined by water or mere atoms since our bodies are 98 percent water or 100 percent molecular; for it is precisely in *how* they arrange themselves that some molecules end up constituting living consciousness and others the petrified stones or swirling plasma or the hydrogen, oxygen, and carbon molecules from which all conscious, living matter comes and to which it can all be reduced. The association of complexity with mature adulthood and civilization, and of simplicity with childhood, is everywhere evidenced today in the commercial marketplace. Consumerism reduces identity to its own commercial behaviors and leads to an identitarian psychology in which quite literally we "are what we buy"— we are the brands we consume (chapter 5). Shopping and consuming are not an aspect of behavior but define the meaning of life.

The preference for the simple over the complex is evident in domains dominated by simpler tastes—fast food and moronic movies, revved-up spectator sports and dumbed-down video games, for example, all of which are linked in a nexus of consumer merchandizing that the infantilist ethos nurtures and promotes. Many of those lionized and rewarded by commercial culture today, heroes to the child consumers who are prime targets of marketing, are themselves behaving like the kids for whom they are supposedly role models. In an acute and quite astonishing *New Yorker* profile of the celebrated basketball player Shaquille O'Neal (at the time still the strongman of the then indomitable Los Angeles Lakers), Rebecca Mead describes how "American culture is increasingly geared to the tastes of teen-age boys" by showing how Shaq lives the life of an unformed teen, utterly secure in the "simplicity of his tastes." She shows how in "many ways his life style is a thirteen-year-old's fantasy existence," how he "has surrounded himself with cousins from Newark and old friends from high school, who share his interests in goofing off, breaking stuff, making noise, shooting guns, and driving a wide range of motorized vehicles." She introduces us to a buddy in the posse which envelops him like a childhood security blanket: he recalls with boyish glee the "food fights, where Thomas, the chef, will come in from the grocery store with all these things, and Shaquille will break a whole watermelon over my head, and I'll hit him with a pudding cake." Shaq keeps a huge video collection ready for his extensive TV watching, including the whole Little Rascals series and countless Kung Fu movies. His friend recounts how "Shaquille likes to wake me up with a pillow smash to the face. You know how you get to being sound asleep, and someone smashes you in the face with a pillow? It's so funny."[16]

Is it? Maybe at thirteen, but Shaq was over thirty at the time. He is, however, working in a sports culture that prefers its athletes to be foolish playboys. When Shaq celebrated his thirtieth birthday party with red balloons at the foot of his driveway, a red carpet with Superman logos projected in spinning light in his living room, long tubular balloons in red and yellow and blue as decoration, and a cake with O'Neal depicted as Superman as the party's climax, he was acting out a role the corporation that employed him helped design and perfect.[17]

Mead reaches exactly this conclusion from her observations about O'Neal: "Basketball itself is marketed with teen tastes in mind. The theatre of a Lakers game has an adolescent-boy aesthetic: goofy and overheated . . . whirling spotlights . . . high-fiving; the snippets of roaring rap music and of the teenboy anthem 'We Will Rock You' by Queen."[18] If John Stuart Mill with his Aristotelian sense of complexity preferred "poetry to pushpin," America today has been induced to prefer the new hot-dogging star-centered basketball of precocious high-school players to the old, team-centered basketball of defense-minded coaches where experience counted and skill meant more than razzle-dazzle. A simple rather than a complex game. No wonder youth-obsessed film industry celebrities sit courtside in New York and Los Angeles, and even seemingly grown-up stars such as Spike Lee and Jack Nicholson decorate "celebrity row" on both coasts, seen at NBA games with the same regularity that athletes appear in juvenile movies and on rock albums.

Basketball in its new simplified, high-speed, offense-minded form is only the most popular and perhaps global of the many sports that in their commercial incarnation today both benefit from and reinforce the infantilizing inclinations of the current corporate ethos. Sports in the commercial setting offer insistent consumables that demand and are reinforced by infantilization—whether it is of thuggish soccer fans in England hypocritically condemned by the owners who sometimes seem to welcome if not actually incite their behaviors, or of twenty- or thirty-something television viewers in the United States wooed by goofy beer ads targeting their puerile fantasies and encouraging their teen taste tendencies. While there are certainly athletes like NBA players Bill Russell and Michael Jordan from earlier eras and Channing Frye or Steve Nash today[19] who whatever their age are thoughtful and grown-up, able to treat their sport as an adult profession, this is not apparently what the companies that have transformed athletics into pure circus entertainment have in mind: the norm is increasingly the infantilized athlete controlled by the supposedly adult corporate owner indulging in infantilizing tactics in the name of the bottom line. As ever before, the excuse is "we are only giving people what they want."

Former Philadelphia Eagles running back Terrell Owens was eventually run off his team for unprofessional behavior that included insulting his quarterback Donovan McNabb. Yet his juvenile antics were tolerated for years on a succession of teams, and while there was much tut-tutting about his unprofessional media-pandering, it was Monday Night Football that arranged for him to do a pregame skit with television's *Desperate Housewives* actress Nicollette Sheridan, who appeared in the Eagles locker room wearing only a towel.[20] The various professional associations make a fetish out of applying tough rules against recalcitrant players, but tolerate and benefit from media-mongering player behaviors that increase the audience for their sports and enhance the revenue for their member teams.[21]

Yet it seems apparent that the corporations that control spectator sports manipulate the game and its environment to maximize consumer sales, giving people not what they want but what they want them to want. Basketball games are forty-eight minutes long, which does not allow much time for affiliated commerce (beer, banners, peanuts, and popcorn for starters, and then the blaring ads and MTV music), so time-outs which "officially" last sixty seconds are allowed to run for minutes at a time, leaving the television advertisers plenty of time as well. A three-quarter-of-an-hour game can last several hours nowadays. In college basketball, even during the NCAA tournament Final Four games, the time-outs actually end after sixty seconds and the games stretch out into eternity only when they are televised.

It is not just basketball. *New York Times* sportswriter William Berlind gives a startling portrait of a typical baseball-club locker room that makes "the boys of summer" a study in literalism and suggests Rebecca Mead's description of Shaq is typical of sports in general rather than specific to basketball or to Shaq. The New York Mets baseball-team clubhouse, designed to "help the players relax and bond," Berlind reports, is "a cross between a frat house rumpus room and a Chuck E. Cheese's." It is a place where players hang out "in the windowless rooms, in which the air-conditioning is always on full-blast, the flickering blue lights give the players a pasty, somewhat sickly aspect as they watch TV, play John Madden's video football on Nintendo 64, read tabloids, get massages and eat."[22]

Sports today, with its preference for fast and simple over slow and complex, discloses the ambiguity of an infantilist ethos that dumbs down adults even as it accelerates the maturation of children into "empowered" consumers. Adult athletes are treated like children and behave accordingly; children are pushed to grow up into profit-generating "adult" athletes as fast as possible, regardless of the consequences to their bodies or their spirits. More and more often, star athletes skip college to join their chosen professional teams right out of high school. Where children's play was once a vital domain of spontaneous activity in which the young had fun while developing their bodies through a variety of physical endeavors from tree climbing and hopscotch to stickball and tag, it is fast becoming preprofessional training ground for commercialized professional sports. As Michael Sokolove has written, "Left on their own, children are natural cross-trainers. They climb trees, wade in streams, play whatever sport is in season and make up their own games."[23] But the early specialization foisted on them by commerce makes them less fit—"one-trick ponies" as Brendan Sullivan, director of Headfirst Baseball, calls them,[24] at greater risk of injury and cut off from the playful aspects of sport that traditionally afford purposeless pleasure.

The infantilist ethos works in a purposefully contradictory manner—pushing kids to grow up fast into professional profit-turning athletes who can then reembrace the childishness their professionalization compelled them to abandon. The trained teen is the perfect marketing target: old and disciplined enough to spend, and sufficiently conditioned to make music or movies or athletic moves—but young enough to embody the puerile taste required to generate global consumer needs. Ironically, where once top-down authoritarian societies imposed professional sports training on juveniles in places like East Germany and the Soviet Union, today it is free-market societies that do much the same bottom up, motivated less by national or ideological hubris than economic greed.

Sports, like entertainment generally, is an obvious but hardly the only domain where simple trumps complex. The transformation of hard news into soft news, and soft news into infotainment, is an old story made worse by talk radio and cable television, neither of which owe anything to broadcasting's once weighty civic standards. Journalist Michael Massing recently asked whether "The End of News" was impending, in the first of two articles for the *New York Review of Books*. Yet iconic broadcast journalist Edward R. Murrow's polemic against the loss of autonomy and integrity on broadcast news (memorialized in the recent film *Good Night, and Good Luck*) is sixty years old, suggesting that the infantilizing of broadcasting is not exactly a novel development. Cable news has, however, accelerated the dumbing down, creating what Massing has called the "Fox effect" (after Rupert Murdoch's Fox News approach) which is visible throughout the industry.[25] The Sinclair Broadcasting Group, which controls sixty-plus stations with access to as much as a quarter of the American television-viewing audience, notoriously instructed its eight ABC affiliates not to run a Ted Koppel *Nightline* segment on which Koppel read the names of the one thousand Americans (the number is now approaching three thousand) killed in Iraq. Too hard for viewers to deal with, and perhaps also in keeping with "the various steps the administration has taken to suppress coverage of US casualties."[26] Even in serious newspapers, complex issues are increasingly marginalized. The *Los Angeles Times* no longer has a labor news reporter, nor anyone specializing in issues of poverty.[27]

Most newspapers are losing money, and finding it more and more difficult to compete with television and the internet, which are in turn finding it increasingly tricky to accommodate hard news. PBS begins to look like CNN, while CNN looks more like Fox, even as Fox turns into ET (Entertainment Tonight), each of them drifting away from the adult standards by which they once defined themselves. In a hilarious but distressing interview with former Clinton staffer Paul Begala and conservative journalist Tucker Carlson on the (now defunct) television show *Crossfire*—a purportedly serious political opinion forum whose very title indicates how far from complexity and nuance television news has come—the Comedy Central Network comic Jon Stewart reminded his hosts that they were supposed to be more than political hacks.[28] When a comedian has to remind serious journalists of their responsibilities, the bottom is falling out of serious broadcast journalism.

Learning and growing are hard; they always feel in the first instance like you are losing something. Remaining ignorant and youthful is easy; it requires nothing but indulging the pleasure principle. For the merchandiser this does not mean taking pleasure in the child's play but taking profit from the child's pleasure. For simple pleasures entail big-time profits. As Erica Gruen (then a Saatchi & Saatchi Interactive researcher) noticed, what is called the "lucrative cybertot category"—kiddies on the web—offers a "medium for advertisers that is unprecedented. . . . [T]here's probably no other product or service that we can think of that is like it in terms of capturing kids' interest," precisely because when kids go on-line, they enter the "flow state," that "highly pleasurable experience of total absorption in a challenging activity" which means "there is nothing else that exists like it for advertisers to build relationships with kids."[29]

FAST over SLOW

The preference for easy over hard and simple over complex issues naturally in a preference for fast over slow. The world of kids is a hare's civilization in which tortoises have no place. It has been seventy-five years since philosopher Bertrand Russell wrote *In Praise of Idleness*, and since that time the "pleasure of slowness," Milan Kundera observed not long ago, "has disappeared." Kundera proposes that "speed is the form of ecstasy the technological revolution has bestowed upon man,"[30] and ecstasy, like speed (the eponymous drug for people who think they are cool), is a specialty of the young. Kundera makes technology the culprit, but technology is always a tool, and while it has features that catalyze speed, speed is something the infantilist ethos demands from both technology and capitalism. Fast food, fast music, fast film-editing, fast computers, athleticism in which speed alone counts, digitalization where speed is the primary objective, the fast-track life (even where it is actually a no-growth road to nowhere)—these are the ever more embedded trends that dominate popular youth culture and commerce worldwide. In India, the new generation of fast consumers call themselves "Zippies."

James Gleick, who writes about speed, observes that the modern Olympics reflect "an obsession with time that is more finely grained and intense than ever in human history. It has a weird effect on the Olympics. The Games themselves have been twisted by our obsession with time and our control of it."[31] Gleick's study of speed rests on the premise that "the modern economy lives and dies by precision in time's measurement and efficiency in its employment." Business is always making "a grab for a few extra seconds of your time. . . . With fast ovens, quick playback, quick freezing, and fast credit."[32] Fast translates into instantaneity, which, Gleick observes, "rules in the network and in our emotional lives: instant coffee, instant intimacy, instant replay, and," bringing us back to what is perhaps infantilization's greatest departure from the Protestant ethos, "instant gratification."[33]

In a more recent book about "thinking without thinking" called *Blink*, Malcolm Gladwell tells us that snap judgments and instant impressions carry both dangers and utilities. Although Gladwell argues that lightning judgments and first impressions may actually represent mental shortcuts rooted in slowly accumulated experience—something akin to wisdom— the first impression the book itself leaves behind is one of fascination with instantaneity, a catering to the pop-cultural vitality of the idea of speed.[34] "Insta-books" are in fact ever more common in the publishing industry, where a record of sorts must have been set in 2006, when an insta-book about Jennifer Aniston and Brad Pitt of more than two hundred pages was written in just one week.[35]

Fast edits and jump cuts in films and videos as well as the instant pop-up ads that blitz the internet all exhibit the same frenzied obsession with speed. Compare Hollywood films of the 1930s where scenes could last for tens of seconds or even a full minute without a single edit or change in camera angle with today's music videos and comic-book and digital-action films where no scene lasts more than a second or two without a snip here and an edit there. In today's film and video, multiple jump cuts per second are the norm for hyperactive directorial control freaks among whom faster has become a form of cinematic tyranny, imagining as they do that youthful audiences saddled with their media-induced attention deficits crave such speed—even as they themselves reinforce the addictive tendencies. Speed is a drug like any other that must be taken in ever higher doses just to maintain its hold over the psyche.

Digitalization encourages and facilitates both speed and nonlinearity, the latter a kind of artificial rupture in temporality in which our "normal" linear experience of time is deconstructed into nonsequential fragments. Ruptures in temporality may well catalyze art and creative innovation, to be sure (the Best Picture Oscar-winning film *Crash* is an example), but are corrupting to normal consciousness and to responsible and predictable behavior of the kind traditionally associated with mature adulthood.

Seen from the perspective of adulthood, speed has become the paramount modern form of youthful vanity: time whipped, time mastered, time accelerated, time overcome. Whether in teen film series starting with *Terminator, Back to the Future,* or the *Matrix* trilogy through recent series such as *Final Destination* and *X-Men,* or through electronic devices permitting "time shifting" of television and cable programming (TiVo) and music listening (iPods), we are now hurried time travelers as malcontent with the idea that "now" can contain our anarchic temporality as we are with the idea that a particular space can contain our spastic bodies (as our gadgets liberate us from fixed spaces). All the small luxuries of our slow yesteryear's youth for which pace defined virtue—oatmeal, chess, mashed potatoes, love letters—are now available quicktime: not just fast but instant, from instant to blitz chess and instant messaging (Gleick's instantaneity). What is the message of instant messaging with its abbreviated happy-/sad-face emoticons, its inventive contractions, and its furious pace, other than the message of being in a hurry? Kids will instant message for hours as if they have but seconds; the mad seconds accumulate, leaving them plenty of time to compose sonnets: but they content themselves with sentence fragments. For the person on the other end is waiting, and probably multitasking and might go away any sec now, and time's a flying, so hurry up!

With the perceived victory over time comes the illusion of victory over death—not just the would-be magic of cosmetic surgery and the promised immortality of cryonics but the total liberation from time that comes with instantaneity: ceaseless instant change, change so fast that it bypasses every terminus and overshoots the stop signs that might otherwise signal death's approach. Shopping itself partakes of the illusion that time can stand still or vanish completely: clocks are never seen at the mall (nor in casinos), where vendors hope shoppers will feel as though time is standing still while they shop or gamble. Fast food means eating (fueling up) is almost instantaneous. "Conspicuous consumption stems from a fear of death" concludes a dour trio of sociologists—with "shop till you drop" both an exultant boast and a reminder of what can happen if shopping is ever allowed to end.[36]

Video games too depend on rapid neurological response and instant reaction to stimuli. Such games are intrinsically tied to the perpetuation of childhood and represent one of the most successful sectors of merchandizing to children and turning adults into consumers of children's commodities (more on this below). But even as measured by speed alone, intelligence in the world of digital games is associated with the rapid firing of extant synapses rather than the forging of new synapses that constitutes traditional associative intelligence (putting together and making sense out of the raw information generated by fast neurons). Where once intelligence was equated with wisdom and deliberation, with the deliberate privileging of slowness and the intentional expenditure of time's wealth, today smart is too often about quick. To be counted as bright, you have to be a quick study, reach conclusions in the blink of an eye, short-circuit the deliberative process (bor-ing!), and cut to the quick. College and Law Board exams, like all modern tests, are timed—a recent proposal to make them open-ended was quickly shot down.

Making a virtue of what seems to have become a necessity, we have our own modern Panglosses to reassure Candide that speed is good. Steven Johnson regards our fast-moving video-game planet as the best of all possible worlds in which everything bad is actually good for you. He initially proposes that succeeding in interactive video games takes time and hard work, just the way the old Protestant ethic said good things should. Earning the goods needed to go to the next level "takes time—a lot of time." Except, as Johnson also acknowledges, "you can buy a magic sword or a plot of land—entirely made of digital code—for hundreds of dollars on eBay,"[37] and thus circumvent time and hard work altogether. That's the new technology, a fool's tool with which you can buy time—in order to circumvent time and with the hours "saved" rush on to victory or more shopping.

Nowhere is the acceleration of time more apparent than in the domain of "news." If news is what is new, in an era of high-speed happenings only the "latest" and "newest" count as truly new. News cycles that lasted weeks and fortnights in the eighteenth and nineteenth centuries, when monthlies reported happenings messengered by stagecoach and steamboat at a leisurely lunar pace, have progressed in the same ponderous but sure way that compound interest accumulates. In the first half of the twentieth century, when daily news cycles were being driven by the telegraph and news ticker and wire services, and newspaper dailies took over from weeklies, the pace took off. In the last half century, hours, minutes, and seconds have come to dominate the now clichéd 24/7 news cycle in which instant communication and media digitalization that move literally at the speed of light give cable news networks and the internet (to which traditional print media are fast migrating) their powerful but deeply counterproductive edge.

Fast here is by no means better or even particularly appropriate. The news cycle now moves faster than the news, with twenty-four-hour-a-day cable services and blogs demanding more content than the lumbering real world can provide. "The Pope is dead" is but a single news item which more or less speaks for itself, and needs no reiteration. Which means the real story must be surrounded by a shroud of faux stories: "The Pope will (one day) die, what then?" And "The Pope is sick, he might actually be dying." And "The Pope *is* dying." And "The Pope is nearly dead." Then "The Pope hasn't died yet, after all!" Then "But now he *really* is dying. Really." And afterward, "How the Pope died," and "The Pope died a week ago," and "A new Pope will be chosen by the Papal Conclave." And finally, "How long before the new Pope dies?" With the news cycle outracing the news, the news must recycle the few legitimate "big stories" it has, rerunning the stomach-churning images of the fire/demonstration/trial/accident/election/shooting/indictment/murder/resignation/plague/funeral/coup all day or for days (weeks) at a time. Natural disasters (Katrina or the Indian Ocean tsunami), human disasters (Princess Diana dead, the Pope dead, Terri Schiavo dead, the Kyoto global warming treaty dead), celebrity trials (O. J. Simpson, Scott Peterson, Michael Jackson, fill in today's "blank") can quite literally fill weeks of programming—all aimed at the grown-up kidults whom the marketplace has targeted and whose wanton attentions can only make them, despite their natural gifts and proclivities, attention deprived and intellectually challenged.

Indeed, according to a *New York Times Magazine* writer (he ought to know!), the 24/7 news cycle, generating "much more news and much faster news," has helped create "a kind of widespread attention deficit disorder" in which new is trumped by newer, and newer superceded by newest, which—instantly superceded—becomes not the news but "what Russell Baker calls 'the olds.'"[38] Once news outruns the natural progression of our lives, it must be invented or rehearsed. Repetition cast as invention (news flash: study reveals teen girls do less well in school because they are obsessed with boys!), and repetition fully acknowledged (. . . on the anniversary of 9/11, the beginning of the Peterson trial, the end of the Peterson trial . . .), dominate the unending hours in which the video clips are run and rerun until the most excruciating images turn into irritating clichés.[39]

Speed has killed news and corrupted telecommunications more generally as it defines the supposed virtues of wireless phones, BlackBerry communicators, and the internet. These forms of communication put us in touch instantaneously with people removed from our sociophysical environment, but remove us from the social spaces in which we physically exist. In this they contribute to the annihilation of public space already underway. The image of cell-phone users falling into a private world with their cell partners, and thereby turning open spaces into private living and bed rooms and literally eclipsing public space, is not some hysterical public citizen's nightmare; it was a ubiquitous cell-phone company advertisement that ran for months on television at the start of 2006. The ability to jump from one person to another, whether on email, instant messaging, the cell-phone, or call-waiting, can detract from the kind of serious one-on-one relationships that demand time, continuity of attention, and commitment. Speed here means shallow, superficial, forgettable, meaningless. A kid's game. No wonder these new "instant communication technologies" are for the most part shunned by the elderly who are deeply immersed in relationships and have no need to hasten the slow walk to oblivion, even as the very same technologies are adored by the young seeking to find or change relationships of which they have yet to learn the value.

With so much current commercial activity representing an extreme to which we have become addicted, speed approaches pathology. So we end up normalizing the pathological in our everyday lives. This is not just attention deficit disorder but *compulsory* attention deficit disorder, defined by a culture in which we are dissuaded from concentration and continuity and rewarded for pursuing jump-cut lives. One job, one spouse, one career, one home, one personality over a whole lifetime seem so monotonous and, well, from the kids' perspective, so *bor-ing*. Enduring commitments, like enduring tastes, do not lend themselves to the faddishness on which consumerism depends. New friends, new families, new lovers, new homes, new fashions mean new commodities, new credit cards, new shopping sprees, new products, and hence new purchases. Keeping up the daunting pace of change is hard: the infantilist ethos helps, since kids are quick.

The emblem of the consumerist preference for fast, which has become the emblem of American style consumerism for the rest of the world, is of course fast food. Fast food has been much misunderstood, even by its critics. In Eric Schlosser's book *Fast Food Nation*, much of the focus is on *what* we eat, its overall quality, and how it affects our health as well as the international economy and the environment, crucial topics all. But fast food's essence is not *what* it is but *how* it is: its speed, to which everything else including its quality and variety or lack of quality and lack of variety is linked. If there are as yet no fast caviar cafés or fast truffle shops, it is not because caviar and truffles are expensive, but only because complex foods demand well-developed palates and by their very nature demand to be consumed slowly. Oyster bars are a compromise between speed and mature taste, and coffee chains like Starbucks invite a certain leisure— along with wireless multitasking. But for the most part, most consumer outlets are about fast while much of what we experience as complex pleasure requires that it happen slowly. To consume is not to experience but to appropriate and swallow for purposes other than intrinsic pleasure, the way dogs eat.

There is actually a restaurant in New Jersey called Stuff Yer Face, and fast food generally is about stuffing your face: about nutrition, fueling up, taking in the calories, food as an instrumentality, eaters as mere animals responding to biological imperatives. Big Macs, fast fries, and doughnuts give a certain pleasure of course—grease, salt, and sugar are tasty. But their virtue is precisely that their rewards are quick and brief, and do not call for slow savoring. A fast read or fast sex may also have certain virtues, but the quality of the pleasure they afford is not among them (that's why premature ejaculation is premature—it comes before the pleasure can be experienced and suggests a lack of erotic maturity). Speed-reading Proust or skimming Whitman makes no more sense than accelerating a vacation, rushing lovemaking, or chug'a'lugging Hennessy. The things we most care about we do most slowly: speed-reading and zipless fucks are actually oxymorons, not because reading and lovemaking cannot be done in a hurry but because doing them in a hurry corrupts what they are about.

Fast tandoori and fast tacos are in fact available in London and Los Angeles and elsewhere, and fast does not have to mean tasteless or mono-cultural. The point is not to privilege the highbrow or insist on a hierarchy of foods. For gourmet fast foods differ little from fast burgers and fast fries in their ultimate impact on culture. Being "fast" means we scarcely taste them anyway. It really is not a question of class, since McDonald's itself, although predominantly down-market in the United States, is up-market in Moscow and Peking and perfectly middlebrow in many European cities. The point is the speed with which food is bought and consumed, the radical informality and asociability of the consuming process, the contrast between what we do when we eat and what we do when we (say) break bread together or dine or share a repast. Dining cannot be hurried without impeaching its integrity as dining; Mama Napoli's sweet sausages cannot be consumed like hotdogs in a face-stuffing contest and keep their character as Mama's sweet sausages meant to evoke an evening's family dinner on Mulberry Street. Thanksgiving at Wendy's isn't possible, even if Wendy's hires a four-star chef and puts turkey, sweet potatoes, and cranberry sauce on real crockery—unless you have two or three hours and an extended family at the ready, in which case why would you be at Wendy's?

Fast food has been slow in coming. It had its origin in TV dinners where marketers first discovered there was money to be made in helping along and profiting off the American family's time-compressing impatience with family dining. The growing addiction to quick food-preparation and easy multitask eating led quickly to watch-the-tube eating, do-your-home-work eating, call-a-buddy eating, answer-your-email eating, and shop-the-Home-Shopping-Network eating. Dining was not the point anymore, communion and ritual were wholly beside the point. It was about getting another task out of the way, fueling up for other activities. Business and trade have always put pressure on schedules and families: under the Ottoman Empire, fast kebab street vendors catered to traders and travelers in a hurry. This wasn't about dining either, but it was a prudent supplement for busy folks at busy times in what was otherwise a serious dining culture. But dining is about sociability, eating as ritual and food as symbol, with the dining table as a kind of secular altar to the family home and hearth. Today, the TV or the computer screen have taken over the ritual function of household altar, and eating is solitary and passive. According to the Nutrition Education Network, up to 40 percent of American families "never or seldom eat together, and that segment is growing."[40] The figures worsen as children get older. It is as if the Roman Catholic mass had been reduced to chewing on communion-wafer gum.

Fast food's content is relevant to fast food's essence then only inasmuch as kids' preferences for fast over slow are complemented by kids' preferences for simple over complex and bland over spicy. Sugar and salt and animal fat trump sour and pepper and olive oil in seducing kids (young and old alike) into taking a couple of minutes to stuff their little (and large) faces. Finger-licking good rather than taste-enhancing delicious; the real key to fast food is the informality and speed with which it is eaten, the ritual-free but highly efficient processing of fast-fuel energy necessary to other youthful activities such as i-messaging, video games and television watching, and (in time) sex and the ardors of shopping. Sugar and caffeine fixes are to a flagging shopper what a whiff of salts is to the woozy prize-fighter.

These kid characteristics have adult marketplace parallels, of course. Mall food-courts are designed as quick pit stops where shoppers can refuel on the run without borrowing too much valuable time from the spending sprees they are supposed to be embarked on. It is not an accident that suburban malls host no serious restaurants where shoppers might be detained for hours at a time from their consumer rounds. In the same manner, urban and suburban fast-food emporiums facilitate fast eating for business workaholics for whom a French three-hour lunch or a Spanish leisurely noontime repast at home with the family impairs the efficiency of the full work day. The Fundación Independiente in Madrid has launched a campaign to get rid of such long lunches. The foundation's president said pointedly, "In a globalized world, we have to have schedules that are more similar to those in the rest of the world so we can be better connected. These Spanish lunches of two to three hours are very pleasant, but they are not very productive."[41] Even seemingly leisure-minded hangout establishments like Starbucks or sports bars offer television and wireless internet connectivity so that customers affecting to chill can in fact engage in ongoing laptop and Bluetooth or BlackBerry multitasking, video shopping included, over a laid-back latte grande. Customers can be busily engaged in several places at once even as they seem to be kicking back in one single place.

The three primary pairs of infantilization, easy over hard, simple over complex, and fast over slow, contain and entail a host of affiliated dyads that merit at least passing mention. Easy and simple and quick privilege pure play over work—something the ethos of infantilization encourages—although, as we have seen, it may prefer play to work most when it can convert work into play. Nowhere is the conflation of work and play more evident than in the commercialization of recreational athletics that has increasingly turned youthful players into full-time, in-training preprofessionals, that has turned school and collegiate athletics into a commercial farm-team system for professional sports, and has at the same time made professional athletes into children whose behavior is not only infantilized but celebrated in its infantilized form. Twenty-five years ago, Neil Postman was already using the disappearance of children's games and transformation of kids' sports into "the business of adults" as evidence for what he called the "merging of children's and adults' values and styles"—a prescient account of what I understand as infantilization.[42] The other side of the infantilization of adult athletes is the professionalization of children's play in the hope of making a profit.[43] Critics fault the "greedy kids" or their greedy parents. But it is the entertainment corporations that own and profit from professional sports that seem to be "guilty of tempting adults to turn back the calendar of children."[44] Kids are not growing up faster: they are being grown up faster so that they can work at what they would otherwise be playing at in order to feed the craving of the empire of commercial sport for new talent.[45]

Yet even as the kids are brought along too fast, encouraged to overtrain and overspecialize in a manner that hurts their bodies and impedes their natural playfulness, the athletes they become not only cultivate kiddie pleasure but are helped to do so by their employers who understand the connections between controlling athletes and conditioned puerility. This is not simply about childish players, but about management preferences for pliable athletes who leave the adult stuff (like trades and wages and union benefits) to the owners or to their own professional agents who are less interested in their clients' careers than in maximizing their own profits. The players absorb the message in a hurry so that the burly men who make millions playing kids games into middle age have a hard time growing up.

Infantilization plays out across the board in consumer society, also privileging images and pictures over words. It is not that words are always vehicles of complexity and truth-seeking—a picture can be worth a thousand words, and words can become tokens of simplification, propaganda, and manipulation. On the whole, however, we have built democratic institutions as well as science, philosophy, and literature (hence, some might argue, civilization) around deliberation and common conversation. Language offers common ground (if sometimes common obfuscation as well). It probably discloses as much of truth—however little that may be—as we are likely to achieve. The preference today for pictures is, in any case, rarely a preference for images as surrogates for the persuasive power of language, but more often a way around that power: a way to short-circuit mature modes of communication whether they are pictorial or linguistic.

Infantilism's preference for simple, easy, and fast gives it an affinity for certain political forms over others. Like consumerism itself, it attaches itself more readily to solitaries (or packs of solitaries) engaged in common behaviors such as shopping than to communities that deliberate together before they act together. By the same token, the infantilist ethos is fortified by an ideology of entitlement in which human beings are seen first of all as individuals—what political scientists might call rights-bearing legal persons—rather than as family members, lovers, kin-people, or citizens of a civic community. This ideology is closely associated with American individualism and the modern ethos generally, and it spurns the ethics of obligation and responsibility that place the individual in a circle of sociability in which identity is given in part by association with and duty toward others. It did not please many Americans, whether they were Catholics or not, that the new Pope Benedict XVI (when he was Cardinal Ratzinger of Munich) wrote bluntly about modernity's "dictatorship of relativism . . . which has as its highest goal one's own ego and one's own desires."[46] Yet Pope Benedict was offering not just an indictment of the entailments of the infantilist ethos but an accurate portrayal of its biases as well, and one that cannot be written off as an expression of his own antique moralist biases (which, ironically, smack of the Protestant ethic).

The ethics of narcissism promote and reflect a preference for the timeless present over temporality itself—whether past or future. The cult of now has always been an American temptation. Immigrants have long found their way to American shores as an escape from the burdens of prejudice and error of the kind Voltaire associated with history. America was, in Tom Paine's words in *Rights of Man*, "life as in the beginning of the world"—life liberated from the cumulative burdens of time, the possibility of starting over again fresh. This penchant for the near over the remote and the instantaneous over the enduring long insulated the United States from the conservative habits of cultures wed to their own pasts and paralyzed by the historical yoke under which they labored. But embodied in an infantilizing ethos, the liberation from time has become an obliviousness to history and a foolish ignorance of mortality. Birth identity is erased, because it is the American promise that birth does not matter. Americans insist where they come from is irrrelevant. Death too is erased (cryonics!), because—oblivious to the future and guaranteed immunity against the aging process by the consumables we purchase—we are happily ensconced in the timeless present and hence momentarily immortal.

In each of these cases, the infantilist ethos tracks elements already present in the modern psyche, but takes away their ambiguity, treating them as instrumentally virtuous, because they are necessary to the success of consumer capitalism in distress. The ethos consumerism needs embraces puerility but without nuance, and it shills for childishness but without recognizing the saving virtues of childhood. In rationalizing puerility, it cites the obligation of producers to give consumers "what they want" and the rights of consumers to exercise their "freedom" through the marketplace.

As thoughtful critics we can and must debate the distinctions by which children and adults are separated into paradigmatic groups at odds with one another; we can see the moral insufficiencies of traditional notions of what it means to be grown up (ridigity, conventionalism, closed-mindedness), and the protoethical aspects of some of childhood's ideals (freshness, spontaneity, playfulness). There is little doubt that so-called grown-up cultures can draw from childhood's more attractive features at least some of their animating mature values. Easy, we have suggested, can also mean simple and unencumbered as in natural, pure, and innocent, while hard can mean opaque, turgid, and complicated. Adult cultures seek ways to make their artifices seem "natural" and to make complexities read as simple—transparent and lucid. The Protestants and above all the Puritans were protesting precisely against the over-articulated iconography and opaque liturgy with which Catholicism had, through its worldly institutionalization, come to problematize and obscure the truths of simple Christian faith. Protestantism was hence both a return to Christianity's "simple" roots even as it represented an evolution of Christianity made possible by such advances as movable type and adult literacy, which gave large populations direct access to vernacular translations of the Bible so that they could engage the "word of God" as mature adults, rather than having scripture spoon-fed to them like children.

Play may be a silly exercise in pretending, but it can also entail a sense of exploration, freedom, and spontaneity: in its evolved form it yields the play that is a sermon, a mass, or a theater piece. Play thus elaborated may become what religion and art share and hence what philosophers such as Hegel and Nietzsche find precious in them. Even the Christian celebration of work disdains anal obsessiveness, lugubrious earnestness, and joyless exertion in favor of a kind of holy exuberance that transforms its work into holy purposefulness: just think of the young Christian hero in the film about the 1924 Paris Olympics (*Chariots of Fire*) exclaiming ecstatically that he runs—plays, works, and lives—for the glory of God.

Even instant gratification can suggest a capacity for living fully in the minute, while deferring pleasure can be a cover for alienation from activity and disengagement from life. Psychoanalysis aims at (among other things) searching out, identifying, and overcoming such apparent ",virtues" with which neurotics may rationalize what is actually repression and psychic disorder. As Herbert Marcuse has observed, for Freud civilization itself is necessarily synonymous with repression—the "transformation of the *pleasure principle* into the *reality principle*." In the first instance, this means if humans are to survive they must become adult by moving from (in Marcuse's gloss) immediate satisfaction to delayed satisfaction, from pleasure to restraint of pleasure, from joy (play) to toil (work), from receptiveness to productiveness, and from the absence of repression to security.[47] Yet Freud himself is dialectical, believing that "because of this lasting gain through renunciation and restraint . . . the reality principle 'safeguards' rather than 'dethrones,' 'modifies' rather than denies, the pleasure principle."[48] That is to say, civilization ultimately conserves a vital element of the id's pleasure principle by subjecting it to the constraints of the civilizational superego. This is Erik Erikson's point when he considers the relations of toys to reason, and of playfulness to mastering reality.

In the same manner, the entire catalog of dichotomies I have organized around the child and the adult is subject to dialectical inversion in the manner of Freud: the child's pictorial imagination may conjure fantasies, but it can also disclose truths ("a picture is worth a thousand words") as readily as adult words can obscure them ("it depends on what the meaning of 'is' is"); which is to say, words serve lawyers and liars as well as philosophers and prophets. Artists and photographers have often made images vessels of truth. Reason quite notoriously has its vices (abstraction, deracination, affectation, and rationalization), while feelings and sentiments quite famously have their virtues (concreteness, authenticity, immediacy, and honest affect). In short, as in most such simple oppositions, moral valence in the opposition between the childish and the adult turns out to be dialectical. Neither side of the dichotomy carries the whole of moral truth.

Yet all of these caveats do not alter the overwhelming historical evidence suggesting that major civilizations and religions, while they certainly encompass and conserve modified forms of childhood's innocent virtues, and work hard at protecting their innocent manifestation in children, nonetheless share a common conviction that the time must come when adults put away childish things, civilize their instincts, and grow up. If children cannot become parents, the children of children cannot thrive. One might even argue that this passage from being and behaving as the children of parents to being and behaving as the parents of children is bound up with what we mean when we speak of a people as civilized. The conscious association of human sexuality with reproduction might be said both to diminish pleasure (responsibility, anxiety, and repression quickly replace hedonistic enjoyment) and enhance happiness, opening up the way to our sense of belonging to a permanent community (a species) that outlives our individual lives.

The pleasure principle, unadulterated, destroys the life it pleasures, grasping, seizing, and hurting at will—in Freud's images, mindlessly slaying fathers and bedding mothers at desire's first impulse without thought to consequences. That is why civilizations, although they may prize aspects of childhood just as individuals do, and even work to find a place for them in some modified form in adult culture, will lean institutionally toward the disciplining of impulse and insist on measuring the worth of childhood by adult standards. Not even Freud, so sensitive to repression's potential to sicken us, is willing to surrender its civilizing proclivities unless that yielding can be achieved without regression to infantilism.

The culture of modern consumer capitalism has thrown all this Freudian (and Protestant) baggage to the winds. For the first time in history, a society has felt its economic survival demands a kind of controlled regression, a culture that promotes puerility rather than maturation. The strategy does not represent a countercultural campaign to recognize those features of childhood that might be sources of virtue (innocence, authenticity, creativity, spontaneity, and playfulness). On the contrary, it is a campaign to repress those features of childhood in favor of others that make adults vulnerable, manipulable, impulsive, and irrational. This strategy makes good commercial sense, since the market does not infantilize out of an ethical love for childhood and its putative virtues but only out of an instrumental need to sell unnecessary goods to people whose adult judgment and tastes are obstacles to such consumption. On the other hand, it makes little sense ethically or civilizationally.

Civilization may wish to encourage spontaneity, even impulsiveness, as prods to creativity and invention. When the market and its infantilist ethos cultivate impulsiveness, however, it is *directed* impulsiveness. Retailers do not draw the young to malls or theme parks or multiplexes to encourage them to socialize or hang out or cruise as they might "naturally" do, but to put them to work shopping, to direct their play to commodities and for-pay entertainment, to turn the impulse to socialize into an impulse to consume. Merchandisers sometimes cultivate kids to help them determine taste (in so-called buzz marketing, for example), and marketers depend on the taste of the young for gossip and peer interaction to turn them into agents of taste. As clear-eyed observers of the Tom Hanks character in the movie *Big* know, the twelve-year-old in the adult's body may look like he's having innocent fun, but in fact a smart company is instrumentalizing fun and using the Hanks character as a tool for shaping public tastes and selling the latest goods. Its aims (largely unnoticed in the movie) are neither innocent, nor finally much fun.

The marketers turn Peter Pan into their Pied Piper, pretending to free the young from the constraints of adult discipline in order to impose on them the discipline of the consumer market. The Pied Piper of Hamlin lured away the children of the village because their parents would not pay him for ridding them of their rats. The marketplace's Pied Piper lures away the children because their parents are "gatekeepers" who stand in the way of their children's induction into the hall of consumers. As the Pied Piper once did, the market today pretends to empower the children it seduces, telling them they will be made potent by the disempowerment of their elders. Freed from possessive parents, they are actually incarcerated in a ubiquitous mall of the juvenile mind.

In his *The Culture of Narcissism*, Christopher Lasch worried about the displaced paternalism represented by the welfare state, treating intelligently with a theme that has become a conservative staple. What A. V. Dicey (cited approvingly by Milton Friedman) said about the state mirrors Lasch's anxiety: although, Dicey writes, the "beneficial effects of State intervention" may be "direct, immediate, and, so to speak, visible," we must be wary of its "evil effects" which are often "gradual and indirect, and lie out of sight."[49] Yet what is more worrisome today, when the evils of the state are so widely noted and the virtues of the market so uncritically embraced, is the invisible paternalism represented by consumer capitalism's advertisers and merchandisers. These wily advocates of the infantilist ethos—very much like the former celebrants of the benevolent state—claim to be "freeing" children from parental bonds in the name of autonomy when in fact they themselves are taking the parents' place as taste- and trendsetters, with "evil effects" that are the more dangerous for being "gradual and indirect, and . . . out of sight."

The Joe Camel ads for cigarettes that have given way to the slick beer ads featuring turtles, parrots, and other kiddie staples, like the roadside playpens at McDonald's and the Peter Pan–themed rides of Disneyland (pirates and cowboys and Indians all still there a hundred years later) are designed not to help children remain children but to "help" children become grown-up consumers of cigarettes or lite beer or Big Macs or Disney's whole lifeline of products from animated films to new-town utopias like Celebration, Florida. Disneyland sells childhood mythology in order to reap grown-up profits. The play at the theme park is pay as you go, a relatively passive "ride" experience that happens *to* you in return for your dollar. In these new theme-park playgrounds that now occupy the leisure time of cash-carrying kids, parents are reduced to the role of minders with wallets.

There is of course irony in an "adult culture" which is intensely serious and very grown up—what is serious if not the bottom line?—in how it conspires to use childhood playfulness, its innocent spontaneity and simple feelings, to sell all it has to sell. The outcome is a more childish, a less free, and a more undisciplined civilization—not really the "disappearance of childhood" (as Neil Postman titled his book a generation ago), but the disappearance of adulthood, because childhood is so much more profitable to the economy of consumerism.

A related paradox is evident in America's workaholic marketplace, where "leisure time" and "playful spectatorship" are anything but leisurely or playful, and where people actually work longer hours than their compatriots anywhere else in the industrialized world, not for the glory of work but for the supposed rewards of play. No people work harder at play or expend more energy on leisure than American consumers. Leisure means anything but lazy here. No French-style, thirty-five-hour workweek in the United States—the abbreviated Gallic workweek mandated by law now being ridiculed in those parts of Europe anxious to imitate the United States. No six-week summer vacations where business literally comes to a nearly summer-long halt in world cities like Berlin or Madrid. No original "slow food" in the manner of the charming Italian movement that affects to put a roadblock in the way of McDonald's.

In the postmodern capitalist economy it's hard work creating the easy life. A full-service shopping society needs consumers with a lot of leisure, but in fact leaves them little time for anything but consumption and the hard work that pays for consumption, so that they rarely feel leisurely or free. Vacation destinations and the travel to reach them are anything but vacations from shopping. There is shopping underway at airport malls and train-station malls, shopping at theme-park and casino facilities, shopping all along the highways leading to and at the tourist destinations to which they lead, shopping at every grand hotel lobby, and shopping on television and the internet when you get to your room.

The consumer of the cornucopia of spectator commodities available from a hardworking, overproducing entertainment industry must work even harder than the producers to take it all in. Can any consumer keep up with the movies, television programs, internet offerings, video games, music downloads, and athletic competitions that constitute the modern marketplace's new bread and circuses? It makes for disciplined work for an individual to stay abreast with any one of these sectors. Yet unless she does, the market economy falters. No wonder leisure, squeezed between the extended hours of work, often feels like a full-time job. If as Dan Cook has declared, childhood makes capitalism hum, the kids better get to work.

4

Privatizing Citizens: The Making of Civic Schizophrenia

> Libertarianism is a political philosophy for Peter Pans, an
> outlook on the world premised on never growing up.
> —Alan Wolfe[1]

> The distinction between private and public coincides with
> the opposition of necessity and freedom, of futility and per-
> manence, and finally of shame and honor.
> —Hannah Arendt[2]

AS THE PROTESTANT ethos once shaped a culture conducive to
work and investment, the infantilist ethos today shapes a culture
conducive to laxity, shopping, and spending. Where once Americans worked harder than almost any other people, today Tom Friedman
worries about the "quiet crisis" in which the "tendency . . . to extol consumption over hard work, investment, and long-term thinking" creates an
America whose vaunted productivity is in decline and where kids "get fat,
dumb, and lazy," squandering the very moral capital the Protestant culture
once promoted and sustained.[3] As I wrote after 9/11, "President Bush
squandered a unique opportunity [back then] when the nation cried out
for engagement and the president . . . urged them to go shopping. . . . To
relinquish fear people must step out of paralysis. The president suggested
they step into the mall."[4] Americans still work hard—harder than others in
the industrialized world; but they also work harder to find time to shop
than workers in, say, continental Europe where 35-hour workweeks, six-

week vacations, and welfare-state benefits undermine the old Puritan ethos and give succor to a new and indulgent brand of European consumerism there as well.

The pervasive new ethos of infantilization is not, however, the only factor in our era's hyperconsumerism. It has both generated and been reinforced by affiliated ideologies including privatization, branding, and total marketing that buttress consumerism and contribute powerfully to the infantilizing project. Among these, none is more salient than the ideology of privatization, a fresh and vigorous expression of traditional laissez-faire philosophy that favors free markets over government regulation and associates liberty with personal choice of the kind possessed by consumers. In its latest guise, privatization ideology takes aim squarely at the public and those democratic philosophies that created the last century's prudent balancing of capitalism and popular sovereignty, with fateful consequences for citizens.

Privatization strategies have shaped the dominant political paradigm at least since the 1980s when President Ronald Reagan and Prime Minister Margaret Thatcher adopted them as the official political philosophy of conservatism. These strategies assail the idea of collective social entities even as they celebrate the private and the personal and have recently become dominant in Western Europe and Asia where communitarian and welfare-state models had long been popular. Long before Reagan and Thatcher, early social science critics of the public interest such as David B. Truman were insisting that "in developing a group interpretation of politics . . . we do not need to account for a totally inclusive interest, because one does not exist."[5] There was no need to take account of the common good in discussing interest theory because there is no such thing. Politicians like Margaret Thatcher simply asserted that "there is no such thing as society."[6] Skepticism about government and society accompanies a renewed and quite astonishing faith in the endless capacity of markets to "coordinate human behavior or activity with a range and a precision beyond that of any other system, institution, or social process."[7] These market strategies reinvented classical laissez-faire economics and political libertarianism (sometimes called neoliberalism in Europe), attacking large, bureaucratic government as an inflexible and inefficient adversary of the liberty in whose name it affects to operate.

Liberty here has a negative connotation: to be free *from*, not to be determined or controlled by someone else's power or will. As the feared seat of visible power in earlier centuries and more recently as the recognized locus of collective will, government has been the entity associated with power and will, the enemy of liberty and personal choice as seen from this libertarian perspective. Milton Friedman, the compelling libertarian economist, offers definitive language. Nearly a half century ago, he contested the prevailing social welfare (statist) ideology of the time by insisting that "every act of government intervention limits the area of individual freedom directly and threatens the preservation of freedom indirectly."[8] Put into practice, this means, as Ronald Reagan was to argue, when it comes to liberty government is always part of the problem rather than part of the solution. This libertarian ideology rationalizes the privatization strategy that has become a crucial ally of infantilization in commercial society today.

Yet in the name of abstract personal liberty, libertarians and privatizers actually pervert and undermine real autonomy, because as Hannah Arendt has argued, "political freedom, generally speaking, means the right 'to be a participant in government,' or it means nothing."[9] Although when Milton Friedman was first writing in the 1950s, laissez-faire liberalism was out of fashion and (coming out of World War II) the idea of benevolent government had few critics; today it is government that is out of fashion, and one can say (with Jedediah Purdy) that "in the wake of an era when it has been common to hope for too much from politics, the greater and more dangerous temptation is now to hope for too little from public life."[10] The educator Maxine Greene, worth noting because she is an altogether practical person whose life has been spent in education and teacher training, is typical of those who, because they actually apply freedom as a tool in the setting of social change, challenge the abstract notion that freedom is always negative.[11] Instead, Greene argues, freedom needs to be addressed dialectically: for it always draws us into a moral and political nexus for which thin "negative" constructions are simply insufficient. Freedom is not just about standing alone and saying no. As a usable ideal, it turns out to be a public rather than a private notion. The insistence that it is private has been the occasion for what in quite distinctive ways both Walter Lippmann and John Dewey termed a kind of "eclipse of the public."[12]

Dewey's and Lippmann's concern with the vanishing public (from differing political perspectives to be sure, Lippmann much more conservative than Dewey) made clear that liberty itself had evolving meanings that reflected changing social and political circumstances. There is no need to argue, as Isaiah Berlin did, about what freedom "actually" means in some abstract or essentialist way. The early English liberal idea of freedom was negative in the sense that it was oppositional: it faced a public sphere of church and government that was hierarchical, authoritarian, and in need of radical dissent. In associating liberty with the absence of external impediments on motion, Thomas Hobbes was offering a fitting rebuke to the tyrannical monarchies that obstructed potentially free citizens and constrained the free movement of people and goods. The early liberal notion of liberty enlisted a metaphor: the fiction of the unencumbered self understood as a bundle of desires and passions seeking to be left alone. It did so because it confronted actual political and religious autocracies that would not leave people alone. Its aim was to liberate "subjects of servitude" from the hold of tyrannical government. In the classical liberal construction, servitude was defined by manacles and muscles—the restraining of the body—so that liberty was necessarily construed as what Maxine Greene appropriately calls "old rebellions against mechanism, schedules, clocks, crowds."[13] Liberty here becomes synonymous with revolution: overthrowing things and liberating people from the grip of tyrants.

In its time, this understanding of liberty helped establish free republics and tolerant societies. Construed in a narrow liberal fashion, the natural-rights approach to liberty offered a powerful remonstration against medieval tyranny and early modern ecclesiastic orthodoxy—the tyranny over the body and mind that defined traditional autocracy. The arbitrary rule of masters over slaves and of kings over subjects was broken by liberal insistence (embodied in the American Declaration of Independence, for example) on the fiction that men were born free (were "naturally free") and could be "legitimately" constrained and coerced by others only with their own consent. Freedom experienced as resistance to impediments on motion captures both Hobbes's conception and more recent liberal understandings of liberty under duress from tyrannical modern regimes. Thus, Jean Paul Sartre wrote paradoxically that he had never felt more free than during the Nazi occupation of France, when his sense of liberty's meaning was enhanced by the climate of repression in which it could find expression as resistance. Still more recently, English playwright Tom Stoppard, reflecting on middle Europe under the communists, has observed that it was far easier to feel free in composing samizdat works of protest against a communist regime than in composing uncontested works of dissidence in a free bourgeois society where anything goes, praise or protest, as long as it earns a profit. Václav Havel, the Czech Republic's theater guru cum president, has drawn similar conclusions based on his experience as poet and politician.

Yet a historically appropriate theory of liberal rights useful in freeing men from tyranny is not so easily converted into a theory of civic participation useful in justifying democracy and grounding justice in societies that have long been free, at least in the formal legal sense. This has been the primary paradox of politics in the last century. Neoliberals, libertarians, and privatizers seem to be reverting to a notion of freedom useful in opposing tyranny—and perhaps useful in nurturing the emergence of democracy, say through doctrines of international human rights today—in order to challenge the legitimacy of democratic governance itself, that form of government the old negative liberty helped establish and legitimate. But nowadays, the idea that only private persons are free, and that only personal choices of the kind consumers make count as autonomous, turns out to be an assault not on tyranny but on democracy. It challenges not the illegitimate power by which tyrants once ruled us but the legitimate power by which we try to rule ourselves in common. Where once this notion of liberty challenged corrupt power, today it undermines legitimate power.

Liberty is a value conditioned by history. Freedom from constraint, so important in resisting tyranny, cannot be a formula for moral liberation or political engagement in more democratic times. Libertarians like Friedman and Reagan are political atavists wedded to conceptions of liberty and government dangerous to modern democracy. In the last one hundred years there has of course been a cycling and recycling of arguments about the proper balance between public and private. But from the time of Adam Smith, there have been those (Smith himself, a more nuanced thinker, not included) who have construed liberalism to mean that the social contract itself is suspect.

In the first half of the nineteenth century in England and on the Continent, and in the period after the Civil War in the United States, when government was puny and capitalism emerging as mighty, a kind of raw and brutal market ideology prevailed that was celebrated by some as social dynamics (Auguste Comte) and condemned by others as social Darwinism, but acknowledged by all as the central reality of the times. Paltry little government in that era could hardly dominate anything, let alone economic markets: America's fledgling federal government was portrayed dismissively as "the President plus the Post Office." But markets, especially as they grew dominant in Europe after the Congress of Vienna and after the Civil War in the United States, created an extraordinary productivity; yet rather than that competition and freedom promised by laissez-faire liberals, these same markets also produced cartels, monopoly, and inequality. Such anarchic forces ultimately endangered not only democracy but the capitalist system itself. Henry Ford had understood that the sort of capitalism that could not pay its own workers enough to buy the products it produced was likely to founder. Entrepreneurship could not flourish by creating monopoly conditions that crushed competition and market exchange. By the end of the nineteenth century, both the Europeans and the Americans came to understand that government's role was to secure the conditions that capitalism needed in order to flourish, but which left to its own devices it inevitably tended to erode (the famous contradictions of capitalism).

In the United States, Presidents Teddy Roosevelt and Woodrow Wilson, and in Europe Prime Minister Gladstone and Chancellor Bismarck, took aim at market anarchy, reasserting sovereignty's prerogatives and rescuing capitalism from its contradictions through prudent antitrust legislation and ongoing monetary regulation. The 1920s saw another period of market exuberance where the new mass production yoked to colonial global trade allowed capitalism once again to outrun its democratic overseers, leading the great social theorist and philosophical pragmatist John Dewey to wonder whether the "great public" had gone missing altogether and to notice that politics was itself tending "to become just another 'business': the special concern of bosses and the managers of the machine."[14]

This era where private trumped public proved to be a brief and unstable interlude between the Progressive Era and the New Deal. Perhaps more compellingly, World War II allowed both the Allies, mostly democracies, and their enemies, nationalist dictatorships all, to renationalize large parts of their economies and reassert the power of government oversight over faltering market economies. National defense and social security were the twin public goods that emerged from the war as defining traits of the old and the new democracies and, in Europe, of the new European Community. These goods were left intact until recently when, in the story told here, they have been subjected to the antipolitics of privatization.

The seeds of this antagonism were planted earlier when in 1944 Friedrich Hayek published his influential *The Road to Serfdom*. One could have wondered then whether that dark road about which he worried was more likely to wind its way to doom through the newly intrusive impediments of the regulatory welfare state or through the market's frenzied anarchy. In any case, by the 1950s the New Deal and the war economy along with the counterparadigm of Soviet communism (and its vanquished totalitarian cousin fascism) had begun to spur laissez-faire liberals, long dormant, to reassert their penchant for markets. They busied themselves building an ideological movement on Hayek's market ideology that was to culminate in the policies of Ronald Reagan and Margaret Thatcher. For most opinion leaders and intellectuals in that era, in the words of Milton Friedman's dissenting work *Capitalism and Freedom*, seemed "overwhelmingly persuaded that capitalism was a defective system inhibiting well-being and thereby freedom." As a consequence, there was "a tendency to regard any existing government intervention as desirable, [and] to attribute all evils to the market."[15]

The wheel turns. Today laissez-faire liberalism is again triumphant and Friedman's text is no longer a radical and heretical sermon but the standard bible of the Washington (and global market) consensus. From where we stand now, social welfarism and it sources in the New Deal and the Great Society appear to have run their course and the ideology of markets is dominant. Yet this hardly means that neoliberalism's political theory, sundered from its justifying history of constitutional founding, is any more convincing today than it was during the Depression or in the cowboy climate after the Civil War. Or that it manages human welfare in the marketplace with any more efficiency or liberty than it did one hundred years ago. At war with the democratic history it once helped inaugurate, laissez-faire liberalism continues to mistake popular sovereignty for illegitimate coercion and to confound the public weal with the repression of liberty. It forgets the very meaning of the social contract, a covenant in which individuals agree to give up unsecured private liberty in exchange for the blessings of public liberty and common security.

The sanctity of the market means, in the description of David Harvey, a critic of neoliberalism, that "state interventions in markets [once created] must be kept to a bare minimum because, according to the theory, the state cannot possibly possess enough information to second-guess market signals [price] and because powerful interest groups will inevitably distort and bias state interventions [particularly in democracies] for their own benefit."[16] Market philosophy is more than a threat to democracy, it is the source of capitalism's most troubling problems today: its incapacity to satisfy the real needs of the poor and its tendency to try to substitute faux needs and manufactured wants for the missing real needs of consumers in developed societies. It is these issues that ultimately have put consumer capitalism in jeopardy.

Yet today's neoliberals—neither radical in the manner Milton Friedman and his liberal Chicago School allies once were, nor responsive to historical realities as the first English liberals of the seventeenth century were—seem uncomprehending in the face of such perils. They have apparently accepted that in its declining period of obligatory consumerism, the democratic state stands in the way of the infantilist ethos and the privatizing ideology necessary to keeping the consumer busily engaged. In good faith, they talk about liberty, but as realists their concern is with shopping. They appreciate, if perhaps only intuitively, that privatization ideology helps to rationalize and facilitate consumption by privileging personal choice. They oppose government regulation advanced in the name of equality, fairness, and justice because they are worried, as political scientist Robert Westbrook observes, about the "crisis of 'overproduction' in an economy no longer tested by the tasks of capital accumulation but by the challenges of finding markets for the prodigious output of its factories and farms"[17]—and nowadays of its service and information technology industries. Neoliberals know they make war not on illegitimate power (the old visible tyrannies) but on legitimate power (visible democratic citizenship) in order to privilege a market power that is both illegitimate and invisible, but crucial to the selling of goods, which they firmly believe is indispensable to the survival of capitalism. Their rhetoric focuses on the tyranny of the state, but they contest not public tyranny but the public good because the public good and the private goods of late consumer capitalism have contradictory purposes and stand in fundamental tension. Capitalism must come to terms with a system of overproduction that William Greider has described in his *One World, Ready or Not* as "an explosive cycle of renewal, migration and destruction that is typically ignited by human invention," and seems poised in the name of its survival to put at risk the democratic system that bore and nurtured it.[18]

Times change, and with it the threats that democracies face. Tyranny is not what it once was in the parts of the world we now call free: it is not a matter of vicious tyrants and totalitarian parties and illegitimate states. At least since Alexis de Tocqueville toured the tumultuous America of Andrew Jackson in the 1830s, tyranny has exhibited to us moderns a deceptively fresh face. "Fetters and headsmen," Tocqueville had already noticed, "were the coarse instruments that tyranny formerly employed; but the civilization of our age has perfected despotism itself. . . . [M]onarchs had, so to speak, materialized oppression; the democratic republics of the present day have rendered it as entirely an affair of the mind." Nowadays, it is not just the power of public opinion about which Tocqueville worried but of the marketplace itself that has created conditions under which, in Tocqueville's phrase, "the body is left free, and the soul is enslaved."[19]

Tocqueville was worried about a tyranny of the majority that could be associated with democracy, but the psychological reality he captured begins with the fact that constraint itself is aimed not at the free body but the liberated consciousness.[20] The modern tyrant hopes to impede our aims, divert our purposes, and reformulate our goals. He is not the democratic majority or the public good, he is the enforcer of consumer capitalism's need to sell. His instrument is not the state but the very market about whose vaunted liberty he boasts. Can it be then that in the new battle for consciousness, the ideology of liberalism has as its true purpose the liberation of the body from public goods in the name of subordinating the soul to the selling of endless private commodities? Does the grinning postmodern Peter Pan who is the new boy hero of buzz marketing work to free the young from convention and deadweight adulthood? Or only to free them from the moral authority of gatekeeping parents and a watchful democratic state in order to indenture us to private consumerism?

To oppose this perverse use of liberty as a cudgel against our collective and moral will, against democracy itself, we need to recall and reaffirm the language of positive or moral liberty. That is to say, in the traditional language of Rousseau, Kant, and Dewey, we need to understand that there can be no viable idea of public liberty outside of the quest for a moral and a common life defined by purposes that are to some degree public in character. There can be no securing of liberty that is not also grounded in moral limits and hence in education and civic participation. In the current political climate of globalizing markets, free trade, and mandatory privatization, and under the sway of the infantilist ethos, this strong view of liberty is unpopular, maligned, permanently under siege. This is not to point to some conspiracy of boardroom managers manipulating political theory to the advantage of the bottom line. Marketers are not *that* smart. Nor do they have to be. The emerging cultural ethos does the work for them. For when we deploy private liberty against public power in a democratic regime, even if we think we are upholding our "rights," what we are really doing is to assail not tyranny but democracy.

To be politically relevant, liberty in our era must be experienced as positive rather than negative, must be public rather than private. This means education for liberty must also be public rather than private. Citizens cannot be understood as mere consumers because individual desire is not the same thing as common ground and public goods are always something more than an aggregation of private wants. Champions of the idea that consumers are democratic citizens have tried to have their civic cake and consume it too by talking about consumer sovereignty and a "consumers republic."[21] Yet a republic is defined by its public-ness (*res publica* meaning "the things of the public"), and what is public cannot be determined by consulting or aggregating private desires.

The consumers' republic is quite simply an oxymoron. Consumers cannot be sovereign, only citizens can. Public liberty demands public institutions that permit citizens to address the public consequences of private market choices. Being permitted to choose among a plethora of automobile brands does not permit a choice in favor of public over private transportation or in favor of fuel-thrifty rather than fuel-wasting engines. Asking what "I want" and asking what "we as a community to which I belong need" are two different questions, though neither is altruistic and both involve "my" interests: the first is ideally answered by the market; the second must be answered by democratic politics. When the market is encouraged to do the work of democracy, our culture is perverted and the character of our commonwealth undermined. Moreover, my sense of self—me as a moral being embedded in a free community—is lost.

Liberty understood as the capacity to make public choices (in Rousseau's terms to engage in "general willing") is a potential faculty that must be learned rather than a natural one that is exercised from birth. Rights are certainly moral claims, but their effective exercise rests on competence and hence on learned skills of citizenship. That is why Tocqueville spoke of a necessary "apprenticeship of liberty" which he called the most arduous of all apprenticeships. It points to the core meaning—now lost to most educational institutions in America—of *public* schooling in the "liberal arts." The liberal arts are the arts of liberty necessary to the exercise of citizenship in a free republic. Jefferson and John Adams were political adversaries, but they agreed with Madison that in the absence of competent citizens, bills of rights were but pieces of paper. If democracy was to live beyond the parchment of a written constitution, competent citizens had to be educated in common schools and public universities.

The logic of democracy may begin with the positing of rights and of a theoretical "natural condition" in which women and men are "born free," but it depends for its implementation on civic learning, public participation, and common consciousness that put flesh on the bones of our potential liberty. The new forms of tyranny we face today derive less from traditional modes of hard autocracy that enslave the body in the name of owning things than from new soft modes of merchandizing and entertaining aimed at manipulating the spirit in the name of selling things. Compulsive shopping speaks to new forms of market coercion that are difficult to discern, let alone contend with, because they allow us to "feel free" even as we yield gently to their subtle bottom-up compulsion. The market does not tell us what to do, it gives us what we want—once it gets through "telling" us what it is that we want and helping us to want it (that's marketing).

I cited Max Weber talking about the iron cage of modernity. He wrote over a century ago. For late consumer capitalism in crisis in a postmodern age, a different cage comes to mind, that of the African monkey trap I also described in chapter 2—the trap in which the monkey is caught only by its own unwillingness to let go of the nut it seeks to wrest from the trap. Is this coercion? Is the monkey free or not? The infantilist ethos does not manacle our hands, it encourage us to tightly grip the chains by which we are held fast. All we need do is let go. How much more fiendish is this box than Weber's iron cage?

Privatization is more than just an economic ideology. It acts in league with the ethos of infantilization to embrace and reinforce narcissism, personal preference, and puerility. It misconstrues liberty and thereby distorts how we understand civic freedom and citizenship, often ignoring and sometimes undermining the very meaning of public goods and the public weal. To the degree Hannah Arendt is right in arguing that political freedom is defined by participation in government rather than freedom from its reach, privatization has not only diminished our capacity to shape our common lives and determine the character of the civilization in which we want to live; it has made us less free.

Civic Schizophrenia: The Psychopathology of Privatization

Why is freedom, when treated as wholly private, so unrewarding, even destructive? It is implicated in a disturbing paradox: it foments a kind of civic schizophrenia that divides the choosing self into opposing fragments and ultimately denies legitimacy to the fragment we understand to be "civic" or "public"—the self associated with our capacity to exercise public freedom. Privatization ideology treats choice as fundamentally private, a matter not of determining some deliberative "we should" (a kind of "general will" produced by citizens interacting democratically) but only of enumerating and aggregating all the "I want's" we hold as private consumers and creatures of personal desire. Yet private choices do inevitably have social consequences and public outcomes. When these derive from purely personal preferences, the results are often socially irrational and unintended: at wide variance with the kind of society we might choose through collective deliberation and democratic decision-making. Although they accurately reflect private wants and wishes—what philosophers call "first-order desires"—they are quite literally dysfunctional with respect to our common values and norms (expressed in what philosophers call "second-order desires" that reflect whether we really embrace our first-order desires as desirable).

Privatization turns the private, impulsive me lurking inside myself into an inadvertent enemy of the public, deliberative we that also is part of who I am. The private me screams "I want!" The privatization perspective legitimizes this scream, allowing it to trump the quiet "we need" that is the voice of the public me in which I participate and which is also an aspect of my interests as a human being. All the choices we make one by one thereby come to determine the social outcomes we must suffer together, but which we never directly choose in common.

This explains how a society without villains or conspirators, composed of good-willed but self-seeking individuals, can produce a radically commercial culture which many of those same individuals despise and for which no one is directly responsible even though more than a few may be said to contribute to its making. Consumer capitalism does not operate by producing self-conscious advocates of duplicity who render consciousness false by getting individuals to establish an unjust society they do not really want. Rather, it generates an ethos of schizophrenia that helps condition the attitudes and behavior it requires for its own survival. It fosters "me" thinking on the model of the narcissistic child and discourages "we" thinking of the kind deliberative grown-up citizens recognize as wisdom and that constitutes what James Surowiecki (business columnist for *The New Yorker*) has called "the wisdom of crowds"—a wisdom that rests on "diversity and independence" that allow "disagreement and contest."[22] Consumerism thus builds psychic monkey traps into its free-range marketplace. If the attitudes and behaviors that result turn out to undermine other important cultural values, which however are extraneous to capitalism's concerns—however deeply relevant they may be to moral and spiritual frameworks and to the shaping of an ideal public culture—too bad.

Freud gets at what appears as a version of the same paradox in his *Civilization and Its Discontents* where he observes that the adult ego, which is normally overseen and regulated by the mature superego acting as civilization's guardian against the impulsive id, is subject to a rear-guard action by the regressive id. Freud postulates an "antithesis between civilization and sexuality," whose consequence is that "civilized society is perpetually threatened with disintegration."[23] For "the original infantile stage of conscience . . . is not given up after the introjection into the super-ego, but persists alongside of it and behind it."[24] The id is impelled by its will to privatized or personal liberty to act against civility and hence against civilization.

In our era of late consumer capitalism, the infantilizing ethos works in this very way to reverse the civilizational valence, encouraging a version of the communal id to displace the communal ego and in place of a civic commons establish an anarchic commercial playground. The ethos does not despise civilization, it is merely indifferent to it. It is single-mindedly devoted to consumer capitalism and so encourages id-driven individuals to indulge in behavior—however corrupting to civilization—that is useful to consumerism. Regression becomes a necessary tactic of the mandate to consume, infantilization a condition for capitalism's success. No one is to blame. There is no "false consciousness." The system cracks around fissures that have developed between the requirements of me and we, of id and ego, of its economic mandate and its civilizational value system. These pairs were once adjudicated and harmonized in our society by a Protestant ethos that encouraged civilizational norms useful both to culture and capitalism: this was Puritanism's virtue as an ethos.

Today, however, culture and capitalism are set asunder by an infantilist ethos made the more effective by its alliance with a privatization ideology corrosive to civilization in its own right. We are encouraged to withdraw from our public selves into the sanctuary of "I want," to secede from the public sector and fence ourselves in behind walled communities in which we deploy private resources to acquire what were once public goods such as garbage collection, police protection, and schooling by treating them as private commodities. President Bush was blamed by many for his market response to Hurricane Katrina in early autumn 2005, but only in an advanced market society already privileging private philanthropy and market voucher programs would his preference for religious philanthropy and housing voucher approaches have any legitimacy at all in responding to a public disaster on this scale. The market had already played a role in weakening New Orleans's defenses against category-five hurricanes: wetlands that once protected the city had been carved up and overdeveloped, safety standards for levees had been pushed aside as too expensive or circumvented by corruption, and the city itself had followed a path of urban development in which the safest land had been secured for commercial development while the lowest-lying, least-protected districts (like the Ninth Ward) had been left to the poor (those least likely to be able to flee a hurricane).

Philanthropy is a form of private capital aimed at achieving public outcomes, but it cannot substitute for public resources and public will in confronting public calamities. In the admirable private efforts of superwealthy American stars such as Oprah and Bill Gates to render assistance to the poor in New Orleans, there is also something dismaying. First a privatizing ideology rationalizes restricting public goods and public assets of the kind that might allow the public as a whole to rescue from their distress their fellow citizens who are in jeopardy; then the same privatizing ideology celebrates the wealthy philanthropists made possible by the market's inequalities who earnestly step in to spend some fragment of their market fortunes to do what the public can no longer do for itself. Better philanthropy than nothing, but far better than philanthropy is a democratic public capable of taking care of itself with its owned pooled resources and its own prudent planning. The private philanthropist does for others in the larger public what they have not been enabled to do for themselves, as a public; democracy, on the other hand, empowers the public to take care of itself.

The services we traditionally think of as public are not merely public in how they are paid for under democracy, but in how they operate. When garbage collection, health care, police protection, education, and disaster relief are privatized they actually are subverted. You cannot protect a few in the midst of general insecurity (ask those who fled urban drugs and crime to the suburbs); you cannot educate a few in the midst of societal ignorance (ask the corporations that turned their back on public education but are now looking for "educated workers"); you cannot collect garbage or preempt disease in one place and let it fester in another (ask the First World victims of diseases like SARS and the West Nile virus, hatched in faraway societies without adequate garbage collection or public health programs). Rescuing victims through individual philanthropy cannot be a substitute for helping citizens avoid victimization through effective public governance in which citizens share real power.

The paradox of public and private that sets capitalism against civilization works to defeat common aspirations by "empowering" private wants. We lose the capacity to shape our lives together because we are persuaded by the prevailing ethos that freedom means expressing our desires in isolation. In the arena of education, for example (which I will examine more closely below), the defects of public schooling are thought to be remediable by the virtues of private parental choice. Through vouchers we are able as individuals, through private choosing, to shape institutions and policies that are useful to our own interests but corrupting to the public goods that give private choosing its meaning. I want a school system where my kid gets the very best; you want a school system where your kid is not slowed down by those less gifted or less adequately prepared; she wants a school system where children whose "disadvantaged backgrounds" (often kids of color) won't stand in the way of her daughter's learning; he (a person of color) wants a school system where he has maximum choice to move his kid out of "failing schools" and into successful ones.[25]

What do we get? The incomplete satisfaction of those private wants through a fragmented system in which individuals secede from the public realm, undermining the public system to which we can subscribe in common. Of course no one really wants a country defined by deep educational injustice and the surrender of a public and civic pedagogy whose absence will ultimately impact even our own private choices. Certainly that is not what we opt for when we express our personal wants with respect to our own kids. Yet aggregating our private choices as educational consumers in fact yields an inegalitarian and highly segmented society in which the least advantaged are further disadvantaged as the wealthy retreat ever further from the public sector. As citizens, we would never consciously select such an outcome, but in practice what is good for "me," the educational consumer, turns out to be a disaster for "us" as citizens and civic educators—and thus for me the denizen of an American commons (or what's left of it).

Robert Reich gives expression to this same paradox when he describes the Wal-Mart philosophy of low-priced goods and low-priced nonunion jobs in terms that show that consumers are complicit in the destruction of the very healthy communities and good jobs which, as citizens, they cherish. "Today's economy," says Reich, "offers us a Faustian bargain: it can give consumers deals largely because it hammers workers and communities. . . . The easier it is for us to find better professional services, the harder professionals have to hustle to attract and keep clients. The more efficiently we can summon products from anywhere on the globe, the more stress we put on our own communities."[26]

Wal-Mart (perfecting the strategy of earlier catalog and big-box retail giants like Sears, Roebuck and Company and Montgomery Ward) sets the consumer in us against the citizen in us, pitting our private interest in obtaining cheap goods against our public interest in having a just and community-sustaining capitalist economy that produces secure high-paying jobs and preserves local communities with robust retail sectors— sectors that are often at the heart of a local community's civic life.[27] Thus do the ethos of infantilism and the ideology of privatization privilege the consumer in us over the citizen is us. Thomas L. Friedman grasps what he calls this "multiple identity disorder," but, favoring market solutions, implicitly rejects the notion that civic identity with its public concerns trumps consumer identity with its private concerns. Hence all he can do is scratch his head over the "multiple identities—consumer, employee, citizen, taxpayer, shareholder"—that are called up by the dilemmas of Wal-Mart economics, without being able to prioritize them politically or recognize that the very meaning of political sovereignty is to establish the priority of public over private. As with so many modern commentators, Friedman simply omits these crucial political concepts from his discussion of modern markets in a globalized world, as if power was irrelevant in the marketplace, or there were no difference between legitimate public power and illegitimate private power.[28]

What this blindness to power inspired by the convergence of privatization and infantilization does so effectively is to tilt the contest between public and private, guaranteeing that the private "me" will trump rival public goods, and that the consumer "me" that dwells ever more schizophrenically within each of us will triumph over the would-be citizen "we" dwelling nearby. For the dilemmas Friedman treats as neutral are in fact already skewed by the new ethos toward the private sector, suggesting not only that consumers are better defenders of liberty than citizens but that consumers are better citizens, that they do the work of citizens better than citizens do that work (a point of view that will be considered in detail in the final chapter). This has been the well-intentioned but disastrous tactic of private-sector do-gooders from the time of the National Consumers League in the early twentieth century to today's advocates of the citizen consumer and the champions of corporate responsibility. It was President Bush's failed tactic in responding to Hurricane Katrina. Urge shoppers to lobby via their dollars and euros and yen to somehow spend their way to the better world that government is supposedly no longer fit to seek; urge managers to "do well by doing good" by being responsible and giving time off for workers who do community service, and by thinking about the needs of the communities in which they reside—right up to the moment the bottom line dictates that their do-good companies abandon them for more profitable climes abroad. Such approaches have an obvious appeal in their goodwilled, philanthropic impulses, but they fall far short of either matching what democracy can do or even rescuing capitalism from what ails it. Capitalism has been crippled by the loss of its partnership with democracy, and cannot be restored to good health exclusively through internal civic goodwill or market-side reforms.

Infantilization acts to reinforce the preference for the private and the puerile by treating the impetuous, grasping child as the ideal shopper, and the shopper as the ideal citizen. It inculcates in adults an obligation to give free rein to the "I want!" and "Gimme that!" that both disclose and consti-tute the infantile id. More than simply an option, puerility is regarded as a necessity of capitalism's survival and hence a mandate of the zeitgeist—which is, of course, the ethos of infantilization. That ethos is thus endowed with a benevolent, even a sacred character, much as work and investment once had Protestantism's fervent blessings. The result is a ver-itable "cult of the child" widely recognized in the media as such.[29] There is to be sure much tut-tutting at Hollywood's celebration of comic book porn like *Sin City* and a good deal of oh-my-ing at the inanities of Howard Stern talk radio and gross winner-take-all, who-can-actually-eat-the-worms? reality television. But there is no serious resistance by consumers to a marketplace geared to children any more than there is resistance by consumers to a Wal-Mart geared to low-wage, minimal-health-insurance, no-future jobs. What resistance there is comes from what the market casts as "special interest" groups such as parents' groups and unions. That such groups are regarded as "special interest" rather than public interest is itself a sign of the triumph of the market.

Indulging our civic schizophrenia, there is the quiet knowledge that what's bad for us in common is good for the bottom line and just fine for me, for my bottom line (the price I pay for goods), for my stock portfolio, and for the long-term value of my property (and, for that matter, for my church's property). We mutter our wan complaints about a violent and salacious pop culture, even as we count its economic blessings and (with a wink) enjoy its enticing products. We worry about corporations exploiting kid cravings for sugar, fat, and salt even as we welcome convenient medical studies "discovering" that fat is not really a health hazard after all, so that fast-food company stakeholders can satisfy themselves that selling pizza and burgers in schools does not really hurt anyone.[30]

A new genre of books is emerging that—with a perverse if inadvertent nod to Nietzsche's transvaluation of all values—argues everything you thought was dumbing down the kids is instead making them brighter: that those inane video games actually make teenagers smarter and those multi-plotline television series geared to attention-deficit viewers actually encourage complexity of thinking and nonlinear logic. Steven Johnson for one does not beat around the bush: his book is called *Everything Bad Is Good for You*.[31] As we have already seen, philosophers and religious leaders have always understood that generally speaking what feels "good" for you as a "first-order desire" you yourself often judge "bad" for you as reflected in your "second-order desires." It is via second-order desires that we second-guess our initial impulse, saying something like "I don't really *want* to want what I just wanted." Of course, as a child (first-order desire) I would like to have grown-ups tell me that everything bad for me is really good for me (smoking, drinking, drugs, laziness, aggression, affect-less sex, and violent video games), but as someone who wants in time to grow up (second-order desire) I am glad they do not.

Philosopher Harry Frankfurt puts it this way: "Besides wanting and choosing and being moved to do this or that, men may also want to have (or not to have) certain desires and motives. They are capable of wanting .

to be different, in their preferences and purposes, from what they are."[32] Reflective self-evaluation of our "free choices" is what really makes us free. We are divided within ourselves by what we want and what we want to want. What we want is usually private, what we want to want is frequently public. John Stuart Mill associates the capacity to subject what-we-want, to what-we-*want*-to-want, with character. "A person whose desires and impulses are his own—are the expression of his own nature, as it has been developed and modified by his own culture—is said to have a character. One whose desires and impulses are not his own has no character."[33] Character is of course a function of maturity, and its absence a sign of persistent puerility.

Examples abound of how this civic schizophrenia, when combined with an infantilist ethos and the ideology of privatization, can defeat the commonweal. I want a Hummer that is bigger and meaner than everything on the road; but we need (the civic me wants) a country (and I want to live in a country), and we must have a world (and I want my children to live in a world), where someone else's car does not protect its occupants by killing me and mine, where the nation is not oil dependent on foreign countries with whom the United States ends up going to war to protect our energy imports, and where the global environment is not degraded by fossil fuel by-products. You want the best health services that you can buy for you and yours alone, but you want to live in a country where everyone is protected from plagues and viruses because health is a public not a private good, which means that where some are at risk all are at risk. I want a career in youth marketing where I can find a niche in targeting five-year-olds, but I don't want to live in a society where kindergartners are targets of manipulation and exploitation, and I certainly don't want *my* five-year-old targeted.

As a career marketing executive for, say, Nickelodeon, I work to open kids up to the influencers I can buy and control—celebrities, athletes, or friends and peers I can pay to be "buzz" leaders—and avoid the gatekeepers I can't buy (moms and teachers, for example);[34] but as a citizen I want to live in a country that protects kids from exploitation and marketing, and I want the influencers to be tough gatekeepers like pastors and teachers and imams and moms—the very people I am trying to freeze out of the influence circle in my work as a marketer. As a producer of films for the global market, you want adults everywhere to retain childish tastes and impetuous movie-going habits (repeat viewers of blockbuster films are what make the big bucks!) that guarantee profitability to your films; but as a parent you don't want your own children to be addicted to violence, porn, comics, video games, and fast-food tie-ins—and you certainly don't want to be addicted to such tastes yourself when you have turned thirty or forty and are yourself a parent of kids.

This exasperating civic schizophrenia has actually infiltrated the banking industry and put the economy itself at risk. As individuals Americans like to spend, and the infantilist ethos conditions them to spend more and more. Yet the collective result of this permanent spree is a nation that no longer saves, a growing international debt, dependency on foreign investors, and a currency crisis that not only lowers the value of the dollar but threatens economic meltdown. A report from the civic research organization Demos makes explicit the tie between privatization (choice defined as consumer spending) and infantilization (targeting and exploiting the young as big spenders). Between 1992 and 2001, Demos reports, "average credit card debt among indebted young adults [25–34 years old] increased by 55 percent," while "indebted young adult households" were spending roughly one quarter of their income on debt payments (running ahead, even, of the U.S. government!) and going into bankruptcy more than ever before. Younger adults (18–24 years old) saw a sharp rise of 104 percent in their credit-card debt over the ten years from 1992 to 2001, with indebted households spending nearly 30 percent of their income (doubled from 1992) on debt payments.[35] Not even bankruptcy can stand in the way of the credit industry's single-minded ambition to "empower" shoppers, whatever the social costs. Ninety-six percent of those who declared bankruptcy in 2001 received offers for credit cards, car loans, and mortgages in the same year their debts were discharged. One-half of those got more than ten offers a month.[36] The United States now has a net saving rate of less than zero, and the latest consumer banking scam is to offer credit shoppers a "savings incentive" in which for every dollar spent with a consumer credit card, a penny (or the change on a dollar) is put into a savings account. Now spending is the new form of saving.

It seems clear then that what we wish for one by one—to spend rather than save—is not intended when aggregated as a referendum on America's global fiscal viability; yet this is in fact exactly what it has become. Undeliberated private choices engendered in part by the convergence of the consumer mandate to spend and the focus on youth consumption result in undeliberated and often dire public consequences. Even the savings banks from whom we might expect to receive encouraging messages about the public benefits of saving have grown schizophrenic, peddling credit and debit cards rather than savings accounts, joining in the chorus of infantilizing voices instructing people to spend—spend beyond what they have, beyond emptied savings accounts, spend themselves into deep debt, because the capitalist economy counts on that spending for its survival however much the national economy is damaged by it. (The banks have figured out how to make credit- and debit-card spending earn more than the modest profit savings accounts once generated through reinvestment of saved dollars.) And so, in the twisted logic that emerges from the schizophrenia induced by privatization, producers pursue their rational individual interests as sellers, consumers pursue their interests as buyers and, presto, consumer capitalism flourishes right up till the moment the national economy fails, and with it, capitalism itself.

To keep global capitalism growing at the pace its survival requires, the keepers of the capitalist ethos must export America's own puerile spending mania. Lenin once argued that capitalism could survive only by pushing across national frontiers and establishing a global imperial presence. In an era of overproduction, capitalism consumerism faces the same challenge. Nations that sell their goods to the United States but have less robust domestic consumer economies and hence import too few overproduced American goods (contributing to the egregious American trade deficit) are of particular concern to those in charge of American capitalism's destiny. In ongoing trade discussions with China, the Treasury Department under former secretary John W. Snow was insisting not only that the Chinese "speed up the privatization of state-owned companies, including banks," but that "China needs to get people to spend more and save less."[37] This is of course the very mantra of consumer capitalism in decline: never has the passing of the Protestant ethos been more apparent. In India, growing wealth and a modernizing highway system that is accelerating the pace of change, are seen by Indians and Westerners as turning "India into a society in a hurry, enslaving it to the Western notion that time equals money."[38] Although India is still a nation where half of children under four years old are underweight, it is increasingly being regarded as the great Eastern hope for rescuing Western consumerism. It may be "stealing" Western jobs, but in doing so it is creating a domestic foundation for increased consumer spending that can only help Western vendors of infotainment, services, and other goods in the long run.

Yet as private consumerism spreads around the world, the idea that liberty entails only private choice runs afoul of our actual experience as consumers and citizens. We are seduced into thinking that the right to choose from a menu is the essence of liberty, but with respect to relevant outcomes the real power, and hence the real freedom, is in the determination of what is on the menu. The powerful are those who set the agenda, not those who choose from the alternatives it offers. We select menu items privately, but we can assure meaningful menu choices only through public decision-making. We choose what kind of car we drive, but it was the automobile, steel, rubber, and cement industries through their influence on Congress that chose a highway-based private transportation system, taking away the option of efficient, egalitarian public transportation (intra- and intercity fast rail, for example). Moreover, it turns out that increasing the number of choices on a given menu has diminishing returns, even for private liberty. Addicted to quantity and the panacea of more, we like the idea of maximizing the number of choices we can have, associating it with liberty. But psychologists teach that there are limits to how many choices we can actually entertain as well as limits to our capacity to calculate the benefits of alternative possibilities. Saatchi & Saatchi CEO Kevin Roberts, who ought to know, writes that "People are overwhelmed by the choices they face. Forget the Information Economy. Human attention has become our principal currency." He cites Nicholas

Negroponte at MIT media lab about the real nature of choice: "I don't want 500 television channels," says Negroponte. "I just want the one channel that gives me what I want to see."[39]

What Kevin Roberts fails to see, however, is that the choice between five hundred television channels and a channel I really want to watch is the choice between private and public goods. Public television in the United States and state television in Europe try to offer at least one or two choices that meet the standards of collective choice and public accountability, although they are under pressures of privatization and commercialization that threaten to turn them into just one more private choice among thousands. The choice between public and private transportation introduced above raises the same issues. Choosing between public and private transportation is not only easier but more compelling than the private choice between endless brands of automobile in a city (such as Los Angeles, for example) where private transportation has been the only option. *Consumer Reports* regularly surveys over 220 car models: does this really enhance our freedom? It also tests 250 breakfast cereals, 400 VCR models, 500 health insurance policies, 350 mutual funds, and 35 showerheads. Surely this is choice overkill—what Swarthmore College social theorist Barry Schwartz argues is "choice overload" in a world where more can actually feel like less.[40] And of course it is a cliché of the old wisdom that the choices which really matter to us, that is to say, "most of what people really want in life— love, friendship, respect, family, standing, fun . . . does not pass through the market" at all.[41]

Along with Barry Schwartz and others, Columbia University scholar Sheena Iyengar has suggested that "more choice can be worse than less choice," since as the number of options increase, choice becomes more onerous and less liberating.[42] Does having all the brand choices ranked by *Consumer Reports* or being offered five hundred or more television channels really make us feel freer? How many channels are enough? How many kinds of soap? Do I really want or need to select among thirty-five models of showerhead? As Schwartz concludes, "when faced with overwhelming choice, we are forced to become 'pickers' . . . relatively passive selectors from whatever is available."[43]

Private choice can be overwhelming. But even when we are under-whelmed, empirical studies show that "regardless of intelligence," people "do not always choose well."[44] In a telling (and quite comical) California test, given the choice of three anonymous 401K portfolios among which, unbeknownst to the participants, the portfolio they actually owned was included, only one in five people chose their own portfolio as best for them.[45] Similarly, experience demonstrates that whether an alternative is treated as *opt in* (you have to say expressly you want it for it to be selected) or *opt out* (you have to say expressly you do not want it for it to be excluded) can have a significant effect on decision making—which is why those pretending to enhance "choice" may actually influence a client to spurn a preferred alternative by offering it only as opt in, thereby favoring inertia. As many as three-quarters of Americans favor organ donation, but opt-in requirements mean that less than one-quarter actually exercise this preference in their wills.[46] On the other hand, while most consumers dis-like solicitation calls on their home phones, government opt-out require-ments give telemarketing firms the edge. Consumers retain a formal "right" not to be called (by opting to put their names on no-call lists), but "choice" (no surprise!) favors the marketers, who have recently won the additional right to intrude on wireless cell-phone lines unless users opt out.

Finally, it would seem that maximizing the number of choices we make in private and segmented domains that are not really crucial to human happiness while limiting the choices we are able to make in public domains that are significant allows a private market system dominated by consumption and the faux liberty it supposedly entails to distort and cor-rupt what we care about and how we live.

This is not false consciousness. We do actually want what we are allowed to choose privately. But we are nonetheless worse off and have less liberty despite having more private choices, since those choices are in a domain where the real decisions are not being taken. We want what we choose privately, but we want even more to be able to choose the public agenda that determines what our private choices will be. Even "Sophie's choice"—decide which of your two children the Nazi concentration camp commander will kill—is a choice of sorts. But not a choice Sophie would ever choose to make, let alone use to identify or define her "freedom." Indeed, a critical distinction between public and private liberty is that it is precisely through democratic participation and the ensuing government intervention that we regulate private choices to constrain their negative sides, and that we focus on the public things that really matter to us as members of a civic (and civilized) community. As a private consumer, you can choose to live in Mexico City's or Los Angeles's or Mumbai's smog-enveloped downtowns, or to live (if you can afford it) on the surrounding mountainsides where the air is better. But why should you not also decide whether Mexico City or Los Angeles or Mumbai legislate clean air standards such that you will not be forced to choose between living downtown or in hillside suburbs in order to breathe? Contrary to intuition, by constraining choice in the private sector we can actually facilitate the sense of liberty we feel. This may explain the paradoxical phrase Rousseau used to capture his crucial conception of public liberty—that we can actually be "forced to be free."[47] That is to say, our truly determinative public choices can be enhanced by restricting the domain of our trivial private choices. A ban on private automobiles in downtown urban centers restricts my private freedom to drive around as I please, but creates an urban environment far more conducive to the health, safety, and (even!) shopper-friendly concerns I have, which as a citizen I will regard as more important and liberating than my private freedom to drive where I please.

Whether overwhelmed by too many private market choices, or disempowered by the lack of real public choices about what sorts of decisions need to be on our agenda, we end up riven by a deeply schizophrenic sense of liberty. We are internally divided and dissatisfied with both our private and our public options. Like the alcoholic who tries to hide the bottle from himself or the professional pornographer who puts security locks on his home studio and bars his kids from access to the internet to prevent them from watching the noisome commodities he produces for a living, we find ourselves loathe to embrace in public the kind of society our private desires continuously create. Yet we are unable and unwilling to "disempower" (if that is what it is) those private desires, because we continue to be seduced by the claim that producers are not only giving us what we want but (as they like to say) "empowering" us in the process. For satisfying private desires does feel good; and helping consumer capitalism survive may also seem to be a good thing for everyone. Our selfishness is rationalized and excused, while the public goods after which we still yearn are construed as liberty-destroying and disempowering. In the process, the public goods and the democratic institutions by which public goods are secured get delegitimized. In this way, through the magic of marketing, such profoundly public terms as *liberation* and *empowerment*, once reserved for a civic discourse associated with democracy and citizenship, are made over into tools of consumerism and merchandising—the new banners of a "consumer revolution" whose aim is to destroy the public selves (citizens) our political revolution once constituted.

It is the peculiar toxicity of privatization ideology that it rationalizes corrosive private choosing as a surrogate for the public good. It enthuses about consumers as the new citizens who can do more with their dollars and euros and yen than they ever did with their votes. It associates the privileged market sector with liberty as private choice while it condemns democratic government as coercive. It promotes a new and malevolent variation on the eighteenth-century laissez-faire doctrine of the "invisible hand" by which Enlightenment economists once postulated that the pursuit of private desire by selfish individuals would result in the greater good of all. Privatization ideology today encourages us to believe that the market is not only efficient and flexible but can somehow turn its regressive impulses to the service of what is left of the idea of the public good. At the same time it pretends that the traditional instruments of our civic empowerment, our democratic institutions, are actually means to our enslavement. The logic is internalized, however, where it can operate in a stealth fashion by deploying civic terms like *liberty* and *empowerment* in a private context that actually robs them of their public functions.

Privatization is a kind of reverse social contract: it dissolves the bonds that tie us together into free communities and democratic republics. It puts us back in the state of nature where we possess a natural right to get whatever we can on our own, but at the same time lose any real ability to secure that to which we have a right. Private choices rest on individual power (brute force), personal skills (randomly distributed), and personal luck. Public choices rest on civic rights and common responsibilities, and presume equal rights for all. Public liberty is what the power of common endeavor establishes, and hence presupposes that we have constituted ourselves as public citizens by opting into the social contract. With privatization, we are seduced back into the state of nature by the lure of private liberty and particular interest; but what we experience in the end is an environment in which the strong dominate the weak and anarchy ultimately dominates the strong and the weak, undermining security for both—the very dilemma which the original social contract was intended to address.

The Costs of Privatization: Commercialization, "Externalities," and Equality

The wholesale privatization of goods once regarded as public has actually long since run its course, at least in sectors whose public character has always been ambiguous, and where efficiency, competition, and equal opportunity can be used to rationalize marketization. These sectors include transportation, first with the railroads and more recently the airlines and highways (toll "fast lanes"); housing, where public housing's reputation has been marred by inefficiency, poor design, high-rise slums, and the undeniable costs of having people live in "homes" they do not own; and in education, where despite the great American rhetoric of public schooling, private and parochial schools have always competed with public schools and where nowadays parental choice (via vouchers, charter schools, and other market mechanisms) has become a cry not just of neoliberals but of minorities seeking to insulate their children from supposedly failed public schools.

In each of these sectors, as well as in striking new arenas such as space exploration and federal disaster relief, what was once a public trust has become a setting for competition where profits are thought to do a better job of securing goods than supposedly abstract notions of the commonweal.[48] A brief review of each will put a little flesh on the bones of the privatization argument. It is worth noting, to start, that even in these domains where privatization is widely accepted, it has produced consequences pernicious to one of its putative goals: a healthy pluralistic society. For privatization has inevitably been accompanied by commercialization, a neglect of public costs written off as "externalities," and an acceleration of the inequalities already pervasive in market society.

An important rationale for privatizing is that it supposedly replaces the "monopoly" of government with a pluralistic and diversified sector of private competition; whether the reality that it yields is actually diverse or is dominated by a homogenizing commercial culture is hence of considerable importance. The transfer of public power to private hands often is associated with a devolution of power; but in fact privatizing power does not devolve but only commercializes it, placing it in private hands that may be as centralized and monopolistic as government, although usually far less transparent and accountable, and also pervasively commercial. Water privatization has been sold as a remedy to public corruption and as a prompt to conservation. When water costs more, people use it more prudently. The reality is privatization has merely privatized corruption and inequality without providing more adequate supplies or even turning much of a profit.

Parks, schools, and other formerly public institutions find it difficult to withstand commercialization, as cities and states lose their tax revenues. Bryant Park behind the New York Public Library in midtown Manhattan, for example, has become a public space run like a business, with user fees and ads from sponsors.[49] Park users may welcome the improvements, and write off the advertising as a necessary cost; but the cost is "necessary" only because private users refuse as citizens to pay and appropriate taxes (the way the French do, for example) to keep up the parks publicly. The same is true with respect to a privatized school system, which may appear to offer parents more local choice than a regional public school system mandating a single neighborhood public school for each child.

Even public schools can fall prey to the logic of privatization, inviting Channel One to run commercials in history class in exchange for the use of borrowed television equipment and supposedly educational news programming (Channel One News). Parents across America frustrated by the public underfunding of their public schools may not even mind that new public school facilities now carry names like the ShopRite of Brooklawn Center (in Brooklawn, New Jersey), Rust-Oleum Field (in Vernon Hills, Illinois), and Eastern Financial Florida Credit Union Stadium (in Broward County, Florida), given that the corporations in question put in hundreds of thousands of dollars toward construction.[50] But again, such privatization opens the doors to a commercialization of educational institutions that in time infects schools both public and private, and that creates a less pluralistic and diversified learning environment. And in every other case, the excuse is not a preference for corporate-named facilities or TV ads in the classroom, but desperate need in the face of too few public revenues to meet the needs of schools and their pupils.

In the same manner, public universities and colleges in search of private funding often find themselves subservient not just to the monopoly of the state (which at least is authorized and legitimate) but to a monopoly of the marketplace as well. The state monopoly nowadays controls schools and universities without funding them properly—the egregious "unfunded mandate" that is the No Child Left Behind policy of the Bush administration, for example; or that uses funding to force encroachments on the free space of schools (as when the federal government threatens to penalize schools that do not admit military recruiters by withdrawing funding).

They assail government monopoly, but the corporate interests willing to make up shortfalls in state funding in exchange for informal control over the climate and content of education are themselves monopolistic. As the share of operating revenues coming from state and local taxes for public universities declined on average from 74 percent in 1991 to 64 percent in 2004, the president of Pennsylvania State University spoke ruefully about "public higher education's slow slide toward privatization."[51] Falling revenues engender desperate measures. Naming rights over athletic facilities as well as academic buildings and even over fellowships and chairs and academic departments are put up for sale to the highest bidders, eating into academic integrity and scholarly autonomy. Cola company contracts are negotiated that allow corporations to buy an exclusive right to sell a single brand of consumables in return for multimillion-dollar gifts, making a farce of the ideal of a campus insulated from outside pressure where choice is supreme. Corporations that boast about free consumer choice in the marketplace team up with universities that boast about free intellectual choice in the classroom in order to constrict both. Energy companies pay for learning materials tainted by corporate biases that undermine objective research and learning—the ExxonMobil company providing materials on conservation, for example. Corporate research funding for academic science privatizes what is supposed to be public research, and allows research results and patents to be sold for private profit.[52] Yet as state funding continues to decline and universities increasingly "become huge research empires that need continual infusions of cash to sustain their personnel and overhead costs," privatization becomes a condition of academic survival.[53]

In 1980, the federal government participated in the commercialization of higher education by passing legislation that licensed universities to sell research for profit. At West Virginia University, Kmart endowed a chair focused on retail marketing (training store managers?). At Stanford University, among America's most elite higher education institutions, a Global Climate and Energy Project was funded by a $100-million grant from Exxon.[54] And finally there is the sad case of Channel One, a soft-news high-school network originally developed by Whittle Communications which offered free telecommunications hardware (on loan only) in return for access to high-school classrooms for nine minutes of soft info-tainment programming laced with three minutes of hard advertising. Schools availing themselves of this devil's bargain (throughout most American states, in over 12,000 high schools representing 8 million students) have mostly been poor inner-city institutions which can least afford to squander classroom minutes on ads or to reenforce the commercial supersaturation of children already deeply immersed in commercial media outside school.

As privatization commercializes the sectors it "frees" from public monopolies, it manages to conceal the social costs of the private market transactions it endorses. By calling such costs "externalities"—Milton

Friedman uses the phrase "neighborhood effects"—economists give the impression that such costs are not part of the internal accounting by which market efficiency and productivity are to be measured. In the United Kingdom, for example, market-oriented governments in the 1970s and 1980s rationalized cutting rail service to smaller towns and villages across Britain based on diminishing passenger usage and ticket sales. This efficiency-based cost cutting omitted any reckoning of social costs—of "externalities." Yet the society-wide impact of these cuts was devastating as measured by the damage done to the quality of rural life and thus English culture, as well as to the preservation of a national communications network inclusive of all citizens—something deemed important to national morale. At the same time, the cutbacks added to pollution and traffic congestion by eliminating a key alternative to automobiles in rural areas. What is desirable from the standpoint of a market consumer may be untenable from the standpoint of a citizen. What serves the bottom line of a private rail corporation may not serve the aims of a national transportation system. A market system that recognizes only profit and treats all other values as externalities to be ignored can devastate a civilization on the way to assuring a return on investment.

Privatization also places invisible costs on taxpayers and allows market institutions to appear more cost efficient and inexpensive than they are. A report produced by the nonprofit group Redefining Progress, based in Oakland, California, has created the Genuine Progress Indicator, an alternative assessment of the economy. Authored by Jason Venetoulis and Cliff Cobb, "The Genuine Progress Indicator, 1950–2002 (2004 Update)," reports that the GDP overestimates the health of the economy by $7 trillion. Unlike the GDP, the GPI weighs the quality of the economy as opposed to merely its quantity. The GDP, for example, suggests that from January 2000 to January 2003 the economy grew approximately 2.64 percent (or $272 billion). The GPI, however, which factors environmental abuse and national debt into the equation, estimates economic growth in this period at a miniscule 0.12 percent, a $212 billion decline over three years. Another report, "The Ecological Footprint of Nations, Update 2005," also published by Redefining Progress, measures whether or not the global pop-

ulation is living within its ecological means. The report answers no, showing that while the earth's biological capacity stands at 42 acres per person,
on average we use 57 acres per person. The United Arab Emirates, Kuwait,
and the United States exceed their biological capacities. In a comparison of
continents, North America and Western Europe have the greatest ecological footprints and run negative ecological balances.[55]

The American market system has become a paragon of how to socialize the costs but privatize the benefits of a supposedly private market
economy. Many of the pilots trained by the U.S. Air Force end up in jobs
with commercial airlines; their expensive taxpayer-supported flight education results in lower training costs for the airlines, and commensurately
inflated "profits" which do not count the public costs of learning to fly.
Taxpayers are assessed for training pilots, commercial airlines reap the
rewards. Much the same thing happens in the new corporatized military
security sector, where mercenaries and other professional security personnel are hired by private companies only after they have completed their
highly technical training in public military forces. Socialism when it comes
to costs (the now classic Chrysler Corporation bailout), but market capitalism when it comes to profits. Ironically, firms that are politically connected to the governments by which they hope to be bailed out do better
than those without such connections.[56]

This (literal) passing of the buck from private to public—another form
of so-called free riding in which a beneficiary of public services refuses to
pay their cost—is most evident in the security domain where a sector once
deemed quintessentially public is fast being privatized, with consequences
yet to be reckoned. Functions many would associate with the very essence
of statehood—of both sovereignty and the social contract which grounds
it—are being outsourced and subjected to market forces. These quintessential functions include social security, individual (police) security, and
national (military) security and represent a striking expression of privatization run amok. It is probably not an accident that social security privatization is being debated in the United States at the very moment when
neighborhood policing, civil prisons, and military security are also being
subjected to radical privatization in ways that suggest not merely a recali-

bration of how the state undertakes its public responsibilities, but an assault on the very idea of a democratic sovereign state's legitimate functions.

Market arguments rarely confront "free riding" and "externalities," and almost never focus on these larger democratic issues. For example, while there was a great deal of discussion about whether the privatization of social security proposed by the Bush administration in 2005 was economically viable or technically feasible, the costs of President Bush's proposed changes measured by the vitality of civil society and the integrity of democracy were scarcely calculated or deliberated at all. The real question here is whether a nation that depends on its civic sector for its democratic oxygen can afford to allow the civic trust embodied in social security to be suffocated. When a public social insurance and pension policy is turned into a private bet where personal and private market decisions determine who does well and who does badly, irreparable harm can be done to democratic common ground and to what was once called the promise of public life. The promise of social security ameliorates the distorting traces of class, race, and gender which can play out so dismayingly in the private realm.

Privatization, whether of education, housing, or social security, makes us less of a public. As Margaret Kohn writes in her thoughtful study of privatization and free speech, "public space plays an important role in fostering democracy by preserving opportunities for political speech and dissent and providing a shared world where we can potentially recognize one another as citizens."[57] When we privatize public space, we not only undermine citizenship; we opt for market Darwinism where private investors may prosper but others will lose, rather than for social justice where all are equally protected. Privatization demeans the "us" as an "it" (big government, bureaucracy, "them") and imagines that consumers and citizens are the same thing. But social security is not merely a technical scheme to give private workers a pension and disability and death benefits, to be toyed with and altered in accord with today's economic fashions. It is an emblem of civic membership in a common polity; a reflection of the benefits that come with the responsibilities of citizenship. We pay in as working, tax-paying citizens not just to guarantee ourselves private pensions but to guarantee a fair social system and public justice to all. Yet today even tax collection is being outsourced by the federal government. In the countries of the European Community there has been much alarm at economic proposals that in the name of economic efficiency and market philosophy demand the rollback of the social security plans associated with the core meaning of European sovereignty. Although the French "no" vote in June 2005 on the new European constitution was animated by several competing motives, many on the left who abandoned their leadership feared that the new Europe endangered the social contract implicit in the French welfare state.[58]

Physical security is perhaps even more essential to the meaning of sovereignty than social security. Yet here too recent decades have witnessed the outsourcing and privatization of police functions in developing and developed nations, led again by the United States. More than one-sixth of prisoners incarcerated in the United States are held in for-profit prisons, whose interest is neither in punishing lawbreakers nor in rehabilitating citizens, but solely in making a respectable profit for shareholders—which may mean reducing services, cutting costs, and lowering salaries in order to compete effectively with other private firms. At the same time prisons are being privatized, the hiring of private security guards and the building of closed and gated communities are increasingly common features of American suburbs trying to wall themselves off from urban blight, and of middle- and upper-class compounds in developing countries like the Philippines or South Africa. In cities like Paris and London, the valence is reversed, with wealthy inner-city enclaves trying to wall themselves off from beltway banlieue where immigrant populations are to be found in oppressed and sometimes violence-ridden ghettos. Walling in or walling out communities of the poor turns out, however, to be ineffective in deterring crime: most urban maladies, from drugs and gangs to guns and juvenile delinquency, have followed retreating middle-class populations from inner- to outer-suburban rings and into the green zones beyond. And suburban ghettos do not insulate inner-city elites from violence and mayhem, as the French learned in the autumn of 2005. Privatization of security simply does not work very well.

Moreover, walling off communities of the poor while privatizing security for the well off also fractures the commons and corrupts democratic citizenship. It undermines the public security function itself, whose legitimacy depends entirely on its being commonly constituted and commonly enforced. Distributing the benefits of security based on class or income or allowing subgroups within a polity to develop their own private security forces actually abrogates the social contract.

Despite the impact on the social contract, the United States is pioneering the way in privatizing not just police security but national defense and global security. In Joseph Heller's *Catch-22*, written nearly fifty years ago, the exasperated Milo Minderbinder exclaims: "Frankly, I'd like to see the government get out of war altogether and leave the whole feud to private industry." What was then a cynical joke from a weary World War II flyboy is today the cynical realism of the Department of Defense. As military recruiters in America desperate for recruits reach down into the ranks of teenagers to find uncritical soldiers to fight its unpopular wars (an irony of an age of infantilization), government invites private industry to play an expanding role in America's global military presence, not just in Iraq and Afghanistan but at military bases throughout the world and even in the United States. Perimeter security at domestic bases has been added to the many logistical functions being outsourced to private firms, while American Ambassador Khalilzad in Iraq is protected not by the nearly 150,000 in-country troops, but by private security guards from Blackwater USA.

That is another irony in an American administration that has consistently bemoaned the supposed "surrender" of American sovereignty by "liberals" to the United Nations or NATO, and has been reluctant to put a single American soldier under the command of a friendly Canadian or British officer, but is apparently more than willing to outsource its fundamental national security to private firms whose announced interest is necessarily (and quite properly) their own bottom line. Don't trust the UN, trust Brown & Root. Don't consult France, consult Military Professional Resources, Inc. Don't call on Europe to rebuild Iraq, contract with DynCorp. Don't ask the Marines to take care of the ambassador, ask Blackwater.

Like every other constitution in the world, the American constitution makes it plain enough that the primary function of government is to "provide for the common defense." As Brookings analyst P. W. Singer writes in his indispensable study of national security privatization called *Corporate Warriors*, providing for security "was one of the most essential tasks of a government. Indeed it defined what a government was supposed to be."[59] Yet today more than seventy major firms, many of them American, do over $100 billion a year in sales to undertake the functions of what once upon a time was the sole function of sovereign states. Halliburton's Brown & Root Services has done business in an alphabet soup of states including Afghanistan, Albania, Bosnia, Croatia, Greece, Haiti, Hungary, Italy, Kosovo, Kuwait, Macedonia, Saudi Arabia, Somalia, Turkey, Uzbekistan, and Zaire, much of it (though not all of it) on behalf of the United States government. That its former CEO, Dick Cheney (who received a $37 million severance contract from Halliburton when he left), has been America's two-term vice-president during a period when Brown & Root has received lucrative contracts from the U.S. government certainly raises serious conflict-of-interest issues, but they are the least of the kinds of improprieties that arise when a transparent, accountable government shifts essential public security functions to a private firm.[60]

Private security firms have also been used in recent years as a surrogate for public security inside the United States. Following the devastation of Hurricane Katrina in New Orleans, and the subsequent breakdown of law and order, when even the United States government and its disaster response agency (the Federal Emergency Management Agency, or FEMA) were conspicuously missing in action, private security firms leapt into action. Blackwater USA dispatched "150 heavily armed Blackwater troops dressed in full battle gear" to New Orleans, with some of its employees patrolling the French Quarter "in an unmarked car with no license plates."[61] Additional security forces were hired from DynCorp, Intercon, American Security Group, Wackenhut, and Instinctive Shooting International (an Israeli outfit) by private businesses and wealthy homeowners wanting to protect their property. At the same time, the federal government was putting out no-bid contracts to private firms such as Halliburton, Bechtel, and Fluor, leading Senator Richard Durbin of Illinois to complain that public officials "are worried because we hear about no-bid contracts in the Katrina areas going to the same companies that they went to in Iraq without the kind of accountability that we have to demand."[62]

Sovereignty is usually defined as the legitimate monopoly over force exercised by a state, entailing that only a state can exercise sovereignty. The essence of the democratic social contract is that individuals and groups surrender their "right of nature" to exercise force in the state of nature to a sovereign body they themselves constitute, in order to protect themselves from others deploying the same anarchic natural force. When sovereign states "outsource" the security function, they in effect cede back to the state of nature the very powers that constitute their own legitimacy. They do what every social contract theorist from Hobbes to Rousseau to the American founders say cannot be done: they alienate "inalienable" sovereignty, and hence negate inalienable rights.

As Singer states the problem in practical terms, when states empower private actors to undertake security functions, the danger is "that empowered corporate actors themselves will become competitive not only with weak local states but also to the national interests of other powers, including even their own home states."[63] When President Karzai of Afghanistan hires private security guards to police his vulnerable presidential presence, we can write it off to a tribal state that does not yet have a fully trustworthy national army. But when the United States outsources scores of military and security functions in both Afghanistan and Iraq to private firms, and entrusts the security of its own in-country representatives to them, how is that to be explained? At best this is to hire mercenaries to do the job of citizen soldiers. At worse it is to outsource American sovereignty and the state's inviolable and hence impossible-to-delegate responsibility for national security. As the *New York Times* editorial page has commented, "It's one thing for the military to outsource food and laundry services to private firms . . . but it's quite another to outsource the actual fighting."[64]

Despite such concerns, several contract workers have, for example, been implicated in the abuses at Guantanamo Bay and Abu Ghraib prison, proving that "private contractors are now carrying out highly sensitive duties that until very recently were the province of government agencies only."[65] The abuses of outsourced security include not only civil rights violations, corruption, and lack of transparency, but the danger that private mercenary forces will be used to undermine rather than assure the peace, to overthrow weak emerging democracies rather than to secure them. While this is not common, Singer reports that rogue private security firms have been found "working for violent nonstate actors," and have even been known to help train and supply terrorist networks.[66] Sakina Security Ltd., a now defunct British firm, helped train Muslim holy warriors as part of a "Jihad Challenge" program it marketed, while Mexican drug cartels were able to obtain counterintelligence and weapons assistance from another private security firm, Spearhead Ltd. Kelvin Smith, an employee of the American government, "ran a side business" that turned out to have trained at least six members of Al Qaeda.[67]

Among the private security firms working in Iraq in 2004 were not only Blackwater USA, but Custer Battles, ArmorGroup, and Kroll Security International. Custer Battles, which had 1,300 employees in Iraq, "subscribes to the 'faster camper' theory of security," referencing "the musty joke about the ravenous bear that invades a campsite: To survive, it is not necessary to outrun the bear, only the slowest camper."[68] The slowest campers in Iraq turn out to be Iraqi civilians, of course, which suggests one more reason why private security firms may not be the ideal vessels of sovereign American security objectives in that nation. Barry Yeoman notes that by using private companies the government can perform military jobs in Latin America and presumably elsewhere "that would have been politically unpalatable for the armed forces." This not only makes clear that "so far, the Pentagon has failed to prove it can take responsibility for either the actions or the safety of its private-sector soldiers,"[69] but more importantly suggests that security privatization affords an egregious evasion of democratic safeguards.

Equal access to power and security is among democracy's chief virtues. But private markets are notoriously indifferent to equality and it is clear, in a portrait cited by Singer, that "these khaki and Brooks Brothers clad mercenaries endorse the idea that power belongs to those who can afford it."[70]

That privatization flourishes in a period when equality is not a priority hints at both a cause and an effect relationship, with arrows that point in both directions. Because government is an equalizer that redistributes goods, secession is always a temptation for the haves, above all when they stop considering their own public interest in sustaining public goods, and engage in private bookkeeping that reckons the individual costs and benefits for them associated with government. If you live in London and are wealthy, why not cut rail service to Yorkshire and Dorset villages? Why not institute a traffic-congestion control system that effectively taxes the poor and benefits the rich by allowing automobile access to the inner city only to those willing to pay £5 a day, or able to keep two cars (with an odd and an even license plate, allowing them to get around the odd/even plate-number restrictions on inner-city access)?[71] Privatize the public highways with high-speed toll lanes—so-called Lexus lanes, because they are only for those who can afford them. And if the public domain becomes too unrewarding, simply move to a gated community and buy your own security, your own education, and your own garbage collection services, and leave the low-tax-base/high-service inner city to rot—complaining all the while about the "double-taxation" you endure by "having to" pay both low-end public taxes and the cost of high-end private services for yourself and yours. Or if you live in a Third World emerging society plagued by anarchy, crime, and corruption, buy your own mercenary security force and pay *it* to be the government; or better yet, pay it to take over the government, overthrow the government, or protect you from the government's armed forces (as in Papua New Guinea). In the bold new post-sovereign market world, the "sovereign right" to use force belongs not to the people constituted by a social contract, but to those able to pay for it— a familiar old recipe, harking back to Hobbes's "war of all against all."

The United States is by no means alone in privatizing security functions. In places like South Africa, where violence has become the greatest threat to the vibrant new democracy there, whites and middle-class blacks increasingly fed up with urban crime, carjackings, robberies, and street murders have also turned to private policing and gated communities. In South Africa this is less a consequence of aggressive privatization ideology than of perduring inequalities and the failure of public authorities to stem the crime wave. But the cure worsens the symptoms and leaves their causes untreated. In the words of one commentator on South Africa, while "government plainly needs more capacity, for both social justice and criminal justice," its defects have led to an "increased privatization of law and order" which in turn "reflects the hollowing out of government's functions." For whatever the causes, and in South Africa they may go back to "the failure of the state, both during and after apartheid . . . to create jobs, health care, housing, and education accessible to the vast majority of the population," the fact is that "when justice and social-control methods are ceded to the private sector—to private security firms, to vigilante groups, to simple mob justice . . . democracy becomes an empty promise."[72]

Inequality is built into the market system, which too often becomes a race to the top for those who are wealthy, and a race to the bottom for everyone else. Inequality is not incidental to privatization, it is its very premise. The implicit tactic employed by the well off is to leave behind those who get more in public services than they contribute as taxpayers in a residual "public" sector (a kind of self-financing leper colony that cannot self-finance) and throw in with those who have plenty to contribute in their own private "commons." The result is two levels of service—two societies—hostile, divided, and deeply unequal.

Not surprisingly, then, privatization ultimately attaches to politics itself. Politicians are merchandized and sold as commodities to a public regarded not as a body of public citizens but as a clientele. Public opinion research turns into private opinion polling where those polled are asked not for their deliberative judgments as citizens but only for their spontaneous private prejudices. Although experiments in "deliberative polling" show that citizens can and do change their minds, even on hot-button issues such as capital punishment, when exposed to rational argument and the values and rationales of others, such approaches are written off by privatizers as "manipulative," which in their minds justifies focus groups that work to filter out intermediate deliberation in favor of unmediated first impressions.[73] Parties and politicians alike are branded, so that what one *calls* a policy or an idea becomes more important than what it is or does (chapter 6). In recent years, Democrats in the United States have hired linguists like George Lakoff and theologians like Jim Wallis to help them "rebrand" their "product" in response to what they believe has been the successful branding of Republican positions by supposed political "geniuses" like Karl Rove.[74] These techniques are now spreading to Europe and even to emerging democracies such as Iraq.

The "selling of the president" (and the presidency) began with the television age and the first televised presidential debates between Richard Nixon and then underdog John F. Kennedy, but has led since to a wholesale marketization of the political in which politics is reduced to a science of manipulation that may or may not be effective, but leaves the public—regarded exclusively as a political consumer base—deeply cynical about the character and capacity of its leaders and its democracy.

The bottom line today is that the federal government "spends about $100 billion more annually for outside contracts that it does on employee salaries," with government agencies such as NASA and the Department of Energy acting more like what two commentators called "contract management agencies" than functioning government actors.[75] President Bush's response to the devastation that followed Hurricane Katrina was to invite private philanthropies and civil society groups along with a motley collection of corporate contractors to play a major role in what was a national disaster in need of national governmental intervention. Halliburton, one of the corporations providing (among other services) for security in Iraq, ended up as a player in New Orleans as well—on the basis of contracts that were not even let out for bidding. As with social security privatization, the justifications for such arrangements are always based on pricing and efficiency; given the calamitous inefficiencies of FEMA, the president's logic after Katrina might even seem rational—although in fact it failed the people of New Orleans, victims, survivors, and rebuilders alike. But an equally costly consequence of the failed privatization response was its unscrutinized impact on democratic sovereignty and on public values. Even political analyst Martha Minow in her judicious study of privatization called *Partners, Not Rivals*, while she identifies among the values that are at risk "equality, due process and democracy," ignores sovereignty.[76]

Yet the ultimate question raised when the recovery of a traumatized city is left to the market or when prisoners are incarcerated in for-profit prisons, is not just whether the solution "works" (it does not), but whether the state can farm out the obligation it has to the commonweal (New Orleans) at all; whether the sovereign right of violating a citizen's liberty (incarcerating prisoners) can be outsourced for any reason whatsoever, given that the legitimate monopoly over violence and an inalienable responsibility for the commonweal are defining features of sovereignty.

Even minimalists such as Milton Friedman or Robert Nozick who distrust all government acknowledge that the right to life and liberty can be yielded only to a public authority in whose collective decision-making (general willing) I myself am represented. In short, when politics, liberty, and security are privatized, it is sovereignty itself that is being outsourced, and this is quite simply an oxymoron. For it returns us not to that "free market" about which neoliberals fantasize but to a veritable state of wholesale anarchy—Hobbes's state of nature where force and fraud are the cardinal virtues.

PRIVATIZATION IS UNDENIABLY a feature of our times and may be pernicious in its own right, but does this prove its affinity to the infantilist ethos? Examining the dynamics of privatization as we have done here suggests that private relates to public as childish stands to the adult. Prioritizing the individual and rendering community private in a way that makes it look like an aggregation of individual wants and needs is a puerile way to construct the social world. Obviously individualism and narcissism are not synonymous, but the reduction of a commonweal to a series of private first-order desires and the trivialization of the common good as nothing but aggregated discrete private interests can be thought of as a kind of regression.

The social contract and the res publica it creates are mature forms of social organization: how adults associate themselves when they have learned the limits of anarchism, the inadequacies of individualism, and the realities of interdependence. In William Golding's harsh novel *Lord of the Flies*, the absence of adults among a marooned group of children precipitates an erosion of social norms and a breakdown of the social contract that leads to brute anarchy and the domination of the strong over the weak—as perfect a picture of Hobbes's state of nature as can be imagined. Pursuing the Hobbesian metaphor as played out by Golding, we are, so to speak, born solitary and self-assertive, we learn sociability and cooperation. Selfishness is inbred, altruism is learned, and civility a patina layered onto our narcissistic core by experience, education, and the shaping forces of democratic citizenship. We begin scarcely able to distinguish the world from our grasping selves. We acknowledge the loving otherness of the mother, but otherwise remain wrapped in a cocoon of infantile sensibility. In time we come to see that we can only flourish as developing selves inside communities of common purpose of which the family is but the first instance.

Privatization reverses this journey to maturation. It re-privileges the "me" and stands with rather than against narcissistic childishness. Community and the public good are about the "we." Marriage, the family, the clan and society are products of reproductive and social maturation. Yet from the point of view of private consumer society, these agents of adulthood are little more than obstructive gatekeepers to be circumvented or overcome. The market prefers bachelors and bachelorettes, kiddie consumers without social ties other than the ones marketers give them. Adulthood defined by agency, autonomy, and independent judgment is not a friend of consumerism. Capitalist paternalism today aims less at disempowering workers than at infantilizing consumers—in the paradoxical name of consumer empowerment.

The linguist George Lakoff, who is cited above as a Democratic Party advisor and who believes "framing issues" is the key to marketing candidates, offers a typical consumer society political frame that treats government paternalistically and casts citizens as children. He claims that the Republicans purvey a "strict father" model of political leadership and urges liberals to offer a "nurturant parent" model in its place, not seeming to notice that in both cases government plays the role of dads and moms catering to simpering juveniles (a.k.a. citizens). What a perfect scheme for an age of privatized politics, where the real power of meaningful public choice is taken away from citizens in return for giving consumers trivial power over private choices. "What do you want to spend your allowance on?" queries the patronizing parent, affecting to give his teen freedom, all the while knowing that real power and thus real freedom remain with the parent who decides whether or not there is an allowance and how large or small it will be.

It is hardly surprising that private money has gained so dismaying a hold on electoral politics in the United States, where politics is understood as a form of consumption and politicians themselves are parental dolls— so many Barbies and Kens—on sale to kiddie citizens who then allow themselves to be "parented" by them.[77] Rising election costs reflect politics as consumerism. In 2005, in the United States, spending totals on elections did as much to nourish civic cynicism as buy seats:

HOUSE

Party	No. of Candidates	Total Raised	Total Spent	Total Cash on Hand	Total from PACs	Total from Individuals
All	1054	$407,461,716	$237,829,973	$322,106,551	$141,268,765	$228,977,852
Dems.	567	$181,343,922	$106,551,126	$143,221,910	$59,679,939	$107,888,312
Repubs.	460	$224,834,130	$130,098,637	$178,754,059	$81,566,672	$119,918,509

Based on data released by the Federal Election Commission on June 1, 2006. Table from the Center for Responsive Politics, www.opensecrets.org/overview/stats.asp?Cycle=2004.

SENATE

Party	No. of Candidates	Total Raised	Total Spent	Total Cash on Hand	Total from PACs	Total from Individuals
All	131	$272,062,026	$122,670,384	$201,367,512	$38,815,777	$200,987,518
Dems.	61	$150,838,381	$65,057,670	$112,484,532	$18,357,868	$117,624,012
Repubs.	60	$117,951,060	$54,682,416	$85,275,552	$20,128,360	$80,534,984

Based on data released by the Federal Election Commission on June 1, 2006. Table from the Center for Responsive Politics, www.opensecrets.org/overview/stats.asp?Cycle=2004.

Neoliberals may object to such spending in principle, but in practice they are among the big spenders to "buy" seats in Congress, and are otherwise not exempt from these games. Even as they work to get government "off the backs of the people," they construe its functionaries as the people's parental guardians. It is in this sense that privatization is a kind of regression: in the first instance, an infantilizing of citizens construed now as both grasping customers and needy children; and then in time a dissolving of social bonds, the denial of the other, and a return to the *Lord of the Flies* where kids are pitted against kids in a war of all against all that is both metaphoric (kids as consumers) and real (kids as soldiers).[78] This vision may be sold as progress—liberation from public monopoly—but it represents cultural and civilizational regression. Citizens are grown-ups. Consumers are kids. Participating in the civic discourse that allows enemies to live together calls for adults; children are more easily taught to kill. The dark side of the "empowering" of children is their empowerment as soldiers—a practice in those parts of the world where children are too poor to be seen as potential consumers.

Grown-up citizens exercise legitimate collective power and enjoy real public liberty. Consumers exercise trivial choice and enjoy pretend freedom. Consumers even when childish have a place in a free society and express one part of what it means to live freely. But they do not and cannot define civil liberty. When they are defined as doing so, free society is put at risk. Privatization does not just reenforce infantilization: in the realm of politics, it is its realization.

Globalization as the Outsourcing of Privatization

As privatization serves infantilization and regression by privileging the personal over the public and private liberty over public liberty, privatization is in turn served by the changing character of the modern world—perhaps most significantly by globalization. Globalization effectively outsources privatization. That is to say, it takes the ideological claim that markets should be sovereign—a claim that is countered within nation states by the claim that only the state can be sovereign, that only a public (a people) can claim sovereignty—and globalizes it. In the anarchic international arena where there is no popular sovereignty but only an international state of anarchy, the argument for market sovereignty is unopposed. On the global level, the idea of the commonweal has no traction since there is no global political body to legitimatize or reinforce it.

The primal economic forces that the public sector traditionally regulated and controlled within states have now escaped their sovereign boundaries. The battle between democracy and markets, between public and private, that still persists within states has no international counterpart. There markets are trump, citizens nonexistent, and global sovereignty a dream. In the absence of even a hint of a global citizenry, there is and can be no democratic flywheel to moderate the capitalist whirlwind. Adults may still battle for control of markets within states, but in the global arena producers and consumers are sovereign and children rule.

The Europeans are giving up their cherished welfare-state security nets because they cannot see how to protect them even within an economically integrated Europe, let alone in a wholly deregulated global market society. How can citizens be protected within frontiers in a world of producers and consumers without frontiers? If undocumented workers challenge national labor laws in markets without borders, what can be done to regulate runaway consumption in markets without borders? Labor mobility has freighted once sovereign states with impossible burdens. The same mobility applies to marketing and those at whom marketing is aimed, and propels laborers into a "race to the bottom" even as it propels consumers into a monkey-trap world of endless and totalizing consumerism.

Globalization transforms the terms of the argument. Within nations, markets are always vulnerable to the powerful doctrine of political sovereignty (the idea that the state has the right to regulate the economy rather than the other way round). Within France or Japan or the United States, privatization must contend with arguments for sovereignty, democratic regulation, and public goods. In the global arena, markets are free from all constraint, rational or otherwise, in fact as well as in theory. Democratic governance is nonexistent. There are no global citizens, only global consumers; no global states, only global capitalist firms; no commonweal, only an aggregate of what individuals and nations and consumer markets want; no global cultural or national identities which are by definition parochial and local, only the new, hollowed-out identity conferred by brands.

Globalization turns privatization from an aspiration into a reality. It is a time traveler, taking capitalism back to a period when governments were too weak to contain its market energies, its market inequalities, and its market anarchy, as in the first half of the nineteenth century in Europe, or after the Civil War in the United States. Global relations are private relations among individuals, groups, and states in the absence of transnational or supra-sovereign associations.

The new realities of interdependence having thus permitted economic markets to escape the confines of democratic oversight, not even the most hegemonic sovereign state can today pretend to regulate or control its market economy or contain and discipline finance capital. The government of that has-been hegemon the United States of America can no longer prevent either specific jobs or whole industries from hemorrhaging abroad. As privatization assails the legitimacy of popular sovereignty from within, globalization from without steals from it its very essence.

Globalization leaves markets free from any need to justify their anarchic ways, whether they breed prosperity or misery, new investment opportunities or an eclipse of national social programs, more productivity or fewer jobs, greater private liberty or greater social injustice. Being dialectical, globalization in fact tends to produce all of the above. Tobacco companies, child porn movie makers, or manufacturers of violent video games may face attacks of local conscience that lead a municipality here or a national government there to crack down and prevent them from fishing for kid customers and consumer pedophiles within particular communities. But there is nothing to prevent them from trolling the global market sea for customers in localities and societies with less fastidious mores; or better yet in the interstices of global markets where the cry "free trade" silences all parochial critics and signals the starting line for the notorious race to the bottom.

Whatever battles are to be fought, then, must also be fought globally. Civic schizophrenia is more than a disease of infantilized market societies. It is an affliction of the global marketplace. A therapy that addresses the affliction only within the boundaries of nation states is likely to be insufficient. Either democracy must be globalized or globalization must be democratized. There is no other way. At the end of the final chapter of this study I will confront this challenge directly.

If privatization in its global manifestations is the most important ideological ally of infantilization, it is not the only strategy capitalism pursues in the age of consumerism. Consumerism is equally dependent on and perhaps addicted to an identity politics that is wrapped up in merchandizing, marketing, and above all, branding; these characteristics played out over the long term diminish rather than increase diversity, and have the effect of totalizing and homogenizing what affects to be a pluralistic market society.

5

Branding Identities:
The Loss of Meaning

The primary objective [of "brandscaping"] is not to sell the
product but to generate a fascination with the brand; to get
the customer to identify with the world of the brand, creating a brand awareness and providing it with a deep set emotional core.

—Otto Riewoldt, *Brandscaping*[1]

I N THE CENTURIES when capitalism was developing as a remarkably
productive system of economic organization rooted in work, investment, saving, and deferred gratification, an identity politics associated
with the Protestant ethos emerged that was perfectly suited to capitalism's
needs. Post-Reformation man, a hardworking Puritan ascetic with eyes
focused on the next life but also pursuing a Christian identity in this one,
embraced a robust notion of agency and a spirited grittiness that effectively married his Sunday church-going morality to his weekday capitalist
productivity. In time, other forms of identity organized around nationality, race, and ethnicity, overtook the more autonomous understanding of
identity associated with Protestantism, which associated the Christian
calling with some degree of free will. For the last several hundred years
these sociocultural (so-called ascriptive, or nonvoluntary) forms of identity have competed with if not dominated economic identity and self-
made civic identity.

Capitalism in its late consumer phase, preoccupied with selling goods to customers who may neither need nor desire what is for sale, is well served neither by the forms of identity embodied in the Protestant ethos, nor by the cultural identity politics of the last forty years. Hence, consumerism has attached itself to a novel identity politics in which business itself plays a role in forging identities conducive to buying and selling. Identity here becomes a reflection of "lifestyles" that are closely associated with commercial brands and the products they label, as well as with attitudes and behaviors linked to where we shop, how we buy, and what we eat, wear, and consume. These attributes are in turn associated with income, class, and other economic forces that may appear to permit choice but are in fact largely overdetermined by demographics and socioeconomics and are beyond the control of individual consumers. Ultimately this deep commercialization of identity responds to and reflects the infantilist ethos in significant ways. Because commercial identities tend to be simplistic and heteronomous (determined from the outside), as well as associated with celebrity and whim ("I wanna be a rock star!"), they reinforce the infantilist ethos, undermining agency, community, and democracy.

Branded lifestyles are not merely superficial veneers on deeper identities but have to some degree become substitute identities—forms of acquired character that have the potential to go all the way down to the core. They displace traditional ethnic and cultural traits and overwhelm the voluntary aspects of identity we choose for ourselves. We may choose to be an athlete, for example, but we are branded as a Nike athlete by the Nike swoosh—hardly a voluntary identity though we may "choose" to wear it in return for free gear or for Nike's corporate support for the event in which we compete. This displacement of a chosen or even a traditional given identity by a brand identity is facilitated by American mobility and suburban life, which uproot individuals from traditional communities and local civic life and make them susceptible to the thin commercial appeal of a brand. This takes place despite the fact that we nominally choose what we buy and hence may be thought to choose the identity with which what we buy saddles us.

In the course of the 1970s and 1980s, these new commercial identities have been to some degree generationally defined by a succession of time periods with commercial signatures. The postwar baby-boomer generation was defined by the fecundity of its defining reproductivity, but in time it reappeared in a language that defined its critical relationship to culture and consumerism—the "spoiled" Sixties generation known variously as "hippies," the "Woodstock generation," and "flower children." These earlier generational categories at least referred to cultural attitudes and behaviors or demographic factors (the "counterculture"). The following generation went temporarily unnamed, but when it was eventually dubbed Gen X, it found itself defined more by commerce than by culture. Pointing to those low-birthrate offspring of the 1960s who some called self-indulgent slackers, it actually defined a generation that in cultural historian Paul Fussell's description wanted to "hop off the merry-go-round of status, money and social climbing" that had characterized the baby boomers of the previous generation.[2] Gen Y succeeded Gen X and was intended to portray a generation almost entirely in terms of consumption. Gen Y grew up in the tech boom of the 1990s and was ready to hop back on the consumer train. Saatchi & Saatchi CEO Kevin Roberts cites "kids born between 1979 and 1994" with the "biggest discretionary spending power of any teen demographic in history," kids who are keyed in on "technology."[3] In Japan, Gen Xers have been called the "thumb generation"—because those under twenty-five are defined not by the "content of their character" but by their affinity for mobile text-messaging by thumb and by the social relationships that grow out of it.[4] In India, young entrepreneurs identify themselves as "Zippies," the children of neoliberal market reform of the kind celebrated by Thomas Friedman. Zippies are between fifteen and twenty-five years old, kids with "a zip in the stride," who are oozing "attitude, ambition and aspiration" and are "cool, confident and creative."[5] It is this generation, feeling "no guilt about making money or spending it" which, first in Japan, and now in India and China, has become the target of youth marketing and signaled the success of infantilization as a marketing strategy across the globe.[6]

These evolving demographic categories quickly found their advertising counterparts in explicitly commercial slogans such as "the Pepsi generation" or "the Wired generation," or by association with strong lifestyle brands such as Ralph Lauren (upper-income suburbanites affecting a kind of faux American landed aristocracy), The Body Shop (environmentally conscious health enthusiasts), or Calvin Klein (hip and hot teens whose bodies more or less reduced to sex are their passports to the good life). Branding also comes via surrogate identity television shows such as *Cheers*, which reproduced itself in countless real-life bar settings around America where people not only watched their screen favorites but played out their behavior; *Sex and the City*, that both captured and helped shape the attitudes of young, educated, me-focused, men-obsessed working women; *The Sopranos*, aimed at would-be tough guys romanticizing New Jersey gang life as a form of suburban diversion; and most recently *Sleeper Cell*, exploiting fear and patriotism in the context of terrorism, and *Desperate Housewives*, a study of the comical pathos of modern suburban life which so many Americans like to revile and emulate.

Lifestyles are branded and brands stand in for lifestyles which take the place of character of the kind that once was the marker of identity. Every brand has its demographic so that companies such as Urban Outfitters, Gap (with its babyGap family add-on), Banana Republic, and Rolex try not only to attract a particular tranche of consumers but to persuade them that the good life for them must be defined by wearing or eating or using the brand in question. As Alex Kuczynski, author of the *New York Times* "Critical Shopper" column, has written, Ralph Lauren offers "the power of implied ancestry."[7]

Modern branding is no longer a matter of effecting a market transaction: "A transaction is like a one-night stand," states a book tellingly titled *Emotional Branding*, "and it's never going to be as satisfying or rewarding as falling in love. A transaction makes the cash register ring once. A relationship makes it ring again and again. And selling takes on a new dimension when you put it in the context of a relationship."[8] Marc Gobé, in his own version of emotional marketing also called *Emotional Branding*, is not quite Max Weber, but he does offer a snippet of eye-opening social theory in which he distinguishes the "old economy" from the "new economy." The old economy is "factory based" and "capabilities-driven" and hence "production-focused" on manufacturing actual products, while the new economy is "consumer based" and "consumer-focused" and hence concerned not with manufacturing products but "creating brands."[9]

Brand identities need not be consistent in every detail across international frontiers as long as the brand relationship is preserved: McDonald's is low end and hence directed at the lower middle class and the poor in the United States, but upscale and trendy in Russia, while comfortably bourgeois in Japan. It wants to make fast food homey and accessible everywhere. American establishments may use "high culture" international branding in their attempt to go upscale: French table wines that are pedestrian in Paris or Brussels may lend the appearance of class to a hotel dining room in Iowa City or Detroit. The object is to displace traditional ascriptive identities associated with place and birth that are divisive and hence unsuited to the global marketplace—a twenty-something Turkish Kurd who is a Muslim—through contrived brand identities without borders: a twenty-something MTV-watching Pepsi drinker.

Naomi Klein was one of the first to confront branding critically, observing in the mid-1990s that "what most global ad campaigns are still selling most aggressively is the *idea* of the global teen market—a kaleidoscope of multi-ethnic faces blending into one another: Rasta braid, pink hair, henna hand painting, piercing and tattoos, a few national flags, flashes of foreign street signs, Cantonese and Arabic lettering and a sprinkling of English words, all over the layered samplings of electronic music." Yet the differences over which ethnic nationalities and religious and racial factions continue to murder one another around the world are treated by consumer commerce as faux, while the common commercial identities marketers are trying to establish are treated as real, as what Klein calls a "third notion of nationality—not American, not local, but one that would unite the two, through shopping."[10]

Pop sociologists have given commercial identity rooted in spending habits a certain cachet with terms such as *yuppies, soccer moms,* and *bobos,* which subordinate character to spending and lifestyle. These identities cross national and ethnic boundaries and so are potentially to be found in Jakarta, Java, and Johannesburg no less than in Munich, Milan, and Muncie.

Yuppies are the young urban professionals who gave foreign cars, fancy restaurants, and urban homesteading their cachet. Soccer moms presumably describe multitasking suburban women trying to "do it all" in a society that permits them to be professionals as long as they remain moms, housekeepers, and (most essentially) shoppers. And bobos, the coinage of journalist David Brooks (self-described as a "comic sociologist, but now an editorial page columnist for the *New York Times*"), fastens onto the "bourgeois bohemians" who manage to blend the hippie counterculture of the 1960s with the hardworking, meritocratic mainstream culture of the 1990s. Bobos are found in all developed commercial societies, from London's Sloane Square to Paris's rive gauche American-style malls, mimicking the great Mall of America in the Twin Cities suburb of Bloomington, Minnesota.

Amazon's review of Brooks's book *Bobos in Paradise* paraphrases him by depicting bobos as consumers who "sip double-tall, nonfat lattes, chat on cell phones, and listen to NPR while driving their immaculate SUVs to Pottery Barn to shop for $48 titanium spatulas. They tread down specialty cheese aisles in top-of-the-line hiking boots and think nothing of laying down $5 for an olive-wheatgrass muffin."[11] This pop-cultural characterization of identity is as laden with product placements as the latest Hollywood blockbuster, and its primary markers are consumables.[12] It is as if the character of the age of Enlightenment were to be identified by the wines served to Voltaire rather than by *Candide*, or the meaning of Romanticism captured by Coleridge's favorite pipe tobacco rather than his heroic poetry. The new, broad demographic categories used by marketers and their journalist avatars reject traditional sociological categories, ignoring class, race, and gender. As a consequence, they lack academic credibility. But that does not prevent them from dominating the rhetorical landscape of the consumerist era and shaping the puerile ways in which we think about who we are in terms of what we buy. Vice President Al Gore was judged more by his style-challenged ineptitude at color coordinating his wardrobe than by his policy-wonkish eptitude in defining his platform in the 2000 election. And Senator John Kerry later insisted the Democratic Party needed to be "unbranded" to win elections again.[13]

Other presidential elections suggest how potent the new consumer identities have become. Politicians like Britain's Blair, France's Sarkozy, Russia's Putin, and Iraq's Chalabi are as defined by their style and brand as by their policies.

In the new world of lifestyle identity, the products manufactured and services rendered in the old industrial economy are no longer even the critical measure of the brand itself. In the definitive Brand Keys' Customer Loyalty Leaders survey of 2004, the number one brand, overtaking Avis, was Google—a company which sells no physical product yet has a stock value that has reached $400 a share and represents a potent commercial force simply by offering a gateway, *the* gateway it would like to think, to the new world of digitalized information. Among the top nine in 2004, there was but a single company purveying hard goods (Canon Office Copier, itself in the communications hardware business). The rest traded not even in consumables such as Pepsi or Pizza Hut, but represented information or communication companies like Verizon and Yahoo! (and at number 14 the on-line bookseller Amazon) or service establishments like Avis and Hyatt Hotels. Brand no longer tracks content, it tracks fads, fashions, hip ways of living and doing. In the view of Al Ries, the president of Ries & Ries brand consultancy, brand is "a fad thing. [Now it's Google.] Next year it will be something else."[14]

TOP 50 BRANDS MEASURED BY CUSTOMER LOYALTY IN 2004 (2003 RANK IN PARENTHESES)[15]

1. Google.com (2)
2. Avis (1)
3. Verizon Long Distance (4)
4. KeySpan Energy (9)
5. Samsung Mobile Phone (7)
6. Hyatt Hotels (19)
7. Sprint Long Distance (3)
8. Canon Office Copier (8)
9. Yahoo.com (14)
10. Miller Genuine Draft (5)
11. Ritz-Carlton Hotels (17)

12. PSE&G (15)

13. Amazon.com (12)

14. Marriott Hotels (13)

15. Swissotel (NR)

16. Discover Card (27)

17. Diet Pepsi (31)

18. Budweiser (16)

19. Motorola Mobile Phone (10)

20. Coors (NR)

21. Netscape.com (59)

22. Sony Ericsson Mobile Phone (93)

23. Capital One Credit Card (29)

24. L. L. Bean Catalogue (20)

25. Wal-Mart (33)

26. Skechers (NR)

27. New Balance Athletic Shoe (22)

28. Miller Lite (87)

29. Starbucks (6)

30. Radisson (48)

31. BP Gasoline (79)

32. Inter-Continental Hotels (NR)

33. Sears Catalogue (30)

34. Verizon Wireless (37)

35. Schwab.com (26)

36. Diet Coke (47)

37. Mobil Gasoline (25)

38. T-Mobile Wireless (76)

39. Bell South Long Distance (28)

40. Adidas Athletic Shoe (23)

41. ETrade.com (42)

42. J. Crew Catalogue (54)

43. FedEx (50)

44. Westin Hotels (73)

45. Excite.com (35)

46. Hilton Hotels (36)

47. HotBot.com (34)

48. Sanyo Mobile Phone (NR)

49. MSN.com (38)

50. AltaVista.com (51)

Like so many traditional consumer product companies, Kodak, a firm whose traditional profits rested on film for traditional cameras and are now under siege from new digital photographic technologies, is not even on the top 200 brands list. With an eye on the new branding philosophy, and a hoped for comeback, it recently shifted its focus from cameras to girls' identity politics, deciding that by opting for cameras that are both giveaway and throwaway (the money is in developing the film!) it can "remain a beacon to teen girls across the nation, letting them know that it's really okay to be themselves."[16] And not just across the nation, but across the world. After all, Kodak is in competition with competitors such as Fujifilm, and must also do well in Asia and other global markets.

Similarly, beer companies are moving away from the brews that established their brands. Brewers are moving toward "drinks that may be beer in name only," limited-edition beverages often served in novel packaging like Moonshot (a caffeinated beer from New Century Brewing), B^E ("B to the power of E") and Tilt (both of which are 6.6 percent alcohol, cocktail-style beers), and Utopias, a 25-percent-alcohol brew from Sam Adams that is served in a weird bottle that looks like an inverted goblet and sells for $100 a serving (the "Utopias" label is presumably plural because drinking one or two of them makes you see double).[17] Making it obvious that they are selling a boyish and cartoonish masculine identity rather than beer per se, the brewers run puerile ads featuring hot girls, talking frogs, and collegiate geeks clearly directed at celebrating and sending up young men. Their target audience is underage in more ways than one.

Thus brands are gradually dissociated from the specific content of the products and services they label and reaffiliated with styles, sentiments, and emotions at best remotely linked to those products and services. In the process, they become compelling new purveyors of infantilism, where marketers seek to give their products, whether they are colas or political parties, the imprimatur (quite literally) of "mommy." How capitalism moved from its original focus on generic products to this preoccupation today with product-dissociated brands offers important insight into the use and meaning of brands under the influence of the infantilist ethos. For their appearance is more than a random accident of market anarchy.

Historically, capitalism began as a system in which specific goods and services, generic in character and reflecting real needs in a free market-place, were produced and sold. The producers were secondary to and wholly subsumed to their products—goods such as whale oil, bricks, steel, wagons, coal, soap, guns, skirts, petroleum, railway cars, pumps, candles, candy, motors, and so on. All products were in today's parlance "generics," and firms competed to control production and distribution through back-room deals, cartels, monopolies, and trusts—where the better part of dis-cretion might actually be concealing the identity of a would-be player like Standard Oil Company. Generic products ideally left room for only one dominant player in each generic sector. Salt was salt was salt, what was the point of having two or three salt companies?

To the degree monopoly was successful, there was hardly a need to dis-tinguish one producer from another. Oil was Standard Oil, steel was Carnegie, film was Kodak, soup was Campbell's, and so on. But the suc-cess of capitalist markets (with the help of government antitrust regula-tion) in checking monopoly and assuring competition meant that by the beginning of the twentieth century in both Europe and the United States, a number of producers making the same product and offering the same services were vying for market share. To distinguish themselves from one another, they began to "trademark" their goods and services in the hope that customers would prefer one salt or oil or gun company to another, initially for "rational reasons" involving claims about who provided the "best" (quality) or "cheapest" (price) or "most trustworthy" (reliability) version of the product or service being marketed.

Advertising and marketing in the first instance aimed at providing infor-mation about goods, but as consumption grew and producers multiplied, the arguments for preferring one trademark over another necessarily grew more manipulative. In an agrarian society (the United States before 1870, Europe until say 1848, India until the 1960s) the essentials were for sale more or less as generics. Monopoly firms hardly needed to advertise at all. You wanted oil, you bought from Mr. Rockefeller. You wanted to send a letter, you went to the U.S. Post Office. You wanted salt or calico, you dropped in at the general store and asked for salt or calico. But when gasoline was offered by competing companies and mail and communications became the provenance of private as well as government companies (Pony Express, Western Union, eventually UPS and FedEx) and salt and calico were offered by firms competing around quality, price, and reliable service, consumer discretion became a reality and influencing and shaping it a major business in its own right. Purveying the generic was no longer enough; a trademark had to offer a "generic-plus."

Goods were proliferating not just because of expanding demand but in order to "satisfy needs that no one knew they had," as William Leach notes in his indispensable and revealing portrait of early commercial culture called *Land of Desire*.[18] In 1890, Leach reports, 32,000 pianos were marketed, in 1904 it was 374,000; where earlier there had just been plain old spoons to be sold, by the turn of the century there were berry spoons and sugar spoons and soup spoons and salt spoons and mustard spoons and on and on. "In just six years, between 1899 and 1905," Leach writes, "American food output grew by nearly 40 percent. The quantity of cheap artificial jewelry doubled between 1890 and 1900."[19] Suddenly there was choice, and under these circumstances, where the original product (a spoon) or service (a mail-order catalog) was more or less indistinguishable from that offered by other competing companies, the specific trademark had to offer an add-on defined by quality, price, consistency, trustworthiness, and customer service. Such qualities still remained tethered to the generic product or service, usually by terms like *more* and *better*. You could buy stuff offered at the general store, but who could say for how much? At Woolworth's it would always be for a predictable nickel or dime. Ford made a better car. Western Union offered more reliable communication. Baldwin made better pianos, but Chickering or Brewster made them cheaper. Sears Roebuck had more goods at better prices than Montgomery Ward (or vice versa).

A critical change was underway. Thorstein Veblen saw in these developments "one of the most significant mutations in man's history" in which
industrial capital was being superceded by business capital where investment for gain overtook "commitment to industry and workmanship."[20]
The Protestant ethos was morphing before the astonished eyes of newly
"empowered" consumers. Markets were being taken over, diversified,
propagandized, and manipulated in the name of consumer choice.
William Leach borrows department-store magnate John Wannamaker's
phrase "the land of desire" both as the title of his book and to describe a
culture of consumer capitalism which, its freedom rhetoric notwithstanding, was "among the most nonconsensual public cultures ever created."
Because it was "not produced by 'the people' but by commercial groups in
cooperation with other elites," and because it "raised to the fore only one
vision of the good life and pushed out all others,"[21] its effect was to diminish American public life and the role of democratic consent even as it
trumpeted a new consumer marketplace dedicated to serving customers—
much the way those who market to children today trumpet kids' "empowerment." Trademarks were the instruments by which the new mass
market corporations founded on business capital helped create "fables of
abundance"[22] and pushed their vision for a "land of desire" in order to
compete with one another for the lion's share of it. They announced the
coming dominion of consumers over producers even as they secured
the dominion of advertising and marketing over both producers and
consumers.

Trademarks were only a way station on the road to brands, however.
For trademarks still hued fairly closely to generic products and services
and would prove insufficient to the task of awakening desires people
didn't know they had. To do this would require enlisting emotion and
imagination in the service of the new mass consumer society which was
producing goods faster than it could produce a palpable sense of need for
them. As early as 1901, anthropologist Margaret Mead's mother, an advertising expert named Emily Fogg Mead, had grasped that what was required
for consumer capitalism to succeed was the "diffusion of 'desire' throughout the entire population." Defending the new business of advertising,
Mead—sounding remarkably like Saatchi & Saatchi CEO Kevin Roberts a

century later—enthused "we are not concerned with the ability to pay, but with the ability to want and choose," which means opening up "imagination and emotion to desire."[23] A contemporary of Fogg's draws the obvious conclusion: "Without imagination, no wants, without wants, no demand to have them supplied."[24] Here was the critical transition from capitalism as a production-based system where saving was the leading virtue, to capitalism as a consumption-based system where spending would become the leading virtue; the transition from a necessity driven and static rural life to a mobile and urban discretionary culture of "the automobile and airplane, motion pictures and radio, the electric light and appliances, bottled soft drinks and canned soups."[25] A transition, in other words, from a system that serviced wants to a system that produced wants.

For such a revolution, trademarks did not suffice. Brands were born as stepchildren of the entrepreneurial competition that followed the age of cartels and trusts. Not surprisingly, Proctor & Gamble with its monopoly on household products being challenged by new competitors was the first to codify a "brand management system" back in 1931. Brands took advantage of the way in which trademarks had first become substitutes for generics by making them literal synonyms for generics, so that Bayer, Clorox, Jell-O, Vaseline, Band-Aid, and Kodak were in time to become synonymous with aspirin, ammonia, sugar gelatin desserts, petroleum jelly, bandages, and cameras. The aim was no longer to tell folks what was for sale but to show them why they needed to buy and stick with a particular brand of what was for sale—better yet, get them to buy it whether or not they needed it. This meant making them feel loyalty to the brand by associating it with feeling: with loyalty per se—not feeling for this or loyalty to that but generic feeling and generic loyalty. Feel at home with the brand because the brand is part of the family, feel the brand is trustworthy because there's a ringer for the faithful family dog Spot right there in the ad. Pancake mix was a generic recipe of eggs, flour, shortening, and sugar, but Aunt Jemima wasn't just eggs and flour, but sugar-and-cream-and-everyone's-dream of that nonexistent childhood nanny with whom you could feel secure without guilt or racial self-consciousness. Where trademarks traded in generic goods, brands traded in generic sentiments, emotions which had little to do with the goods and services themselves but were surgically attached to them by professional market doctors.

Modern brands pursue this logic relentlessly. Coffee is coffee is coffee, and it is clear to Starbucks, for example, that "consumers don't truly believe there's a huge difference between products" so the real goal is "to establish emotional ties."[26] Starbucks founder Howard Schultz knows quite well that he is not really selling coffee any more than the brewers are selling beer. Rather, what is at stake is "the romance of the coffee experience, the feeling of warmth and community people get in Starbucks stores."[27] Nike too is "leveraging the deep emotional connection that people have with sports and fitness. . . . [A] great brand raises the bar—it adds a greater sense of purpose to the experience."[28] Not products but emotional leveraging, manipulated lifestyles, and the shaping of human purpose define the new corporation. As Nike founding CEO Phil Knight suggests with typically naïve bluntness: "For years we thought of ourselves as a production-oriented company, meaning we put all our emphasis on designing and manufacturing the products. But now we understand the most important thing we do is market the product. . . . Nike is a marketing-oriented company, and the product is our most important marketing tool."[29]

This radical inversion of the traditional capitalist relationship between goods and services (a company's products) and marketing (how it sells its products) represents a remarkable step forward, one requiring targeting and infantilizing consumers in a fashion utterly foreign to productivist capitalism. While Naomi Klein points amusingly to what she calls the "deep New Age streak" of the corporate world, much more is at stake than tree hugging and whale songs.[30] The economics of late consumer capitalism would seem to mandate a system in which Nike is competing with Disney rather than Reebok, and in which brands are to be understood in terms of experience, lifestyle, and emotion, and it is these qualities that must be sold, while the products themselves remain either wholly unnecessary in themselves or differentiated from similar products by marketing alone.

No one is more instructive about the new consumer ideology associated with the infantilist ethos than Saatchi & Saatchi CEO Kevin Roberts. "In the beginning, products were just, well . . . products."[31] Bricks are just bricks, and one brick is hardly to be differentiated from another; but bricks build homes and fireplaces and can be made to evoke a sense of safety and sanctuary. The brick company that is in the "home building" business—there's a brick brand worth buying. Marketers in India, where floor tiles are as important as bricks, have learned the lesson well. Rival tile manufacturers face the challenge of competing with one another while their brand logos are buried on the underside of their tiles, never to be seen by consumers once floors are installed. Brands must therefore aim at "attracting and capturing the hearts and minds of Indian households," something that requires more than a review of ceramic tile properties.[32] As Marc Gobé writes, if you want your brand to make a connection, "give me a F-E-E-L-I-N-G (not stats or lists of numbers)."[33]

Oats are no different than bricks or tiles. When the Cheerios brand name was growing stale in the early 1990s, Kevin Roberts persuaded fustian General Mills Cereals executives that Cheerios was simply not to be regarded as a "common oats" breakfast cereal; it was rather to be regarded as a "member of the family" and hence "an enduring expression of a mother's Love for her family." By "emotionally branding" its cereal, General Mills bonded with its customers and in no time at all, according to Roberts, sales shot back up again.[34] In the same vein, General Motors, manufacturer of the specialty auto brand Saturn, was pleased in its heyday (the company and the brand are in decline) to advertise that it had "persuaded 44,000 customers" that they should "spend their vacations with us, in a car plant." Saturn and its customers too had become members of a single family—one with whom consumers were more than pleased quite literally to go on vacation. Some might even say that brand loyalty verges on the cultish. Advertising executives are the first to agree. Douglas Atkin has written a book that argues that "cults are a rich and legitimate source of insight for the creation of brand worship," that "brands are the new religion."[35] He concludes, not as a critic but as an advocate, that "alongside alternative religions, brands are now serious contenders for belief and community."[36] When Jihad takes on McWorld today, it's not religion against commerce, it's religion against religion.

Television news in the United States plays by the new rules of this new understanding of what Atkin calls the "spiritual economy" in which the "need to belong and make meaning" dominates the world of material commodities.[37] The morning "news" shows such as the *Today Show* and *Good Morning America* started in an earlier era (*Today* in 1952) as semi-serious news programs featuring journalists like John Chancellor and Tom Brokaw. But it became apparent in the 1980s that the news, hard and soft, was merely the vehicle for the star brands the television networks were marketing in order to enlarge their audiences by playing on the deep "need to belong."[38] What was once the Fourth Estate—civic journalism's critical role vis-à-vis the three traditional estates or classes of the political realm—is now little more than real estate, commodity capitalism selling infotainment in order to maximize advertising revenue in order to satisfy corporate stockholders.

It is not news but personalities like Katie Couric and Diane Sawyer and Al Roker who are nowadays put on display. The shows target women (70 percent of the morning viewing audience) and, as media critic Ken Auletta points out, insist on the "likability" of their anchors above all. *Today* includes periodic forecasts, but mainly to offer a platform for their jolly star Al Roker, whose most important job "is not to provide weather reports but to play a character—friendly, jokey—called Al Roker. The weather is beside the point."[39] In the new brand marketing, the product is always beside the point when compared with emotions, feelings, and connections. So when Porsche offers its new Cayenne S Titanium edition, is anyone surprised that the small print in its big eye-catching ads reads "the Cayenne S Titanium Edition . . . is not made of nor does it have any parts made from titanium." Why would it? Brands are experiences, and brand experiences need to be "staged."[40] *Good Morning America*'s former producer Shelley Ross actually had a script for her stars that cast anchor Charles Gibson as "Dad," and hence "Patriarch," with Diane Sawyer as "the lover of all culture" and newsreader Robin Roberts as "the best friend."[41]

Naomi Klein has reported in depth in her *No Logo* on what she calls these "'brand vision' epiphanies," which she found under every marketing stone she turned over. Polaroid is no longer a camera but a "social lubricant," IBM sells "business solutions" not computers, Swatch markets time rather than watches, and Diesel Jeans is a lifestyle "movement." The idea is to embody a set of values, to deploy "attribute brands"—not to actually manufacture something, but, as Naomi Klein insists Tommy Hilfiger is doing, to be "in the business of signing his name."[42] Many brands today revolve around celebrities and personalities, from those like Michael Jordan and Larry King who *are* the brand, to those like Richard Branson (Virgin) and Phil Knight (Nike) and Bill Gates (Microsoft) who by turning a product into a celebrity reputation have, to a considerable degree, Martha Stewart style, *become* the brand.

Think of Michael Jordan or Oprah or even the slightly tainted Martha Stewart as walking, breathing name brands associated with no particular product other than the ones they create, perform, "act" in, or are paid to shill for.[43] If they move a product, it is because those who purchase it are meant to think they are buying and acquiring the attributes of ("becoming") Jordan or Oprah—much as those ancient warriors who once consumed their slain enemies believed they might imbibe their virtues.[44] Think too of the new breed of celebrity politicians who have converted their iconic entertainment business trademark (Arnold Schwarzenegger and his potential challenger Warren Beatty) into political brands and sometimes (as with Tennessee's ex-senator Fred Thompson) converted political brands back into entertainment trademarks. Anything, everything, anybody, even nothing, can be branded, including, say, water, or even sand.[45] Or the homeless: a "clever" kid has invented what he carelessly calls "Bumvertising" utilizing signs held by the homeless in which the reverse cachet of the destitute sells whatever you want it to sell.[46] Or pets: Nickelodeon, the kids' cable channel, is selling out its dog sweaters with its signature SpongeBob SquarePants character embroidered on them, while celebrity Paris Hilton dresses her chihuahua as "an expression of herself" (and her product line).[47]

Not even an industry as substantive and serious as publishing is immune. Some observers suggest that prudent best-selling authors in the mass market ought no longer to think of themselves as producing books; rather, books produce mass market best-selling authors. It is the authors who are the new brands, whether they write fiction, nonfiction, or faction. Stephen King or Bob Woodward or Tom Clancy or Danielle Steel or Ann Coulter sell *themselves* first, and their books or book titles second. Things are not so different in France, with pop-cultural authors turning out a stream of books and memoirs and essays in which their brand names and *Vogue* magazine photos are what move the product.

Celebrity branding trickles down and can compel less popular authors to think about their careers in antiliterary ways. In a 2005 Authors Guild symposium on "Platforms and Publicity in a Packed Marketplace" (the title alone tells the story), author E. Jean Carroll, already better known for her column in *Elle* magazine than her books, gushed not about fellow author George Carlin's books but about his book tour (it "was great") and his appearances (they "were great"), concluding that "the day is coming when the book will not be the platform. The book is starting to be ancillary to the platform." As with the weather on news television, the book is beside the point. Speaking with casual spontaneity from the authoritative podium of the Authors Guild, Carroll sums up the spirit of the age of brands: "The book is like, eh, it's out of print. Frrpp [sic]. Everybody wants to be on the websites and they want to get on the cable TV, they want to get on the radio, they want to get on Sirius [the satellite radio network]. The book is on the outside now. It used to be on the inside, everything swam around that, now the book is on the outside."[48] The product's on the outside, the book producer and the producer's brand are on the inside.

In his boyish enthusiasm, Kevin Roberts has made the implicit meaning of brands explicit, codifying the meaning of the many different examples surveyed here and effectively writing the next generation's branding bible under the title *Lovemarks*. In it, he is happy to recognize marketing not as capitalism's tool but as its new essence—emotional propaganda that hijacks authentic emotions and sentiments and employs them in wholly instrumental ways to sell products to which neither producers nor consumers (absent Kevin Roberts's stratagems) otherwise are likely to have much interest, and for which there is in any case little inherent demand. Roberts believes that the time has come for a third-generation term for *trademarks*, one which improves on *brands* in the same way *brands* once improved on *trademarks*. His candidate is *lovemarks*—brands that consumers are in love with, and hence which are "owned" not by corporate managers or stockholders but by consumers themselves. To put it more plainly, lovemarks are brands with which consumers can be made to fall in love and then persuaded to "own" by savvy advertisers and canny marketers like Kevin Roberts, Richard Branson, Phil Knight, Tommy Hilfiger, and Howard Schultz. Their job is to immerse products and services in a nonspecific sentimental miasma from which "emotional decisions" can "naturally" arise (natural as a creation of artifice, and emotional decisions as irrational and nondeliberative and hence scarcely decisions at all).

It's "love for sale" in the most literal sense, for corporations are selling love rather than a substantive product—as with the LOVE postage stamp that is now a favorite of the U.S. Postal Service and which seems less a payment for services rendered than a Post Office feel-good brand emblem that embodies some marketer's idea of happy communication. Once a consumer buys into love or "lovin' it" (the famous McDonald's slogan), a lovemark is born. The product itself as originally defined by rational needs and actual wants is no longer the point. In the era of lovemarks, the first step is to fully embrace emotion by disowning rationality and knowledge as features of brand marketing. Since "human beings are powered by emotion, not by reason" (or since children are powered by emotion, not by reason), the key to the new marketing (and implicitly, the key to the old marketing as well) is to make "consistent, emotional connections with consumers" so that they make their shopping choices based on emotional decisions of the kind manifest in expressions such as "I like it, I prefer it, I feel good about it." So Starbucks sets out to "establish emotional ties," while Nike endeavors to "leverage emotional connections." Kevin Roberts is merely their mouthpiece when he writes that of all the emotions targeted, "Emotion Number One, the most fundamental of them all," was and is (imagine this single word in bright screaming crimson drawn out over two full otherwise blank pages of *Lovemarks'* psychedelic layout):[49]

L   O   V   E

It's that simple. As in Roberts's chapter 4 (its title borrowed from you know where), "All You Need Is Love." That is especially what children

need. From the moment in 1997 when Roberts became CEO of Saatchi &
Saatchi, he practiced what he preached. He recalls that his big idea was
that "Saatchi isn't an 'advertising agency' but an 'Ideas Company.'" "We
need to stand for much more," he announced to his enthralled associates.
"Much more." What "we needed to stand for," he explained, "was love."[50]
Not only did every brand his firm serviced need to become a lovemark
stand-in for love, but Saatchi & Saatchi—was it not also a brand?—had to
do so as well. What more archetypical brand is there in a postmodern consumer economy in which brands are all that get sold than the brand that
sells brands—Saatchi & Saatchi itself. The puzzled economist will wonder,
in the words of another pop song, "What's love got to do with it?" but this
is only to misunderstand the economics of the age of infantilization.

In Roberts's marketing lexicon, Lovemarks entail trustmarks and rest
on creating a monopoly over a set of affiliated sentiments including mystery, sensuality, intimacy, respect, and loyalty; that is to say, "loyalty
beyond reason"—an extreme formulation which cynics might mistake for
something resembling "my country right or wrong" or "blind patriotism"
or "irrational exuberance" or "undying loyalty" to, say, the Communist
Party or Al Qaeda. Yet Roberts is only taking the new rhetoric of marketing to its natural climax. His competitors use the same overheated language, persuaded with Daryl Travis "that all successful brands have their
own singular, little sweet spot in the brain of their prospects and, hope-
fully, a warm spot in their hearts. This sweet spot holds both the facts and
feelings of what makes you different from your competitors."[51] They are
convinced, with Marc Gobé, that "the challenge is to evolve the existing
concept of corporate identity (C.I.), which is 'corporate-driven' toward an
emotional identity (E.I.), a people-driven approach."[52] For Gobé, too,
brands must "resonate emotionally in our lives." Why? "Because emotions
are quite simply the conduit that best connects brands with people, elevat-
ing our perception of a product or service to the level of aspiration." Gobé
prepares the ground for Roberts: "*Corporate-driven messages*," he says with
emphasis, "*need to be replaced by people-centric dialogues.*"[53] Lovemarks are
the archetypical product of a people-centric dialogue.

That loyalty in brands is blind to facts and reason is evident for Roberts
from the now notorious misjudgment made by the Coca-Cola Company

in 1985, when the company stumbled into one of the worst marketing blunders of all time. After careful market research focused on blind taste tastes unrelated to brand, it proposed to its customers a new formula to be called New Coke. What it failed to understand, Roberts instructs us, is that Coke's customers "didn't care" about taste or whether or not the new formula might "in principle (or even in fact) have tasted better"! They were "inspirational consumers" attached to the classic Coke brand, and by failing to understand this, the Coca-Cola Company had nearly jettisoned the very essence of its precious brand asset. New Coke failed not as a tasty beverage but because it was an oxymoron and embodied a kind of betrayal of its consumers' deepest loyalties.[54]

The label on the outside of the Coke bottle was the measure of what was inside, while what was inside—as with books and Cheerios and the morning news—was on the outside and beside the point. The lesson applies to everything, including supposed "essentials" such as education. The New School of Social Research in New York, a legendary graduate program founded in 1919 by John Dewey and others, and transformed into an international center for social philosophy and research by refugees from Nazi Germany in the 1930s and 1940s, changed its name a few years ago to New School University. It had opened new programs and swallowed up once autonomous institutions like the Mannes College of Music, Parsons School of Design, and Actors Studio Drama School and needed subsequently both to integrate this anarchic diversity of programs and signal its new status as a real university. Its fans and customers rebelled, however, while the general public expressed confusion. Bowing to consumer pressure and brand loyalty, in 2005 it reclaimed its original brand—once again, just The New School.[55]

It is not in the products, then, but in the names and the brands they represent that the commercial value of consumer companies resides. Coke's unhappy experiment was no fluke. A company that ranks brands, Interbrand Corporation, has Coca-Cola at the top of its list, and placed its brand worth "upward of $67 billion." Not for its factories and bottling plants and recipes but "for the words 'Coca-Cola' and 'Coke' if the Atlanta firm lost its mind and decided to sell what may be the most recognized brand name in the history of commerce."[56] At the 2004 meeting of the World Economic Forum in Davos, Switzerland, a press release was issued under the title "Corporate Brand Reputation Outranks Financial Performance as Most Important Measure of Success" in which it was claimed that "Corporate reputation is a more important measure of success than stock market performance, profitability and return on investment, according to a survey of some of the world's leading CEOs and organization leaders. Only the quality of products and services edged out reputation as the leading measure of corporate success." The release reported estimates that set brand value at "40% of a company's market capitalization."[57]

Kevin Roberts offers a personal example to drive home the new loyalties that have taken him from brands to lovemarks. He has always loved the dandruff shampoo Head & Shoulders, he confesses. Now he's gone bald, but he goes right on using it. There's no reason to stay with it, but this is what it means to "love" the brand. This kind of "loyalty beyond reason" is real and present in everyday life, but it is usually associated with impulsive children rather than mature adults. Try wresting an old raggedy doll or tattered blanket from a six-year-old with the promise of a brand-new and much better replacement doll or blanket!

The challenge of instilling brand loyalty is of course a key reason why companies are so very "eager to court young consumers and their parents." They are even "targeting a new marketing outlet: preschools." Ford Motor Company printed 100,000 posters focused on safety in the home and "of course, in the car" for preschool, child care, and kindergarten institutions, while Pizza Hut is offering branded preschool reading materials (literature is not exactly the natural provenance of the pepperoni and sausage chain). But with more than four million American children in preschool or child care, the opportunity for corporations to establish brand loyalty is proving irresistible.[58] "More than ever," reported the *New York Times*, in introducing an essay on luxury products for tiny tots, "babies are staking their own wee claim on the luxury goods market, as parents eagerly swaddle their children in clothes, accessories and other assorted products with designer pedigrees."[59] To suggest that babies can "stake their own claim" to anything is obviously absurd if not downright perverse, but when corporations aim to establish brand loyalties in wee babies, as Christian Dior does with a program to loan designer dresses to toddlers, such hyperbole is to be expected. According to a mother whose daughter was the beneficiary of the program, "having your child offered a dress is such a social thing, it means you are in a certain special social echelon."[60] In the same spirit, American Girl, the doll company, has opened a restaurant/boutique chain devoted to the dolls and their young fans (consumers) with locations in Los Angeles, Chicago, and New York,[61] touted by Julia Moskin in the *New York Times* article "It's the Hottest Place in Town, and Dolls Eat Free."[62]

Marketing to the very young is not restricted to the United States. There is a youth "entry point" that firms are seeking to exploit around the world. Maria Papanthymou reports enthusiastically on a survey showing that "young people are becoming an increasingly desirable target audience for marketers in Russia" since in Russia, as elsewhere, "young people are highly oriented towards prestigious consumption and are very responsive to brand communication. Besides, youth's lifestyle is becoming more and more a reference point for consumption culture." As with identity branding elsewhere, the survey suggests that in Russia too "the description of an ideal youth brand is in tune with the respondents' description of the ideal self." Papanthymou seems to arrive instinctively at the language of Kevin Roberts when she concludes that the survey's findings confirm "the fact that the emotional components of the brand's image and the social implications of the particular product are much more important than the product's functional benefits."[63]

The lovemarks approach to brands and identity is then global in reach. Whether in Russia or the United States, however, it suffers from another trait that helps define the distorting effects of the infantilist ethos on society: it entails and produces inauthenticity. As Papanthymou observes, it hijacks the sentimental force of authentic emotions and attaches them to products and services whose "functional benefits" are simply irrelevant. Bricks are not the same thing as home and hearth, and can actually be used to destroy, say, glass houses, or to enclose extermination-camp ovens, or build those proverbial brick shit houses, though these are hardly the sentimental associations advertising executives are hoping to impart. Nor is Cheerios really a member of the family, any more than are Al Roker and Head & Shoulders. It would be a bizarre family indeed in which such brands were given a place next to Fido at the hearth or even stuck in a bowl with the family guppy, let alone made to supplement or substitute for Mom and Dad. Associating them with a mother's love is to hijack love and trivialize mothering. This of course will not stop ambitious corporations and hustling political parties from marketing maternal sentimentality.

In the new world of brand identity, values are transvalued through trivialization. Inauthenticity becomes a kind of simulated authenticity. Faux sentiments and commercially contrived emotions have been a special feature of the Disney Company's approach to what it calls "imagineering." Roberts admiringly cites Walt Disney saying "I love Mickey Mouse more than any woman I've ever known."[64] And Celebration, Disney's foray into new-town construction in Florida, offered clients faux representations of diverse architectural styles pasted onto common suburban construction models. More tellingly still, it promised buyers the lure of "instant traditions."[65] Hotel architecture in Las Vegas and Atlantic City as well as at Indian casinos in New England and theme parks in France and Japan specializes in reality-re-imagineering and faux imaging. In Las Vegas one can experience the Manhattan skyline or a Paris landscape without leaving one's rental car, while just outside Paris at Euro Disney one can experience Main Street USA from a "German" cafe. In Manhattan's Times Square one can walk through a sanitized urban funscape that feels more like a suburban Las Vegas mall. London Bridge is in the Arizona desert, and the old British ocean-liner the *Queen Mary* is in a San Diego dry dock. All the originals are now cardboard cutouts—authentic imitations that simulate Mom and the *Queen Mary* alike. The world becomes a carnival hall of mirrors where everything is a reflection.

Television has become parareality's medium, sponsoring "parasocial" and "pseudopersonal" relationships with shopping network hosts, news anchors, campaigning politicians, and reality-show personalities who are experts in simulating faux social realities. They look into the viewer's eyes and speak impromptu to her from their hearts even as they actually are staring into an anonymous camera lens and reading words from a tele-prompter contrived in a script conference by invisible writers for whom "authenticity" is an excuse for simulation and "reality" an invitation to invention.[66] As cultural commentator Jerry Mander has noticed, the United States was the "first culture to have substituted secondary, mediate versions of experience for direct experience of the world."[67]

Neal Gabler's book title *Life: The Movie* is no mere flight of rhetorical fancy, but a clue to a novel ontology in which being itself is displaced from its source to its simulated representation on the screen. Gabler writes about the conquest of reality by entertainment, about a "republic of entertain-ment" that took root in Jacksonian America in the 1830s and has culmi-nated today in entertainment which is "the governing cosmology" through which all forms of identity and celebrity are mediated.[68] The con-ceits of this new world in which image and reality are no longer to be dis-tinguished are captured by Peter Weir's 1998 film *The Truman Show* in which hundreds of hidden cameras turn Truman Burbank's "private" (to him) life into a transparent show in which every element is scripted except Truman himself who thinks his life is "real." Clay Calvert describes this as *"mediated voyeurism"* in which the *"consumption of revealing images of and information about others' apparently real and unguarded lives"* becomes the basis not only for entertainment but for the subversion of privacy and discourse.[69]

Voyeuristic reality television defines and embodies postmodern con-sumerism. Like Chauncy Gardner in Peter Sellers' touching film *Being There* (from the Jerzy Kosinski novel), the whole world now "likes to watch"—primarily because consumer capitalism wants it to and helps it to do so, able to earn more from consumers who watch than consumers who do. Everything from sex to sports to politics becomes an affair of specta-tors. Sex is so much about watching—whether it is *Sex and the City* in the United States or *Canal Plus* high-end porn in France or juiced-up advertis-ing or charged video games or the popular "Upskirt" sites on the internet that purvey endless images from hidden cameras (in shoes and stairwells and wherever they can be secreted with their lenses peering upward) of women's private parts now made globally public on the World Wide Web.

Voyeurism has taken over team sports, engaging passive armchair viewers in a clash of branded teams with whose victories and losses they are supposed to identify, even though players are bought and sold without reference to the cities in which they play other than that conferred by the cold cash nexus—a fact reinforced today by the private corporate names that identify what were once publicly defined arenas. Politics too, even for aficionados, has become a spectator sport, where democracy is something we watch on TV rather than an activity we engage in. Political zealots are defined as television news junkies who spend all their time watching C-SPAN, cable news, and the multiplying political websites and blogs that constitute the new virtual civil society. When some of Howard Dean's virtual supporters, cultivated and captured by the internet, failed to show up to vote at the Iowa caucuses in the 2004 Democratic primaries, a deep confusion in the young about the difference between virtual politics and a real electoral campaign became apparent.

Voyeurism is not then just a peculiar feature of modern media, or an odd feature of our increasingly virtual lives. Modern media and our increasingly virtual lives are rather defining features of late consumer capitalism. For consumer capitalism now owns identity and reality, needing them as marketing instruments in a failing consumer market that moves goods (and hence produces profits) with ever greater difficulty. By the same token, it is not technology that determines politics and economics, but politics and economics that determine technology. Behind their interaction is the ethos of infantilization and the power of brands the ethos has harnessed.

Virtual identities and faux loyalties are encouraged when products move away from their generic character and are associated with secondary sentiments that are made primary. The marketing war of vodka brands offers an instructive example. Grain alcohols are only marginally distinguishable by taste and quality. Trying to emerge from the pack, France's Grey Goose Vodka prudently launched a 2005 advertising campaign that brought an "independent film" legend, Robert Redford, and sponsored a film series Redford produced for his Sundance Channel, into the marketing fray. The series paired great "iconoclasts" in documentary films that gave "intimate, unpredictable portraits of ground shakers who have transformed our culture through their passions." Grey Goose Vodka was not looking to pair Einstein and Mother Teresa, or Churchill and Stravinsky of course. The company was reaching for pairs emblematic of the good life, as envisioned by Grey Goose Entertainment. Its "creative pairings" included fashion designer Tom Ford and artist Jeff Koons; actor Samuel L. Jackson and basketball legend Bill Russell; and chef Mario Batali and film producer Michael Stipe. A related contest promised tickets to the L.A. premiere of the films and a "$1,000 shopping spree."[70]

In 2006, Lexus enlisted public broadcaster Charlie Rose in another infomercial-style crossover: "The Road to Innovation" conversation series that drew a parallel between innovation and inspiration in conversations Rose held with celebrities such as George Clooney and Michael Eisner and innovation and inspiration as defined by Lexus automobiles.

A relatively new social networking website called Orkut plays on this new inauthenticity in novel and facile ways, offering a place where those lucky enough to be chosen to join "a community of friends and trusted acquaintances" can instant message and interact.[71] A "trusted acquaintance" is of course an oxymoron, but as a marketing gimmick it works well in a world starved of trust and hungry for communication. In the words of the Orkut website,

orkut is unique, because it's an organically growing network of trusted friends. That way we won't grow too large, too quickly and everyone will have at least one person to vouch for them.

If you know someone who is a member of orkut, that person can invite you to join as well. If you don't know an orkut member, wait a bit and most likely you soon will.

We look forward to having you as part of the orkut community.

Orkut uses "buzz" (informal person-to-person "selling") around faux "community" and "trust" to compete with other young people's websites that seem more "anonymous" and hence less cool.

The lessons of all the examples surveyed have both been absorbed and distilled into a philosophy of marketing being taught anew by Kevin Roberts, Daryl Travis, Marc Gobé, and Matthew Ragas, all of whom proffer an array of faux emotions and sentiments to be cultivated in selling brands even where (especially where) the emotions and sentiments do not grow out of products but are attached to them the way rockets are attached to the space shuttle to propel it into space. Except the rockets effectively become the payload, self-justifying ends in themselves.

This brings us back to the heart of the problem with branded identity in an infantilizing consumer society. As he labors to glamorize and give classical credibility to his marketing of love, Roberts cites among others Longfellow, Voltaire, Ruskin, and Erich Fromm (as well as Walt Disney and Homer Simpson). In doing so, he steals the force of the term from its authentic sources and instrumentalizes it, subordinating it to commercial use. Unlike the trademarks once identified with generic goods and services, brands in their lovemark incarnation displace product generics with purloined emotional generics to put them to work on behalf of brand loyalty and shareholder profitability. Cheerios becomes a member of the family not because the family is in need of reinforcement and baked oats simulate and take the place of dogs and cats and other family-enhancing pets, but because by associating a generic oat cereal with family love, advertisers hope its sentimental force may rub off on the product and invest it with a brand meaning it otherwise lacks.

The proof of the strategy's efficacy comes with product placement in films where the aim is not only to sell the product but to exploit its emotional message. Thus, for example, in Jim Jarmusch's award-winning film *Broken Flowers*, Bill Murray throws a cute child at breakfast a sweet line about how he should watch his Cheerios (Murray might filch a spoonful!)—the Cheerios label working as much to lend emotion to the scene as to sell the brand.

Musical revivals on Broadway often convert the generic references of the original production into product placements for sponsoring companies, with the caveat that this is intended only to enhance realism. In the 1966 original of *Sweet Charity*, a waiter asks his customer "A double Scotch, again, sir?" In the 2005 revival, the query is "Gran Centenario, the tequila?" with the brand for sale in the lobby at intermission. Hormel Foods Corporation, the maker of Spam, not only endorsed the hit musical *Spamalot*, but licensed its name to the show and introduced a new Golden Honey Grail flavor Spam to the New York market. Yahoo! joined Hormel as a *Spamalot* sponsor, with the brand written into the script (a yahoo in the show yells "Yahoo!" and the company appears as a "make-believe" sponsor of an on-stage routine).[72]

If brand name can shape or even stand in for identity, then to figure out "who you are" you must decide where (and for what) you shop. That is modern branding's simple secret. There is no "illusion." Consumers are knowing conspirators, so it is not exactly a matter of false consciousness. In the postmodern form of consumer identity, appearance is everything. A homeowner from the wealthy Georgia suburb of Alpharetta who is interviewed in the *New York Times* seems to acknowledge that he engaged in "creating the illusion of history." He knows that the thick columns that "hold up" his house are hollow; he knows that the new-town historical society is located in an old Queen Anne house relocated from another venue. The 74-year-old Neal Martineau admits to being involved in "architectural bullying" whose point is to prove he is "better than you are." "I'm faking it here," he admits. "I have property that does not have enough meadow to feed a horse, but I call it a horse farm." He sees that automobiles convey status, so Martineau drives a Mercedes, "indicative of who I am." Since it makes him feel important, he is "happy to wear [sic] a Mercedes."[73] A typical member of the "relo" (relocation) class, where identity is as slippery as mobility is constant, Martineau understands that cars are not so much driven as worn—identity signifiers from the outside because the inside is empty. Clothes, cars, clubs, churches, they are all the same: Kathy Link, another "relo" product uncomfortable in still one more new anonymous suburban venue, is also searching for a brand identity. Having joined a local country club in her new community of Medlock Bridge, she admits "We haven't found a church. We went church shopping."[74]

In a commercial society where identities are linked to cars that people "wear" and churches they "shop" for, it is little wonder that identity can be bought, borrowed, or stolen. Identity theft has become a universal concern among credit card and internet users, and hence at banks and credit services. But it can no longer be assumed that the term is merely a metaphor for the abuse of stolen plastic. As the television advertisements warning against identity theft show when they portray a thug's callous baritone emerging from a sweet old lady's mouth, a stolen commercial identity may effectively mean the loss of your own "voice." By the same token, when data-collection services such as Acxiom, Seisint, and LexisNexis buy and sell information about individual consumer buying habits, credit ratings, and shopping behaviors (among other things)—usually without the knowledge or consent of consumers—more than privacy is at stake.[75]

Whole urban neighborhoods can undergo a shift in identity, as has happened (in Adam Gopnik's vivid portrayal) with Times Square in New York. In Manhattan's defining entertainment district, a mass commercial culture of "national brands and eager shoppers" has become a "replacement of an authentic 'popular' culture, of arcades and Runyonesque song-pluggers." Gopnik discerns at once that branding Times Square is part of the strategy of selling to children: "This decline [of Times Square] allowed for the emergence of the real hyperdrive of the new Square, the arrival of what every parent knows is the engine of American commerce: branded, television-based merchandise directed at 'families' (that is, directed at getting children to torture their parents until they buy it)."[76]

Putting faux values at the core of identity exacts a price, however. Over time, parasitism drains its objects of their own authenticity and meaning, and leaves the new identities insubstantial and unrewarding. If Cheerios is about Mom, then Mom is about Cheerios, and moms who are about Cheerios (or soapsuds or Katie Couric) may eventually cease to be "real" moms at all, and become as phony as their brand use—at which point depreciated moms can no longer be fit subjects to which Cheerios can attach itself as it seeks brand credibility in a faux association with maternal nurturing. So that when Tide also decides to associate itself with Mom as chief cleaner-upper and dirt cop who keeps the family healthy, it may not want Cheerios to be poaching on and undermining Mom's credibility, any more than Cheerios wants Mom to be commercially overexploited by Tide. Both companies hope to play off of (steal) some patina of the authentic essence of motherhood which is embodied in the real and proper meanings of motherhood—love, loyalty, and trust "beyond all reason." Yet in exploiting these borrowed attributes, the companies help drain them of their meaning. While it makes sense for a mother to love her children beyond reason and for kids to love their mothers the same way, it makes no sense for us to love Cheerios or Tide or Head & Shoulders or Coke beyond reason. In fact it is downright stupid to do so. Childish. The adult will like Cheerios because of its taste and nutritional value and use Head & Shoulders to control dandruff, not because he is in love with a label. In the end, consumers will become cynics and disdain both the products attached to Mom and the sweet ideals of motherhood. Yet bereft of traditional identity and skeptical of brand, this may mean not that they will become liberated but only deracinated.

This is why children and teens make such responsive target-subjects for branders. Alissa Quart has thus argued that "teens and tweens are perhaps more open to altering or branding their bodies than adults. The idea of a permanent change to the body—made practically overnight—appeals to adolescents, people who are by definition shifting identity daily. . . . Many teenage cosmetic surgeries emanate from self-aversion, camouflaged as an emblem of self-esteem and normalcy. The girl who chooses cosmetic surgery chooses obsession with the body and mastery over it rather than an attempt at the transcendence that means forgetting the body."[77]

Although the marketers claim to be purveying emotion rather than reason, and while they are certainly trying to evoke emotion in consumers, they themselves are actually acting rationally, employing a powerful form of instrumental reason—that is, emotion rationally deployed in the name of profits. Their concern with girls' body image, for example, is the quite rational one (for them, not us) of selling goods and keeping the corporations they serve (and consumer capitalism) afloat. Producers absolve the customer from rationality so they can sell her on doing what suits the producer's rationality: making money. Their task, Kevin Roberts acknowledges, is to impact a consumer who in effect says, "you've got three seconds to impress me. Three seconds to connect with me, to make me fall in Love with your product."[78] *Make* me fall in love with your product. Even the customer knows the love affair is the responsibility of the producer and its marketing agents rather than his.

Making consumers fall in love depends on parasitism, however, which not only draws *on* but draws *down* our society's stock of values—using up, trivializing, and demeaning them, without putting anything back in the bank. To the extent families are in decline, Cheerios will not help raise them up again in the way that, say, a law making it harder both to get married and to get divorced might do. Or as family counseling might do. Or having a child. Or even as buying a cocker spaniel might do. "Loving" Head & Shoulders or Coca-Cola is good for the brands but bad for love. Lovemark purveyors are romance thieves, playing on love for all the wrong reasons. Indeed, they operate much the way propaganda and ideological brainwashing do: they turn proper emotions to improper objects. "Love of Cheerios" or "love of Tide" is little different than "love of the Fuehrer" or "love of the Party." When we speak of "loving God" we mean something like "God is love," but when we speak of "loving Head & Shoulders" we don't really mean "Head & Shoulders is love." We imply rather that love is a con, love is a trick, love is a whore, love is for sale. Hire Saatchi & Saatchi or Doyle Dane Bernbach and they will buy love for your brand. Hire Marc Gobé's d/g* world wide, his image and "brand creation" firm, and you will put his "new paradigm for connecting brands to people" to work for *your* brand.[79]

Kevin Roberts reports eagerly on his success with a Lexus video advertisement in which a pregnant mother traveling to the hospital with her husband gives birth in the car (conveniently stopped in front of a Lexus dealership) with the help of a Lexus salesman. Naturally, Lexus provides a loaner for the couple to continue their journey, cleans up the birthroom sedan, and becomes a part of the family: yes, the infant girl is named Isabelle Alexus.[80] To Roberts this suggests Lexus has gone from brand to lovemark, participating now in the miraculous act of creation. To more skeptical observers it can only suggest borrowed sentiment, faux feeling, displaced emotion, and unearned love. Not a lie exactly, but something worse: mere bullshit—in the technical sense.[81] It is impossible in this new identity politics to know if a "Lexus family" is defining Lexus in terms of the family, or the family in terms of Lexus. In any case, it presumably speaks to Lexus's success at branding that Tom Friedman could employ it as a synonym for successful Westernization and globalization in *The Lexus and the Olive Tree*.

The aim of these branding strategies is then precisely to establish identity as one more crucial product of the consumer marketplace. Roberts reproaches critics who worry that "brands are taking over people's lives," which they regard as a "bad thing," by insisting that in reality "it works the other way. Maybe life is taking over brands."[82] That Roberts may be right testifies to the power of the infantilist ethos. From the innocent wearing of T-shirts featuring celebrity names or displaced logos—(the unwrenching T-shirt version of Edvard Munch's wrenching painting *The Scream* is perhaps the locus classicus)[83]—to the new "reality shows" in which participants engage in excruciating (and hence riveting) public displays of identity envy, the market becomes a setting in which deracinated young moderns look for roots.

OLDER SOURCES FOR NEW REALITY SHOWS

Lifestyles of the Rich and Famous (Robin Leach)

Password

Hollywood Squares

What's My Line?

The Dating Game

Candid Camera (becomes) Punk'd (Ashton Kutcher)

MORE RECENTLY

Hulk

The Surreal Life (seven celebrities live in house)

The Osbournes

The Anna Nicole [Smith] *Show*

Big Brother 6 (eight strangers in fake house studio, get kicked off by spectators)

I Want to Be a Hilton

Celebrity Fit Club

The Apprentice (Donald Trump)

Fire Me, Please

Dancing with the Stars

American Idol

Kill Reality (reality stars make movie *The Scorn*)

Extreme Makeover

Made

True Life

Diary

I Want a Famous Face

The Swan

Date My Mom

Room Raiders (dating)

The Real World (seven strangers taped living together, originally
    from Dutch version)

Fear Factor

The Bachelor

The Bachelorette

Survivor

The Amazing Race

Reality television purveys an identity sweepstakes in which everyone is looking to be transformed into somebody else at least in the gaze of those watching television. Most shows permit a kind of metaphoric transformation as on *The Apprentice*, where by winning the Donald Trump sweepstakes and avoiding being "fired" you end up not only as a Trump employee but as a kind of junior Donald Trump sharing in the many celebrity perks of being Trump; or where by competing for the affection of a made-for-TV bachelor or bachelorette you have a chance yourself to become if not happily married at least "famous," as in famously rejected. Or where you win fame and fortune (a genuine career in entertainment) by seducing America with your voice on *American Idol* (a show that began in the United Kingdom).

A few shows even dare to promise actual transformation into a famous other—most egregiously on shows such as *I Want a Famous Face* and *I*

Want to Be a Hilton, but also on "makeover" shows such as *The Swan* and *Extreme Makeover* where self-image-challenged wanna-bes opt to undergo radical makeovers, including invasive surgical procedures, in order to look like their favorite stars, or minimally like someone (anyone?) other than who they are. In the manipulative fashion detailed earlier, participants subjected to this commercial image-mongering are treated as if they are being empowered rather than exploited by these "opportunities" to remake themselves as someone else. The results would be comic if they were not representative of trends so deeply disorienting to identity and so painful to the individuals being exploited. After all, these are not medieval circus freak shows but participatory extravaganzas in which thousands vie to participate and millions watch in awe and envy. Thus, for example, in pursuit of a celebrity look on the reality television show *I Want a Famous Face,* "a plus-size woman gets tucked, lifted and lipoed in hopes of looking like Kate Winslet. A professional Britney Spears impersonator goes in for Britney-size breasts. Most freakish of all, identical twins *both* want to look like Brad Pitt."[84] Another "contestant," a man from Long Island, has "his 'man-boobs' reshaped so as to appear more like Arnold Schwarzenegger."[85]

Branding and privatization turn out to work in tandem. As identity moves away from public categories rooted in religion and nationality and toward commercial categories associated with brands and consumables, identity itself is privatized (though hardly individualized!). To brand a public institution is effectively to privatize it. Over the last twenty years, institutions from sports stadiums to colleges have been renamed, branded, and effectively both privatized and commercialized. In chapter 4 we looked at the privatization of educational institutions: it is worth noting here that naming and rebranding have now become a part of the way in which "tax-exempt, non-profit institutions of higher learning [are] increasingly explor[ing] relationships with commercial ventures either as partners or affiliates."[86] In its most extreme form, this can involve the actual renaming of a school to "honor" a donor (Glassboro State College in New Jersey reborn as Rowan University), or lead universities to imitate professional sports teams and their host cities and sell naming rights for their arenas. The cola companies already "own" exclusivity of product and advertising at many public universities: until 2005, Rutgers University served and advertised only Coca-Cola (in 2005, it converted to Pepsi), the University of Maryland served and advertised only Pepsi. When their teams met, it was no longer a school sporting rivalry but the continuation of the cola wars.

When a sports stadium like New Jersey's Brendan Byrne Arena is renamed Continental Airlines Arena with its Continental logo visible from above to Continental Airlines flights on the glide path into Newark's Liberty International Airport, more than a name change has occurred. A public governor's association with a public sports arena is transformed into a billboard for a private company. This does to public arenas what the transformation of urban public squares into private commercial malls does to civic space. Stores and shops that once coexisted in downtown public spaces with civic, religious, educational, and political institutions in a healthy civic congruence—the old ideal of the agora—now reappear inside walled, protected private commercial spaces that bar protesters, unwanted strangers (urban youth, minorities), and nonshoppers and transform the agora into a unidimensional commercial arena. Rebranding is more than name-deep: it alters the character of the civic environment and allows commerce to trump every other activity, whether recreational or civic.

Even when they do not carry the name of a public figure, most sports arenas traditionally carry names with a public resonance—Memorial Coliseum, Fenway Park, Veterans Stadium. Today corporations such as American Airlines, FedEx, Reliant Energy, Philips Electronics, Invesco, Dunkin' Donuts, Bank One, and Lincoln Financial Group pay on average between $5 and $10 million a year for the right to affix their commercial logos to a public stadium or arena.[87] Even in civic citadels like San Francisco with a reputation for protecting public space, branding deals eventually get signed in the name of fiscal survival. San Francisco fought a losing battle for almost ten years to preserve the traditional civic identity of its 49ers football stadium as Candlestick Park. In 1996, it yielded to 3Com in a multimillion-dollar deal; but it was the first city in America to take back its "maiden" name after a "corporate divorce." At the time, San Francisco supervisor Tony Hall said: "We do not need to prostitute ourselves at the feet of the NFL franchises. . . . [Candlestick] is our . . . Colosseum. . . . it's part of our background, part of our culture." San Francisco even considered a bill to prohibit sale of naming rights to "any publicly owned monument, building or park."[88] Yet in 2005, based on "need" (too few revenues, a public aversion to public taxation fueled by neoliberal privatization ideology), the city cut a deal for $6 million with Monster Cable Products, Inc., even though this meant redubbing Candlestick "Monster Park." The contract runs until 2008, when the city (it again insists) will really ("permanently") allow the stadium to revert to "Candlestick."[89]

Denver has a similar story, having tried unsuccessfully to resist the sale of naming rights to Mile High Stadium, a civic favorite. In 2001, despite public petitions opposing it, naming rights were sold to Invesco for twenty years for $120 million. In a compromise with the riled citizenry, the new name was to be Invesco Field at Mile High. Colorado media continue to call the stadium simply Mile High, although given that the Colorado Rockies baseball team plays at Coors Field, and the Denver Nuggets basketball team plays at the Pepsi Center, the commercial name seems likely in time to prevail.[90]

A San Francisco sportswriter asks plaintively, "In a real sense, don't we, the public, have a mutual interest and shared ownership in these teams and facilities?" To him, "offering naming contracts to the highest bidder" is wrong.[91] But with the Arizona Diamondbacks playing baseball at Bank One Ballpark (now Chase Field) and the Philadelphia Eagles playing football at Lincoln Financial Field, it is clear that the economics dominate the politics and the civics of late capitalist consumer society, with college teams relentlessly following the same fiscal logic, pressed on by the public defunding of public education and public government. In 2004, Boston College played North Carolina in a football bowl game at the Continental Tire Bowl in Charlotte's Bank of America Stadium.

Money is in the first instance the proximate driver of these deals. But how much fiscal difference can a few million dollars paid out by the renaming of Candlestick add to San Francisco's $5-billion-a-year budget? In reality, the renamings are part and parcel of the rebranding of our commonweal—our public goods (res publica)—as a privateweal, a collection of special economic and corporate interests that now define what it means to be an American: not the citizen but the consumer, not the civic participant but the customer, not the loyal fan but the loyal customer. The transition is perfectly described by the trajectory of the American capital's football home (of a team with its own naming problems, the Washington Redskins): first in urban Washington, D.C., RFK Stadium after the historical political legend Robert F. Kennedy; then, in the new facility in suburban Prince George's County, Jack Kent Cooke Stadium after the visionary builder who died before his dream opened in 1997; and then, in 1999, succumbing to the seductions of commercial branding, FedExField, turning the stadium into one more logo'd palace where the selling of a corporate brand to loyal consumers takes precedence over sharing the fortunes of a football team with loyal fans.

Branding public arenas is relatively new. The first naming sale was by Buffalo back in 1972 when a local company, Rich Foods, paid the modest sum of $1.5 million to attach its name to the Buffalo Bills football team arena. Sixteen years later there were still only two other corporate names on stadiums. But since then, as Daniel Kraker writes, "companies large and small, famous and obscure, have snapped up 62 stadium names."[92] Boston's legendary Garden (where the Celtics basketball team plays), for example, became the FleetCenter, which allowed the clever Fleet Bank to buy naming rights to Boston's "fast lane" electronic toll system, so that the fast lane became—with happy corporate redundancy—the Fleet Fast Lane. How fleeting corporate identity can be, however. For today still another corporate bank merger has meant that the FleetCenter must now be branded TD Banknorth Garden—which, however, ironically allows fans to refer again to the old (Boston) Garden of yesteryear.

No name is too trivial, no logo too tawdry. Providence has its Dunkin' Donuts Center, while what was once perhaps America's most celebrated football team, the Pittsburgh Steelers, now must tolerate a giant Heinz ketchup bottle planted next to its stadium. Corporations are interested in more than naming things. In 2004, the producers of *Spider-Man 2* tried to cut a deal with major league baseball that would have allowed Spider-Man logos to be imprinted on the bases and previews of the movie to be screened between innings.[93] The deal was killed only after a public outcry led by veteran sportswriters, but the writing is clearly on the bases.

Kraker observes that "in the last few years, the name game has rapidly spread outside the athletic sphere and into the public sector. In cities across the country, the nomenclature of our civic landscape—from our parks to our high school scoreboards—is up for sale. The trade magazine *IEG Sponsorship Report* estimated that in 1999 alone, 50 cities inked deals totaling $100 million with corporations willing to sponsor public assets. . . . Throughout the country, hospitals, parks, libraries, performing arts centers, theaters, convention centers, fairgrounds, high school sports facilities and shopping malls are available for the right amount."[94] Today cities like San Diego have special departments set up to handle corporate branding sales, while Massachusetts is exploring selling naming rights to public parks including the park that is the site of Thoreau's Walden Pond.[95] Police cars, fire engines, and parking meters are currently being treated as potential billboards by revenue-desperate cities, which may perhaps one day find it prudent to put up for sale their own historic city names: Boston as "Fleet Bank Burg," Providence as "Dunkin' Donut Demos," Paris as "Destination Euro Disney," and Baghdad as "Halliburton Hamlet."

Brand America

Far-fetched, yes, but the fetish of branding in an age of infantilism and privatization has infected every part of the once public sector in more than just the United States. A recent profile of Larry Ross explaining how this successful marketing executive took a "bungee jump for God" and helped turn religious public relations into big business carried the title "Christianity, the Brand."[96]

If religions need marketing, it is not surprising that nations now regularly treat their public images as brands, both distorting and trivializing their character and making them consumables for infantilized "citizens." Early in his first term, English prime minister Tony Blair captured the hip flavor of his New Labour politics by talking about "Cool Britannia" rather than "Rule Britannia." The French lost their bid for the Olympics to the English in the summer of 2005 in part because they failed to brand the nation with the marketing clarity of the English.

The United States of America has taken branding seriously for a long time, having gone so far as to create a Department of Public Diplomacy and Public Affairs within the State Department which not only treats America as a brand, but argues that the country's fortunes may depend less on policy realities or traditional identity and behavior, than on brand marketing by experienced advertising and marketing executives. Democracy becomes less a system of governance than an enticing brand logo aimed at turning friends and adversaries alike into consumers of America *the product* (democracy? Prosperity? Mom and apple pie?). As with consumer marketing in general, the producer of Brand USA works hard to convince consumers (Iraq, Afghanistan, Middle Europe, the Middle East) that "the message is one of empowerment, not American domination or even tutelage."[97] Karen P. Hughes is the latest Bush administration Brand USA promoter, a more nuanced marketer than her predecessors. She emphasizes "listening" before pitching the U.S. trademark—a proven marketing technique in which customer "needs" are heard, shaped, and factored into a message about the value of what is being sold.

Branding has become a staple of electoral and party politics. From that first inkling in 1966 that running for the presidency could be regarded as a branch of marketing (see Joe McGinniss's *The Selling of the President, 1968*) to Senator John Kerry's suggestion in 2005 that the Democratic Party needs to "unbrand" itself and then rebrand itself "more effectively" to regain its sway over American electoral consumers, party politics has become, among other things, an exercise in consumerism.[98] Keeping brand purity by staying on message is a common preoccupation on the left and the right. Justifying his attacks on Republicans who will not toe his "no more taxes" line, Republican opinion leader Grover Norquist seizes on marketing prudence: "When you have a brand like Coca-Cola, and you find a rat head in the bottle, you create an outcry. Republicans who raise taxes are rat heads in Coke bottles. They endanger the brand."[99] Vice president Gore was worried about his brand in the 2000 election—not about rat heads but color-coordinated electoral outfits that would lift the Gore brand out of the blahs. In 2006, alleged Congressional pedophile Mark Foley nearly sunk the Republican brand without ever leaving his computer.

Brand America feels like a metaphor, yet it is much more than that, not a game version of politics but politics itself reconceived as the new public relations specialty known as public diplomacy. Public diplomacy not only defines a new office in the State Department, but has become an academic specialty with its own university departments. Its aim is to frame a global marketing strategy for Brand USA. The office of Public Diplomacy and Public Affairs at the State Department has clearly been regarded as a marketing center and has been staffed by marketing and advertising executives. It has assiduously followed the advice of Bush's former (ultra-conservative) Public Broadcasting Board of Governors chairman, Kenneth Y. Tomlinson. Tomlinson turned aside criticism that President Bush was running a national propaganda machine obsessed with image rather than policy by asserting, "We should not be ashamed of public advocacy on behalf of freedom and democracy and the United States of America."[100] The bipartisan character of this brand approach to politics is evident in the branding work being done by liberal Democrats such as Keith Reinhard, who as CEO of advertising goliath DDB was responsible for, among other successes, McDonald's "You deserve a break today" campaign. Reinhard has developed a program called Business for Diplomatic Action in which he acknowledges that (as rock-star philanthropist Bono also said to the World Economic Forum) Brand USA is in trouble, which is clearly a problem for business.

In a reversal of the traditional strategy by which business attaches itself to the luster of Brand America, Business for Diplomatic Action wants to help rebrand America by associating it with the luster of business. Because American brands "continue to exert a fascination among young people from Damascus to Jidda," says John M. McNeel, a Business for Diplomatic Action board member, "corporations can bring their inherent pragmatism, optimism and resourcefulness to provide the people of the [Middle East] region with real examples of our desire to see the Middle East progress on a path to a better future."[101] The irony of Business for Diplomatic Action's well-intentioned initiative is that even "public" diplomacy is being subjected to privatization and outsourcing. At the same time, corporate brands are seeking their own "civic" luster. Marc Gobé's naïve book called *Citizen Brand* (the companion volume to *Emotional Branding*) urges companies to grasp "the fact . . . that brands must communicate who they are, and if they become true Citizen Brands, with aims of social responsibility as a core element of their corporate mission, they must—very tactfully, of course—communicate this point of view!"[102]

Originally, the office of Public Diplomacy and Public Affairs went the other way, trying to win private-sector marketing experts over to the public job. The first director of the office was Charlotte Beers, who won the right to help rebrand Uncle Sam's America through her success in branding Uncle Ben's Rice years earlier. Beers, unlike backers of the Business for Diplomatic Action initiative, understood that a country isn't exactly rice: "This is the most sophisticated brand assignment I have ever had," said the former head of advertising giants J. Walter Thompson and Ogilvy & Mather. But at the same time, branding is branding so that Beers understood the job required her "to redefine what America is" for foreigners who have been misled by resentment at actual American policies in the world and hence were "misled" about the brand.[103]

Beers set about making cheerful videos about happy Muslims in America, but her Panglossian approach was deemed simpleminded and ultimately failed because too many Arab nations refused to broadcast her products locally. After less than two years Beers quit. She was succeeded by someone with more experience in government. Margaret Tutwiler, a former State Department spokeswoman who had been ambassador to Morocco, came into the post embracing a 2003 bipartisan congressional report called "Changing Minds, Winning Peace," which had concluded that few minds were being changed and that "America's prestige had dwindled, that its good works were largely ignored and that it lacked strategic direction in its message." Tutwiler acknowledged a few months into her job that it would take "years of hard, focused work" to remedy the problem.[104] Too many years for Tutwiler, it seems, for just a few months later she quit and took a much cushier job at the New York Stock Exchange, a brand with its own problems, but hardly as formidable as those of Brand USA.

The latest appointee to the brand-burnishing office is Karen P. Hughes, President Bush's longtime friend, personal advisor, and campaign manager, signaling rising frustration and a rising sense of the importance of the mission as well as the need to have a marketer in place not only friendly to the CEO but in a position to influence the product. Hughes has listened well, but the message she is hearing is that much of the Muslim world sees the United States as one of those faux Gucci watches sold on the streets of Manhattan, a knockoff purveyed by hypocrites and swindlers that carries the brand logo but lacks the real product's defining character. Treating America as a brand puts image before substance and tries to influence brand consumers by associating the product with sentiments and emotions that have no necessary connection to the nation being pitched. In selling America, Karen Hughes takes a page from Kevin Roberts and Cheerios brand marketing: Cheerios wants be about Mom rather than boring old oats, Karen Hughes wants America to be about Mom rather than about nasty old Guantanamo Bay or Abu Ghraib. Introducing herself on a "listening" tour of the Middle East as just a regular "working Mom" rather than as a Bush intimate associated with policies Muslims deplore, she hoped to divert attention from earned resentments to unearned sentiments.[105]

As astute an observer of American policy as political scientist Sibley Telhami seems also to play Roberts's game when he defends public diplomacy by insisting that "the best-lasting public diplomacy isn't propaganda. It's more about creating a level of trust."[106] Yet when a nation strives to create trust through public relations rather than policy, that *is* propaganda. Trustmarks are contrived by marketing gurus rather than earned by positive outcomes. Guantanamo Bay and Abu Ghraib prison make poor trustmarks; while FEMA—never mind M-1 tanks and bunker-busting bombs—is definitely not what Kevin Roberts had in mind when he contrived "lovemarks." Not for want of trying on the part of Karen Hughes, however. Hughes has claimed to represent a more "humble" approach to branding, but has nonetheless called for "rapid response" teams in the Middle East to deal with what Secretary of State Condoleezza Rice understands to be "misinformation" about and "misinterpretation" of American policies abroad. Rice cited the example of a *Newsweek* story about a controversial and contested incident supposedly involving the flushing of a copy of the Koran down a Guantanamo Bay toilet.[107]

As Rice's comments suggest, the branding approach prizes communication over content, and assumes that a poor image is always the consequence of poor advertising. Democrats and liberals too, no less than Republicans and libertarians, focus on "communicating" properly—framing and reframing positions and finding the right words to describe what are in truth often the wrong positions. Democrats attack the Bush administration for being out-imaged by Osama bin Laden. "How can a man in a cave outcommunicate the world's leading communication society?" asks a frustrated Richard Holbrooke.[108] Linguist George Lakoff moonlighting as a Democratic Party advisor believes winning votes is all about *framing* what you do rather than about *what* you actually do. Republicans, he admonishes, have branded their kind of leadership "stern father" leadership, leaving the Democrats to look like bad parents.[109] What they need to do is rebrand themselves as nurturing parents (a less gendered and hence politically correct version of "they're playing Dad, let's play Mom!"). This game fails to notice that both the stern father and the nurturing parent images infantilize voters by substituting p/maternalism for democratic politics, shoving aside the idea of active citizenship, whose practioners are not the pliant children of their leaders but the sovereign citizens of the communities in which they live. The language of grown-up democratic politics moves necessarily away from the brand game and back to democratic political theory and practice, where branding appears as what it is, an insidious corruption of democratic ideals and practices.

The United States is hardly alone in approaching its global image in terms of brand marketing. America's critics and enemies purvey their own brand images on Aljazeera and the internet. Moreover, they grasp as clearly as the Department of Public Diplomacy and Public Affairs what is at stake in Brand USA: they beg, borrow, and steal its image to their own ends at every turn, and they mangle, manipulate, and mix it to their own purposes whenever they can. Seeking to buy into the market value of the American brand's attractive side without being trapped by its downsides, for example, Muslim businessmen in France have engaged in a brilliant species of branding hybridization, borrowing a look and a logo from American brands like Coke, but rebranding them through clever add-ons and reformulations—Mecca-Cola, for example, an unsubtle but effective knockoff of Coke sold in France, North Africa, and elsewhere.[110]

Similarly, America's fast-food paradise is pleasantly plundered by another French-Muslim chain trying to get the goodies without paying the downside price: Burger King lives on in Beurger King, a successful new French fast-food outfit featuring halal beef and waitresses in hijabs that plays on an idiomatic term "Beur" (second-generation immigrants from the Arab North African Meghreb) to borrow a little American brand razzle-dazzle without being tainted by the full Brand USA association. This partial parasitism borrows positive sentiments from ambiguously situated American brands even as it distances itself from the American downside. A backhanded compliment to the power of the branding idea.

As the reputation of Brand America falters, even true red-white-and-blue American-based brands accustomed to associating themselves with Brand USA to enhance their commercial images around the world are tinkering with their branded Americanism. Jihadi websites refer to Pepsi as an acronym for "Pay every penny to save Israel." No wonder the American brand Heinz tries nowadays to sell its ketchup in the United Kingdom as a British brand, while the quintessential American brand SPAM cultivates local accents and cultural references in its advertising abroad. In a mirror move by a non-American company, Nestlé—a Swiss company that worked hard and long to be perceived in the United States as American by selling Toll House cookies there as "a brand that America trusts"—now seeks to distance itself from the United States.[111] With a 2003 Global Market Insite poll showing that over half the world's consumers in Europe and Asia "mistrust" American brands, and fully twenty percent actively avoid them,[112] Brand America has become a dubious marketing tool.

McDonald's, closely associated with Brand America, has learned this the hard way. As a frequent target of enemies of the United States, it has been making adjustments. In Athens terrorists shot rockets through a local franchise, and in France the antiglobalization organization ATTAC focused early on McDonald's as everything wrong with globalization American style. Its moral leader, a French farmer named Jose Bové (partially educated in North America, however), actually tore apart a McDonald's under construction in Millau and went (heroically) to jail for it. In its recent efforts at marketing, McDonald's has prudently embraced "glocalism"—go global locally—by custom fitting its global menu and fast-food service to local tastes, decors, and pricing structures. Serving wine and "McLutèce" burgers (with Emmenthaler cheese) in its Asterix-branded French franchises but "Maharaja Macs" made of lamb in Hindu India and kimchi burgers made of fermented cabbage in South Korea, where cabbage is a national favorite, McDonald's now aspires to muddy the very image it once assiduously cultivated as an agent of America and America's pop-cultural McWorld. Camouflaging itself in local color, McDonald's is just a local boy now, its global aspirations and its association with American cultural expansionism well hidden.

In France, at the time perhaps the most intractable of the 121 countries where it operates, McDonald's responded to ATTAC in 2002 by going native—and not just by serving McLutèce burgers. With its adversary, Mr. Bové, being turned into a French folk hero who with his bushy mustache and mighty physique bore an uncanny resemblance to the emblematic Gallic comic-book figure Asterix, the global burger franchiser bought the rights to Asterix. With his sidekick Obelix, Asterix (a historical figure who opposed the Roman occupation of Gaul) would assume the marketing role played in America by the clown Ronald McDonald. The idea was to put a native cultural imprimatur on McDonald's culturally alien *malbouffe* (junk food). This bold strategy, the equivalent of Châteauneuf du Pape buying Mickey Mouse to market its Beaujolais in Los Angeles, capitalized on McDonald's earlier campaign featuring a slogan boasting: "McDonald's, born in the United States, made in France." To many French consumers this looks like "the bad food giant has taken over the indomitable Gaul," but to Grégoire Champetier, McDonald's French marketing director, it was just a matter of helping "integrate McDonald's into French culture."[113]

Anthropologists have suggested that glocalization is another form of "creolization" by which local cultures colonized by McWorld's imperial economy fight back by countercolonizing the colonizer. I will give this claim greater attention in chapters 7 and 8 on resistance, but what seems clear from the experience of McDonald's with Asterix is that local culture exacts cosmetic changes in return for accepting and legitimating the alien culture in a fashion that allows the dominant alien culture to succeed.

The identity politics of the twenty-first century is then part and parcel of the infantilist ethos. It mistakes brand for identity and consumption for character while treating Americans as consumers of Brand USA rather than as the free citizens of a democratic republic. Yet despite these strong claims, I do not mean to suggest that markets and the businesses that operate in them have any intrinsic hegemonic interest in shaping identity or controlling behavior. As with everything else associated with the infantilist ethos, the purpose is not to govern subjects or turn citizens into subjects; only to create a culture conducive to selling goods by treating citizens as customers—customers, however, who no longer "naturally" want or need what the market must sell to them in order to survive. Instead, they must be impelled to buy branded goods that reflect wished-for lifestyles. Discouraging adult autonomy is finally just a marketing strategy for encouraging puerile attitudes. But marketing becomes everything when identity itself is shaped to its needs and the whole world is subordinated to consumer society's marketing requirements. For the result is not merely a society that is privatized, commercialized, infantilized, and branded, but one that is increasingly totalizing in its commercial embrace of our lives, sucking up the air from every other domain to sustain the sector devoted to consumption.

6

Totalizing Society:
The End of Diversity

The arts and sciences, less despotic though perhaps more
powerful than government, fling garlands of flowers over
the chains which weigh [people] down . . . causing them to
love their own slavery.

—Jean-Jacques Rousseau[1]

IN THE FIRST decade of the new millennium, consumers find themselves trapped in a cage of infantilization, reinforced by privatization
and an identity politics—call it an identity antipolitics—of branding. It
is not necessary to label them victims of what earlier leftist critics called a
kind of soft totalitarianism to see that their freedom may be compromised. Nor need we insist that they suffer, in the consumer choices they
make, from what Marxists once liked to call "false consciousness" in order
to suggest they may not be getting the social outcomes they wish for. The
history of the brutal realities the term *totalitarian* captured certainly
argues strongly against using it metaphorically to dramatize the lesser
forms of manipulation that characterize market relations today. Nor does
"false consciousness," calling up images of people who literally do not
know what they are thinking, willing, or doing, apply to today's focused
and knowing shoppers.

Yet there is something disturbingly flattening—not totalitarian, but
nonetheless both totalizing and homogenizing—about consumer society

under the subtle shaping influences of the infantilist ethos. And there is something defective about consumer choice when it repeatedly entails collective outcomes that are neither willed nor intended by individual choosers. Consumers are not citizens, and when a system pretends that they are, peculiar and even perverse things happen to decision making and to democracy, as well as democracy's commitment to diversity.

Critics of capitalism in the postwar period, especially those German neo-Marxists associated with the so-called Frankfurt School, were already worrying—a little hysterically if also rather presciently—about the ways in which the successes of late capitalism seemed to them to be cloaking new and subtle forms of repression in the marketplace. If the market, with its hidden monopolies and invisible coerciveness, was "free," then maybe freedom had (as the French philosopher Michel Foucault suggested) become a smoke screen for repression.

The Enlightenment had created worlds of liberty, privacy, and tolerance unknown to earlier societies. The new liberal ideologies that helped emancipate eighteenth-century men and women were oppositional (their targets were absolute monarchy and an authoritarian church). Since their ambition was to overthrow entrenched forms of political and ecclesiastical tyranny, their rhetoric was negative—suspicious of power and distrustful of government, even when it became democratic. But though it was understandably seditious in its oppositional phase, liberalism offered at best an ambiguous foundation for affirmative governance. Its intrinsic political promise was shot through with contradictions which were in part a reflection of the Enlightenment's own ambivalences about power. Reason ruled—after all, it was the Age of Reason—but reason had become predominately instrumental. David Hume had snatched it from its noble classical perch as the defining human faculty that gave men access to the laws of nature and God, and reconceived it as a faithful slave of the passions—an adjunct, as it were, to man's animal nature and to the power required for the satisfaction of animal interests. Tied to impulse and hence to power, reason could be made to rationalize manipulation, legitimating and even concealing the sharp edges of the new forms of coercion it facilitated.

In Jean-Jacques Rousseau's ironic phrase, so-called liberal institutions of the modern cultural ethos might in truth do little more than fling "gar-lands of flowers over [our] chains," causing men "to love their own slav-ery." Similarly, in that famous commentary in which he at once praised and warned against the ambiguous potential of democracy in America, Tocqueville had proposed that, in the new dictatorship of public opinion, "tyranny leaves the body free and directs its attack at the soul."[2] In the same Rousseauist vein, Foucault would later argue that in modern times power had come to work "without recourse, in principle at least, to excess, force or violence."[3] Citing such liberal and liberating institutional devices as the prison "panopticon" propounded by liberal philosopher Jeremy Bentham (a circular prison floor plan that allowed prisoners to come under the full-time surveillance of omnipresent guardians stationed at the circle's center, without entailing any physical encroachment on prisoner space), Foucault discerned a new form of liberal coercion which "assures the automatic functioning of power . . . so the perfection of power should tend to render its actual exercise unnecessary." The idea was to guarantee that prison inmates were "caught up in a power situation of which they are themselves the bearers."[4]

The question raised here by these earlier suspicions about liberalism's stealth coerciveness is whether the market itself, the driver of consumer capitalism's ambitions, may not harbor soft forms of manipulation its lib-eral character conceals; whether the market's vaunted pluralism is belied by an uncoerced uniformity in its actual offerings—in, for example, what these earlier critics called the "culture industry." The so-called dialectic of Enlightenment that Frankfurt School critics thought they had uncovered in private liberty was something less than liberating in its modern cultural manifestations. For, in its incarnation as bourgeois culture, the liberal ideology that had once overthrown kings appeared to be corrosive to pub-lic if not to private freedom; it seemed to turn equality into a source of leveling mediocrity (a critique associated earlier with John Stuart Mill, Nietzsche, and later Walter Lippmann); and it appeared to make choice a servant of constraint—not of false consciousness but of unintended consequences.

Max Horkheimer and Theodor Adorno (in their classic *Dialectic of*

Enlightenment) had identified a culture industry which no longer reflected the standards of "art" but generated instead a "monopoly" under which "all mass culture is identical." Under these conditions, they argued,

> the people at the top are no longer so interested in concealing monopoly: as its violence becomes more open, so its power grows. Movies and radio need no longer pretend to be art. The truth that they are just business is made into an ideology in order to justify the rubbish they deliberately produce. They call themselves industries.

The new culture industry, purveying the myth of what I have called consumer empowerment, claimed

> that standards were based in the first place on consumers' needs . . . [a] circle of manipulation and retroactive need in which the unity of the system grows ever stronger.[5]

In 1964, with this postwar leftist ambivalence about Enlightenment as backdrop, Herbert Marcuse proposed the controversial thesis that late capitalism was producing "one-dimensional men." Nurtured by a society in which "a comfortable, smooth, reasonable, democratic unfreedom prevails," one-dimensional men were being molded by a "productive apparatus [which] tends to become totalitarian," especially inasmuch as it determines "individual needs and aspirations."[6] Marcuse resorted to the hyperbole of totalitarianism to portray what he called "a non-terroristic economic-technical coordination which operates through the manipulation of needs by vested interests." This new form of liberal coercion encourages what I have identified as infantilization's defining civic schizophrenia inasmuch as it "obliterates the opposition between the private and the public existence, between individual and social needs."[7]

In producing a totalizing environment for consumers, consumer capitalism rendered much of what passed as freedom as mere illusion. Marcuse's critique was intentionally provocative, by conventional standards well over the top, especially in our postmodern era today after the fall of communism as a governing political system. After all, *false consciousness* had for a long time been the suspect term the far left used to delegitimize the desires and wants of workers and ordinary citizens when they failed to desire and want the things the far left thought workers and ordinary citizens were supposed to want.[8] Thus it seems perfectly sensible to suggest that in using the potent concept "totalitarian" to portray market tendencies toward conformism that were nefarious but something less than toxic, Marcuse was confounding mildly manipulative forms of persuasion associated with marketing and advertising with the kind of virulent repression that defined and set apart fascist and communist regimes.[9] When extremist groups like the Baader-Meinhof Gang and the Red Brigade in West Germany cast themselves (in Paul Berman's description) as enemies not of liberalism but of "the real Nazism, the Nazism that had survived Nazism, the Nazism that was built into the foundations of Western life," this was rhetorical overkill, a linguistic trick that betrayed both rationalism and liberalism, and rationalized violence and outlawry.[10]

Marcuse seemed to be treating what at worse was a commodification of values as a kind of stealth surrogate for oppression on the scale of the Holocaust. He was indulging in the kind of excess that permitted people to dismiss his underlying criticism. Calling markets totalitarian was like calling President Nixon or Charles de Gaulle back then fascists—a kind of sloganeering that let politicians off the hook for the much more modest but real and indictable sins they had actually committed.

Yet forty years after the publication of *One-Dimensional Man*, there is considerable evidence to suggest that the ubiquity of consumerism, the pervasiveness of advertising and marketing, and the homogenization of culture and values around an infantilizing commerce together have created a cultural ethos which, although not totalitarian, robs liberty of its civic meaning and threatens pluralism's civic vitality. Combined with privatization and branding, this commercial homogenization has made us less free as citizens and less diverse as a society than traditional liberals conceive us to be or than traditional capitalist producers and consumers think we are.

In the 1950s a longshoreman named Eric Hoffer won a certain celebrity for writing about totalitarian "true believers" who threatened the free-market liberalism.[11] Today free-market liberal marketers write about the need to make true believers out of consumers. In his book on how to cult brands, cited earlier, Douglas Atkin praises marketing that makes "customers become true believers." His position as an enthusiast is worth citing at length, because it makes a far better case for calling consumerism totalistic than any critic could. Atkin writes:

> We've reached a unique intersection in society that favors marketers. On one side, established institutions are proving to be increasingly inadequate sources of meaning and community. On the other, there has been a growth of a very sophisticated kind of consumerism. Marketing is reaching its maturity in terms of shrewdness and artfulness. Billions are being spent on gratifying a discriminating audience with complex and subtly crafted brands. The confluence of these two trends is leading to these commercial creations being embraced by a population disillusioned altogether by less satisfying, and often less trusted organizations. Alongside alternative religions, brands are now serious contenders for belief and community.[12]

Atkin is not alone. In the previous chapter, we cited Matthew W. Ragas bragging about the power of cult branding. Others, like Douglas B. Holt, talk about how brands have "become icons."[13]

This new ethos of consumer totalism has developed not because there is a conspiracy among capitalists to undermine liberty or an invisible party of persuaders pushing for conformity. It has happened because, as with infantilization generally, the ethos of our times privatizes our lives and immerses us in an environment of total marketing and ubiquitous advertising where goods are marketed everywhere and available at all hours, quite literally in our faces all the time. The intended consequence of the new totalism is that consumers buy consumables and services they do not necessarily need or want than they would in a traditional town square or agora where shopping was but one of a cornucopia of human activities. In such an environment, consumers are more likely to think their citizenship begins and ends with how they spend their income in the market-place, while corporations can believe that good deeds (or bragging about them) can turn them into "Citizen Brands, with aims of social responsibility as a core element of their corporate mission."[14] Such strategies privatize democracy itself.

I want to argue here that this has happened because the infantilist ethos envelops and penetrates each of what philosophers like Jürgen Habermas have called our "life worlds," those spheres of activity and thought and purpose that define us as free beings. The evidence is everywhere: media salesmen who themselves speak glibly of "ubiqui-TV"; and newspapers, not just television, crowded with infomercials, with the once sober *New York Times Magazine* carrying not only a regular shopping column by Rob Walker which, like this book, is labeled "Consumed," but is itself consumed by extended "magazine article" infomercial-style layouts that cannot be clearly identified either as news or advertising—articles pushing teen, tween, girl, toddler, and pet fashions; that same magazine now supplementing its weekly fare of the forgettable with an extended section called "The Funny Pages" that patronizes readers without being particularly funny; an expanding global culture of McWorld that seems unstoppable even in Western civic cultures (e.g., France) pitted against it, even in Islamic religious cultures (e.g., Iran) or truly totalitarian political cultures deeply hostile to it. Shanghai is today more cluttered with advertising slogans and corporate logos than it was with communist propaganda slogans and one-party state propaganda banners a generation ago, though it remains a one-party communist state.

The infantilist ethos totalizes by affording commerce a universal access to every part of life and every sector of our "life world" in ways we can only experience as homogenizing and flattening. Were commerce not associated in neoliberal ideology with freedom, and were the content of commerce to be defined by politics or ideology or religion rather than consumer products and consumer brands, we might even forgive Marcuse for mistaking our condition for a kind of gentle market totalitarianism. After all, when religion colonizes every sector of what should be our multidimensional lives, we call the result theocracy; and when politics col-

onizes every sector of what should be our multidimensional lives, we call
the result tyranny. So why, it might be asked, when the marketplace—with
its insistent ideology of consumption and its dogged orthodoxy of spending—colonizes every sector of what should be our multidimensional lives,
do we call the result liberty?

The market consciously aims at exerting a firm and encompassing grip
on time and on space, controlling each and every of our waking moments
and infiltrating the psyche's most remote and private geography. This is
the necessary condition for capitalism's success: an all-consuming people
who shop or think about shopping, who conceive or exercise consumer
wants, all the time. Consumerism is totalizing rather than pluralistic
because pluralism offers space to something other than shopping, and
diversity means periods of time when people are not shopping. Compare
a modern suburban mall that is the only common space in those suburban
deathscapes where more than half of America lives today with the traditional town square or the village commons. On the town square, mixed in
among the shops and stores and commercial establishments, could once
be found a schoolroom and courthouse, a post office and library, a village
theater and churchyard, each mirroring the rich human variety that constituted a democratic community's essential character. Now reimagine
Thornton Wilder's *Our Town* set in the video-game lobby of the local
multiplex (*Our Mall?*). The mall of America has become the mall that is
America; and that mall that is America threatens to colonize every other
world in which people may aspire to live.

In the style of the countercultural 1960s, Herbert Marcuse's rhetoric
exuded hyperbole. But his instincts were acute. For as the infantilizing
ethos has both produced and been produced by a spirit of capitalism that
favors pervasive consumerism, it appears to have produced a parallel and
reinforcing homogenization of taste. In reducing civic liberty to a whining
and whimsical "I want" that trumps every other human sentiment, the
infantilist ethos has declared war on variety. Although it cannot outlaw
them, it has hurried to out-rush, outflank, and dominate every attitude
and behavior that does not conduce to shopping. Unlike the state, which
uses its monopoly over legitimate force to guarantee diversity, the market

uses its suasion to enforce commercial monopoly. And when "I want" becomes "I want the brands and brand identities that marketers want me to want in accord with what marketers explain to us are what I really want," consumers may indeed have arrived at a kind of consciousness that, if not precisely false, is inconsistent with their deepest wishes for the commonweal to which, as public citizens, they aspire to belong. It is not so much false consciousness as divided consciousness—that civic schizophrenia to which we have alluded earlier.

In a book with the telling title *Preference Pollution: How Markets Create the Desires We Dislike*, the economist David George has spelled out the ways in which the marketplace has used its capacity to satisfy "first-order desires" (as Harry Frankfurt calls them in a passage I cited in chapter 4) even as it ignores the "second-order desires" that constitute what we might understand as our genuine will. It gives us what "we want" (my earlier example of big gas-guzzling, pollution-spewing SUVs) but pays no attention at all to what we *want* to want (energy independence and clean air). By serving desire, it feels free to engage in "unrestricted persuasion" with respect to first-order desires, thinking in doing so it legitimizes free will.[15]

In the subtitle of her book *The Overspent American*, Juliet Schor proposes to tell us "why we want what we don't need."[16] What needs explaining, however, is why so often *we don't want what we want*. Why what we want is not really what we *want* to want (what our social selves want). If, as Harry Frankfurt insists, "to have a free will is to be moved by desires that one wishes to be moved by," then market persuasion directed at first-order desires isn't really freedom at all.[17] This is not a matter of false consciousness, but of second consciousness (what we want to want) trumping first consciousness (what we want). I want another vodka . . . except on second thought I don't want to be an addict or an alcoholic, so I don't really want another vodka after all. Yes, I really want a drink, but I really don't want to want a drink. Part of how market totalism works is to make the realm of first desires the only legitimate realm of choosing. In old-fashioned moral language, the empire of impulse is allowed to trump the empire of will, and then is rewarded with a crown called liberty. What is missing, however, both in the old moral language and in David George's economist talk, is that first-order desires tend usually to be private, and second-order desires tend to be public. We speak first as "me" and only then consider the "we."

In this chapter, I will try to show then that the infantilist ethos tends to homogenize taste and narrow rather than expand variety. With consumerism infiltrating and conditioning every nook and cranny of the larger society, the market takes over our lives. This totalizing impact on consumers is hardly comparable to the impact of political totalitarianism on its subjects. Privileging first-order desires is not the same thing as tyranny. And resisting consumer totalism is possible and possible at far less cost than resisting totalitarianism, although doing so, it turns out (see chapter 8), is difficult all the same. Why? Because consumerism's totalizing tendencies unfold out of sight, and consumerism colonizes time and space under the banner of choice. Because homogenization emerges from market choices that are seen as competitive and pluralistic. Remember the African monkey trap: if all we need to do is "let go" of our chains, what need is there to break them?

Forms of Market Totalism

There are five forms of market domination that constitute the substance of my argument that consumer culture has a totalizing although not totalitarian impact on our lives. I will argue that the consumer market is *ubiquitous* (it is everywhere); that it is *omnipresent* (it is "all the time" and aspires to fill up all time); it is *addictive* (it creates its own forms of reinforcement); it is *self-replicating* (it spreads virally); and it is *omnilegitimate* (it engages in active self-rationalization and self-justification, eroding the moral bases for resisting it). Together, these five characteristics give markets a power over our lives and thoughts, bodies and souls, that rival but are not the equivalent of more traditional forms of totalitarianism. Yet although they are less toxic because they operate under the putative legitimacy of market freedom and depend on civic schizophrenia for their success, they are the more difficult to resist and overcome. Their dangers, above all the loss of genuine diversity in a marketplace which, although pluralistic, monopolizes consciousness, become apparent as these characteristics are elaborated and documented.

UBIQUITY

In the traditional liberal view of society, life offers many discrete spheres of activity for human beings whose values, cultures, and life purposes are historically plural and empirically diverse (pluralism is a fact rather than an aspiration). In surveying the spheres in which justice might play a role, for example, political theorist Michael Walzer gave us a representative typology which considered not only the marketplace defined by money and commodities, but other spheres, each with its own values and goods, defined by merit (office in the ancient sense), by work (workplace), by leisure (recreation), by education (school place), by kinship and love (family or home), by divine grace (religion), by respect and recognition (friendship), and by politics (public or civic space). Like other liberal "Lockean" thinkers upholding a fundamentally "pluralist conception of goods," Walzer wished to describe and justify "a society where no social good serves or can serve as a means of domination."[18] That is to say, Walzer gave the fact of human pluralism a prescriptive thrust, arguing that "there is no single set of primary or basic goods conceivable across all moral and material worlds."[19]

Now as a theory, private market philosophy shares this commitment to pluralism and variety. Those who propound the virtues of the market boast of its openness to pluralism (courtesy of competition), especially as compared to the state's defining monopoly over force and law. Yet the liberal democratic state employs its monopoly over legitimate force to assure a pluralism of spheres and the sanctity of individual rights and of the domain of privacy rights, while the consumer marketplace tends to colonize every sphere and sector, even though it maintains the fiction of pluralism. Although it does not initially make a moral claim for its omnipresence, by aspiring to occupy every space and all spaces, it effectively precludes the possibility of coeval spheres of human activity. Commercializing capitalism mandates the infiltration and permeation of noncommercial spheres in order to maximize profitability. It is quite literally everywhere, colonizing every life sphere in which we live out our daily routines. On sidewalks and walls and buses and trains, in schoolrooms and bedrooms and restrooms and trams, on big screens and pod-screens and TVs and phones, carved into haircuts and written on skin, codified as trademarks and brandmarks and lovemarks—ciphers for human identity consumed by desire, a spirit perfectly captured by the *New York Times* in the title of a book review of a philosophical study of desire, "I Am, Therefore I Want."[20]

Ubiquity is a powerful term, but as with so many ideas examined here, it is not my coinage but that of the marketers. A journalist surveying telecommunication conglomerates introduces a story on MTV networks under the title "I Want My Ubiquitous Conglomerate."[21] His ubiquitous conglomerate—which is itself a subsidiary of the still more elephantine Viacom—includes MTV, MTV2, Nickelodeon, Comedy Central, TV Land, and Spike in the United States, and 111 channels around the world, including 19 brand-new channels in Europe, Asia, Latin America, and Africa. The question posed by this newsman's story is "Once you are everywhere, where do you go next?" Meanwhile, *Newsweek* takes note of the new competition for small-screen television (on cell-phones and iPods) by shouting "Only one thing is clear: the race is on toward ubiqui-TV."[22]

A recent advertising campaign slogan for Samsung's new cell-phone television portrays ubiqui-TV as a privatization of public space: we watch a variety of people nominally "in public" turn their spaces into privatized viewing rooms for their handheld Samsung miniscreens, while a tagline urges us to "imagine the world as your living room." The annihilation of public space, a feature of many of the new technologies, from cell-phones and BlackBerrys to video games and global positioning auto maps (no more turning to "the public" to ask directions), has become a virtue among privatized consumers for whom the presence of public others is a distraction from consuming private behavior. The only thing quasi-public that follows you into the privatized sanctuaries that the gadgets carve out of the public husk is commerce itself, since the wormholes through which you must travel in making your escape must always be purchased. What is public—trees, wind, architecture, sounds, other people—is free: commercially supported solitude must be bought, which is of course the point.

Those seeking the sanctuary of electronic screens and headphones may imagine themselves seeking out the diversity of what is offered in games, films, and music, and eluding the sameness of the outside world; yet, bought electronic content is far more homogenous and limiting than the actual pluralism of our natural life worlds, even if for some people it also feels more vivid and "real." At their best, movies cannot be more heterogeneous and varied than the real worlds they aspire to capture. All of Hollywood at its best is not the equal in variety or originality of a single summer day's walk in a public park.

Art originates its own varied worlds, of course, and this discussion of public diversity is not intended as a comment on the aesthetic. It is variety in the literal sense with which I am concerned, actual variations in experience and diversity of life spheres. Not pluralism within but pluralism among the many sectors in which we think, feel, work, and live. It is this kind of variety that public space guarantees and which markets shrink. For everyone ends up watching the same selection of programs offered them by the same "ubiquitous conglomerates" sponsored by the same consumer companies aiming at dominating the same economic markets.

In France, consumers have discovered, it is not the market that assures cultural variety in television programming or rescues the movie industry from the scourge of ubiqui-TV. It is instead the state telecommunications quasi-monopoly over television that does so. Though market-obsessed Americans will rush to call such state intervention Orwellian, the French recognize that a state-sponsored rule that prohibits the showing of films on public television on Wednesday and Saturday evenings (the primary movie-attendance nights) is what secures the balance between movie attendance and television watching and (yes, through coercion) generates greater variety in French cultural life. It is likewise the state in France that subjects American films to import quotas (as if they were vegetables, Hollywood complains), not to prevent French audiences from being exposed to American pop culture, but to salvage a little space for French culture—pop or otherwise—in the face of the American market onslaught which, if the market alone prevailed, would mean that French audiences would be exposed to nothing but American films, TV, and pop culture.

Alone among its allies other than Israel, the United States opposed the 2005 UNESCO Convention on Cultural Diversity because it insisted and insists that the free market is a better vehicle for global cultural diversity than transnational regulation. Yet the global marketplace has facilitated an asymmetry in cultural power in which the United States (Hollywood) dominates. French cultural minister Renaud Donnedieu de Vabres defended the convention by noting that "Hollywood movies account for 85 percent of movie tickets sold around the world. In the United States only 1 percent of shown movies come from outside the United States."[23] Does the United States defend the market mechanism then because it assures diversity or because it assures American cultural dominion and the ubiquity of its commercial products?

Ubiquity means everywhere. Everywhere means anywhere, so that any space not yet occupied by the market can become a target for commercial takeover by specialists for whom an unbranded space is an unfulfilled potential. There is no such thing as a blank slate—a tabula rasa—in today's ubiquitous marketplace. Every blank space invites a brand logo or an advertising slogan; every skin patch invites a commercial tattoo;[24] every silence invites a noisy come-on. Marketers figure out how to hook products and brands to movies and songs; to make whole TV stations advertising boards (MTV, like VH1, is a shopping network for the music industry in which, we have seen, rock around the clock becomes shop around the clock on 111 channels [and counting] worldwide). They try to enlist the five senses in every campaign, recently seizing on the idea of "embedding aromas" in packaging, "hoping the way to the purse is through the nose . . . targeting as many of the five senses as possible."[25]

The most unlikely places have recently been transformed into advertising venues. A production of the musical *Stomp* in the Orpheum Theater in New York offered a three-minute staged advertisement for a tourist organization called Visit London. Live commercials in live theaters? They can now be found in Dublin and Hamburg as well as Manhattan. Why? Because, according to one advertiser, "They're a captive audience. They can't switch channels or change over or walk out once the thing is started."[26] And if live theater works for marketers, why not live sheep? Hotels.nl, a Dutch on-line reservations firm, has been buying space on sheep at one euro per ewe, to spread its message around Holland. Despite fines levied by angry local municipalities, the practice—founded by an English firm called Easy Green Productions that puts ads on sheep blankets—is growing.[27]

As companies trade, merge, cobrand, and exchange, they try to create content monopolies over the multiple screens we nowadays watch from dawn to midnight. Those Samsung cell-phone screens, so seemingly plural, are conduits to common content, and the firms that control or sponsor content seek a monopoly on that commonality. The Disney Company (and its ABC broadcast subsidiary) is partnering with Steve Jobs's Apple Computer company to put Disney content on Apple's latest iPod video players. Their rivals, such as Google Video (which purchased YouTube at the end of 2006 for $1.6 billion) and RealNetworks, compete for the same eyeballs, every digital pipeline looking for its own monopoly over content—right around the world. And so *Newsweek*'s "race is on toward ubiqui-TV," where virtual ad-driven watching never stops courtesy of multiplying media technologies—wristwatch, phone, iPod, computer screen, wi-fi connectivity, television sets large and small, and old-fashioned movie screens. Real-world advertising has been everywhere seemingly forever, of course: above public urinals, aloft on blimps and biplane banners, on school bus roofs and parking-meter poles, in school and college campus student centers, on sports arena billboards, all over "public" transportation, and still everywhere on those old-fashioned outdoor billboards.

There are more and more circuits, more wires, more "pipes" to deliver virtual content, but less and less pluralism of content. The internet has already entangled us in a World Wide Web that has become a surrogate reality. Futurologists in the mould of George Gilder have gone a step further in quest of ubiquity, imagining an electronic network built into and coterminous with the atmosphere, an "ethersphere" into which anyone can plug: presto! universal wi-fi absolutely anywhere. Using the nearly infinite bandwidth beyond what is commercially exploited today, no one will ever have to be off-line again; we can all be hooked together into a virtual "telecosmic" network through which, however, our actual connections to actual publics are obliterated.[28]

Web games target youth, but players abound in every generation—millions of kidult gamesters participating in "persistent" (permanently on and available to players who log on) on-line games. A fifty-four-year-old on-line player of Star Wars Galaxies complained when the manufacturer changed the format and rules that it had ruined the "wonderful second life together" she and fellow gamesters had developed—destroying in the words of the story's reporter, "a camaraderie and friendship with other players that were far more important than the play itself—relationships that can be hard to replicate in 'real life.'" Other distraught players complained of feeling "violated" by the format changes, one gamester saying "for them to just come along and destroy our community has prompted a lot of death-in-the-family-type grieving."[29] When a gamester's virtual life takes precedence over an adult's actual life, it is hard to imagine that our real civic or social communities are being benefited.

Gilder's vision of a ubiquitous telecosm is no futurologist's fantasy. In October 2005, Philadelphia chose EarthLink "to build and manage a wireless network spanning the entire city." Chicago, Miami Beach, Milwaukee, and Portland, Oregon, are also exploring municipal wireless networks, and Google recently offered to "make all of San Francisco wireless for free" (well, not exactly free, but to be paid for by advertisements targeting users).[30] Around the world, where many countries including South Korea, Canada, Israel, and Japan already have a greater percentage of their population with access to broadband than the United States (which now ranks sixteenth in broadband access), public wireless networks are likely to prove even more seductive. Consumers will deem this progress, since it will appear to enhance their capacity to communicate, buy and sell, and access entertainment. But so will marketers, who will understand that the telecosm offers them ubiquitous access to customers and endless possibilities for marketing. Here and there, an artist or a dissident will use universal access to call out crowds into the streets to make a happening or foment a demonstration, but the dominant use of and economic purpose behind the telecosm are necessarily commercial. The aim of those who finance and establish it is to use the customers who think they are using it. The new media advertise their "pull" capacities—tell us what you want, we are here to empower you—but their viability depends on their "push" capabilities, their success at selling products, services, entertainment, knowledge, and other stuff.

Born of competition and rooted in entrepreneurship, consumer markets today have become monsters of monomania. With "everything for sale" (the title of a book by Robert Kuttner on markets), rival spheres come under attack, and "Government stands impeached and impoverished, along with democratic politics itself."[31] There is only one paradigm— "Unfettered markets are deemed both the essence of human liberty, and the most expedient route to prosperity"—and hence but one value (profit), one activity (shopping), one identity (the consumer), one para-digm of behavior (market exchange), one life world (commerce) that qual-ify as legitimate.[32]

Unsuspecting subscribers to what probably is America's most presti-gious magazine, The New Yorker, must have read their August 22, 2005 issue with growing puzzlement; for there were hundreds of red-and-white peppermint targets everywhere: on the cover, in the reading matter, among the ads, and threaded into the layout and design right to the back cover. The New Yorker had discovered cobranding: the wealthy wannabe-up-market discount firm Target (facetiously pronounced in the French fash-ion as Tar-zhay) had purchased this issue of the actually up-market New Yorker from cover to cover (for $1.1 million), a singular monopoly on advertising that intruded on layout and design of the magazine and obscured the traditional boundary between advertising and editorial con-tent. Well-known illustrators such as Milton Glaser, Ruben Toledo, and Robert Risko offered drawings as part of what The New Yorker called its "project."[33] For that week at least, Target was The New Yorker and The New Yorker was Target, their brands merged, their logos married, their content intertwined. For one moment in time, under cover of design ingenuity and creative advertising, in a single magazine at least, a retail company had achieved advertising ubiquity. Only *Pravda*, the official newspaper of the Communist Party in its Soviet heyday, could boast such total penetration— except that its relationship to the party was always fully acknowledged.[34]

OMNIPRESENCE

The consumer market aspires to be everywhere, but it also wishes to be ever present, occupying time with the same fierceness that it conquers space. In modern consumer societies, the store is never closed, the pitchman is never silent, and the opportunity to engage in market exchange is never suspended. This is a kind of reverse Sharia in which the rules of every competing social sector, whether religious or political, are overwritten by the rules governing shopping. Islamic Sharia, like Puritanism with its Sunday blue laws, might decree "no shopping on the Sabbath," or "no acohol or dancing permitted, ever!" Market "Sharia" decrees "no *no*-shopping days permitted, stores permanently open!" and "alcohol and dancing and everything else that can be bought permitted, encouraged, ordained, everywhere and always!" Shops and malls that once were open five or six days a week now are open seven days a week, with added hours on selected evenings and holidays, and early openings (five or six in the morning, even one minute past midnight) on those special shopping days like Black Friday (as in "profitable" or "in the black") right after Thanksgiving on a day when nearly ten percent of all holiday purchases are now made in the United States, many at predawn morning sales. (Electronics Monday—get your gadgets, on sale!—has recently followed Black Friday as the season's second most rewarding shopping day.) "Religious" holidays from Christmas and Easter to Passover and Ramadan have joined other holidays like Halloween and Kwanza and Valentine's Day as occasions for commerce that spread across ethnic and national boundaries, their "holiness" an excuse only to stop working (producing) in order to ramp up consuming.

In a front-page post-Thanksgiving story, in language mimicking the hysteria that accompanied reports on Hurricane Katrina, the *New York Times* recently reported: "Across the country, millions of Americans mobbed discount stores, raced into suburban malls and swarmed downtown shopping districts in a retail ritual that appeared to set a record for sleep deprivation." As if he foresaw the actual breakdown of civilization in the antics of his marauding customers, a lonely early morning Black Friday store clerk featured in the story is seen trying to control a mob of shoppers clutching for cut-rate computer hardware, shouting "Civilized! Civilized!" over and over again, even as customers continuously "lunged at one another" for a share of the booty.[35] The aim of this frenzied all-night market "doorbusting" is commercial omnipresence, an environment of total shopping.

To measure commercialism's contemporary omnipresence is to chart the actual minutes and hours spent each day by Americans or Germans or Japanese during which they are exposed to commercial media messaging and invited to identify themselves in terms of what they buy and eat and drink and wear. The numbers, as they impact on the young, are particularly daunting. Measured by the time allotted to them, commercialism's pedagogical competitors—education, parenting, socialization by church or civic group—come out on the short side. Teachers struggle for the attention of their students for at most twenty or thirty hours a week, perhaps thirty weeks a year, in settings they do not fully control and in institutions that are often ridiculed in the popular media. (*Animal House* has become a more popular emblem of the modern university than the ivory tower.) Pastors, rabbis, imams, and priests get an hour or two a week with that ever smaller minority of their congregations that actually attend services. Parents are embattled "gatekeepers" at best, who year by year watch their hold on their children compromised, eroded, out-flanked, and eventually wholly loosened by their rivals in the marketplace who often target them as impediments standing in the way of access to children, or try to exploit them as conduits to children. The true tutors of late consumer capitalist society as measured by time are those who control the media monopolies, the aggressive content purveyors, shameless lords of the omnipresent pixels, who capture sixty or seventy hours a week, fifty-two weeks a year, of children's time and attention.

The Kaiser Family Foundation's 2005 survey of eight- to eighteen-year-old American youngsters found that "the total amount of media content young people are exposed to each day has risen to eight and a half hours."[36] In an attention-deficit modern society, this is as oppressive a temporal totalism as can be imagined, one in which commercial branders and love-mark propagandists control our civilization's commercial ethos by controlling time itself. With "direct and indirect spending by young people 18 and under in the U.S. account[ing] for roughly $1 trillion a year," marketers necessarily become subversive adversaries of adulthood who inculcate puerility in the young, from tots to teens to dumbed-down adults, in the name of maintaining market viability.[37] The culture of puerility legitimates it all in part simply by owning the clock.

To own the clock is not always to display it. Malls are stubborn in their disdain for clocks, and manage to own time by operating outside its discipline. If shoppers do not know what time it is, they can never spend too much of it on shopping. A mall with a public clock is as rare as a train station without one. The now notorious 24/7 news cycle that puts "all news all the time" on dozens of cable channels, internet stations, and satellite radio and television transmissions announces that news time is all the time. "All the time" is another way to achieve no time at all. The original meaning of the "news" was to convey a sense that from time to time something "new" happens that merits a "news" report. All news all the time is no longer news at all, but commercial infotainment geared to commerce rather than to information. The then executive vice president of scheduling at CBS acknowledged the obvious, that "in a hyperactive society with so many choices, viewers are used to being entertained every minute."[38] To maximize content, while using up more and more of the day and still retaining the focus of attention-deficit kids, content providers must dumb down, speed up, fast cut, and jump cut—putting a premium on speed (see chapter 3) and a preference for repetition. For these purposes, 24/7 is inadequate. There are literally not enough hours in the day for a totalizing consumer culture that needs to fill every available second of psychological time to overspill capacity.

In responding to multiple technologies, young people are developing multitrack minds that accommodate multitrack media, adding hours to the clock. A successful marketing strategy must think bigger than twenty-four hours a day. A study commissioned by Yahoo! from OMD Worldwide found that by exploiting the multitasking typical of fast-moving young people, it is possible to get "members of the My Media generation [to] fit up to 44 hours of activities in just one day."[39] In an infantilist culture, time itself is elastic, for electronic gadgetry like TiVo and iPods allow consumers to "time shift" their consumption of content. Hence, young people can respond to advertisements about gear on their television screens (the Home Shopping Network), even as they research comparative pricing on another channel (Googling stuff), and "buzz market" stuff to friends on still another (i-messaging them)—a three-for-one multitasking that lets them do an hour's consumer labor in twenty minutes. This is not some trick of Einstein's special relativity theory: in the cyclotron of marketing, desires can be propelled to speeds that exceed the speed of light, after which anything is possible.

The younger the target consumer, the more effective the assault on time. While adults can mute, filter, or otherwise elude or ignore advertising, "the first survey of American children by Mediamark Research Inc. has found that children differ from adults in one way that should interest advertisers: most of them aren't skipping TV ads." They do not mute their sets during ads, and they do not time shift out of commercial space as adults do. Nearly 60 percent of 5,400 six- to eleven-year-olds said they watched ads the same way they watched programs.[40] Commercials themselves have a timeless quality, merging with television, web-based, and video-game content, to digest more and more of a typical child's daily schedule. American television ads today "eat up eight minutes of a sitcom and 16 minutes of a drama."[41] Executives are dropping song-themed lead-ins and credits to make still more time for commercials. Since the younger demographic may not even recognize the difference between commercials and content, the two become commingled in children's programming—something, we have already observed, the Target campaign in *The New Yorker* achieved for adults.

Singular content such as a Nike swoosh can appear on marathon runner sweats in a race being watched by a kid with a Nike swoosh knit yarmulke while he downloads a clever Nike commercial onto his iPod. The commercial time-space continuum is expandable. Its eyes are those glow-ing diodes that stare at us day and night, green or red peering optics that are always on even when the gadgets they sign for are off, reminders that the commercial time-space continuum is never "off," only hibernating or paused or, if you try to turn it off, like your computer, recycling into the "restart" mode, waiting, ever ready for you to log on again and get on with the consumers' virtual life. Like all the other systems of the market econ-omy, the selling system default mode is set permanently to "opt in." There is no opt-in switch, you are in until you opt out. Except there is no opt-out switch either, so you are forever in. This is a kind of "passive consuming," a system mode which, like car restraints and safety cushions, works with-out the will or input of the user. The market economy is in user mode all the time, and deploys wares and marketing without the consumer having to do anything at all. A perfect selling machine.

When new technologies are introduced, they are introduced to repli-cate in new media the same old commercial messages and the same old message monopolies. "With each new medium," writes family finance expert Nathan Dungan, "there is one more outlet for advertisers to reach people—especially impressionable young people."[42] An illusion of diver-sity based on technological variety covers up the actual homogeneity of content, whether commercial or merely commercially sponsored. In 1996 a new deregulatory Federal Communications Act was passed, supplanting the 1934 act. It was precisely the logic of technical "spectrum abundance" that motivated deregulation and rationalized the emphasis on market activity, though the reality was that control of content was narrowing in a world of vertical integration and global media monopolies. More and more time and more and more space for a less and less varied content.

Broadband originally held out the promise of greater variety. Every television channel yielded increased transmission time capacity by a factor of six. But digitalizing broadcast spectra so that one old analog station can yield six digital channels does little to increase the variety or cultural diver-sity of content. Changing the format for the mechanical and electronic reproduction of music from roller tubes to player piano to 78, 45, and LP vinyl records, and then to tape and disc and iPod download, has done little to increase the variety of music consumed (there may be more variety, but format change has not been the spur). Likewise, digitalization has done little for diversifying content. Cable television and satellite radio offer dozens of different varieties of music, but the economics of recording and the monopoly ownership of telecommunications companies continue to shrink musical taste. What can be heard (an extraordinary variety) has little impact on what people actually listen to (a narrow spectrum) so that the potential pluralism of the technological architecture is unrepresented in the public's listening habits. Likewise, showing movies on cell-phone or iPod screens does not release viewers from Hollywood's comic-book blockbuster approach to films, but secures it over viewers 24/7. Whereas, according to media critic Jodi Kantor, traditional large-screen television "is meant to cut a neat hole in your day" during the time you watch a movie or a game or the news at day's end, "small-screen television fills the ragged holes that already exist in your routine: the 37-minute train to work, the 6-minute line at Starbucks . . . the stretches spent in the bathroom."[43] What she does not notice is that the moments of time occupied by these ragged holes represents what up until now have been the moments that have eluded commercial media omnipresence. Filling the ragged holes secures the media's temporal monopoly. There is no longer anywhere to hide: iPod and cell-phone, wireless network and telecosm, are everywhere with you; there is no longer any moment in which to take sanctuary, time belongs to the market.

ADDICTIVENESS

Another indicator of the totalizing and homogenizing character of consumer culture is its apparent addictiveness. Addictive behavior places the addictive object in the forefront of both consciousness and subconsciousness in a manner that can obliterate rival interests. In the first instance, it is a medical and psychological issue. But in a hyperconsumer society, it has a cultural and economic dimension, as is apparent in this technology expert's comment on a four-year-old playing a video game, "who was so excited about finding words in the maze that she got addicted, in an arcade-ish way" to the game.[44] My use of the term *addiction* is not metaphoric: addiction is ubiquity's core psychology and hence an ideal means to securing market omnipresence. For addiction leads to repetitive behavior in which the addicted subject returns to the same obsession over and over again, so that it encompasses time as well. The consumer society prospers on addictive behavior, selling tobacco, alcohol, medications (legal drugs), and of course state-sponsored and casino as well as on-line gambling (estimated to be a $10-billion-a-year business), in theory because consumers "want" these "goods," but in fact because it is profitable to do so.

Much the same is true for the selling of sugar-saturated sodas and candies and grease-laden fast foods to the young. By helping to create desires and habits which, if not actually addictive, turn consumer desire into ad-reinforced craving, consumer capitalism gets consumers to want the very things, become addicted to the very things, it needs to sell. Do eleven-month-old babies "need" electronic learning toys like the V.Smile video-game console or the handheld Leapster game system? Do babies "want" "Baby Einstein" and "Brainy Baby" videos? Or BabyFirstTV programming to while away the hours when they turn six months old? What is clear is that the firms that make these "learning toys" and "educational" programs need to sell them, and want parents to believe that unless they buy the educational cartridges the marketers call "smartridges" that "turn game time into brain time" their kids will fail in life. The V.Smile was named Best Toy of the Year by the 2005 toy industry trade show, and is marketed under ad copy reading "You'll never get into college if you don't play your video games!"[45]

Business spends over $11 billion a year in its "advertising assault" on "children, teens, and young adults." Some of this is to sell about $20 billion a year in toys, and alarmingly, marketers are now introducing digital music players and digital cameras for three-year-olds—"Mommy, Help Me Download 'Farmer in the Dell' to My MP3 Player" proclaims a *New York Times* "news" headline![46] The greater proportion of the sum continues to be spent by the food, beverage, candy, and restaurant industry whose aim, if not quite addiction, is not only brand loyalty, but sugar, salt, and grease dependency. Fast-food chains vie for the superburger record, with Hardee's 1,400-calorie Monster Thick-burger and Wendy's 1,000-calorie triple cheeseburger trumped by Ruby Tuesday's 1,780-calorie Ultimate Colossal Burger. Meanwhile, Pizza Hut boasts a Full House XL pizza with 2,240 calories.[47] Schools are equipped with vending machines that sell sugar-rich sodas, with cola companies offering some percentage of the take as a bribe to school systems to overcome resistance based on the health of children. It is not exactly addiction that is at stake, but "the American Beverage Association knows it has hard-wired America to drown the salt and grease with sugar."[48] The food and beverage industries continue to introduce new products aimed at children. In 1994, only fifty new food products were developed for kids; ten years later, in 2004, 470 new products were introduced, "a rate far greater than that for the increase of new products in the total market."[49]

Alcohol, naturally addictive, is also heavily marketed to the young. Binge drinking has become a peril on university campuses across the world, and in the United States it finds commercial sponsorship in extensive television beer advertising geared to teen taste (girls, gags, and geeks mixed in with talking turtles) as well as in the new fashion of collegiate drinking games like Beer Pong, in which contestants try to throw Ping-Pong balls into beer cups with the "losers" being "compelled" to guzzle beer. Anheuser-Busch introduced a "Bud Pong" game in 2005, "promoting Bud Pong tournaments and providing Bud Pong tables, balls and glasses to distributors in 47 markets, including college towns like Oswego, N.Y., and Clemson, S.C."[50] Outrageous websites (not beer-company sponsored, however) with names such as www.collegedrunkfest.com "feature rules, merchandise and pictures of wild parties, with some students naked and others hugging the toilet."[51] The site is a kind of unending virtual spring break venue made up in equal parts of porn and foolishness, all explicitly linked to heavy drinking. Breweries and distributors are themselves more prudent, offering a "responsible drinking" text for their marketing, but the irresponsible subtext is teen consumption, binge drinking, passive athletic spectatorship, and alcohol-induced sex (featured in dozens of on-line porn sites, portraying putatively drunk women engaging in "forced" sex and simulated rape).

Addiction is a clinical term, and many observers use it in speaking of consumer behavior. But even without invoking it, we can task the consumer market with an ambition to attach every natural human need to an artificial commercial product, so that for the need to be fulfilled the product must be purchased. The aim is commodity-based addiction, day and night (omnipresence is a synonym for addiction): no sleep without Ambien and no wakefulness without No-Doz; no passive evening spectatorship without TV and no midday athletic prowess without all the right gear; no nighttime colds without NyQuil and no daytime sniffles without DayQuil. Every mental and emotional state demands a commercial facilitator, ideally one on which a dependency can be bred. Think of a typical young man's evening out at the local mall's sports bar: no cool without Ralph Lauren, no hook-up without Nokia, no fun without Bud, no buzz without nicotine, no pickup without Heineken, no chat without the overhead bar TV screen, no getaway without the Miata, no Muzak without Bose, no high-thread-count sheets without Martha Stewart, no intercourse without Viagra, and no see-ya without the trumped up buddy call on Verizon. Even big-ticket items in the Third World call for big-ticket commercial facilitators: no war without Blackwater, no democratization without Halliburton, no reconstruction without Bechtel. Eventually, the generics become indistinguishable from the brands so that it becomes redundant to mention both: Pepsi means youth, Kodak means memories, Hummer means macho, Sony means games, iPod means music, Microsoft means computers, Google means knowledge, and Nike means sports.

Children once skipped rope, played house, hopped scotch, said Simon, sticked ball, and otherwise entertained themselves with more or less whatever the living environment conditioned by their imaginations could offer up. Today, play is commodity facilitated and consumer sponsored, a question of expensive gear, electronic video games, internet entertainment— all the right equipment regularly reengineered in new and improved versions that demand constant repurchase and have the potential to induce addiction. Youthful consumers get hooked on the gear and the peripherals if not the games.

Addiction itself is commodity based: no addiction therapy without web-based health sites and self-help books and novel medications aimed at depression or bipolarity or anorexia or the latest illness of the week that can be associated with addiction. To need and to shop become synonyms: "I Shop, Therefore I Am," wails April Lane Benson, editor of the self-consciously Cartesian takeoff subtitled "Compulsive Buying and the Search for Self."[52] Apple computers are thus being sold under the slogan "What G4 are you?" And even Porsche is blurring the boundaries between consumer choice and what sounds like addiction: "Suddenly the line between want and need seems so arbitrary" runs the tag line for Porsche's new Cayman S (a car also featured in the television series *The Sopranos*), followed by this afterthought: "Priorities give way to pure desire."

What this means is that for every discretionary want converted into a pure desire need, a dollar is somewhere earned; and for every need converted into an addiction identified, two dollars are earned over and over again—one for the addictive purchase and the second for the addiction treatment. The idea is a market economy that dominates every other human sector by making other sectors dependent on consumption for their enjoyment: recreational gear, workplace gear, arts gear, educational gear, even religious gear, define an all-encompassing marketplace. An iPod costs what an inexpensive guitar does, but the guitar is a one-time expense that can lead to a lifetime of music making, whereas the iPod is a one-time expenditure that can lead to a lifetime of shopping—iPod upgrades, music downloads, headset enhancements, and so on. Since consumerism aspires to a world in which people are consumers all the time, addiction is commerce-friendly. Addiction to consumer products, to gear and peripherals and to games and goods, is good, but addiction to consumerism itself—to shopping—is better.

Compulsive shopping is certainly more today than a rhetorical phrase or a tired shopper's joke. A Stanford University study reports that "up to 8 percent of Americans, 23.6 million people, suffer from compulsive shopping disorder," an affliction associated with "out-of-control spending" that "rips apart relationships and plunges consumers into overwhelming debt and bankruptcy."[53] Googling terms such as *shopping addiction* and *shopoholism* turns up hundreds of help sites, dozens of books (mostly of the self-help variety), and a growing medical literature that extends all the way to

Russia and China.[54] The figure of twenty-four million compulsive shop-pers in America suggests something approaching a pandemic. Except that in the medical lexicon of consumerism, the addict is not an aberration but a product of the marketing industry. Addiction is not a pathology in need of therapy, but an industry ambition calling for reinforcement. The infan-tilist ethos is itself at least in some part an ethos of addiction, and the twenty-four-million-strong American compulsive shopping vanguard suggests that the ambition has succeeded, not just metaphorically but clinically.

The Illinois-based Proctor Hospital runs an addiction recovery pro-gram (the Illinois Institute for Addiction Recovery) that, among more tra-ditional varieties of addiction such as drug dependency and alcoholism, for example, also treats compulsive shopping. "Compulsive shopping or spending," the IIAR at Proctor counsels on its website, "may result in interpersonal, occupational, family and financial problems in one's life. In many ways the consequences of this behavior are similar to that of any other addiction. Impairment in relationships may occur as a result of excessive spending and efforts to cover up debt or purchases. Persons who engage in compulsive shopping or spending may become pre-occupied with that behavior and spend less and less time with important people in their lives. They may experience anxiety or depression as a result of the spending or shopping which may interfere with work or school perform-ance."[55] This is a lucid definition of how a totalizing consumer economy can come to dominate consciousness.

Most therapy programs naturally treat shopping addiction as a psycho-logical illness. The IIAR Proctor Hospital is unusual in that it acknowl-edges there are "social and cultural factors" at work that "tend to increase the addictive potential of shopping and spending," which include the "easy availability of credit and the material focus of society in general." These factors "encourage people to accumulate possessions now and worry about financial responsibility later." Highlighting the branded iden-tity theme raised in earlier chapters of this book, the IIAR also notes that "society places a strong emphasis on one's outer appearance and many media personalities promote spending money to achieve a certain look that will bring about happiness." The IIAR at Proctor website also cites on-line shopping and cable shopping shows which allow items to be "pur-chased and ordered by express delivery to arrive quickly without the buyer having to leave home or personally interact with anyone else."

Other web-based therapy groups (Prioryhealthcare.com, Medscape's WebMD.com, and HypnosisDownloads.com, for example) also see shop-ping addiction as psychological. Thus, the Yahoo! Health website for shop-ping addiction offers a typical self-help support group rooted in webchat that eschews any discussion of the culture of commerce. An indication of the daunting challenge of distinguishing addiction from normal shopping behavior, even to well-meaning health groups like the one on Yahoo!, is the site's "note" reminding visitors that "this group is NOT for people who like to shop and want to chat about purchases, this is for people who have a problem."[56] Perhaps the difference is not so obvious. Robert D. Manning, a serious and scholarly critic of the place of credit in the United States, has even suggested that dependency on credit has itself become addictive, as is evident from the subtitle of his book *Credit Card Nation: The Consequences of America's Addiction to Credit.*[57]

If the web is a source of therapy, it also creates its own addictive pathol-ogy. In Redmond, Washington, the home of Microsoft, a company called Internet/Computer Addiction Services "is a pioneer in a growing niche in mental health care and addiction recovery."[58] Skeptics may believe that "obsessive Internet use does not exact the same toll on health or family life as conventionally recognized addictions." However, there are mental health professionals who "support the diagnosis of Internet addiction" and who argue that "a majority of obsessive users are online to further addictions to gambling or pornography or have become much more dependent on those vices because of their prevalence on the Internet."[59]

Addiction is not just an American phenomenon, a by-product of Amer-ican hyperbole and the American penchant for medicalizing cultural prob-lems and dealing with them through self-help programs. In the United Kingdom, the website www.addictions.co.uk cites a 1998 Mintel market-ing study that reports "almost one in four Britons admits being addicted to shopping," with "twice as many women as men" saying that they "frequently set off on a shopping expedition even though they had nothing specific in mind to buy."[60] This help site says shopping addiction is more than just a kind of "retail therapy" in which people treat other disorders and "unpleasant realities" with the buzz that shopping can bring. Real shopping addiction, however, results in an "overwhelming sense of shame, remorse and guilt accompanied by feelings of hopelessness and helplessness," and leads not only "to despair" but often to still "more addictive behaviour resulting in more self destructive feelings." These in turn generate "high levels of debt, fear of discovery and retribution leading to more denial and desperate acts to cover up the behaviour. For those closely connected to the sufferer life becomes frightening and unpredictable with a growing sense of uselessness and the belief that the sufferer is deliberately causing chaos and a feeling of desperation sets in."[61]

In Russia, which has shivered through a fifteen-year consumer capitalism cold shower (all consumerism all the time), and has established little in the way of mitigating democracy, shopoholism has also become a well-publicized problem. An essay in the Russian on-line magazine *Pravda* reports that shopping addiction is a "mental and spiritual disorder" that is now common "mostly with women," one that has recently "been shaping up as an epidemic." The piece cites "researchers" who include the psychologist Nadezhda Yugrina who have "found out that about twenty percent of German women acknowledge their insuperable desire to buy something all the time." The piece offers undocumented claims suggesting that "the addiction has conquered 40 percent of American women, whereas 52 percent of British females said they found shopping a lot more enjoyable than sex." The author is more prudent about Russia itself, writing that "there is no such statistic data as far as Russian women are concerned, although the passion for shopping has been developing in Russia steadily."[62]

Unsurprisingly then, shopping addiction appears to be as global as shopping itself. For while it is widely recognized as a pathology of advanced market society, it may be that it is in fact simply market society itself writ large, the perfect image of its defining ethos, hiding behind a rather flimsy screen of self-deprecation (to the degree "addiction" still counts as a pejorative). The infantilizing aspects of shopoholism seem clear enough. Therapists report that they are "seeing a growing number of teenagers and young adults as patients, who grew up spending hours on the computer, playing games and sending instant messages. These patients appear to have significant developmental problems, including attention deficit disorder and a lack of social skills."[63]

Addiction to video games and to on-line multiplayer games is not only growing, but is an implicit goal of game manufacturers. I earlier referenced Sony and LucasArts' on-line game Star Wars Galaxies, citing reports that changes in format and rules had led to a kind of "virtual despair" among the virtual players affected. The other part of this story is that the controversial changes were made expressly in order to dumb down a game thought to be too complex and text-based for younger players. Nancy MacIntyre, then LucasArts' senior game director, complained about the original game that "there was lots of reading, much too much, in the game. There was lots of wandering around learning about different abilities. . . . We wanted more instant gratification: kill, get treasure, repeat."[64] A perfect recipe for dumbing down consumers and underwriting addiction: kill, get treasure, repeat. Kill, get treasure, repeat. Instant gratification that is ever less gratifying, and that enjoins repetition that is both endless and joyless, as well as murderous and addictive.

Students of addiction agree that addicts can often be "multiaddicted," say to alcohol or drugs as well as to shopping. Thus, shopoholics are often addicted not only to shopping generically, but to the media that facilitate or manifest the fruits of their shopping and that are the primary venues for the commercial ethos of infantilization—video games, television shopping networks, and the internet itself (as well as pornography on the internet). *New York Times* reporter Sarah Kershaw has attributed to unnamed specialists the "estimate that 6 to 10 percent of the approximately 189 million Internet users in this country have a dependency that can be as destructive as alcoholism and drug addiction." The problem has purportedly created "a growing niche in mental health care and addiction recovery" under the diagnostic rubric "Internet addiction disorder."[65]

Therapists query fifteen or more discrete symptoms for the disorder, while firms advertising therapies offer twelve-step programs designed specifically to treat it. At places such as the Sierra Tucson psychiatric hospital in Arizona, the Center for Online Addiction in Bradford, Pennsylvania, and the Illinois Institute for Addiction Recovery at Proctor Hospital in Peoria, Illinois, computer addicts mix in with more traditional populations of cocaine and alcohol abusers. McLean Hospital in Belmont, Massachusetts, one of America's oldest and most distinguished residential treatment centers for mental illness, now has a Computer Addiction Study Center in conjunction with the clinic established there in 1996.[66]

On-line video games played in competition with others across the world (EverQuest, Doom 3, and World of Warcraft, as well as the Star Wars Galaxies game described above, for example) are apparently especially addictive—perhaps because in a game like World of Warcraft it can take up to six hundred hours of play just to rise up out of the game's first levels of play and become capable of slaying the more challenging demons and monsters whose demise players aspire to. An estimated 100 million people worldwide log on each month to interactive computer games, generating subscription revenues of $3.6 billion a year.[67] Time spent on-line, especially by the young, is increasing rapidly, thanks to the games' "persistent" ever-readiness to serve players. The 2005 Internet and American Life Project of Pew "found that teenagers did spend an increasing amount of time online: 51 percent of teenage Internet users are online daily, up from 42 percent in 2000," although the Pew study added that most teenagers "maintain robust networks of friends."[68] Internet addiction converges potently with pornography addiction, since pornography has traditionally always been potentially addictive, whatever its medium, and on the internet it is pervasive. Conjoined with a medium that offers its own addictive solitude, pornography is thus especially troublesome. Some estimate that up to one-third of all internet traffic is around pornography, and addiction here has been associated with the collapse of marriages, the loss of jobs, and self-destructive behavior including suicide.

At the treatment end of addiction, therapies are offered not only for addiction but for those whose addictions have led to crippling debt, for which groups such as Debtors Anonymous offer traditional "healing and health" twelve-step remedial programs.[69] Therapy can work as long as "'compulsive shopping and spending are defined as inappropriate, excessive, and out of control,' says Donald Black, M.D., professor of psychiatry at the University of Iowa College of Medicine. 'Like other addictions, it basically has to do with impulsiveness and lack of control over one's impulses.' "[70] In other words, the medical approach seems to argue, if we are confronted with a pathology of the individual, addictive spending can be treated. But what if we face a pathology of the culture itself? What if the consumer culture that generates a response to pathological compulsive disorders and the consequences they bring (indebtedness and bankruptcy) is itself organized around and even defined by the very pathologies its therapies affect to address? Is not addiction under such circumstances consumption-sustaining rather than shopper-pathological? To the extent that, in Dr. Black's own phrase, "shopping is embedded in our culture," the culture is unlikely to be able effectively to treat it. For the culture is directly complicit in breeding the pathologies that putatively threaten it. It *is* its pathologies, which cannot then be truly regarded as aberrational with respect to its ends. It is the culture itself that becomes aberrational.

Carolyn Wesson wants to help women who shop too much to overcome the "urge to splurge." And in her self-help tome for compulsive shoppers, Olivia Mellan hopes to offer a "winning plan for overspenders and their partners."[71] But if compulsive buying is really only the mirror image of consumer capitalism's compulsive selling, and if debt is less a disease of than a desirable condition for a profitable consumer economy, then authors like Wesson and Mellan, and institutions like Debtors Anonymous or the Illinois Institute for Addiction Recovery at Proctor, are unlikely to have much success—not until the infantilist ethos itself is brought under scrutiny. The *Pravda* article cited earlier calls it "an open secret that shopping addiction is common in the countries with stable economies" since "stable economies generate more shoppers." Behind this open secret is the dirty little not-so-hidden secret that the cultural ethos of consumerism mandates compulsive shopping to satisfy its need for compulsive selling.

SELF-REPLICATION

Addiction is an effective instrument of totalizing commercialism; so is self-replication, that capacity of market entities to reproduce themselves, both virally and in other ways, in the absence of public oversight and regulation. Global corporations that depend on franchising (fast food or coffee chains) aim first to establish a beachhead, then to dominate, in time to suffuse, and finally to monopolize the market in which they compete. A Starbucks wherever coffee is consumed, no rivals; a Café Einstein (once a unique Berlin coffee shop) reproduced as often as possible, across Berlin and then Germany; McDonald's wherever burgers (beef, lamb, tofu, no matter) are to be eaten in a hurry. When there was a single McDonald's in Beijing, variety was served: an alternative to Chinese cuisine had established an entrepreneurial, diversifying foothold. With ten McDonald's in the city, different neighborhoods could partake in the new variety. But with 100 outlets, now nearly 350 across China and still proliferating, diversity is diminished and franchise monopoly at the expense of pluralism becomes a growing danger. There may be natural market limits on franchising (some fast-food chains have, at least for the time being, hit a wall), but there are no natural limits on the ambition to franchise until every sandwich consumed anywhere in Beijing or China or Asia or the world is a quick-eat Big Mac.

Franchising not only aspires to a market monopoly (Coke leaves no room for Pepsi or, for that matter, for tea),[72] but produces homogenization and conformity. Fast food not only replicates itself through franchising, it encourages competitors in the food-service business to pursue fast food, leaving less and less room for rival "slow food" services. Consumer malls worldwide still offer all manner of fare from ethnically inflected fast-food chains such as Pizza Hut, Wendy's, Burger King, McDonald's, Domino's Pizza, KFC, Taco Bell, and Sbarro as well as the local Chinese and Thai chains, but finding an alternative to fast food (finger food served in a hurry to customers who stand in line to buy, and stand or perch on chairs to eat fast) in general is difficult. Traditional restaurants, barring the occasional sports bar, are rarely found in the big-box malls, since eating in such venues is meant to supplement shopping (a fuel stop) rather than borrow serious time from it. The point of fast food after all is its speed, not its recipes. The same is true for the sports shoes sector, where there is competition among brands, but little competition by alternative modes of footwear.

Nearly two-thirds of the shoes sold in the world today are sports shoes, so that there is less variety around the world than ever before. T-shirts and baseball caps as well as blue jeans and athletic shoes are sold under a number of competing (if monopoly-aspiring) global companies, but the overall result is an emerging global "youth uniform" that pinches dress tastes as effectively as MTV and VH1 constrict musical taste.

Commodification is the mode by which a consumer society reproduces itself, working overtime to create uniform monopolies of taste and behavior. To commodify an object is to transform multiple meanings into a singular market meaning, namely the potential of a good or service to be bought and sold. To commodify is thus to colonize, to impose singular meanings on multidimensional goods: "Things never before considered commodities—things that were free, unlimited, or beyond the pale of human commerce—have become commodities today," writes James Ridgeway. "The oceans are being commodified [oil drilling] . . . offshore fishing rights are being auctioned. . . . [T]he sky—the earth's inner and outer atmosphere—is fast becoming a commodity and sold in bits and pieces."[73] Commodification's process is progressive, and progressively corrupting to heterogeneity and the autonomy of other sectors. "Companies can participate in federal programs to buy and sell air pollution rights—in effect purchasing space in the atmosphere. . . . Now, parts of human bodies are commodities as well, from blood to eyes, kidneys, and hair. . . . [E]fforts are being made to commodify not only living things, but . . . life itself, with biotech companies making ownership claims to genetically engineered life forms."[74]

The new electronic and digital technologies permit the ongoing commodification of communication and of knowledge itself. The vehicles that carry knowledge and entertainment and the "pipes" through which communication must pass are themselves commodified goods. The image is free, but the pixels by which it is reconstructed and transmitted are commodities that must be purchased. Thoughts are autonomous—*"Die Gedanken sind frei"* proclaimed the old German student drinking (freedom) song—but when packaged, reproduced, and marketed they are but one more kind of commodity. The internet is a particularly powerful reproducer of consumerism because of its technical capacity to reproduce digital information, and both spread and preserve such information permanently. Try to "erase" an email and its many ghostly shadows or eradicate all traces of a website visit on your computer, and it becomes clear that decommodification and decolonization are far more daunting than the colonizing processes to which they respond.

The computer virus is a useful metaphor for at least one powerful characteristic of commodification: the way in which it not only puts its character at the center, but removes characteristics and identities that were in place prior to infection. Like those multiplying pop ads that efface other underlying images on your computer screen, commodified goods dominate our landscape. Like a virus that may reproduce what is a quite innocent message over and over again until it erases all other message content, and become something other than innocent, commodification works to transform many kinds of goods and services into saleable commodities whose core meaning is their consumability—they can be bought for a price. Marcuse tried to capture the meaning of commodities in the cultural sector this way: "If mass communications blend together harmoniously, and often unnoticeably, art, politics, religion, and philosophy with commercials, they bring these realms of culture to their common denominator—the commodity form." Like a cancer, commodification does not so much kill as crowd out other meanings and values, so that "exchange value, not truth value [or any other kind] counts."[75] What is the tumor but the single mutating cell run amok, reproducing itself over and over again, oblivious to what it may be destroying on the way to a successful reproduction? Television takes over our entertainment sector, crowding out theater and movies. The internet and broadband crowd out television. "Normal" use becomes abnormal, and then obsessive and finally addictive. All the while, consumer capitalism triumphs, seemingly a benign engine of the market sector. Yet its endless capacity for self-replication ultimately destroys alternative sectors and thus erodes variety.[76]

OMNILEGITIMACY[77]

I have wrestled with the terms *totalitarian* and *totalizing* because they are freighted with history's heaviest baggage. Yet the more straightforward terms I have used to depict consumer totalism—*ubiquity, omnipresence, addiction*, and *viral self-replication*—suggest a reality that is perilous enough. What the infantilist ethos succeeds in doing is to rationalize and justify these terms, turning them into acceptable conditions for consumer capitalism's flourishing. Commerce everywhere and all the time enhances our freedom! Addiction is merely a sign of how fervently we want something to which, after all, we surely have a right! Franchising and self-replication manifest and prove the success of a product.

The real purpose of an ethos now becomes apparent: to legitimate the structural features and behaviors capitalism depends upon that might otherwise be thwarted or rejected, if other value systems were pursued (religious, political, civic, artistic). To be compelling, a market society that boasts a theory of pluralism must in practice either obscure its bottom-up forms of coercion or try to legitimate the actual absence of diversity. Legitimation, to lean again on Horkheimer and Adorno's more abstract formulation, often takes the form of a "circle of manipulation and retroactive need in which the unity of the system grows ever stronger."[78]

The ubiquity of commerce must be made to seem a good thing, a widening of our realm of discretion. Addiction must be renamed, authorized, made to seem benign—associated with "need satisfaction," for example. Homogeneity must be reformulated—as healthy value consensus, for example. A cultural ethos that successfully places consuming at its core and shuts out rival spheres must seem to be justified in doing so—and not just in purely economic or instrumental terms. It must be "OK," as the fatuous title of an earlier rationalization of a certain kind of commercial ethos put it: "I'm OK, You're OK."[79]

This is of course precisely the goal of marketing: to impose an omnilegitimacy of good feeling and appropriate sentiment not only on the products and brands it services, but on the marketing process by which it achieves its goal. Marketing itself needs branded legitimacy, the legitimacy of branding, to succeed. The logic described in chapter 5, where loyalty and love are attributed to goods and services in order to endow mere material products with the virtues of a higher spirit, becomes a legitimizing logic when applied to marketing itself and to the consumer culture marketing rationalizes.

When Marcuse wrote about one-dimensional men, he was getting at the character of a society that constrained freedom through "voluntary compliance," where an economic order could prevail in "the absence of terror" courtesy of a "pre-established harmony between individual needs and socially-required desires, goals, and aspirations."[80] And when he identified "today's novel feature" as "the flattening out of the antagonism between culture and social reality through the obliteration of the oppositional, alien, and transcendent elements in the higher culture," he was portraying the workings of a cultural ethos which does not so much reject oppositional values as work toward "their wholesale incorporation into the established order, through their reproduction and display on a massive scale."[81] Marcuse's analysis, preoccupied with libido, explained the Mao jackets which, at the height of the anti-Western cultural revolution in China, became fashion accessories in the couture houses of Paris and Rome; it made sense out of the Che Guevara and Black Panther radical chic that fascinated up-market matrons in Beverly Hills and Manhattan's East Side, matrons whose fortunes successful revolution would obviously obliterate.[82]

Thirty to forty years later, the cultural ethos treats with oppositional values (whether aesthetic, religious, moral, or civic), by turning them into play; and by turning adults into grasping children with aggressively trivialized tastes. Holding market culture together through branded wants and manufactured desires allows consumer marketing to separate us from one another through privatization even as its forges a faux commonality and consensus through common branding. The passive, quasi-addicted children who emerge as archetypical consumers are less one-dimensional

than no-dimensional, because such identity as they possess is entirely heteronomous, a product of what is bought, eaten, worn, and imbibed. This
is not really identity at all, but merely a coat worn to cover nakedness. I am
my Mercedes. I am my Apple. I am my Big Mac. I am my Nikes. I am my
MTV. We are our cars, we are our computers, we are what we eat and
wear and watch. The end effect of the ethos is the eradication of significant differences among consumers, people who inasmuch as they are consumers are clones.

Diversity? Sure, says the market, "whatever." As the hold of consumerism grows, what Horkheimer and Adorno used to call "mass culture" becomes even less diverse. "Under monopoly all mass culture is
identical," they wrote long ago, "and the lines of its artificial framework
begin to show through. The people at the top are no longer so interested
in concealing monopoly: as its violence becomes more open, so its power
grows. Movies and radio need no longer pretend to be art. The truth that
they are just business is made into an ideology in order to justify the rub-
bish they deliberately produce. They call themselves industries."[83] Marx-
ism has long since gone under as a socioeconomic system and (for most
people) even as a critical perspective. But Horkheimer and Adorno were
less Marxists than they were astute sociologists portraying mass culture.
Non-Marxists and anti-Marxists reached their conclusions by different
roads.

Cultural critic Neil Postman contrasts George Orwell and Aldous Huxley on the way to trying to depict the real danger of the kind of mass conformity manufactured by the culture industries: "No Big Brother is
required to deprive people of their autonomy, maturity and history. As
[Aldous Huxley] saw it, people will come to adore the technologies that
undo their capacities to think. What Orwell feared were those who would
ban books. What Huxley feared was that there would be no reason to ban
a book, for there would be no one who wanted to read one."[84] The infantilist ethos generates nightmares more attuned to Huxley than to Orwell:
"Orwell feared those who would deprive us of information. Huxley feared
those who would give us so much that we would be reduced to passivity
and egoism. Orwell feared that the truth would be concealed from us.

Huxley feared the truth would be drowned in a sea of irrelevance."[85]

Fortunately, we are not yet fully propelled into Huxley's nightmare. Other powerful forms of identity continue to rival consumer identity. Unfortunately, many of those identities arise out of antimodern ascriptive identities drawn from religious fundamentalism and ethnic extremism, Jihadic identities of the kind that were the subject of my *Jihad vs. McWorld*. Totalization generates its own contraries, just as conformity spawns rebellion. Nonetheless, consumer capitalism in the grip of marketing continues to risk totalization and homogeneity. The question is whether it is possible to prevent the infantilist ethos from succeeding, to impede its course toward further totalism and privatization, to loosen the hold of marketing and branding on identity, to overcome the civic schizophrenia that has made it so difficult for constructive citizens to work together to overcome the destructive impulses of consumers when acting alone.

For those seeking resistance to totalism, conformity, and privatization, and trying to stimulate opposition to the infantilist ethos itself, it does not help that what were once the most important systemic alternatives to consumer capitalism have self-destructed. As real-world societies and as cultural paradigms, socialism, social democracy, communism, and anarchism have gained little historical traction. Although these paradigms, because they were wedded in theory to equality and justice, are cousins to liberalism, the practices they founded in revolutions, movements, and actual regimes were mostly disastrous. The revolutions ended in failure or tyranny, the movements and parties in hypocrisy and dictatorship, and the regimes in one-party, totalitarian dictatorships. These failures, above all the collapse of Soviet Communism, while good for those who had to live under them and better yet for the history of liberty, have been bad for capitalism in one crucial sense: in the absence of alternatives, capitalism's successes have bred triumphalism and eroded meaningful self-criticism. They have blinded neoliberals and liberals alike to the subtle perils inherent in markets and led them to try to remedy the vices of big government by attacking the virtues of the democratic public. The failure of communism has been mistaken for proof of capitalism's merit, even its invincibility.

Is resistance to the infantilist ethos possible? Are there significant forms of rebellion and opposition already in place despite the infantilist ethos? Can they be made effective? Is there a civic therapy that can treat the civic schizophrenia that afflicts liberty in market societies? The power of dialectic, opposites arising out of the very contradictions against which they rebel, suggests that there might be.

PART 3

THE FATE OF CITIZENS

7

Resisting Consumerism:
Can Capitalism Cure Itself?

Under certain circumstances [the marketplace] held out a
vision of transcendence, however fleeting.[1]

—Jackson Lears

C AN A BALANCE be restored between marketing and life? Is there
a way for capitalism to survive and yet still reconcile itself to a
culture of adults who do more than shop? To meet the real
needs of people who lack the resources to participate in market exchange?
Overthrowing capitalism has never been either a viable or a desirable
option—not at any stage in its long dialectical history (as communists and
Marxists learned from long, bitter experience). So today the challenge is
not capitalism per se but restoring the balance between capitalism and the
many other independent life worlds it once helped establish but now,
dependent on hyperconsumption, it threatens to destroy.

Strategies of ascetic withdrawal, although they have a considerable history, do not appear very effective. Traditional critiques of corrupt culture
often appealed to such strategies: some 1960s hippie dropouts and "down-
shifters" imitated nineteenth-century Quakers and Shakers, advocating
the establishment of utopian communities insulated from the larger society (some Fundamentalist home schoolers aspire to something of the sort

today). A hundred and fifty years ago, Henry David Thoreau sought the sanctuary of Walden Pond as a refuge from the rough materialism of his time. A century earlier, Jean-Jacques Rousseau had established a precedent for all critics of the corrupt modern by instructing readers of his educational novel *Émile* to "build a wall around your child's soul," while Rousseau lost himself in voluptuous intellectual reveries accessible only to the solitary walker (*Reveries of a Solitary Walker*). He was the original modern ascetic pursuing a simple formula: if happiness results from reducing the gap between our desires and the power we have to realize them, it makes more sense to reduce desire than to enhance power—a rationale, perhaps, that has made Buddhism so attractive to Westerners weary of competitive consumerism.[2]

Yet in a cultural ethos as totalizing and insistent as that of push consumer capitalism today, true physical withdrawal is hardly an option. Withdrawal to where? The family hearth is no longer a refuge in a world of virtual commerce where the tentacles of the digital octopus stretch out around the family gatekeepers and into the child's bedroom on computer and television screens. Nor are there any longer those "loci vacuii," or empty places, to which the seventeenth-century political theorist John Locke had suggested those who wished to opt out of a given society or social contract might repair. The once (for Westerners) "exotic" societies explored by Marco Polo now trod the Western path, if a decade or so off the pace. China and India have recently signed contracts with AOL, Google, and Microsoft, and (as pundits such as Thomas Friedman constantly remind us) are the new capitalist behemoths-to-be. Even the least developed parts of the world cannot save themselves from the global consumerism that perches on their doorsteps, awaiting only the abolition of that wrenching poverty which alone insulates them from its sure Midas-market touch.[3] Nor is asceticism ever going to be a successful option for more than a small minority in a society whose ethos is everywhere at war with austerity and self-control.

It might then seem that the ethos portrayed here embodies forces so powerful, so inescapable, so necessary to the survival of capitalism in its late consumerist phase, that they can no longer be resisted or transformed at all. That neither resistance nor withdrawal, neither rebellion nor subversion, neither asceticism nor pluralism, are possible; that we can do little other than acknowledge the ineluctability of infantilization and be content with throwing garlands of flowers over our smooth and comforting chains. In short, it may seem there is no alternative to rationalizing our new condition of consumer servitude as a gentler species of "private" freedom while democracy, commonwealth, and the liberty that is pluralism vanish over the receding historical horizon. This would mean that there are no viable alternatives to modern capitalism's only truly "successful" adversaries, those Jihadist reactionaries who would annihilate the market, and along with it democracy itself.

One of the greatest perils of failing to resist hyperconsumerism in a moderate and democratic way may in fact be how such a failure might privilege more violent, Jihadic, antimodern kinds of resistance that are deeply undemocratic. It is easy to respond to the radical critique offered by Al Qaeda ally Abu Musab al-Zarqawi (during the 2005 Iraqi elections) declaring "a bitter war against the principle of democracy and all those who seek to enact it" and writing off "those who vote" as "infidels."[4] Even within the United States, there are those who use the rejection of aggressive secular materialism to assail pluralism and the modern workings of the constitution. Although Catholic philosopher and polemicist Richard John Neuhaus speaks in the name of democracy against the denuding of the public square by secularist forces and against the "tyranny" of the judiciary over the views of a religious American majority, the notorious intemperance of his notorious *First Things* magazine symposium called "The End of Democracy?" represented a startling rejection of American pluralism in the supposed name of American democracy. It signaled what Damon Linker, himself the former editor of *First Things*, has described as a campaign in which "moral and theological absolutists demonize the country's political institutions and make nonnegotiable public demands under the threat of sacralized revolutionary violence" and "in which citizens flee from the inner obligations of freedom and long to subordinate themselves to ecclesiastical authority."[5]

Yet in the absence of democratic and pluralist critiques of consumerist materialism which is itself so corrosive to democratic diversity, absolutist and dogmatic religious critiques will seem to many people to offer the only road of resistance. I have related elsewhere the price of the struggle between those two equally undemocratic forms of modernity—McWorld and the violent struggle of Jihad to liquidate it—and will not revisit it here.[6] But it is crucial to recall that study's chief lesson: that unless capitalist consumerism and the homogenizing McWorld it produces can be democratically contained and modified, its challengers are likely to be zealots or nihilists with less sympathy for liberty and democracy by far than the aggressive materialists of consumer society who are infantilizing our global marketplace.

The self-correcting dialectics of history, however, may offer ways to respond to infantilization, privatization, and civic schizophrenia—ways that arise out of the very contours that define their logic. Like the forces that once created the Protestant ethos, those that today create the infantilist ethos have some potential to produce their own remedial strategies. Consumerism may have an autoimmune function that yields its own therapies. After all, even Jihad is to a significant degree the product of the modernizing commercial forces it challenges. To personalize this lesson, one might say I am less likely to find a way to remonstrate with consumerism than will my teenage daughter—who is a far more adept and avid consumer, and hence potentially a far more knowing and efficient resister. This is to suggest that while a Jihadic martyr, even if he succeeds in blowing up a mall today, will probably fail to contain consumerism tomorrow, but his brand-addicted son, if he can figure out and come to terms with his addiction, may actually manage to do so. If dialectic means anything, it means that consumers themselves harbor the secrets that can release them from consumerism.

If those who are consumed are to be instrumental in resisting consumption, however, they will in the long term still require large-scale social reenforcement to succeed. Changes will come from the inside out but also from the outside in, much as a successful therapy does. It will require action by reengaged citizens as well as by resisting consumers. The restoration of a healthy pluralism in which human values are multiple and material consumption but one in a cornucopia of human behaviors will in fact quite precisely require a social therapy that treats our defining civic schizophrenia—a civic therapy that restores the balance between private and public, giving our public civic selves renewed sovereignty over our private consumer selves and putting the fate of citizens ahead of the fate of markets. This involves both a restoration of capitalism to its primary role as an efficient and productive way of meeting real economic needs, from supply (or push) back to demand (or pull), and a restoration of the democratic public as the sovereign regulator of our plural life worlds—of which the marketplace is just one among equals. Before coming to this broader social strategy, however, there are important forms of resistance, subversion, and rebellion as well as of market skepticism and consumer consciousness worth exploring. For corporate marketing and hyper-consumerism have already generated significant real-world reactions that once elucidated can perhaps be reinforced. Their collective impact creates a foundation for the serious political and civic work that will also be required.

These dialectical reactions include three quite specifically cultural responses to consumerism that grow out of consumerism itself. I will discuss them under the rubrics *cultural creolization, cultural carnivalization,* and *culture jamming.* They also include two market-side responses that pursue public goods in private market ways, namely the twin strategies of *corporate citizenship* and *civic consumerism,* discussed in the final chapter. These are significant forms of resistance and subversion, the more so because they grow out of the pathologies they address and can be the imaginative products of consumers (often young consumers) and producers (often influential producers) who we think of as "caught up" in a cultural logic of consumerism which they may in fact be capable of subverting. George Soros, Bono, Bill and Melinda Gates, Jeff Skoll, George Clooney, Anita Roddick and many others like them are all primary producers of, and at the same time, are potentially courteous critics and inventive subverters of commercial culture and consumer capitalism.

Cultural Creolization

Consumerism has an aggressive, even totalizing face. It effectively colonizes the plural sectors that define culture's diversity, replacing them with a homogenized environment of marketing, advertising, and shopping—faux feelings and simulated sentiments—as well as common pop-cultural commodities that constrict cultural pluralism. Nonetheless, anthropologists have argued for some time that colonized cultures often react to being colonized by shaping the forces that affect to shape them in ways that alter the cultural aggressor and modify its supposedly "dominant" cultural face. This countercolonizing logic may apply within a culture that is trying to brand and homogenize taste. The process has been called creolization, or sometimes hybridization, and is evident in America's own cultural interaction with the postwar world beyond its shores.

Following World War II, even as the United States "Westernized" and democratized the vanquished Japanese Empire, Japanese culture infiltrated the occupiers. In the gently mocking Broadway comedy hit of an earlier era (subsequently a successful film) *Tea House of the August Moon*, a clever, seemingly obsequious Japanese houseboy, attached to a commanding reeducation officer in occupied Japan, uses his post to inflect with subversive Japanese elements and hence ultimately deflect the happy American ideology being inculcated. Even in defeat, Japan conditioned the American culture being imposed on it. By the 1980s, historians like Paul Kennedy were arguing that Japan was actually reacquiring its status as a dominant power, threatening to displace American hegemony,[7] although by that time Japan was itself being creolized by the America for which it was becoming a dominant automobile and technology supplier.

In a more recent film, *The Gods Must Be Crazy*, a Coke bottle falling from a passing airplane on a !Kung tribesman acquired new indigenous meanings through the ways in which the tribesman received, interpreted, and used it. Anthropologist David Howes suggests that this hybridization process is often invisible when "seen through the windows of the corporate boardroom situated on the twentieth floor of some glass office tower," from which perspective the world "may well look like 'a single place' and alterity [otherness] just another market opportunity."[8] Comprehended from the perspective of the anthropologist who acts as a kind of "marginal native," however, and observed from a "position on the border (looking both ways) rather than in the boardroom (looking up and down)," it becomes apparent that the reception of culture can be as important as the production of culture in how it looks and what finally it means. Commodities that aim at secularizing culture can instead be sacralized by those who receive them—as happens famously with so-called cargo cults[9] and as happened with the Coke bottle that dropped from the sky in *The Gods Must Be Crazy*. Even marketing slogans can be turned against themselves. When Pepsi translated its "universal" slogan "Come alive! You're in the Pepsi Generation" into Taiwanese, it became "Pepsi will bring your ancestors back from the dead," not exactly what Pepsi was looking for.

As Tyler Cowen has observed in his lively account of cultural consumption, culture itself is a moving target and apparent homogenization can conceal what in fact is mere mutability. To Cowen, all culture is fusion culture and no culture is pristinely indigenous, which certainly applies to consumer culture. Cowen thus shows that the "indigenous" music of Zaire, which is putatively under assault from a totalizing global music marketplace, is in reality itself a product (among other things) of the electric guitar, saxophone, trumpet, clarinet, and flute, "none of which are indigenous to Africa," but instead arrived in earlier decades along with Cuban and other foreign influences.[10] Likewise, Trinidad's steel bands, among its greatest "indigenous" tourist attractions but vulnerable according to native defenders to the global marketing inroads of MTV, actually were themselves a twentieth-century by-product of the colonial petroleum market that led in the late 1930s to the replacement of truly indigenous bamboo instruments by steel drums—newly "traditional"—cut from oil barrels. Similarly, those storied Navajo designs and colors, above all the deep red serape patterns with their serrated zigzag lines that distinguish "indigenous" Navajo blankets from all others, actually reflected designs borrowed from "the ponchos and clothing of Spanish shepherds in Mexico, which in turn drew upon Moorish influences in Spain."[11] In sum, as anthropologists such as David Howes, along with Constance Classen and Jean Comaroff,

have observed, culture is "constructed by consumption" as well as by production. Consequently, through the "creativity of consumption," dominant culture homogenization can be countercolonized and turned back
into cultural particularity. Constance Classen cites the surreal artist
Leonora Carrington's charming and ironic jest about how "in the Mexico
of the future one would find tins of Norwegian enchiladas from Japan and
bottles of the 'rare old Indian drink called Coca Cola.'"[12]

While the consumer market may then be inclined to branding and
homogenization, its interaction with the domains it brands and dominates
can also produce new forms of diversity. Seemingly diminished local cultures may actually reappear inside the dominant culture in ways that plu-
ralize it. The rebranded culture re-rebrands the original brand in turn. In
investing itself in every sector, commerce finds itself at least partially
decommercialized by the sectors it invades. Religion as televangelism is
commodified, but commodification is compelled to serve quasi-spiritual
ends and its radical commitment to materialist secularism is compromised. Hollywood had dumbed down the customers it entertains, but the
customers have caused Hollywood to smarten up by supporting efforts at
independent filmmaking that transgress the very conventions Hollywood
helped contrive (see "Reel Change" in chapter 8).

What starts out as one-way homogenization often becomes the two-
way street of hybridization in ways that can advantage diversity. If as
noted above the ubiquitous Nike logo is being stitched into the yarmulkes
of hip kids in New York City, yarmulke-wearing rockers in Jerusalem are
using their own rebranded hip music to win religious converts. Take, for
example, the popular ultraorthodox Jewish singer Gad Elbaz, a twenty-
something self-styled Sephardic "Hasid Rocker," who is a "world-class
hunk" and "Israel's first Haredi heartthrob" from a Hasidic background.
Studying Torah four hours a day, and happily married, Elbaz employs his
"balladeer's voice, hip two-day beard, and pious lyrics [as] a way to preserve Old World traditions in the age of Britney Spears."[13] "He gave me
the power to make you dance," Elbaz sings in "Tonight Is the Night,"
"Open your hearts, disengage from all. Believe in yourself, believe you are
mighty." Elbaz's style is a true example of creolization, drawing on "Arab

rhythms, hip-hop beats, the harmonies of the Backstreet Boys and the bal-
lads of Whitney Houston and Celine Dion," yet marketed with all of the
pop hype of a teenie-bopping gang banger.[14]

Better known and more widespread than Hasidic rock is Christian rock,
which has developed a broad and profitable Christian counterculture
through a rock hardcore (self-advertised "Christcore") Christian gospel
hybrid that has been enormously successful. Christian rock bands with
names like Stryper, Bride, Petra, and Guardian offer every variety of music,
"anything from Metal to Punk to Hardcore (Christcore) to Alternative
Rock" according to www.Christianrocklyrics.com. Wedding heartthrob
pop stars with pop-cultural styles that include (as the Christian rock band
Visual Cliff boasts) "a sonic mix of rock, metal & heavy fusion,"[15] and
Christian lyrics, often taken directly from scripture, these bands lure cool
kids from the cool marketplace to what the secular media often portrays
as a square religious counterculture but is in fact a hip Christian subculture. From magazines like *Contemporary Christian Music (CCM)*, *7 Ball Magazine*, and *Heaven's Metal* to websites like www.Christianmusic.com and
www.Christianrock.net, young people in search of a kind of hot religious
solace that does not ask them to surrender completely their marketplace
cool can find songs like "The Wait Is Over" (number one Christian song of
2005) by the group Disciple, sharing the good news (it takes from 2 Pet.
3:2–12) that "It's our time, the wait is over."

Like oppositional religion, oppositional politics borrowing from the
dominant culture has also invoked the power of rock music. In the 2002
Kenyan election, the opposition featured a rap song that mixed English and
Luo (one of many local languages) in which the Luo term *bwogo* ("scare")
was sung by a couple of twenty-somethings bent on proving they were
unshakable ("unbwogable") in their political commitment to democracy—
to a new regime to replace Daniel arap Moi's corrupt government.[16] Pop
opera composer superstar Sir Andrew Lloyd Webber has been known to
turn his skills to song writing for the Conservative Party in England. And,
also in England, a more virulent but equally effective oppositional borrowing of rock for political recruiting purposes among the young has been a
tactic of skinheads and neo-Nazis. The relationship between British skin-

heads and German neo-Naziis was forged in music in the 1970s and 1980s by Stuart Donaldson (Ian Stuart) and other market-savvy British ultra-rightists. Bands such as Skrewdriver and Skullhead in England, and Böhse Onkelz (Evil Uncles) and Endstufe (Final Steps) in Germany, along with marginal groups that explicitly borrowed their names from the German Wehrmacht such as Stuka (the World War II divebomber) and Sturmwehr (storm troop), drew young people into ultraright movements in England and Germany without pushing them out of pop culture, smart tactics directed toward malicious political ends.

As proof of the countercultural (and in this case antidemocratic) power of rock music cool, the German social historian Klaus Farin recalls that a "third-rate amateur rock band" with neo-Nazi proclivities called Storkraft was vaulted into the public eye in the 1980s because "practically every 14-year old in the country had to get an album by this 'ultra-hard' band if he didn't want to be totally uncool."[17] This was a kind of dialectical anti-marketing that put successful marketing practices to work by transferring the abstract "cool" that comes with heavily marketed mainstream rock music back to a specific political commodity that was anything but cool. The music said mainstream youth market, but the lyrics said down with the mainstream. If marketing could make cold commodities hot by associating them with faux sentiments, faux sentiments could make perverse politics cool. Böhse Onkelz's first album featured a song called "Stolz" ("Pride") that joined English skinhead culture to German ultranationalism: "One of many with a shaved head, / You don't hang back because you have no fear, / Shermans, Braces, Boots and Jeans, / German flag, because you're proud."[18] A later cut called "Türken raus!" ("Turks Out!" copying the Nazi slogan "Juden raus!" [Jews Out!] of the 1930s) by the same band joined neo-Nazism to antiforeign prejudices of the kind that have gained wide traction more recently in Europe—as was evident in the vote against the new European constitution in France and in Holland in 2005, for example. This kind of crude creolization, for all its vicious intent, suggests the possibilities of the countercultural uses of pop culture inside Western secular materialism.

Resisters on the outside utilize creolization strategies as well. Even the most aggressive brands such as Coca-Cola and McDonald's have undergone hybridization in the global marketplace as a result of anti-Western radicals hoping to use Western brands to undo Western hegemony. Mecca-Cola, a French-Islamic knockoff of Coke, has made a significant mark on the beverage market primarily in France and Islamic North Africa, while fast tandoori shops in London rival McDonald's in the Indian and Pakistani communities there.[19] "We can compete with the West and do colas and fast food without buying into American branding" seems to be the boast of those who manufacture hybrids such as the new Islamic Barbie doll ("Razanne," meaning "modest" in Arabic).

Yet these examples also suggest the limits of hybridization as a counterbranding tactic. In Asia, advocates of creolization will see in the "K-pop" (Korean pop) superstar "Rain" (Ji-Hoon Jung) an instance of a local talent attaching himself to but simultaneously indigenizing global music culture. Yet by the time this "Korean Justin Timberlake" and "Korean Usher" finished his adaptation to what he himself called the United States's "dominant music market" and brought his act to the Hollywood Bowl and Madison Square Garden in 2005/2006, the real question was whether Rain was really an indigenous Korean figure or one more assimilated global (read Western) rocker wearing local clothes.[20] Koreans insist he is part of—the personification of—"hallyu," Korea's campaign to provide an alternative regional brand for world pop-cultural products. However, his collaboration with American rap producer P. Diddy raises the question of whether he can preserve his Asian character or will simply become another of many Asian stars who have failed on the way to trying to conquer the American market. The same question can be asked of *Indian Idol*, the Asian television version of *American Idol*, which may posture as a creolization but seems little more than a crude knockoff.

Similar questions can be asked of the many attempts that have been made to glocalize and indigenize fast-food, cola, and coffeehouse companies, and thus to creolize the products that have defined McWorld. The case for creolization has often confounded specific products like burgers and fries, which can be customized and localized, with the essence that defines the products, which cannot. The fast-food brand is not about burgers and fries, it is about speed and consumerist atomization of what were once slow-food cultures. Fast food's toxic cultural impact comes from its speed—the fact that it is eaten on the run, corrupting eat-at-home family gatherings and long sit-down restaurant meals. It makes the social breaking of bread into what is in fact little more than a fuel pit stop for busy capitalist shoppers, whether what is being consumed is a burger, a taco, a tandoori chicken wing, or sushi to go. Fast tandoori avoids the McDonald's label but imbibes and spreads the McDonald's philosophy. Mecca-Cola may creolize Coke, but the Coca-Cola Company's aspirations are imperial and global and their intent is to undermine any indigenous culture that stands in the way of the spread of its product, and Mecca-Cola probably advances this agenda. Thus, in its 1992 corporate report, the Coca-Cola Company noted that Indian tea culture stands in the way of Coke's spread in India and must be treated accordingly.[21] Faux colas presumably undermine tea culture as effectively as the "real thing" manages to do.

A striking example of how a creolized brand can actually contribute to the cultural damage done by a dominant original it is trying to resist can be seen in the Starbucks-like Barista Coffee chain in India. By the end of 2004, Starbucks had opened 8,000 cafés worldwide, with more than 100 in China. It sees a potential of 30,000 cafés worldwide, with up to 5,000 in India alone over the next five years. The Barista chain, with over 130 cafés already operating in India (as of November 2004) can, on the one hand, presumably be deemed a competing local, capable of staving off the Starbucks invasion. On the other hand, Barista's cafés clearly mimic the ambiance and operating philosophy of Starbucks. They target young and well-heeled Indians and offer them, in the spirit of Starbucks, a "home away from home."[22] Whether or not Barista holds off Starbucks, Indian tea culture and the distinctiveness of its cultural rituals are unlikely to be enhanced by the spread of Starbucks-style coffeehouses, whatever their national provenance. With Starbucks or with Barista, Mumbai will become more rather than less like San Francisco or Berlin (where the Café Einstein coffeehouse chain is Starbucks's local rival).

It is this logic that explains why Korean pop star Rain may creolize

American pop music without preventing P. Diddy from Americanizing Korean "hallyu." Witness the case (cited in chapter 5) of McDonald's buying the Gallic comic-book figure Asterix, which has not really Frenchified the Big Mac but has rather concealed it inside a Gallic horse of indigenous comic-book mythology. Then there is the proposed mall projected as a portal to the famed carved stone terraces of the Borobudur Buddhist temple in central Java—the largest such temple in the world and a UNESCO World Heritage site. There, a local governor proposed a mall to be named "Java World"—a kind of Buddhist Disney World that sews a commercial skin onto a religious body. Opponents ignored claims that it would honor religion, understanding it to be a stalking horse for Western-style commercialism rather than a charming exemplar of hybridization.[23]

Such examples point to the greatest deficiency of the creolization argument: it simply ignores the relative *power* of the clashing cultures. Anthropologists and diversity-inclined apologists for capitalist marketing make the age-old laissez-faire assumption about "free exchange" within the mythic frame of prefect market competition where two equally free and equally potent interacting agents sit down and make a deal. We sell you our global market commodities and universal brands, you assimilate, transform, and creolize them, thereby generating new cultures of diversity that continue to reflect indigenous or fusion identities. Deal. You look more like us, we look more like you, and we both end up looking like someone else. Deal. You commercialize us, we decommercialize you. Deal. Yet once the relative economic and cultural power of the intersecting civilizations or in-country subcultures is factored in, the felicitous reciprocity of cultural hybridization is trumped by the infelicitous preeminence of the dominant culture. Indigenous film industries in Mexico, India, and Hong Kong may still be flourishing, and critically acclaimed "independent" films (even when studio produced) are grabbing attention, but the percentage of world screens devoted to American-made product, and the percentage of tickets sold within the United States to comic-book blockbusters that overshadow quality films, continues to grow in ways that make it hard to believe that Hollywood's global muscle is really good for cultural diversity within America or abroad.

Even those who see in Western consumerist materialism a deep affront to their own values and culture have failed the test of resistance, whether by creolization or other methods. Malaysian commentator Farish Noor writes that "Malaysia's Muslim youth, like youth the world over, are both helplessly mesmerized by the charm of global consumerism as well as woefully inadequate to put up any resistance to it whatsoever." Noor remarks that "While the Islamic elite and intelligentsia ponder the weighty questions of Islamic banking and Islamic education . . . , they seem to have abandoned the site of popular cultural discourse and have provided no alternative cultural paradigms whatsoever," making it difficult for youth to "break away from this state of dependency upon Western consumerist culture . . . by themselves." Noor depicts local attempts at preserving Malay culture against Western inroads as "cosmetic," things like decorating a global skyscraper with a traditional Malay facade with the "obligatory Moorish dome and shades of 'Islamic' green paint." But as Noor sees the reality: "Against the mighty weight of MTV and MacDonald's [sic], the Islamic elite have only been able to produce endless diatribes about the evils of Western culture and lifestyle without offering something else in its place."[24]

Noor's insights suggest that when anthropologists and apologists for the dominant culture start talking about market hybridization, one may want to ponder the sorts of "free exchanges" negotiated by pythons and hares. "Oh, yes," exclaim the preening relatives of the hare, "it may seem that our cousin has been consumed, but regard the distended snake, its shape ever so much more like a hare's than a python's. Truth is, the hare has changed the snake as much as the snake has changed the hare!" But wait a week or two, as the python's relatives will learn, and the hare will have vanished and the serpent, happily hissing about the virtues of hybridization as he goes, will slither on in search of new prey.

Cultural exchange may be a form of Schumpeter's "creative destruction," but over time dialectic is trumped by power, and destruction merely destroys, leaving behind an ever more homogenized, monocultural marketplace. Creolization does not create very much: it may sometimes slow the pace of homogenization, but it cannot arrest it altogether. For every Christian rocker who thinks she can use pop music to displace pop cul-

ture's secularism with religion conversions, there is a Christian skeptic
who worries (with considerable reason) that being cool will always mean
being "flippant, irreverent, quick with biting one-liners that exalt self and
embarrass others"; and that far from being designed by hip Christians hoping to strengthen spiritual resolve, "Christian rock was the invention of
big, profit-motivated record companies who were looking for a way of
selling more rock music. By offering a Christianized form, they sold it to
children whose parents would otherwise object."[25] It may seem an odd
source to cite in looking for support of the arguments about the real character of liberty offered above, but the insight from *The Moorings* website
that the devil "and his spokesmen in the media promise you freedom, but
in truth they want to put you in bondage" rings of truth; as does the claim
that "the entertainment industry wants to make you a mindless, helpless,
addicted consumer of their products." Some Christian resisters skeptical
of consumer culture seem to know that creolization may involve what,
borrowing their language, is a devil's bargain at best. This is an insight secular resisters should take seriously.

Cultural Carnivalization

Yet what if the progress of infantilizing consumerism is itself a beneficent
rather than a destructive process, the liberation of consumers from
Weber's cage rather than their incarceration in it? What if, even when it
dominates public space, the mall is a happy, even civic place and shopping
a benign, even invigorating pastime? What if consumerism's defining
industries, marketing and advertising, are less an establishment bulwark
than a theater of rebellion and ongoing change? What if the very puerility
with which critiques like mine charge the modern ethos is actually its saving virtue—an attachment to the playful child that softens the hardening
of capitalism's arteries and makes youthfulness a genuine virtue? Perhaps
consumerism can resist its own petrification by calling on its inherently
playful character and drawing on the sentiments of its inherently carnivalesque heart. In this case, the point would be to recognize and celebrate
consumerism's truly liberating nature.

The surprisingly widespread response that embraces this view among modern cultural critics, including several prominent architects and designers, can be summed up under the term cultural *carnivalization*. The word is borrowed from pagan celebrations of the Middle Ages associated with village fairs that were thought to play a liberating, even transgressive role with respect to established Christian value hierarchies and entrenched feudal political authority. In the rhetoric of philosophers such as Mikhail Bakhtin, carnivalization is borrowed to identify modern forms of inversion, resistance, and transgression in speech and action.[26] Celebrating "temporary liberation from prevailing truth of the established order, it marks the suspension of hierarchical rank, privileges, norms and prohibitions."[27] To cultural historian Jackson Lears, market exchange has long been "associated with a carnival atmosphere, with fantastic and sensuous experience, perhaps even with the possibility of an almost magical self-transformation through the purchase of exotic artifacts in a fluid, anonymous social setting. . . . Under certain circumstances [the marketplace] held out a vision of transcendence, however fleeting."[28]

The trajectory of carnivalization tracks the course of capitalism's evolving ethos. Protestantism acted as a constraining ethos that repressed medieval play in the name of the kinds of self-denial and hard work required by productivist capitalism. Consumer capitalism in the nineteenth century (and especially, according to Lears, advertising in the nineteenth century) once again encouraged such playfulness and eroticism in keeping with the requirements of a new consumerist culture.[29] While capitalism in its more recent incarnation has also concerned itself with control and discipline, carnivalization has persisted as a subtext, reappearing in the playfulness of theme parks and malls, in the mischievous dislocations of urban architecture (think Gehry), in the radicalism of inventive advertising, and in the obsession with youthful spontaneity and rebellion—all serving the new consumerism and giving it an allegedly radical spin. The infantilist ethos contains the core of its own transgression, although the transgression is assimilated so that it serves commercial interests even as it achieves a certain psychic liberation. Cultural critic John Fiske thus reads in mass-produced culture's exploitative oppression "oppositional cultural practices" that make possible "rebellion"—concessions he thinks mass cultural consumption makes to "the carnvialesque" to "evasion" and to "jouissance" as tools by which those the culture aspires to dominate can in fact liberate themselves.[30]

The clown Ronald McDonald is both an apt symbol and a stealth subverter of McDonald's corporate image. A recent television campaign thus used him as a prop in what were clearly intended as ironic ads playing with his juvenile image. Modern consumerism is a kind of carnival, above all for the young who are both its targets and its agents. It sells itself by mocking itself, making fun of products to consumers who no longer take themselves or their tastes seriously. John Kenneth Galbraith once wrote morosely, "We quite literally advertise our commitment to immaturity, mendacity and profound gullibility."[31] Yet James Twitchell, who cites Galbraith, insists that the spirit of carnival consumerism is not involuntary or coerced: "We have not been led into this world of material closeness against our better judgment. For many of us, especially when young, consumerism *is* our better judgment."[32] For Twitchell, it is a "self-evident truth about human nature" that we "like having stuff," so that "getting and spending" has become "the most passionate, and often the most imaginative, endeavor of modern life."[33] Critics—presumably critics like me—will find this "dreary and depressing" (I do), but "it is liberating and democratic to many more."[34] Although Thomas Frank is hardly a friend of mass consumer culture, he is at pains in his *The Conquest of Cool* to show that the 1960s spirit of carnival and rebellion that infected the countercultural "hippie" revolt against business actually infected an important element in the business community itself, including the advertising sector, so crucial to marketing. "Like the young insurgents," Frank argues,

> people in more advanced reaches of the American corporate world deplored conformity, distrusted routine, and encouraged resistance to established power. They welcomed the youth-led cultural revolution not because they were secretly planning to subvert it or even because they believed it would allow them to tap a gigantic youth market, but because they perceive in it a comrade in their own struggles to revitalize American business. . . . If American capitalism can

be said to have spent the 1950s dealing in conformity and consumer fakers, during the decade that followed, it would offer the public authenticity, individuality, difference, and rebellion.[35]

More than just liberating, the carnival spirit of capitalism is vaunted as democratizing as well. For desire itself had been democratized in the founding era of modern capitalist society through the philosophy of empiricism (all our knowledge derives exclusively for sensory experience) and an affiliated associational psychology (our minds are blank slates on which experience writes its history). This philosophy and psychology, associated with early social contract theory, postulated that women and men were mutable creatures subject to desire and aversion, interest and sentiment, in a way that made them all more or less identical—commensurable with one another—and hence equal. As measured by what they thought, imagined, and created, people may be said to differ. Hierarchies like those of Plato or Nietzsche began with this premise of inequality. But in the new empirical philosophy, desires were all commensurable. When the market emerged as the primary life world of modern women and men, it was easy enough, as William Leach has written, to see how "the democratization of desire emerged alongside the cult of the new and the unfolding of the consumer paradise."[36]

Architecture and design have been apt theaters of the carnivalization thesis. Architects such as Robert Venturi and Rem Koolhaas look with a fresh eye at consumer environments and invoke a spirit of democratic liberation in celebrating what to others may look like little more than theme-park vulgarity and tawdry mall commercialism. Relax, have a little fun! Transferred to New York's Times Square or Las Vegas, or even to "the traditional European city (which) once tried to resist shopping, but is now a vehicle for American-style consumerism,"[37] one can see how the shoppers' fun palace might indeed be likened to the medieval carnival. Although I have insisted shopping is the archetypical *private* activity, in his Harvard Project on the City Rem Koolhaas sees it rather differently. In manifesto-style prose, he claims shopping is "arguably the last remaining form of public activity." For it has been able

to colonize—even replace—almost every aspect of urban life. Historical town centers, suburbs, streets, and now train stations, museums,
hospitals, schools. The internet, and even the military, are increasingly shaped by the mechanisms and spaces of shopping. Churches
are mimicking shopping malls to attract followers. Airports have
become wildly profitable converting travelers into consumers.
Museums are turning to shopping to survive. . . . Ailing cities are
revitalized by being planned more like malls.[38]

Koolhaas is of course less a disinterested observer than an activist welcom-
ing a trend that has helped define his architectural and design projects. His
perspective reflects a reveling in consumerism and its taste cultures—
whether of a suburban or theme-park nature—that has been widely recognized, even by critics such as Gary Cross. Although Cross is no fan of
malls, he understands how effective the Mall of America (in Minnesota)
has been with its "themed" clubs and its "shoppertainment" and "enter-
tailing" approach to consumption. "The Mall of America combined shopping, entertainment, and a pleasant, unthreatening crowd experience," he
observes, so that "shopping had become leisure, even a vacation."[39]

Even Los Angeles, the city of angels dreaming wicked dreams—written
off by Adorno and Horkheimer (who wrote *Dialectic of Enlightenment*
there during World War II) as an "anti-city" that was a dispiriting "crystal
ball of capitalism's future"—remains a city of "fleshpots and enchant-
ments."[40] While it repelled many of the German cultural critics who spent
their war years there, it seduced others like Herbert Marcuse, who found
in southern California (to which he came in the 1960s from his post at
Brandeis University in Boston) a hothouse of political subversion and cultural transgression. He half hoped he would find in West Coast soul music
and jazz, or in the politics of subversives like Communist Angela Davis
and the Black Panthers, a response to the homogenizing culture of *One-
Dimensional Man*. Jean Baudrillard, stern critic of capitalist philistinism,
was likewise said to have found "perverse exhilaration" in Hollywood's
Hieronymous Bosch inferno.[41] Certainly Los Angeles knew how to
mythologize itself as a celluloid carnival imitating a real-life circus which,

if indeed it predicted capitalism's future, suggested that the future encompassed a consumer counterculture "that would reject the values of the dominant society" and attune itself instead to "the most important signifiers of late modern youth . . . the various bikers, heavy metal, hip hop, grunge, punks, goths and ravers."[42] For according to Bakhtin scholars Laura Langman and Katie Cangemi, "While these groups differ from each other, they share certain crucial features, they embody and celebrate the carnivalization of everyday life. These liminal anti-structures privilege privatized hedonistic indulgence to provide their members with meaningful, gratifying identities and interactions."[43]

No one has welcomed the carnivalesque interpretation more than James B. Twitchell, whose title *Carnival Culture: The Trashing of Taste in America* (1992) established his ironically self-mocking position. In a more recent publication, he goes to the heart of the case: "The usual academic critic," he writes disdainfully, "sees the consumer as a dumb ox. The producer is the scheming farmer who forces the ox to both plow furrows and then consume the mediocre harvest of its labor. . . . I on the other hand, see the consumer as the wily fox leading the flabby squire on one wild chase after the other."[44] Embracing the marketing narrative about consumer empowerment, Twitchell associates his celebration of consumerism with a rejection of arguments about fabricated or manufactured needs or compelled materialism. "There are no false needs," he vouches. "Once we are fed, clothed, and sexually functioning, needs are cultural . . . if anything, we are not materialistic enough."[45]

I have already cited Gary Cross as an opponent of the "all-consuming century" he excoriates so judiciously, as well as a political critic who believes that consumerism has fundamentally undermined democracy. Nonetheless he recognizes that "no one has found a more effective way than consumerism to help individuals face change and uncertainty."[46] He accepts not only that "consumption often eased, rather than worsened, social tensions,"[47] but that with the introduction of credit cards it "both eased and democratized consumer credit."[48] Even name brands, he suggests, "did more than create dominant companies. They also served to democratize American life at a time when social differences were extreme."[49] Cross notes that in 1939, the Advertising Federation of America called advertising "the mouthpiece of free enterprise" and accused its opponents of wanting collectivism and tyranny.

It has been more than a mouthpiece for America, however. It has also been a poster boy for subversion. Its self-styled role as the carnivalesque bad boy of American consumer capitalism, even as it exercises an appetite for capitalist control over consumption, has been compellingly portrayed by cultural historian Jackson Lears.[50] To Lears, "advertising preserved that fitful promise [of the carnivalesque] down to the twentieth century." For "advertisements themselves became a carnival of exotic imagery," even though pleasure also was being "subordinated to a larger agenda of personal efficiency."[51] In Lears's exquisite portrait, "words like magic and carnival acquire an almost talismanic significance . . . as recurring counterpoints to managerial values." Since "the stimulation of fantasy was central to the expansion of the consumer market," advertising indulged in a kind of sensationalism that "democratized the cult of sensibility and helped reorganize consumption patterns, directing attention from the satisfactions of actual possession to the excitement of anticipated purchase." With an oblique "celebration of the flesh,"[52] advertising indulged the "desire for a magical transfiguration of the self . . . a key element in the continuing vitality of the carnivalesque advertising tradition."[53] This potent tradition led department-store owners "to surround their wares with an aura of oriental exoticism: some goods retained the magical charge of the early modern market fair. P. T. Barnum was the impresario of this world, entrepreneurial advertising its lingua franca. In many ways this world resembled the Rabelaisian realm of Carnival described and imagined by Bakhtin," where we can imagine that the healthy sides of childhood—its playfulness, spontaneity, and innocence—are preserved.[54]

There is then a good deal to be said for consumerism's dialectical capacity to generate transgressive cultures of pleasure, eroticism, and just plain fun which, if employed in the spirit of liberation, may transform puerility into an instrument of diversity and liberation. A society devoted to play may indeed nurture playfulness. To acknowledge this does not require that we reduce the modern celebration of consumerism as a good thing to the self-parodying proportions of Steven Johnson's panglossian tract *Every-thing Bad Is Good for You*. In pandering to infantilization with a booster's passion, Johnson insists that mass culture is "a kind of positive brain-washing" and that we should take seriously Woody Allen's joke in his early sci-fi satire *Sleeper* "where a team of scientists from 2173 are astounded that 20th century society failed to grasp the nutritional merits of cream pies and hot fudge." While Johnson does not quite endorse the nutritional merits of cream pies, he must revel in the recent studies suggesting choco-late is good for us (after all), and he obviously grasps what Howard Stern teaches so well: that shock/shlock sells only if it feels subversive and hence progressive. "Where most commentators assume a race to the bottom and a dumbing down—'an increasingly infantilized society,' in George Will's words," Johnson enthuses, "I see a progressive story: mass culture growing more sophisticated, demanding more cognitive engagement with each passing year."[55] Johnson sets himself squarely against the kind of cultural criticism implied by the idea of an "infantilist" ethos that pur-portedly spurns nuance and complexity. Consumerism's "cultural race to the bottom is a myth; we do not live in a fallen state of cheap pleasures that pale beside the intellectual riches of yesterday. And we are not innate slackers, drawn inexorably to the least offensive and least complicated entertainment available. All around us the world of mass entertainment grows more demanding and sophisticated, and our brains happily gravi-tate to that newfound complexity. . . . Dumbing down is not the natural state of popular culture over time—quite the opposite."[56]

These passages, like George Gilder's misplaced enthusiasm for Protes-tant virtues no longer needed or wanted by consumer capitalism, point to the chief danger that also faces the more judicious and interesting propo-nents of the carnivalization thesis: call it slumming. The romanticization and glamorization of consumer culture may be a diverting option for cul-tural critics, and it captures an aspect of modern capitalism's cultural play-fulness. But for most people, consumerism is a permanent, inescapable, and largely unchosen "lifestyle." Village fairs may have yielded a moment of escape to feudal peasants caged by feudal authority, but life was no car-nival for anyone caught in the web of hierarchy that defined medieval life, even when they were attending a carnival. The New York sophisticates who eat at the upscale Chelsea diner featuring waiters wearing tuxes, a retro cocktail piano tinkling away behind retro menus offering shrimp cocktails, have little in common with the long-distance truck driver pulling off the interstate for a cup of bitter coffee or the undocumented worker who eats diner dinners because she has no kitchen at home and can't afford real restaurants of the kind critics otherwise patronize. The journalist sophisticate will appreciate the diner's late-night carnival ambience and the mall's playground leisure while writing a piece for *Architectural Digest*, but for those with fewer choices, there is likely to be only obesity and diabetes and credit-card debt and various forms of shopping addiction along with a household of goods and gadgets that, because they are unnecessary, are rarely worth their price. The mall may be a critic's liberation, but it can be a teenager's Saturday-night cage (cruising on Main Street is gone) and an aging couple's prison-yard strolling place in suburbs without sidewalks in the land of the vanished public square.[57]

The mall, like the carnival, can be seen as a form of controlled release. It has purposes akin to the theme park or Disneyland. To architect Michael Sorkin, Disneyland is another kind of circus, with Disney as "the cool P.T. Barnum . . . and Disneyland the ultimate Big Top." Not a carnival, really, since "both circus and Disney entertainment are anti-carnivalesque," more like "feasts of atomization, celebrations of the existing order of things in the guise of escape from it, Fordist fun."[58] The question Sorkin and others need to ask, however, is who the carnival is run *for* and who it is run *by*. Like the theme park or Disneyland, the mall is run for paying consumers, by profit-taking producers and marketers. Architects and cultural critics are independents, but they are always at risk of intellectual slumming. Slumming strips environments of their power context, interpreting what to others may feel coercive as voluntary (Twitchell's position) because the slummer—a discretionary user—is autonomous if not actually powerful, and hence feels free. As with creolizing culture, carnivalizing culture is read as if power meant nothing. Read Koolhaas's manifesto again with an eye to power, and it is clear that what he is describing is the very process of market totalization portrayed and condemned above in chapter 6.

Jackson Lears is one of the few who uses carnival imagery to approach consumerism who sees clearly that the agenda ultimately is about control and hence about power. And social theorist James C. Scott, who understands power perfectly, makes clear that the trouble with those like Bakhtin who celebrate carnival is that they miss "the extent to which the speech characteristic of one realm of power is, in part, a product of the speech that is blocked or suppressed in another realm of power. Thus, the grotesquerie, profanity, ridicule, aggression and character assassination of carnival make sense only in the context of the effect of power relations the rest of the year."[59] So after Mardi Gras, Scott reminds us, comes Ash Wednesday. The infantilist ethos may then be a call to carnival, a bit subversive with its appeal to release the repressed child and let her come out and play, but ultimately it is incapable of subverting the power that has produced it as an instrument of control, as an inducement to shop, and as an invitation to addiction.

There is a difference, moreover, between the original idea of carnival and the carnival evoked by modern consumerism. The ancient carnival offered occasional moments of release for those caught up in lifetimes of disciplined drudgery. It offered what the medieval king offered the fool: toothless insubordination in return for permanent fealty. But the modern mall, even if it disciplines the fun by turning recreation into work and leisure into purposiveness, actually promises—perhaps even compels—endless fun and permanent release. Its designers need their customers to sustain the carnival mood all year long, like the cruise line that has grabbed the carnival name. So they push less for release than for addiction. Repose and austerity never come to Disneyland, which is relentlessly Lent-less in its pursuit of permanent pay-as-you-play fun. Rather than a momentary vacation from discipline, release *is* the discipline. Howard Stern's pubescent scatology and regressive sexuality are on satellite radio 24/7, on two channels. Rather than a bump on the road to responsible adulthood, Peter Pan's escapades are now happily ever after.

Similarly, although Thomas Frank's 1960s young advertising execs were rebels, they were rebels *with* a cause, and the cause was precisely the same as the cause of the routinized advertising establishment they purported to overthrow: to secure consumerism as a foundation for the survival of a capitalism. Since it was producing more and more of what its constituents no longer needed, it was in desperate need of new marketing techniques, even if that meant a modest internal corporate rebellion. By pushing the envelope and incorporating rebelliousness, a culture was created in which the violent and vicious and pornographic could be built into controlling media. Some revolution. Today, interactive video games incorporating virtual violence and digital porn are appraised and praised on the sports pages of the *New York Times*.[60]

It seems clear, then, that licentiousness and puerility are what the ethos aims at and intends rather than a permissive holiday from the ethos. How much easier it is for the keepers when their task is to let Peter Pan fly free and keep Wendy cartwheeling under Peter's careless gaze rather than contain narcissism and help children grow up. For the keepers know the risk that comes with helping children grow up: they do not necessarily grow up into consumers. They sometimes become citizens.

Culture Jamming

Cultural hybridization and cultural carnivals offer some hope of dialectical resistance, but are limited by their obliviousness to power and to the purposes of the consumer culture and the ethos that sustains it. "Culture jammers," on the other hand, resist consciously, knowing the power of their adversaries and trying, jujitsu style, to leverage that power in the name of subverting it. They too like fun, if only for its dialectical reversals and subversive turnabouts. Like the yippies of the counterculture who threw money around on the floor of the Stock Exchange and wrote books with titles like *Steal This Book*,[61] they grasp that iconoclasts without hard worldly power must make the imagination their redoubt, messing around with signage and waging a battle of meanings with those who command the signs and symbols. They share a little of early capitalism's outlawry. They are swindlers like Wild Bill Rockefeller, but swindlers aiming to undo capitalism using capitalism's own up-to-date marketing tools. The jammers remember 1968, but it is the *soixante-huit* of the Parisian imagination as interpreted by Guy Debord they prefer. The inscrutable but obviously oppositional Debord, who founded the so-called Situationist International in Paris in 1957 and whose influence culminated in the 1968 student would-be revolution at Nanterre and the Sorbonne, wrote: "Only the real negation of culture can inherit culture's meaning" which, while "no longer cultural . . . remains, in some manner, at the level of culture—but in a quite different sense."[62]

In somewhat plainer words, Kalle Lasn, whose book *Culture Jam* is the bible of this appealing exercise in semiotic resistance, defines culture jamming as aiming "to topple existing power structures and forge major adjustments to the way we will live in the twenty-first century," not by force or insurrection but by changing "the way we interact with the mass media and the way in which meaning is produced in our society."[63] By waging "meme war" (a struggle of symbolic meanings), Lasn wants to give practical import to the memorable 1968 slogan proclaiming *"L'imagination au pouvoir!"* ("Empower imagination!"). Although Lasn appeals to a "ruthless criticism of all that exists," his writing is laced with ironic self-depreciation along the lines of such soft and self-parodying 1968 slogans as "It's forbidden to forbid," "Boredom is Counterrevolutionary," and "I am a Marxist . . . of the Groucho Tendency." If Groucho Marx is a stretch, Lasn nonetheless defines his tribe as

> a loose global network of artists, activists, environmentalists, Green entrepreneurs, media-literacy teachers, downshifters, reborn Lefties, high-school shit disturbers, campus rabble-rousers, dropouts, incorrigibles, poets, philosophers, ecofeminists. We cover the spectrum from the cool intellectual middle to the violent lunatic fringe, from Raging Grannies who chant doggerel at protests to urban guerillas who stage wild street parties.[64]

What jammers do, Lasn reports, is paint their "own bike lanes, reclaim streets, 'skull' Calvin Klein ads, and paste GREASE stickers on tables and trays at McDonald's restaurants. We organize swap meets, rearrange items on supermarket shelves, make our software available free on the Net." Generally speaking, they try to get consumer culture "to bite its own tail."

Like the "idealists, anarchists, guerilla tacticians, hoaxers, pranksters, neo-Luddites, malcontents and punks" they boast they are, they present themselves as "the ragtag remnants of oppositional culture."[65]

Culture jamming activities represent a "demarketing campaign" aimed at a "situationist 'detournement' [echoes of Guy Debord]—a perspective-jarring turnabout" in everyday life. Lasn's jammers agree with those Christian skeptics who deny that the conquest of cool can be the victory of rebellion over consumption since cool is merely the "opiate of our time," whereas culture jamming demands a "movement versus The Corporate Cool Machine" that will "strike by unswooshing America^{TM}."[66]

When Kalle Lasn first started writing about how to practice resistance, he exuded a certain naïveté, offering up Hollywood-style "I'm-not-gonna-take-it-anymore" tactics on the order of "The next time I'm caught standing in a long line at the bank, I'm going to shout cheerfully 'Hey, how about opening another teller.'" Or "subvertising" corporations by getting those who patronize McDonald's to feel "a little guilty, a little sick, a little stupid."[67] Other preferred strategies, as tame as they were cute, included sending spam mail faxers black pages that would use up the offending machines' ink supplies and asking telemarketers for their home numbers to call them back later that evening.

On paper, then, Lasn's proposals hardly amount to resistance, let alone a ruthless critique of all that exists. Yet the jammers turn out to be exactly what Debord and his Situationists were not. In the case of the metaphysical Guy Debord, the theory was opaquely exquisite, but the practice altogether unsatisfactory. On the contrary, culture jamming reads tamely, but has produced a practice that is intriguing, savvy, and at least modestly efficacious, resting as it does not on the random proposals of Lasn's book but on employing the best practices of marketing itself—gripping rhetoric, potent graphics, and imaginative "detournements" of the conventional—to subvert the advertisers, the marketers, and the companies that employ them.

From headquarters in Vancouver, Canada, Lasn and colleagues such as Nicholas Klassen started a glossy, eye-catching monthly called *Adbusters* ("A Journal of the Mental Environment") and launched a set of magazine-

and web-based campaigns aimed at subverting consumerism's most seductive features. To treat with those hysterically merchandized post-holiday shopping days, the jammers inaugurated a "Buy Nothing Day" for the Monday after Thanksgiving every year ("participate by not participating"). To confront television, marketing's irresistible King Kong, they initiated an annual April "TV Turnoff" week. And to take on the commercial media (which have at times refused to run Adbusters anticommercials), they promulgated a "Media Carta" declaration of consumer rights, including a right to media access. They also reached out to potential allies, embracing the "Slow" movement (begun some years ago in Italy as a "slow food" response to fast food) with a "Slow Down Week" every January and with the marketing of books such as *Slow Food* and *In Praise of Slow*.[68] They marketed the design of anticonsumerist logos, including a U.S. flag with corporate logos where the stars should be (see www.unbrandamerica.org) and a gray smog smudge (peel-off and stick-on), a kind of "black spot" of their own invention that can be pasted over conventional advertising and used by street guerillas to obliterate corporate logos.

As an eclectic movement (Lasn boasts that it includes anarchists, rabble-rousers, lefties, and sundry political radicals), the jammers have unavoidably adopted an eclectic politics. This has, however, sometimes led to diversions from the consumerist focus: radical condemnations of American foreign policy in places like Iraq and Palestine, for example, on the tenuous theory that Brand USA is also all about the spinning of bad ideas as good ones. But calling President Bush or former Israeli Prime Minister Sharon terrorists probably does not help critics of consumerism focus on the jammers' primary issue.[69]

Yet Lasn recently embarked on what is perhaps the jammers' most daring and controversial project, one that is directly related to its core anti-marketing theme: a start-up athletic-shoe company targeting the corporate colossus Nike and the defining Nike swoosh that has become a surrogate for identity around the world. With Lasn as its "antipreneurial" founder and CEO, this new "anticorporation" with the antitrademark "Blackspot" (a takeoff on the logo-obliterating smudge) is manufacturing and selling a high-top Blackspot Unswoosher and a "classic" Blackspot Sneaker. The jammers are pursuing their plan to market demarketing with an anticommodity commodity. The shoes are sold in a dozen countries and were featured in the 2005 *Le Salon de la mode éthique*, Paris's anticonsumer answer to runway fashion shows, and itself still another instance of consumer-based anticonsumerism. As might be expected, world-consumer capital California and more generally the United States have the most stores (thirty) offering Blackspots.[70]

Lasn and his jammers are exploiting other anticommodity commodities with an eye to manufacture, including eco-safe bikes, biodiesels, local culture specialty shops, food co-ops, and a portable barcode reader that would allow consumers to check products against a list of environmental and child labor law standards. And yes, there is debate about anti-Starbucks coffee shops and a jammer vodka to compete with all those heavily logo'ed commercial brands. The idea is for activists "to harness the entrepreneurial spirit." While "giant corporations run roughshod over our lives, we whine and complain, protest and boycott. But the one thing we've never done is fight the corporations head on," reads the Adbusters.org website. "For too long we've ignored the market, written it off as enemy territory. Yet, what do mega-corps like Walmart and Coke fear most? Competition. We're talking about a new breed of bottom-up enterprise that does things differently: promotes ethics over profit, values over image, idealism over hype. A brand of grassroots capitalism that deals in products we actually need—and believe in. No sweatshops. No mindfucking ads. Just sustainable, accountable companies. Run by us."

Assessing cultural jamming as meaningful resistance is tricky. It mixes its imaginative antimarketing marketing with an anti-American posturing and a naïve leftist critique of foreign policy. It invites individual inventiveness on behalf of group action, but can seem to subvert the advertising landscape without really changing it. Anyone can be a jammer, which is a virtue. Example? Internet search engines are programmed to permit popup, click-on "search ads" to appear when select keywords are entered. A search for "travel to Miami" might spring an ad for an airline that provides flights to Florida. Here is the jammer angle: the search-engine companies like Yahoo! and Google make their money off charging the advertisers up to $10 a pop each time someone clicks on their ad. Now if scores of jammer net-users click on every pop-up ad in sight, the advertisers will find themselves lumbered with endless costs for people who have no interest in their commodities. They will pay the freight without getting the customers for whom the goods are intended, and the whole pop-up advertising scam will be brought down—perhaps along with the search engines themselves (although that may not be seen as a desirable outcome), which depend on advertising revenue for their survival, according to an article in *Wired* magazine.[71] Jamming in action. If thousands of jammers could be found who could be bothered to play the game.

Yet the underlying question remains whether anticonsumerist activists can actually harness the entrepreneurial spirit (the movement fails here quite conspicuously to use its rebellious alter-meme "antipreneurial"!) without playing the game whose rules they want to subvert. Taking over capitalism with "good commodities" is not the same thing as subverting commodification—indeed it can seem little more than a version of the "corporate responsibility" model limned below. After all, the Blackspot shoe may pretend to be an anticommodity, but an anticommodity is just another commodity—at least when it's a shoe. Blackspot pursues some worthy objectives such as assuring the manufacture of athletic apparel in keeping with safety, environmental, and labor standards. Yet it has refused to disclose earnings or other data on its shoes.[72] Moreover, as critic Rob Walker has observed (in a comment that was posted commendably enough by Adbusters itself, on its site), "That black spot may symbolize a blotted-out logo, but it is also, unavoidably, a logo itself." While Adbusters is actually "trying to sell an antilogo that happens to have a shoe attached to it. . . . [T]he spot and its supposed meaning aren't a byproduct of the campaign—they are the whole thing. But one of the most legitimate criticisms of blind logo loyalty is that it trivializes the logoed item itself: Don't worry about what we're selling, just buy the symbol we've stamped on it."[73] Naomi Klein has also been a critic, arguing that playing the marketing game in the name of antimarketing still expands the crowded and homogenizing space where marketing takes place. "Publications that analyse the commercialisation of our lives," Klein says, "have a responsibility to work to protect spaces where we aren't constantly being pitched to. This can be undermined if they are seen as simply shilling for a different 'anti-corporate' brand."[74]

Lasn is certainly aware of the dangers of faux resistance. He notes in *Culture Jam* how "a lot of people who think they're rebelling aren't," and derides those leftist activists who "have been reduced to the level of little kids throwing snowballs at passing cars." He has unkind things to say about reformers like Ralph Nader and the Public Interest Research Groups network (PIRG) he helped found, as well as about former *Harper's Magazine* editor Lewis Lapham.[75] Yet throwing a "nice" brand of Blackspot sneakers at world bad-boy brand leader Nike does not seem much different than throwing snowballs at passing cars. Indeed if Blackspot ever won an unlikely victory, it would be a victory of superior marketing that the marketing industry would no doubt ape and steal for its own purposes. This is exactly what, in Thomas Frank's account, the 1960s advertising industry did with the countercultural critique aimed at it. Blackspot would be the new Nike, and cool athletes would sign on to its countercultural message the way they sign onto Nike's today. And what would have changed? Indeed it was a Nike ad copywriter who exclaimed in 1966, "Why do this kind of advertising if not to incite people to riot?" As Thomas Frank answered the questions in *The Conquest of Cool*, "From its very beginnings down to the present, business dogged the counterculture with a fake counterculture, a commercial replica that seemed to ape its every move for the titillation of the TV-watching millions and the nation's corporate sponsors."[76] In a more recent best-seller trying to figure out why one-time Kansas Democrats now vote Republican, Frank describes how "the corporate world . . . blankets the nation with a cultural style designed to offend and to pretend-subvert: sassy teens in Skechers flout the Man . . . hipsters dressed in T-shirts reading 'FCUK' snicker at the suits who just don't get it."[77]

The trouble with countermarketing is not that it doesn't work, but that it is a tactic invented by the marketing establishment itself. It is marketers and advertisers who figured out how to mock themselves in order to sell their commodities and who learned to assimilate and sanitize taboo-breaking critics and down-and-dirty adversaries like hippies, yippies, and

Maoists by embracing their transgressions. Volkswagen has a long, successful history of self-deprecating and ironic advertising.

The marketing industry is the master-jammer and engages less in "pretend-subversion" than in instrumental subversion—subversion and transgression as hot sentiments and cool ideals to be associated with commodities to which they bear no relation—as happened with love, Mom, and trust in traditional marketing. Subversion and jamming make a profit, however. If Blackspot can attach a sneaker to an anticonsumerist logo, Cingular can attach an anticonsumerist logo-slogan (flouting "the Man") to a mobile phone and reap the benefits of cool even as it sells product.[78]

There has not yet been a symbol of resistance and transgression that has not been effectively assimilated and reengineered as a marketing slogan or sales logo. The 1970 Buick borrowed countercultural lingo to promise it would "light your fire," while GM's Oldsmobile division was selling "Youngmobiles." Mao Tse-tung jackets became a favorite of the 1970s fashion industry, and Che Guevara portraits (in life and death) as well as the now endlessly reproduced image of Edvard Munch's *The Scream* decorated (and continue to adorn) T-shirts worn by youngsters around the world who have not the slightest concept of their meaning—only their "coolness." Benetton made a reputation in apparel by associating itself with stark, startling, but self-consciously uncritical images: portraits of kids as soldiers, of kids with AIDS, of kids in extremis. Why? On the way to protesting injustice? Or merchandizing death? Or just making a buck? It was not clear that the meaning mattered: the pictures were cruel, hip, stark, and cool. And whatever else happened, Benetton turned a profit.

These examples raise the question of whether a "meme" war can be won against those willing to accept *your* meanings as long as they are attached to *their* products. When Michael Jackson bought the publishing rights to the Beatles' song library and then sold John Lennon's hit song "Revolution" (from the 1968 *White Album*) to Nike, its subversive meaning (if it ever had one) vanished. Phil Knight, former Nike CEO, remembers that "Nike 'got a ton of criticism' for using the Beatles' *Revolution* song . . . as the [Air Max shoe] ad's anthem," but with it the company found its voice, and regained the number-one brand spot from Reebok. "When we started out, we couldn't make up our minds what kind of advertising we wanted. We had different messages for different groups, but there was no overarching theme. *Revolution* captured everything we wanted to do."[79] Paul McCartney griped that "the song was about revolution, not bloody tennis shoes,"[80] but meaning is hard to own, even by those who author it. That is the secret of marketing's success.

No personality better embodies the spirit of modern marketing with its endless capacity to assimilate transgression and turn it into sales than Howard Stern, the former shock jock of morning radio who in 2004 signed a half-billion-dollar contract with Sirius Satellite radio, with a bonus of several hundred million dollars if he could bring millions of listeners with him to pay radio (he could and did when he began satellite broadcasting in 2005). A giant of marketing (his show, his books, his movie), Stern showed how to mainstream pubescent scatology and a childish, if not quite innocent, embrace of pornography and sexual deviance. He turned his violation of taboos into a sign of his honesty and thus enhanced his credibility as a flogger of commodities (including satellite radio). His success is evident in a quite astonishing *New York Times* column on the Stern phenomenon, in which reporter/critic Virginia Heffernan first depicts him with seeming disdain as "an unwashed basement figure, best kept out of sight—a haggard masturbator and morbid misanthrope who must hang out with deformed and desperate men because he can hardly perform with women . . . a mean little pornography-addicted freak whose self-loathing reverses itself only in fits of equally grotesque narcissism, as when he flashes his listeners with a dirty raincoat by disclosing disgusting secrets about himself." Yet it soon becomes apparent that Heffernan is not condemning but praising Stern on the way to deriding Stern's broadcast radio replacement David Lee Roth (the former Van Halen singer). Roth, it turns out, "is far too square" for the morning-radio slot, "surprisingly grating and banal when he's speaking." Listeners, Heffernan concludes, "will miss Mr. Stern's low, unerring, New York–inflected voice—and the depth of weirdness it unfailingly conveys."[81]

Culture jammers face a challenge then. They must share the transgressor's stage with those they mean to combat. Iconic companies like Nike and Coca-Cola are themselves culture jammers, and impressively effective ones at that: for them it's a question of surviving the competition. For all the jammers' subversive brilliance, they are not only in danger of being out-jammed by those they jam, but they are likely, even if they succeed, to add luster to the image of marketing rather than to undermine its culture. If Blackspot somehow makes inroads against Nike, will the marketing of expensive "athletic" shoes to a global market of nonathletes be set back? Or advanced? The danger for the jammers is that they lose even when they win.

There are significant opportunities then for resistance inside the culture of consumerism. Consumer products can be creolized, consumption can be carnivalized, and consumer corporations and their busy marketers can be jazzed and jammed. Monolithic homogenized consumer taste may thus be pluralized; oppressive consumer markets can be made more fun, and put to expressive uses; and the weapons of marketers can be turned to the purposes of antimarketing to help spread antimarketing messages and induce antimarketing behaviors. Yet the ultimate obstacle is capitalism's current plight: caught up in a campaign of survival, it demands obsessive consumerism and addictive materialism to stay viable. As a consequence, the kind of resistance that will cure the ills of hyperconsumerism and civic schizophrenia must help capitalism once again address the real needs of that half of the world that is abused rather than served by it. This will require a transformation of capitalism back into a needs-satisfying economic machine, and a transformation of democracy back into the sovereign guarantor of all domains private, the market domain included. How this might be accomplished is the subject of the final chapter.

8

Overcoming Civic Schizophrenia: Restoring Citizenship in a World of Interdependence

> Enlightenment is Man's emergence from his self-incurred immaturity.
>
> —Immanuel Kant, "What is Enlightenment?"[1]

> The grand, leading principle, towards which every argument unfolded in these pages directly converges, is the absolute and essential importance of human development in its richest diversity.
>
> —Wilhelm von Humboldt[2]

FOR ALL THE power of marketing, consumers are too often willing subjects of manipulation. It is less the efficacy of advertising than the frailty of shoppers that renders resistance so problematic. For in the absence of real wants and genuine needs, consumers often seem to invite the producer of goods and services to tell them what it is that they want. The cynical slogan behind which earnest marketers hide when faced with the tawdry, the harmful, and the meretricious proclaims "Don't blame us, we just give people what they want!" Yet when skeptics reply "It is you, however, who tell the people what they want!" marketers offer the ingenuous response, which contains a seed of truth, that "Yes, to be sure, but the people *want* to be told what they want! They *need* to be shown what they need!"

Thus, eighty years ago in a notable *Life* magazine ad (from the National Advertiser organization) run in 1926, a little guy called Andy Consumer offers a pathetic plea to the big company boys: GO AHEAD AND MAKE US WANT reads the header; followed by a clever text which, in a flattering whine, complains that "sometimes I get mighty mad at advertising—tempting me all the time. I wish it would leave me be. If it weren't for advertising, I wouldn't know what I was missing." At first it seems as if Andy Consumer is on to the advertisers, knows a con when he sees it. Except his message is layered, and he goes on to confess "I begin to see it is advertising that makes America hum. It gives ginks like me a goal. Makes us want something." In other words, advertising won't leave me alone, but that's a good thing, because left to my own devices I don't really know what I want. How much better for ginks like me to be told! "And the world is so much the better" too, Andy concludes. "I guess one reason there's so much success in America is because there's so much advertising—of things to want—things to work for."[3] One can almost hear the cheers echoing down through the century, "Hoo-ray! and ya-hoo!" right up to Thomas L. Friedman's exercise in gee-whiz consumer technology boosterism called *The World Is Flat*.

Yet Andy Consumer has a point. Polls show many people go shopping without a list or a specific purchase in mind. Friedman begins his paean to the new digital technologies that have putatively "flattened the world" (leveled the international playing field) by acknowledging it all happened (in the title of his first chapter) "While I Was Sleeping." With very few needs of the order inspired by hunger or homelessness or nonpotable water, but softly addicted to the pleasures of shopping and needing very much to need, consumers may welcome the manufacture of wants—shopping ideas that come from somewhere else: the shill on the Home Shopping Network, the pop-up ads that interrupt your web searches, the catalogs that cascade into your mailbox week in and week out, the consumer sections of newspapers and weeklies, the *Wired* magazine celebrated and pundit-pushed new technologies that will "revolutionize" our lives.

The challenge is to demonstrate that as consumers we can know what we want and want only what we need; and that, with the rest of our lives we intend to live as lovers or artists or learners or citizens in a plethora of life worlds in which consumption need play no role. Once we resume our lives as complex human beings with diverse wants, only some of which can be satisfied by material consumption, capitalism will be compelled to resume its role as an efficient respondent to real human needs, even if (as often happened in the early history of markets) profits come only further down the road because so many of those who have genuine needs are not in a position to pay in full for their satisfaction. This kind of fundamental change is likely to come only when citizens reassert their democratic sovereignty over the economy, requiring a revolution that is more like a restoration of the situation under which capitalism has historically been most successful. But first we can recognize changes within the marketplace that suggest a healthy starting place for the more radical therapies that are necessary.

Civic Consumerism and Corporate Citizenship

Cultural jamming tries to use inside-the-market tactics to challenge the market. But to those who take seriously the civic side, even when the market seems the only game in town, there are ways to civilize—that is to say "civicize"—markets on both the demand and supply sides. The reforms they champion do not renounce supply and demand in favor of command economy public goods, but use market exchange to produce civic outcomes and public benefits. These market-side reformers see in consumers like the National Advertiser's Andy Consumer an instrument of demand-side power—for example, boycotts—and in corporations a supply-side tool of responsible organizational citizenship that can "do well by doing good." They play the market to change how the market does business. On the demand side, "civic consumerism" hopes to "empower" consumers for real by making them thoughtful and responsible shoppers using collective consumer clout to shape what is sold and how it is sold. They want to turn the aggressive "push marketing" economy that manufactures and sells faux needs back into a satisfying pull economy of real products and services meeting genuine human needs, or at least reasonable human wants. On the supply side, the same logic yields the ideals of "corporate responsibility" as a strategy in which the producers wear civic caps while captaining their corporate vessels, steering companies away from obvious abuses and profiteering selfishness of the Enron variety toward responsible decisions that benefit society as well as shareholders.

Both trends are welcome, though neither is likely to be decisive in reversing the effects of the infantilist ethos, because even civic-minded market approaches ultimately share the shortcomings of the market they wish to transform. Markets are not civic for a reason: their virtue, which is that they reject imposed statist solutions and rigid collective planning, is also their vice—they reject democratic oversight and collective decision-making, and hence make it difficult for market players to realize public goods. Nonetheless, perhaps because Americans have forever wanted to have their apple pie and eat it too, the uneasy blending of private and public that goes by the name civic consumerism has a long history in the United States, if not in Europe or Latin America where the state has generally been entrusted with almost all public obligations. From the beginning in the United States, the market has floated on a rhetoric of civic empowerment, which was frequently seen as a happy synonym for what advertising was meant to achieve. A *Collier's* magazine editorial published in 1930 thus reminded readers that "the old kings and aristocrats have departed. In the new order the masses are master. Not a few, but millions and hundreds of millions of people must be persuaded. In peace and in war, for all kinds of purposes, advertising carries the message to this new King—the people. Advertising is the king's messenger in this day of economic democracy."[4]

It has been a crucial point of the argument here, as well as a constant refrain of cultural critics such as Christopher Lasch and Michael Sandel, that citizens and consumers should not and cannot be confounded. Nonetheless, they quite clearly have been. Historian Lizabeth Cohen narrates the story of what she calls the "Consumers' Republic" in ways that suggest "a century-long trend of entwined citizenship and consumership" is our reality. To her, this means that we have little choice but to accept and perhaps exploit the trend, since "it is unrealistic to assume we can reverse [it]."[5] Cohen recounts that by the time of the New Deal, a consumer movement was underway that Kenneth Dameron could portray in 1939 as a "series of efforts having in common the feeling of dissatisfaction with

goods and services and the marketing practices involved in their distribution, coupled with . . . a demand for information and for protection in the
market."[6] However, this "movement" was less about empowering consumers to protect themselves than prompting government to intervene on
their behalf. The aim was price control (a wartime must), truth in advertising, and consumer product safety regulation, all policies that required
legislative action.

In a later wave of American social action that came in the 1960s, the
consumer movement reemerged as a part of the rights movement, still
directed primarily at inducing government to act. Following such muck-
raking exposés as Vance Packard's 1957 *The Hidden Persuaders* and his 1960
The Waste Makers, John F. Kennedy sent a message to Congress declaring
a "Consumer Bill of Rights." Less than a decade later, after expansive consumer protection legislation had been passed during Lyndon Johnson's
Great Society administration, Richard Nixon released his own "Buyers
Bill of Rights."[7] Though neither of these consumer bills of rights were
enacted as legislation, from 1960 through 1977 no fewer than thirty-three
major bills were passed protecting consumers' rights to everything from
clean air and water to wholesome meat, flame-retardant fabrics, gas
pipeline safety, fair credit protection, poison preventative packaging, and
truth in lending.[8]

What is striking about the consumers' movement story as told by
Cohen is that it is less a story of consumers getting their own through
market action than a story of citizens acting through their legislators to
protect their interests both as consumers and citizens. Much of what she
depicts as belonging to the Consumers' Republic belongs actually to the
Republic pure and simple: the Republic (citizens) acting on behalf of consumers worried about their civic interests. Civic consumerism defined by
its primary goal is actually an instance (and a positive instance, at that) of
restoring the sovereignty of citizens over consumption. This is why, starting with the Reagan and Thatcher administrations in the 1980s and continuing down to the second Bush administration and market-oriented
governments in Canada, Europe, and Asia, the principal project of neoliberals who want to privatize has been to undo the regulatory civic work of

the civic consumer movements of the 1930s and the 1960s. If democrats struggle to restore citizens to their rightful sovereignty, neoliberals struggle to get them out of the way and leave the marketplace to consumers pure and simple whose agenda can be set by advertisers and marketers.

There is, however, a second element in civic consumerism that does not strive to engage government, but is content to use consumer empowerment to achieve its limited social goals. This element in the Consumers' Republic engages in direct consumer action, marked by consumer demonstrations and boycotts. The Civil Rights movement launched an effective boycott of Woolworth's to force integration of its lunch counters, while the National Welfare Rights Organization organized its boycott of Sears, Roebuck in order to secure fair credit for customers on welfare. The aim was not to draw in the government or depend on legislation that was not always enforced, but to induce producers to change policies unrelated to their products out of fear they would lose customers. The idea was not to supercede but to utilize the market.

Cesar Chavez's farmers' union scored a significant success by organizing a countrywide boycott of grapes grown in nonunion vineyards. Pure market pressure also worked in the international arena, where consumer boycotts of goods or corporate stocks of companies engaged with regimes regarded as illegitimate or unjust played a part in overcoming South African apartheid. It also played a role, far more controversially, in the Arab attempt to isolate and destroy the state of Israel, and more recently in the Islamic effort to isolate and punish Denmark through consumer boycotts of Danish goods in response to the publication in a Danish newspaper of cartoons demeaning the Prophet Muhammad. Boycotts are in fact available to any intense minority wishing to make a political point through its pocketbook, whether or not its aims have been legitimized in a democratic election or might otherwise be approved by the larger community. In 2005, an English organization of academics set out to punish Israeli academics for putative sins committed not by them but by a Likud government (a similar boycott was proposed by a higher education professional union a year later). The first boycott was short-lived, but again showed that boycotts are not partial to particular ideologies and can be used to persue liberal or illiberal ideals.[9]

Corporations have responded to consumer boycotts variously, depending on whether they are merely symbolic surrogates for a nation or a policy (as was the case with the boycotts of Israeli academics or Danish companies who had themselves done nothing wrong) or are actually the progenitors of despised policies the boycotts are intent on changing (as with the vineyard owners or the tobacco industry).

Generally speaking, once they are under consumer pressure, companies will prefer self-regulation to state intervention. In 1999, prior to the 2000 elections, a lively debate about the McCain-Lieberman bill which would require cigarette-style warning labels on entertainment products (music, film, video games) highlighted the difference between "voluntary" codes endorsed by the marketplace and the stricter government regulations envisioned by lawmakers. In the entertainment industry for example, bad faith self-regulation is widespread. According to a Federal Trade Commission report, "although the [three relevant industries] have taken steps to identify content that may not be appropriate for children . . . those industries routinely target children under 17 as the audience for movies, music and games that their own rating or labeling systems say are inappropriate for children or warrant parental caution due to their violent content." As a result, "the practice of pervasive and aggressive marketing of violent movies, music and electronic games to children undermines the credibility of the industries' ratings and labels. Such marketing also frustrated parents' attempts to make informed decisions about their children's exposure to violent content."[10]

In 2004, telecommunication behemoths Hewlett-Packard, Dell, and IBM agreed to promote an Electronic Industry Code of Conduct that essays to ban bribes, child labor, unsafe materials, and pollutants. As with the Apparel Code endorsed by many apparel manufacturers, however, enforcement remains the crucial issue. The difference between the state and the market is precisely that the state has a legitimate monopoly on force and is able to enforce its laws, whereas voluntary codes are ink on paper and only as good (or bad) as the willingness of their signatory industries and their customers to live by them. American students protesting the use of child- and low-wage labor as well as unsafe or environmentally dangerous working standards in the overseas manufacture of athletic apparel by American companies have faced these dilemmas of voluntary codes.

One such code has been relatively successful in a domain where the government has been unable to act effectively. In the late 1990s, students on a number of campuses (with Duke University in the forefront) created United Students Against Sweatshops, an organization that now operates on several hundred campuses throughout the United States, and has targeted such major brands as Nike, Reebok, Champion, and Russell who outsource production of the apparel sold on American campuses. Spurning lame self-enforcing voluntary codes, United Students Against Sweatshops has taken on the enforcement function by organizing college and university campuses to boycott manufacturers who fail to live up to the code. They have also lobbied against the "cola" monopolies on college campuses (that exchange monopoly market rights and exclusive access to the marketing use of university logos for big-time donations of cash), again by dint of their consumer power to boycott.

Although labeling campaigns have had mixed results, two such "Consumer Seal of Approval" campaigns stand out: Dolphin-safe Tuna, a movement aimed at forcing tuna fishermen to use dolphin-safe nets so that harvesting fish does not inadvertently lead to the slaughter of these endangered mammals; and Rugmark, an organization that monitors the uses of child or indentured labor in the making of rugs around the world, especially on the Indian subcontinent, and whose seal of approval has come to guarantee a rug manufactured by acceptable standards, which has influenced policies in rug-making nations.

Dolphin-safe Tuna engaged in a long battle with the fishing industry, which had used nets in the eastern Pacific and elsewhere that caught dolphins along with tuna. It culminated in the passage of a number of accords, including the La Jolla Agreement on the conservation of dolphins of 1992 (that included Mexico and the United States), the Panama Declaration of 1995, and the International Dolphin Conservation Act, passed by the United States Congress during the environment-friendly Clinton administration in 1997. The campaign has not achieved its zero-mortality goal for dolphins but has spurred effective conservation efforts.[11] According to the Rugmark Foundation, this global nonprofit works "to end illegal child labor and offer educational opportunities for children in India, Nepal and Pakistan." The Rugmark label is thus "your best assurance that no illegal child labor was employed" in the making of a carpet.[12]

Boycotts have also been used effectively at the local level. Throughout the 1960s housewives organized boycotts of grocery stores with unreasonably high prices due, they believed, at least in part to promotional games for which consumers were in effect being charged. Boycotts have remained a tool of local market pressure. Kalle Lasn's intriguing idea for a portable scanner programmed to read bar codes by measures that give potential buyers a readout on the product's social impact belongs in the civic consumerism category as well as the culture jammer's bag of tricks. Whatever their role in jamming, Blackspot shoes (described in chapter 7) are also an example of affirmative civic consumerism.

Consumer boycotts have generally worked best when used in conjunction with government action. When a company's goods and how they are produced is the main concern, as with Dolphin-safe Tuna and cigarette warning labels, consumers as citizens can speak forcefully to their legislators ("We want new laws!") and citizens as consumers can speak forcefully to the producers of the goods they buy ("Produce *what* we want, *how* we want, or we won't buy!"). It is, however, a merit and a defect of the boycott tactic that it need not concern itself just with the product or service under scrutiny. A boycott might be directed at how or where a service is provided. Boycotts of segregated lunch counters put flesh on the bones of federal antisegregation legislation, they did not protest what was on the menu. Boycotts of apparel manufacturers aim ultimately at spurring government action to regulate apparel imports on the basis of how they are manufatured, rather than at changing the character of the clothes. Even without the cooperation of governments, then, boycott strategies often meet with modest, if not decisive, success.

For Lizabeth Cohen, the Consumers' Republic substantially advanced at least some progressive goals, above all, social inclusion. In its seductive embrace of the notion that equality can advance through prosperity, it has "provided true inspiration to a wide range of Americans," including welfare rights activists and credit critics, and has achieved "decent housing and schools."[13] Cohen remains wary, however. For the "Consumers' Republic's dependency on unregulated private markets wove inequalities deep into the fabric of prosperity, thereby allowing, intentionally or not, the search for profits and the exigencies of the market to prevail over higher goals . . . [so that] the outcome dramatically diverged from the stated objective to use mass markets to create a more egalitarian and democratic American society."[14] The market is finally a device of private goods, which necessarily overshadow public goods. If the demands of both can be accommodated, a blend is possible, but where the two are in opposition, as is often the case, the private must trump the public, effectively negating sovereignty by turning over power to the private domain and the individual producers and consumers who operate in it.

In recent years, capitalism's neoliberal victories have deprived the market of democracy's oversight and regulatory succor. In the international arena, financial institutions such as the World Trade Organization and the International Monetary Fund have actually used the ideal of free trade to make war on civic consumerism. Bottom-up consumer boycotts are often deemed top-down "national boycotts" aimed at official protectionism by the global bureaucrats who run these organizations, and are in fact considered illegal under most international trade and financial exchange regulations enforced by international financial and trade institutions such as the WTO or the IMF. This effectively deprives citizens (and whole nations) of any recourse against the depredations of anarchic global market capitalism. American state governments that have tried to impose restrictions based on safety or other civic considerations on imports from nations in violation of such standards, have been successfully sued under these free-trade provisions, and compelled to abandon their civic agenda.[15]

Civic consumerism has achieved significant results both for civic consumers and thwarted citizens. Yet the problems faced by those who must operate exclusively in unregulated markets have led frustrated consumers to seek out tactics that affirm rather than penalize companies whose practices they aspire to influence. Why boycott when you can also reward? Instead of penalizing companies whose policies or products are regarded as insidious, it is possible to patronize companies whose policies and products are regarded as praiseworthy. Such politics reinforce the other side of market-based civic consumerism: civic corporatism or corporate responsibility. When companies that pay attention to the civic concerns of consumers get rewarded, doing well by doing good is reflected in quarterly balance sheets and company stock and bond profiles. Positive market reinforcement has generated a number of new businesses—among them, "social investing" firms that specialize in helping stock-market consumers find and invest in firms with socially responsible profiles. Typical are the market players at Pax World Funds, whose slogan as advertised on its website is "Principles & Performance." Originally founded by ministers who objected to investing in companies that manufactured napalm during the war in Vietnam, Pax World deploys an investment strategy that appeals in blunt political rhetoric to its target constituency: "We refused to invest in a retail giant because they sold rugs made by children. We divested our position in a Silicon Valley company because of the increased volume of their Defense Department business." Such socially responsible investment firms have proliferated in recent years, as is evident from the extensive membership of the Social Investment Forum, a trade association of social investment companies in the United States. And social investing has gone international: the United Kingdom boasts its own UK Social Investment Forum.

The field has its own journals (*Business Ethics* magazine and *GreenMoney Journal*, for example) and is peopled by companies such as Domini Social Investments, that promise "screening, shareholder activism and community investing." Large pension funds like TIAA-CREF that offer their subscribers a wide choice of investment portfolios (high risk, low risk, domestic, overseas) now include a portfolio measured by social and civic criteria in which the promise is not of extraordinary income but of socially responsible investing. Jeff Skoll, whose progressive filmmaking activities through his company Participant Productions is discussed below, has also established a foundation that invests in social entrepreneurs through three awards programs: the Skoll Awards for Social Entrepreneurship, the Awards for Innovation in Silicon Valley, and the Skoll Social Sector Program Grants, helping build infrastructure for socially responsible NGOs. Much of the work of newer foundations like the Gates Family Foundation (now also in control of the Warren Buffett Foundation fortune) and the (former President) Clinton Foundation aspire not just to do good works but to leverage others to do the same by investing in other socially responsible organizations and institutions.

Finally, there are a number of consumer product companies that try to associate their products with good works, sometimes by reference to the product itself, but more often (in typical marketing fashion) by simply manufacturing a connection between the brand and the good deeds an owner or a corporate board decides to undertake. Benetton produces ordinary (if colorful) apparel, but generates extraordinary marketing by suggesting through the clever use of pointedly political advertising that it is somehow deeply attached to political change in the world—if only because it runs shockingly raw graphics that have little to do with apparel, but a great deal to do with violence, poverty, and sexual and drug abuse. Starbucks is not exactly doing good in the world as it puts corner cafés, luncheon counters, and smaller coffee competitors out of business. But in 2006, it launched two campaigns: the first to "develop a cup using 10% post-consumer recycled fiber . . . the first hot cup to contain post-consumer fiber produced by a process that has received a favorable safety review from the Food and Drug Administration." Using the cup, Starbucks proudly declares, will "conserve 5,000,000 pounds of new tree fiber over the next year." This, Starbucks adds, is just a start to Starbucks's promise to "work with its partners, customers and industry colleagues to further integrate sustainable environmental practices into our business." In the second campaign, Starbucks promises to turn over a nickel for every bottle of Ethos water sold (it acquired the company in 2005) to water-resource projects in the thirsty Third World. Yet Starbucks's water campaign, although it promises up to $10 million to the developing Third World over the next five years, depends on selling bottled designer water in the First World—a peculiar way to address the water crisis, especially given that disposing of all those plastic bottles creates an environmental hazard.

Fast-food chains in the grease and starch, sugar, and salt business now also are motivated to offer a few "healthy" products so they can participate in the war on obesity in which consumers have finally become interested as they watch their children grow fat and diabetic. Cola companies offer sugar-free products even as they work to expand their school-lunchroom presence. Such drinks are now proscribed in French schools, and are coming under greater scrutiny in the United States. This represents what some call a portfolio approach to consumerism, in which customers are offered a wide variety of goods and services, some associated with civic goals they may support.

The connection with public goods is not always very clear and perhaps as a result always vulnerable to charges of hypocrisy. Anita Roddick's Body Shop has long professed a preference for green politics. Companies such as Ben & Jerry's ice cream, (Paul) Newman's Own, Stonyfield Farm yogurt, Whole Foods Market (the grocery-store chain that has committed to using wind energy), Interface, Inc. (the largest carpet manufacturer in the world which has committed to using only reusable or recycled materials), and Starbucks have all grasped the civic possibilities of marketing along with the marketing possibilities of charitable giving.

Corporations understand that good citizenship pays, and that modifying their products and practices in order to attract customers who may otherwise avoid them or seek out rivals is not only a prudent civic practice but good business as well. Their motive may be greed, but that's the point: greed is good in this domain, not because the greedy are posturing narcissists like Michael Douglas's character in the movie of that name, but because greed can be made an engine of responsible social service, allowing producers to make a profit when they respond to socially responsible demands by consumers. Buying bottled water can rescue African children from thirst. Using your credit card can help you save responsibly (pennies in your savings account for every dollar you spend). The policies pay, if in peculiar and self-contradictory ways.

As with civic consumerism, there are market limits on these sorts of corporate responsibility. When it helps profits, it is a no-brainer. When it is profit neutral, it makes for good collateral marketing, and is worth doing. But when it obstructs profits by diverting too much revenue to the pursuit of its public benefits, it becomes problematic. Doing business in socially prudent ways either has to be added to the price the consumer pays, or it reduces profit margins. Someone pays—shareholders or consumers. It has been estimated that a socially motivated consumer will pay a premium of perhaps 5 or 6 percent for socially desirable attributes of a product, but not much more. Similarly, a social investment can pay a little less than an investment made for the return only, but it has to pay something. People give to charity, but nobody *invests* in social trusts to lose money, or buys a bottle of Ethos solely because a percent of the proceeds go to thirsty Sudanese. In the blunt words that the advertisement which Calvert Investments (an investment instrument with "high performance potential and high ethical standards") puts into the mouth of a pretty young woman: "Call me greedy," she says, "but I expect my funds to be as solid as my values."[16] This does not quite reach the quixotry of Groucho Marx's "I have principles! And if you don't like them, I have others!" but it comes close. Indeed, there is no more provocative example of the dilemmas, strengths and weakness alike, of civic consumerism and corporate responsibility than how Hollywood has wrestled with the moral dilemma of its principles—self-imposed by the self-appointed inventor-in-celluloid of America and the would-be conservator of its virtues—and its profits, in whose name it has a habit of corrupting and undermining much of what America really believes in.[17]

Reel Change

At the intersection of civic consumerism and corporate citizenship, there are intriguing efforts underway to work within the market on behalf of cultural and civic goals the market generally corrupts. Notable among these is a movement in the entertainment industry, focused on movies but also including video games and television, which we might call "reel change." Reel change speaks to Hollywood's capacity, as old as the industry itself, to respond to demands for more challenging and socially or morally engaged films whether or not they are profitable or popular (though in some cases they have been both).

It is of course easy enough to charge Hollywood with many of corporate capitalism's worst sins: marketing trash, dumbing down taste, hijacking teenagers as taste-makers, pretending to "empower" its clients, glamorizing violence, and making pornography chic. After all, critics have been complaining forever, and with vociferous ardor for at least the last quarter of a century, about what *Newsweek*'s David Ansen called "the widespread infantilization of pop culture and Hollywood's increasing tendency to cannibalize itself."[18] *The New Republic*'s cultural critic Leon Wieseltier has charged that "Hollywood is significantly responsible for the infantilization of America. Almost all those movies that are not suitable for children are irredeemably childish."[19] And Maureen Dowd has asked mockingly whether director Steven Spielberg might ever be "able to grow beyond the enforced adolescence of current Hollywood filmmaking?"[20] We have already noted that the largest-grossing films of 2001–2005 were comic-book blockbusters.

Like the media generally, Hollywood is subject to the hierarchy of conglomerate ownership that constantly contracts control of the world of images to ever fewer telecommunication Goliaths. Truly independent studios scarcely survive. The Weinsteins' Miramax Studio is now owned by Disney, while the Weinsteins have departed to create a new company; Disney itself merged with Steve Jobs's once proudly independent Pixar and then bought Pixar outright in 2006 (as of this moment—things change rapidly!). General Electric owns both NBC broadcasting and Universal Studios; Time Warner/AOL controls not only Warner Bros. Entertainment but the once independent New Line Cinema (which made the Lord of the Rings movies) as well as HBO cable television (that screens *The Sopranos*) and Ted Turner's CNN and TNT cable networks. Viacom controls Paramount and CBS (although it has recently split them into autonomous operating divisions) along with Nickelodeon, MTV, and the Black Entertainment Network; Rupert Murdoch's News Corporation controls Fox Television, Fox's film studio 20th Century Fox, Fox Searchlight Pictures, and a newly announced genre division (intended to service the youth market with video games, new content-capable cell-phones, and other innovative platforms) as well as Sky Television in Europe, STAR in China, and numerous newspapers and magazines. In short, from all the fresh-faced start-up "indies" (independents) of Sundance's yesteryear, there is only one true independent left in Hollywood in 2006 at this writing: John Feltheimer's Lions Gate Films. And to stay in the business of making quality independent films such as *Monster's Ball, Grizzly Man*, and *Crash* (which won the Academy Award for best picture in 2006), Lions Gate has been forced by the economics of global moviemaking to develop its own version of big-studio trash, including *Saw, Saw II, Saw III*, and *Cabin Fever*, for example.

Yet throughout its history, even studio-dominated corporate Hollywood has found ways to resist what studio-dominated corporate Hollywood supposedly stands for. Long ago in the 1930s, the inmates rose up and took over the asylum, with Charles Chaplin, Douglas Fairbanks, Mary Pickford, and director D. W. Griffith creating United Artists in 1919.[21] In its first half-century, this studio made such celebrated films as *Wuthering Heights, Stagecoach, Spellbound, The Apartment*, Arthur Miller's *The Misfits, One Flew Over the Cuckoo's Nest, Network, Apocalypse Now*, and way before *Brokeback Mountain*, the New York man-boy hustler movie *Midnight Cowboy*. These were all films that helped define Hollywood filmmaking at its best in terms of excellence and entertainment but also with respect to the breaking of taboos and the assuming of a social agenda. Other studios made risky political films such as the nuclear-winter nightmare *On the Beach* (five survivors contemplate the aftermath of nuclear war) and sardonic black Armageddon comedies like Peter Sellers's *Dr. Strangelove* (directed by Stanley Kubrick). A handful of bankable stars including Robert Redford and Warren Beatty used the fame and fortune they acquired from acting to develop film projects that pressed Hollywood's tolerance for politically and culturally transgressive films—notably, Warren Beatty's *Reds* (a semidocumentary narrative history of early Communism) and his more recent satire on congressional hypocrisy called *Bulworth*. Paul Weitz's over-the-top spoof of terrorism, *American Idol*, and the American presidency (called *American Dreamz* with Hugh Grant starring) belongs to this category.

The recent economics of filmmaking, when marketing budgets represent up to a third of the total cost of making big-budget films (producers too appear to believe that consumers must be told what they want in order to want it) and when blockbuster films are often animated kiddie films aimed at a global audience of infantilized viewers, should have made risk taking rarer than ever. Yet the Hollywood system has nevertheless continued to turn out enough films that test Hollywood's boundaries (however modestly) to suggest corporate Hollywood still has the capacity to address if not altogether overcome its own cultural corruptions. A few such films are oddities, the result of a big-name star spending his own money to make a serious movie. This was the case with Mel Gibson's startling (and startlingly successful) *The Passion of the Christ*. Even those unsympathetic to Gibson's self-flagellating and violent portrait of Christ and to what some saw as the film's anti-Semitic undertones must count this film as deeply contrary to Hollywood's usual crass secularism and materialist embrace of filmmaking as profit-grabbing, teen-teasing trash.

Yet, putting oddities like *The Passion of the Christ* or Michael Moore's sardonic radicalism aside, Hollywood has begun in the last few years to offer a quite explicit social agenda, more remarkable because it comes during a period when movie-ticket sales are declining (down in three consecutive years starting in 2003) and independent studios disappearing. The new offerings come not just from the indie film sector—arts films and the sort of movies that passed muster in the early days at Robert Redford's Sundance Film Festival, and today play international film festivals. Rather, they are films made by superstars like Spielberg, including *Schindler's List*, *Saving Private Ryan*, and *Munich*, and new big studio–backed or studio-distributed productions like *The Constant Gardener* and *Syriana* that hint at a wish to honor the standards Hollywood boasts about but rarely lives up to. This is a crucial point; for no trend is of much significance unless the major entertainment conglomerates who exemplify the "blockbuster" profits-come-first mentality are involved.

What remains most intriguing then about Hollywood is that it has demonstrated its own dialectical capacity to generate rebellion and subversion out of its most corporate, market-oriented sectors. Although once-independent studios like United Artists (now under MGM at Sony), DreamWorks (now at Viacom/Paramount), Miramax (now at Disney), and New Line (acquired by Time Warner) have gotten much of the credit for Hollywood's small-scale incendiary rebellion against itself, the real fire—given these patterns of ownership—has actually come from the belly of the beast. The big-studio generators of puerile blockbusters critics rightly revile have also been involved in financing, making, or distributing some of Hollywood's more interesting new millennium fare. Two of 2005's more political and original (if also predictable and formulaic) films, *The Constant Gardener* (about corporate, politically backed corruption by the pharmaceutical industry in Africa) and *Brokeback Mountain* (the well-made and affecting so-called gay cowboy movie), both turned out by James Schamus and David Linde's Focus Features and involving superb directors Ang Lee (who won a 2006 Oscar) and Fernando Meirelles, were funded and distributed by Universal, behind which stands the global corporate megalith General Electric.

Meanwhile, two provocatively political films—*Good Night, and Good Luck* (the Edward R. Murrow film) and *Syriana* (a political thriller about oil and the CIA in the Middle East)—although made at Section Eight (where film artists Steven Soderbergh and George Clooney were partners until they decided to dissolve their partnership at the end of 2006) and funded in part by Participant Productions (a new organization in which former eBay partner billionaire Jeff Skoll plays a crucial funding role), were actually made at and distributed by the graying studio Warner Bros., owned in turn by the Time Warner/AOL conglomerate. Similarly, conservative media oligarch Rupert Murdoch's News Corporation stood behind Fox Searchlight's small quirky 2004 film *Sideways* as well as its 2004 *I ♥ Huckabees* and *Kinsey*, while Sony's big MGM studio made *Capote* (with Philip Seymour Hoffmann's Oscar-winning portrayal of the author of *In Cold Blood*) through its specialty studio (using its United Artists brand, which also made *Hotel Rwanda*). Skeptics will have to confront the reality that this class of small, politically engaged, controversial films won a lions' share of Golden Globe and Academy Awards in 2005 and 2006, shutting out blockbusters such as *King Kong* and *Memoirs of a Geisha*, suggesting that the marketplace was responding favorably to risk taking of a kind investors might shun.[22]

These films will continue to draw varied critical responses from serious audiences, and even the most original among them are compromised by formulaic plots, star dependency, and the demands of marketing to youthful spectators across the globe (which is where movies finally earn their bottom line or fail). And cynics will correctly note that like such big companies as Kellogg's, Hollywood may be doing little more than perfecting the so-called portfolio approach to marketing, that pairs health-corroding trash products that make big bucks with smaller volume healthy alternative products in order to further legitimize their standard consumer fare. Thus Pepsi or McDonald's will offer select low-sugar, low-fat options to rationalize a menu of goodies suffused with sugar and fat, just as Nickelodeon will offer a few responsible educational programs to offset the junk it generally markets to juniors. The overall portfolio of products looks better than the trashy commodities that actually define it.

Nonetheless, it does seem clear that Hollywood at its corporate worst can sometimes generate work reflecting Hollywood at its creative best, work that challenges, if only modestly, rigid conventionalist views of America and the dumbing down of audiences. Perhaps if it is true that the worst needs the best as its rationalizer (the portfolio approach), it is also true that the best needs the worst as its funder. No George Clooney *Good Night, and Good Luck* without the George Clooney *Ocean's Twelve*, no Mel Gibson *The Passion of the Christ* without the Mel Gibson *Lethal Weapon* series, no Oscar-nominated performance by Felicity Huffman for her portrayal of a transsexual in *Transamerica* without her pop-cult portrayal of one of four desperate housewives in the trashy TV series of that name. The studio system tolerates, sometimes even supports, film innovators such as Steven Soderbergh, the Coen brothers, or Paul Weitz (director/ writer of the "terrorist" satire *American Dreamz*) in part because it also uses and exploits their talent for its most commercially rewarding blockbuster offerings (yes, innovator Soderbergh also made *Ocean's Eleven, Twelve,* and *Thirteen*, while Weitz cut his teeth on the charming *About a Boy*).[23] An unlikely screen hit of 2006 was former vice president Al Gore's screen lament on global warming called *An Inconvenient Truth*. A cause for modest hope from some unlikely sources.

Reel change is also evident in the rather more sordid if commercially predictable setting of video games, a domain dominated by kid-conceived mindless violence and civilizational mayhem drawn from every era of history. Whether in popular games like Grand Theft Auto (notorious recently for secreting sex acts inside its program), in massively multiplayer online role-playing games (MMORPGs) such as World of Warcraft and Ever-Quest involving millions of players across the globe, knockoffs of movies like *King Kong* or *Lord of the Rings*, war games set in eras from the Middle Ages down into World War II and the contemporary Middle East and on into the imagined future, video games have become youth-world's favorite recreational addiction as well as the focus—despite a voluntary rating system—of agonized educators and moralists aghast at the medium's crassness. The game genre is shot through with commercialism, in the form of product placements and tie-ins to movies and other commodities. It has recently crossed a line between virtual and real economics: the online role-playing games have (as noted above) spun off the buying and selling (on eBay, for example) in real-world currencies of the virtual resources needed to advance in and eventually win on-line games like World of Warcraft. Unlike the movies, there has been little in the way of rationalization in this domain: these are hardcore games for men-boys interested in surrogate violence and time-consuming, mind-bending, highly competitive, often murderous play.

Yet even in a sphere of such blatant, youth-mongering consumption, there have been interesting attempts at using the genre to counter its pernicious effect and to achieve worthier ends. Proponents of peace can play Food Force, a game in which players pilot a C-130 Hercules cargo plane dropping rice bags rather than a B-1 bomber dropping bunker-busters. And apparently many do: after America's Army (the Army's recruiting video game), Food Force is the second-most downloaded free internet game currently on the market.[24] There are a number of such peace games, not so different from the early (and, as the title suggests, somewhat ambivalent) example of Pax Warrior which simulated the UN peace-keeping mission in Rwanda during the 1994 genocide (a game in which players could hardly fail to improve on the actual record of the United

Nations). Other games challenge players to develop solutions for the Israeli-Palestinian conflict, or—accommodating radical adversaries of the West—offer oppositional solutions rooted in Islamacist war games such as Ummah Defense I and Maze of Destiny, where the aim of players according to the *Wall Street Journal* is "to seek out and destroy the disbelievers." In fact, the games turn out to be fairly rudimentary and generic, with traditional gaming spaceships and robots named to accommodate Islamic Jihadist terminology; a few, however, engage in more virulent forms of play, permitting players to shoot virtual Israeli soldiers, for example (e.g., Special Force and Under Siege).[25]

Then there is the long-lived and much-played series based on the classic SimCity game that allows gamesters to engage in simulated urban and civilization design of a quite creative and altogether pacific nature. Such games are known as "open-ended" because they are aimed less at achieving some winning end than at maximizing ingenuity and imagination along the way. The original SimCity authored by designer Will Wright grew out of a map-making simulation. It gave birth to The Sims, a game in which players simulate a family carving out its own destiny according to loose program rules. The Sims has become one of the best-selling single-player games ever marketed, generating both parodies (e.g., SimBrick in which an ant wanders about aimlessly until it is squashed by a falling brick) and political criticism from both the right and the left, suggesting that it is pushing gaming boundaries. On the one hand, the Sim games are radically consumerist: buying things is the key activity, and the game's human beings are conceived as largely raceless and classless shoppers. On the other hand, the simulation is not programmed in accord with neoliberalism's anti–big government discourse and so is not averse to inviting state intervention on the way to improving a simulated society.

The social significance of games is attested to by the spread of video-game design to academia, in no small part through the influence of leading game design companies such as Electronic Arts. The University of Southern California, the University of Central Florida, Georgia Tech, and Parsons School of Design at New School University (among others) have now launched technical design offerings (and in some cases humanities programs) that pay attention to video games. The World Wide Web on which MMORPGs are played itself has been increasingly touted as a site of contestation and transgression with respect to both governmental and market hegemony. Web logs (blogs), for example, give individuals a digital megaphone, turning private persons into critics and muckrakers. Like so many recent political exposés, the uncovering of James Frey's fabrications in his book *A Million Little Pieces* was the work of a blogger. Along with email and i-messaging, blogging permits point-to-point "horizontal" communication across the world. Where traditional entertainment, broadcasting, and informational services are hierarchically organized in vertical structures where the few speak *to* the many, the new lateral organization of the web and the "democratization of information" afforded by such web search engines as Google allow direct communication among the many, and facilitate potential resistance to hierarchy and top-down authority.

There is little question that new technologies can play a limited transgressive role in the face of privatizing consumer totalism of the sort depicted in chapter 6. More than twenty years ago, I suggested in *Strong Democracy* that the cabling of America for television and such (then) innovations as interactive cable service (Warner-Amex's pioneering "Qube" experiment) could enhance democracy by servicing "civic participation in a strong democratic program that would . . . [link] neighbor assemblies . . . [as well as] individuals."[26] Since then, the democratic and leveling potential of the new digital technologies has been widely noted and celebrated, with booster magazines like *Wired* talking about global "netizens" linked together by a network beyond the control of nations or corporations. Enthusiasts from John Perry Barlow to Steve Jobs have made rebel-branded careers based on the democratic (even anarchistic) potential of the new technologies. As Neal Gabler argues in his ongoing examination of Walt Disney's world, when Steve Jobs (the key figure at Apple Computer and then Pixar Animation Studios) came to Disney in the Disney/Pixar merger, he brought along a democratic "bravado and disdain for traditional business practices."[27] This bravado is typical of many who work the web, whether as bloggers, program developers or, like Joe Trippi,

Howard Dean's campaign manager and web enthusiast, as new digital politicos. After all, the architecture of the web is horizontal, and many of its other features lend themselves both to leveling and resistance against authority. Can it be then that the new technologies are proof of the force Joseph Schumpeter called creative destruction: the capacity of capitalism to cure is own maladies through tumultuous developments it has itself produced? Perhaps.

Yet it is important to recognize that democratic and felicitously anarchic as their architecture may be, new electronic technologies (like all technologies) ultimately tend to reflect the cultures that generate them. In the warring culture of Renaissance Europe, Chinese explosive powder became gunpowder, put to the purposes of slaughter. The internal combustion engine had the potential to move both public and private forms of transportation; its use in automobiles (and the role automobiles played in spawning a mobile, suburban culture) was not determinative but the consequence of adaptation to preexisting cultural factors such as American individualism and the penchant for home ownership and continental sprawl, as well as to a postwar U.S. government commitment to highways (and to the automobile, oil, steel, and rubber industries highways benefit) rather than railways. Whatever the lateral architecture and democratic potential of the new telecommunication technologies, they have in fact been put to commercial and consumerist uses reflecting the corporate structure and consumer biases of the society that facilitated their emergence, a society dominated by the infantilist ethos.

Whatever its promise, the web appears first of all as an electronic mall. The primary form of transgression it facilitates is pornographic rather than political or civic—because pornography pays the freight while civics weighs down profits. Even when it has been adapted to the kinds of political uses for which it seems naturally suited (as in Howard Dean's presidential campaign), it has at least initially done little more than replicate and improve upon traditional political functions such as fund-raising and polling.[28]

Applied technology ultimately gets defined by its uses rather than its architecture. If producers of surplus goods want the new "democratic" hardware and software they develop to become a fresh venue for undemocratic consumerism, if they want to emphasize its marketing potential as a "push" medium that can track and exploit consumer taste (as sites such as Amazon do so effectively), then they will adapt the hardware and software to those purposes. If censors of child porn in democratic societies or censors of democracy in tyrannical societies wish to block, filter, or otherwise control content, then they will find or build programs that let them do that, even where such programs go against the "spirit" and architecture of the technology. Google not only acceded to China's demand that it assure its search engine would not be used by political opponents of the regime or even by independent thinkers, but provided the mechanisms by which the government could block access to prohibited information. Access to infinite strings of knowledge (from which the name *Google* derives) is the web's most cherished virtue, but this virtue turns out to be no obstacle to programmers who want to filter or block whatever a client government may wish to ban. The web's open and democratic architecture cannot and does not guarantee access to subversives and rebels. Type in such treasonous keywords as "Tiananmen Square" or "democracy" or "rights" on Google's China access link, and the endless world of free information abruptly acquires blinders and is closed in by artificial horizons—something Google rationalizes by referring to its respect for local rules and the local authorities that impose them.[29]

There are clear limits then to corporate responsibility and civic consumerism. Even the most civic-minded companies can afford to pay only a 5- to 6-percent premium to service civic goals as well as shareholder profits. We have already cited studies that indicate consumers are likewise constrained in how much of a civic surtax they will pay for commodities produced in civic-minded ways (with an eye to environmental and safety standards, or child labor). The bottom line is a reality for every corporation competing in a global marketplace that makes a race to the bottom easier than a race to the top. The business of business is finally business, while the business of civics is the business of democratic government—for which business cannot be an adequate surrogate. Lee Drutman and Charlie Cray are powerful advocates of responsible business practices, but in the end they recognize that reform depends on the need to "strengthen a citizen-sovereign democracy," which is an affair of effective government rather than of self-regulating companies. Their seven signature proposals for curbing corruption, reigning in the political influence of business, confronting monopolies, and dealing with corporate crime all point to a renewal of popular sovereignty rather than to marketplace solutions based on innovation or creative destruction.[30] Consumer advocate Ralph Nader also turns to government for enforcement of the consumer standards he continues to promote. Breaking the vicious cycle from within remains a daunting task. Media and cultural studies programs as well as the arts themselves, while formidable potential adversaries of monopolistic market practices, have largely been subordinated to those same market forces, making real autonomy difficult.

Religion may be the sector with the most potential for resistance from the outside to the infantilist ethos and its consumerist culture. Despite America's deep engagement in consumerism and the materialist ethos it entails, Americans remain the most religious people in the developed world. The infantilist ethos notwithstanding, a residual Protestant ethos continues to grip the American consciousness. As Harold Bloom has written, "The American religion is pervasive and overwhelming, however it is masked. . . . We are a religiously mad culture . . . a nation obsessed with religion."[31] In a 1989 Gallup Poll, 88 percent of those surveyed said they believed "God loves them." Figures generally show that 40 percent of Americans attend religious services once a week, while 60 percent report they are members of a religious congregation, far in excess of comparable European numbers. Although there is a strong element of individualism and evangelicalism in their religious practices—"I am a sect myself," said Thomas Jefferson, while Tom Paine preferred to believe "my mind is my own church"—Americans also insist that "religion has an important role to play in the public realm."[32]

Yet religion too has been corrupted by consumerism and the infantilist ethos, with televangelicalism and salvation for profit making inroads into precisely those realms of extrainstitutional and individualistic religion that are most archetypically American. Some might even charge that religious paternalism matches marketing paternalism in its treatment of "clients" as needy children. Moreover, when it does focus on the evils of consumerism, American religion, like other fundamentalist criticisms of secular materialism, risks becoming antimodern and antidemocratic as well as anticonsumerist. This was apparent from the assault on pluralism by religious conservatives led by Richard John Neuhaus described in chapter 7. Religion pushed into a corner by aggressive secular materialism can quickly turn reactionary and exceedingly dangerous. Anti-consumerist Jihads may curb materialism, but even when they are American, they will not improve democracy. So while there is surely room for an exploration of religious resistance to the infantilist ethos, there are many obstacles, and in the long run, solutions need to come to terms with the dilemmas of modern capitalism that have produced the infantilist ethos rather than turning their back on modernity itself.

Restoring Capitalism

The hold of consumerist capitalism over us can be moderated on the demand side by "civic consumer" resistance and bent a little on the supply side by corporate goodwill. But the market is ultimately made inflexible by capitalism's intractable survival needs. Unless ways can be found to help capitalism survive and prosper by serving real rather than faux needs, by providing services to those who are not yet consumers rather than those addicted to consumption, no resistance from inside the market is likely to succeed.

From the outset, consumer capitalism's paradox has been that those with real needs are without the means to enter the marketplace, leaving producers with no alternative to fabricating needs among those whose wants it has already oversupplied. The radical inequalities that divide developed societies from within, and continue to carve the planet latitudinally into hemispheres that exist as if on different planets, feed off capitalism's modern "triumph" as consumerism. But where there is real need, there capitalism, forever in search of profits, is not. This puts global capitalism itself in peril, not only because it risks in Jeff Faux's dramatic terms a "global class war," but because in the absence of effective democratic leadership, even global capitalism's successes in stimulating productivity and prosperity will be jeopardized.[33] How then might the market be incited to respond?

There are commodities enough that respond to and efficiently meet the special and real needs of the developing world. For all the wants of that vast world of potential consumers, there are products galore that might secure the health and safety of children, promote the economic potential of women, and support the long-term market viability of whole societies. Just recently, an antidiarrheal oral vaccine called RotaTeq was approved that could save up to a half million children a year in Third World countries. Problem? It costs $187.50 for a series of three oral doses, pushing it entirely out of the marketplace for those who most need it in places like Africa. The same can be said of a whole class of commodities pushed by advocates of Third World aid like Jeffrey Sachs, including nitrogen-fixing plants (to improve poor soil), water recycling devices (for water systems with too much salt), vaccines targeting childhood diseases, and nutritional supplements designed for the millions of children for whom starvation is a permanent and mortal threat.[34] All such commodities might help Third World citizens to pull themselves up by their bootstraps. But for the strategy to work, they have to be wearing boots. In the consumer marketplace, this means being able to pay the price of the consumables they so desperately need.

Recently, a promising commodity specifically designed to address child malnutrition was introduced in the African marketplace. Since malnourishment is a principal contributor to the diseases that afflict and kill the young, addressing hunger is also a way to treat disease. Niger has over 150,000 severely malnourished children under the age of five and 650,000 who are moderately malnourished. A quarter of children never reach the age of five. Aid workers at Doctors Without Borders recently began distributing a 500-calorie "Plumpy'nut" peanut-paste bar developed by French scientist André Briend that can be packaged in foil, is resistant to spoilage, and can be injected with a slurry of vitamins and minerals that saves lives. A couple of foil packets a day is a miracle cure for the starving (proximate normalcy can be attained within a week or two), and an inexpensive foundation for long-term child (and adult) nutrition.[35] Here is a consumer product designed to rescue children from death.

Simpler yet is the mosquito net, an old remedy newly advocated by Jeffrey Sachs, once an ardent partisan of privatization and market strategies, whose recent work has moved in a very different direction.[36] Sachs has focused attention on simple products as exemplars of the kinds of commodities capitalism can produce to meet genuine needs around the world. A favorite example is the mosquito net. Malaria and many other communicable diseases that continue to ravage Africa and other poor regions of the world are spread primarily by mosquitoes. Protecting exposed populations with bed mosquito nets is an efficient and inexpensive prophylactic against these diseases as well as against those even more dangerous infections (such as HIV/AIDS) that attack those whose immune systems are already weakened by mosquito-borne plagues like malaria. Yet even an item as cheap as a mosquito net is beyond the means of those who most need it. It could offer an adventurous company a potentially lucrative market niche, but the risks are considerable and the profits far down the time line in a marketplace that no longer accepts deferred gratification as a standard. Sachs thus must depend for his mosquito-net campaign on international aid organizations and philanthropy of the sort made available by the Gates and Clinton foundations, while capitalism's efficient market mechanisms are more or less shut out.

The crucial question for all such products, from vaccines to mosquito nets, is how to make them a source of profit so that the great engine of capitalism can be turned toward providing them for the markets where they are needed. Currently their claim to attention rests on the ethical entailments of what the psychologists T. Berry Brazelton and Stanley I. Greenspan call the "irreducible needs of children," which effectively create "core rights" demanding a response. But the reality is that moral claims are not sufficient to animate the private marketplace, which moves according to a potential client's capacity to pay rather than on the righteousness of her needs. Capitalism "needs" to be able to address the vast and untapped marketplace of the billions around the world who still have real needs, and it "needs" to move away from having to manufacture faux needs for those whose wants have been largely satisfied. Moreover, this need of capitalism corresponds perfectly to the need of the world's poor to have their own real needs satisfied. Yet the market mechanism itself forbids that the two sets of needs intersect.

In discussing the donation of the greater part of his fortune to the Bill and Melinda Gates Foundation, billionaire Warren Buffett acknowledged that although he is "a big believer in the market system 95% of the time . . . it's done pretty well by me, and the world . . . there are things where the market system is not going to solve the problem."[37] So although only a few of the core or irreducible needs enumerated by Brazelton and Greenspan or fellow psychologist Abraham Maslow are material in character—aimed at nutrition, housing, health, and security[38]—those crucial few remain mostly without impact on the market and on world trade, which continues to focus on the real if fragile market defined by the artificially induced faux needs of the prosperous. Brazelton and Greenspan are correct in arguing that "our society is failing many of its families and small children at present," but only if a way can be found for capitalism to target irreducible needs is this injustice likely to be redressed.[39]

Is it possible for capitalism to revamp its mission within the limits of the modern consumer market? Those engaged in the experiment seem dubious. Jeffrey Sachs no longer seems to put much faith in the market efficiency he once championed, and looks more to significant governmental and NGO participation in prompting the market to make a contribution. He calls on private philanthropies but also on the World Bank, the International Monetary Fund, the World Health Organization, and other international institutions to become active in his campaign to address African disease, poverty, and malnutrition. He relies heavily on achieving compliance with the unmet United Nations Millennium Development Goals, which ask developed nations to raise their foreign aid contributions to 0.7 percent of their GNPs—a modest goal that would nonetheless require "generous" European nations to double their expenditures (from a current rate of about 0.4 percent), and require the United States to increase its aid nearly fourfold (from what is currently less than 0.2 percent).[40] In the absence of such formidable increases in government aid, he worries that real change will not be possible.

Nevertheless, there are three experiments under way that depend on the market itself and that aim at redirecting capitalism by utilizing its flexible potential for change. These include the experiments proposed by three imaginative economic pioneers: C. K. Prahalad's strategy of mining "the fortune at the bottom of the [consumer] pyramid" by turning the world's poor into paying consumers; Muhammad Yunus's idea for lifting women and their families out of poverty through microcredit, a small-loan program for the impoverished to jump-start market development in communities barred by poverty from market participation; and Hernando de Soto's inventive idea of addressing poverty by legalizing informal and black-market elements of the private economy that represent real but largely unrealized wealth among populations that are poor in name rather than substance—if their invisible wealth can be unlocked. Each of these proposals, which I will only touch on here, has the virtue of relying on the market itself to cure what seems to be the market's inability to address global inequalities and use its capitalist potential to treat world poverty and overcome global inequality. Although each, as I will show, finally depends, like almost every reform we have examined here, on some form of government intervention, they remind us of the dynamism of capitalism when it is liberated from a dominant cultural ethos to which it has become tethered, and allowed to serve a system that by addressing real need can accommodate justice as well as prosperity.

In his popular text with the self-explanatory title *The Fortune at the Bottom of the Pyramid*, C. K. Prahalad, an economist at the University of Michigan, seeks to reattach the heavy load of poverty reduction to the engine of what he calls an "inclusive capitalism" by treating the poor as a capitalist "growth opportunity" in which their own collaborative contribution is critical. Although he recognizes that to date "the large-scale private sector was only marginally involved in dealing with the problems of 80 percent of humanity," Prahalad rejects the paternalistic notion of the poor as "wards of the state." Rather, he asks how one might mobilize the "resources, scale, and scope of large firms to co-create solutions to the problems at the bottom of the pyramid (BOP), those four billion people who live on less than $2 a day?"[41]

The virtue of Prahalad's approach is that he begins not with a new but with the classical definition of capitalism—which approaches the eradication of poverty precisely as it approaches every market need: by figuring out how to respond effectively to need expressed as market demand in a manner that earns profits for investors and producers. He turns the challenge of making capitalism work in impoverished settings at the bottom of the pyramid—few are trying to meet the desperate needs to be found there—into a virtue. After all, is there not an inviting market opportunity to be found at the bottom of the pyramid where it is still possible to capture the largest number of unsatisfied consumers left on the planet today, over half the world's population? Although they are without the wherewithal to pay for what they need, Prahalad hopes to enlist the poor as participants in creating the new market that will address their needs. He understands that there is no existing market, and hence few companies willing to invest. The challenge is to create a new market through what is "essentially a developmental activity," converting the poor into potential consumers. This means converting "poverty into an opportunity for all concerned" and calls for a cooperative strategy in which governments, NGOs, corporations, and the poor themselves are engaged in collaborative activity. Prahalad focuses on how the poor see themselves, and believes changes in discourse and self-image can contribute to changes in behavior. A discourse centered on "the poor" and "alleviating poverty" cannot draw investors and producers into low-profit new markets. The "needy" draw pity, not investment; on the other hand, "collaborators" are potential customers.

Prahalad's strategy can be criticized for assuming up front the very changes it must produce in order for it to succeed: if the poor knew how to bootstrap themselves out of their victim status into entrepreneurship, they would not be poor. Yet it is also true that if cultural ethos is about how we see and identify ourselves, then encouraging a language of consumer demand as a substitute for the language of desperate neediness can make a difference. Prahalad has also been criticized for confining his research largely to India and Latin America (Peru, Mexico, Brazil, and Nicaragua) where attitudes toward poverty are already changing and development is already well under way and thus, the challenges of poverty less formidable than in say Africa or the Middle East. Prahalad also cites the work of Unilever's Indian subsidiary Hindustan Lever Limited, but despite persistent inequality, India is well along in the process of energizing its consumer sector and leapfrogging over rivals in the world trade market. Indeed, nowadays, India is often cited as an example of the new competition that lazy old industrial nations like the United States are going to have to contend with (this was a topic of President Bush's 2006 State of the Union speech and is a perennial theme of pundit Thomas Friedman), rather than as an exemplar of the kind of traditional poverty to which markets have not yet begun to respond. Africa is the real test for any theory of market revisionism.

Muhammad Yunus's Grameen Bank, begun in 1976 in Bangladesh (at the time a major site of extreme underdevelopment), is a second example of capitalism's capacity for self-revision.[42] Yunus quickly grasped that to mine what Prahalad called the bottom of the pyramid meant jumpstarting the engagement of the poor in their own bootstrapping operation. Which was to say, doing what Prahalad failed to do, giving them the boots by which to bootstrap. Attitude change would not be enough. Very small loans, often $50 or less, could give people with nothing just enough capital to do something. Such marginal changes could be critical. It was well known in the developed world that the difference between a working head of family and a homeless vagrant might be a month's shortfall on a rental payment. Yunus saw that in the developing world the difference between an impoverished mother unable to meet the needs of her own children and a village dynamo helping the whole community rise up out of poverty might be a microloan of a few dollars, enabling her to start up (for example) a modest cottage-industry basket business. Microcredit can turn the poor into self-employed producers, and transform the needy into viable consumers in the global marketplace.

Like Prahalad, Yunus also understood that discourse and ethos were at stake. His most radical innovation was thus to treat credit as a right, urging banks to rely on trust and the engagement of the bank itself in guiding the client's investment as collateral to secure the loan. Since the loans were labor intensive (the banks stuck around to help make their investments productive), they carried high interest rates, often more than 50 or 60 percent of the original loan. But a $50 loan repaid at $80 after a year that established a real business which lifted a family out of poverty was a pretty good deal for lender and borrower alike.[43] And although Yunus insisted on credit as a right, he also understood that lender institutions had to be sustainable, which is to say at least marginally profitable.[44] This was not philanthropy, but prudent market investment that helped create the market in which it invested.

A decade after Yunus's pioneering work, microcredit has become an important tool of the international aid and development community and has made the Grameen Bank a model of how finance capitalism can contribute to development without altogether slighting profit. The year 2005 was the International Year of Microcredit, widely supported by the IMF, the World Bank, and the United Nations. The microcredit strategy has been used throughout the Third World, and been the subject of some experimental work in Third World enclaves inside the First World, in Los Angeles, for example. It depends on a market logic but conceives of the market as part of a larger world of values and norms for which the wealthy are no less responsible than the poor.

In a third example of what can be called self-reforming market capitalism, the Peruvian economist and head of the Institute for Liberty and Democracy Hernando de Soto has attracted wide attention for his proposal to confront apparent poverty by finding ways to capture hidden wealth in the world of the poor. Market zealots like Margaret Thatcher and Milton Friedman as well as justice-seeking egalitarians like former Secretary of State Madeleine Albright and former United Nations Secretary-General Javier Pérez de Cuéllar have alike welcomed de Soto's effort to bring "dead capital" into the real economy by titling untitled assets and thereby empowering the poor to whom the assets belong as players in that economy.

De Soto's insight was to recognize that if the extralegality of much of the global property system could be overcome so that those who possessed it could use it, invest it, and borrow on it—"own" it in the legal sense—much of what passed as poverty would cease to exist in many places around the world. As a sympathetic critic put it, "the problem with poor countries is not that they lack savings, but that they lack the system of property that identifies legal ownership and therefore they cannot borrow."[45] What de Soto has managed to do is not just (in de Soto's title) to solve "the mystery of capital" but much more importantly, to help "solve the mystery of poverty." The potential energy and the economic value that is "locked up in a house" belonging to a family that lacks legal title to it, if unlocked, "can be revealed and transformed into active capital." For "capital is born by representing in writing—in a title, a security, a contract, and in other such records—the most economically and socially useful qualities about the asset."[46] Turning a house into capital means it can be used as collateral for a loan or the foundation for a business; it means that credit need not be furnished externally by a bank, but can be self-generated by converting the value of hidden capital already in the hands of a potential economic player.

Although de Soto suggests in his subtitle that capitalism has succeeded in the West and failed everywhere else, his analysis tends to prove the contrary thesis, a thesis that has been argued throughout this book: that capitalism is poised to fail in the West—where it produces goods for people with few real needs—but positioned at least potentially to succeed elsewhere and thereby help First World capitalism sustain itself. The challenge is whether it can title untitled Third World assets and give the poor the wherewithal to reward First World capitalism when it responds to their genuine needs.

Nonetheless, as with every other instance of responsible capitalism and civic consumerism described here, unlocking hidden capital is a political and legal rather than strictly an economic task. It is a function of politics and democratic legislation. In fact, in the absence of a political strategy that secures newly manifested capital against exploitation and abuse, the danger of de Soto's ingenious idea is that once the regular economy discloses, legitimizes, and hence captures what de Soto estimates may be up to $8 trillion in formerly extralegal assets, these newly legalized assets are in danger of being taken from their new and rightful long-term owners-by-use and effectively confiscated by dominant players already in the market—for example, monopoly corporations and corrupt governmental officials sitting astride the "legal" market economy and hence in a position to usurp claims to the newfound wealth.

Because he is a believer in markets, de Soto makes the mistake of assuming a "legal" economy that is neutral. Hence, he fails to notice that "legalization" also exposes newly recognized capital assets to the power arrangements that can define both the marketplace and the legal system. As tenant farmers discovered in the United States in the nineteenth century, formalizing their ownership over the land they worked certainly allowed them to collateralize their property, but it also allowed banks and big corporations to expropriate that same property when farmers failed to keep up with high interest payments or fell prey to a hard-luck growing season. What does not belong to you (even if you have used it extralegally for generations) cannot be taken from you (so you can continue to use it for generations to come!). To take title to and own an asset is to become vulnerable to every claim on ownership that corrupt and power-deformed political and market players can tender. Foreclosure, bankruptcy, repossession, and other strategies by which a system eats up the poor work more efficiently when hidden capital is revealed and given a legal title. This is probably one reason why the poor themselves sometimes prefer to hide assets behind extralegality, even if this means they cannot take advantage of legitimacy's benefits. Undocumented workers, for example, remain undocumented in part because they benefit from not having to acknowledge and pay tax on income or risk forced repatriation to their home countries if something goes amiss—as might happen if their status were disclosed.

This is not an argument for extralegality or for leaving assets untitled. It is an argument for insisting that legitimation of undeclared and untitled assets makes sense only when the legal system in question is not tilted to the rich, only when the political system is not dominated by the wealthy, only when the marketplace is defined by genuine equality and undominated power relations. The poor can afford to publicly own their hidden assets only when they publicly own their governments. De Soto's research suggests that in Haiti, the poorest nation in Latin America, the total hidden assets of the poor are worth more than 150 times the total foreign investment made in Haiti since 1804, when it won independence from France. Untitled assets in Egypt amount to more than 55 times the total of direct foreign investment there over its recorded history. Yet, in the absence of major political reforms and an end to corruption, it seems likely that a full accounting of such massive assets would benefit those who already control them extralegally less than it would benefit the exploiters-in-perpetuity who would seek to appropriate them. The people must trust—better yet, control—the legal system in order to benefit from the legalization of their potential assets in the invisible economy.

De Soto is a splendid and innovative economist, but in making capital visible he also has rendered power invisible. For his scheme to work, capital and power must be legitimated and captured at the same moment. Which will work only in a genuinely democratic, egalitarian society. As with almost every other experiment in market innovation scrutinized in the last two chapters, de Soto's depends on the quality of democracy, something the market can itself never guarantee and in its consumerist phase has consistently undermined.

Overcoming Civic Schizophrenia through Democratizing Globalization

Power is the missing constant in almost all of the proposals for capitalism's self-reform reviewed here. Once upon a time, democratization—which genuinely empowers a nation's citizens—rendered private power both public and accountable. Now, globalization often places both real power and its many abuses largely beyond the purview of national governments. The problems are global, democracy remains local. Voluntary codes need enforcement, and adducing standards to which to attach such codes is a function of democratic deliberation, but there can be no effective solutions within the framework of national sovereignty alone because interdependence—what Thomas Friedman calls a flat world—has fatally compromised sovereignty. Protecting children from commercial exploitation demands government regulation and oversight, but that cannot be achieved within solitary nations without encouraging a race to the bottom in which the market ruthlessly seeks out national markets willing to leave children unprotected. Consumer monopolies of the kind toward which Microsoft and Google naturally tend can be prevented only through vigorous antitrust legislation and government intervention in the name both of genuine private competition and the public trust, but there is no global public to entrust, no global legislature to enact regulations.

In other words, civic schizophrenia has to be treated globally as well as locally, but there are only local citizens bounded by their national loyalties, and they cannot rein in the rampant desires of unleashed global consumers. How can toxic substances and drugs, including tobacco and alcohol, be effectively regulated when they can so easily slip the bonds of national oversight? Critics of the American "addiction to oil," including President Bush himself, as well as critics of President Bush who protest his outsourcing of American port security to firms under the sway of "foreign" governments such as the United Arab Emirates, share a common illusion—that control over the production and distribution of oil or meaningful control over national port security anywhere can realistically be exercised by singular sovereign nations, even when they are hegemonic and democratic and even when they expressly choose to exercise it.

This lesson is perhaps most obvious when it comes to questions of global inequality, global rights, and global justice. Whether using the innovations of Yunus, Prahalad, and de Soto portrayed above, or trading pollution emissions on the global market, or forgiving Third World debt as envisioned by the Millennium Development Goals 2000, or rescuing peoples from genocide in places like Uganda, Sarajevo, or the Sudan, market reforms today demand transnational civic and political cooperation as well as international enforcement of a kind that violates the sovereignty both of the transgressing and the would-be enforcer nations.

In a world of interdependence, the sovereignty we seek to recapture is no longer an effective instrument of national democratic will. Citizens remain creatures of nations, while consumers are planetary itinerants. Democracy is parochial, markets cosmopolitan. The remedy is no longer commensurate with the challenge. With markets globalized, consumers are the new branded cosmopolitans who respond neither to the siren call of nationality nor the therapeutic appeal of democracy. A capitalism dependent on shopping turns us not just into children but *global* children. For, in psychologist Allen D. Kanner's wise words, "with the rise of economic globalization, the commercialization of childhood has become a worldwide phenomenon," bringing "sophisticated marketing campaigns, including those aimed at children, to every corner of the earth."[47]

We "kidults" have lots of company around the world. China has almost 300 million children under fourteen, while India has nearly 350 million children—a subcontinent of potential "Zippies" waiting to be rushed into permanent consumerism. In many parts of the world, including much of the Middle East and Africa, more than half the population is under sixteen. These children face three possible destinies, only one of which can promise them liberty or happiness: a harsh life of exploitation as child soldiers, child sex-objects, and child victims where poverty enslaves, starves, or otherwise destroys them;[48] a far more welcome but ultimately one-dimensional, unfulfilling, and unfree life as consumers in the growing world of infantilized shoppers;[49] or a life of autonomy and dignity as empowered citizens of global civil society and democracy. Global victims, global shoppers, or global citizens—with the third option remote because democracy remains locked inside increasingly disempowered sovereign states.

The anarchy and illegitimate power of global markets can only be brought under control by the legitimacy and power of global democracy. In the age of nation-states, Thomas Jefferson (and John Dewey after him) once cried "the remedy for the ills of democracy is more democracy." Today the remedy for the ills of democracy *within* nations is more democracy *among* nations. The paradox is that democratic nations, intent on preserving the vestiges of a sovereignty that has already been taken from them by the brute facts of interdependence, have themselves become the most vociferous opponents of democracy *among* nations—just as once upon a time, supporters of the sovereignty of the states at the time of the

American founding were enemies of the Federalist quest to establish a more effective national union. This paradox leads democracies accustomed to exercising their will through sovereignty to stand squarely in the way of the transsovereign pooling of power that alone can offer their citizens a chance, working across borders, to control their common destiny. Only if they release *their* citizens, can the powers of citizenship be made to count across borders. As Trotsky once warned Social Democrats there could be no socialism in one country alone, today's realists must warn democracy's national partisans there can be no democracy in one country alone. Nor even—imagine the neoconservatives' utopian dream come true—in a world in which every nation miraculously becomes a working democracy, but relations among them remain unregulated.

In the absence of democracy among and between nations, sovereign democracies will feud and fight, and discover and rediscover in the global market only an arena for cultivating national advantages (as they do today). Neither port security nor energy policy nor hidden capital nor child pornography nor undocumented workers nor public health in any given nation can or will ever again be controlled and regulated at the sole discretion of that nation's sovereign citizenry. The world is interdependent not because sovereign nations have wished it so but because, in spite of their wishes, encroaching forces of ecology and technology, capital and labor mobility, crime and disease, and terrorism and war are quite simply beyond their control. Interdependence is not an aspiration: it is the reality.

Individual nations remain crucial players, however, as much in what they can obstruct as in what they can still accomplish. They can still frustrate internationalists and impede the development of transnational democratic institutions, as the United States government has done with its refusal to sign on to the Kyoto Protocol on global warming, a fact that has doomed the promising "carbon trade" market idea pioneered in the 1990s (allowing nations to buy and sell "pollution rights" within an internationally determined quota on the global marketplace), even though that trade has been partially realized on a regional basis in Europe today. Or as India had done in refusing to abide by the nuclear proliferation treaty, most recently with the active complicity of the United States. But even an environmental protocol signed by every nation cannot function effectively without teeth, since it remains susceptible to any nation's decision either to drop out or refuse enforcement on its territory (the dilemma not only of the nuclear nonproliferation treaty but also of the new International Criminal Tribunal and the Land-Mine Ban Treaty). As Thomas Hobbes wrote long ago, covenants without the sword are of no use at all to secure a people's safety. Noncompliers, free riders, and other outlaws will always be happy to sign agreements they wish others to obey as long as they themselves—in the absence of vigorous enforcement—can do as they please.

The market operates on interest alone and market contracts are obeyed only when they must be obeyed. Enforcement depends on making it in the interest of contractees to comply by raising the costs of noncompliance. This is viable only when there is effective enforcement. In a globally inter-dependent world where markets and the illegitimate power exercised by market monopolies are transnational, but where democracy remains national, there can be no remedy either for civic schizophrenia or social injustice. Poverty, for example, is ultimately political, and its alleviation cannot take place without the deploying of democratic power. Yet famines and health plagues today, like earthquakes and tsunamis, cross borders, and to be efficacious democratic remedies must follow them across and beyond the boundaries of one or another individual nation's sovereignty.

There are, Amartya Sen proposes, "extensive interconnections between political freedoms and the understanding and fulfillment of economic needs."[50] The evidence shows not only that "poor people . . . care about civil and political rights," but that the achievement of such rights is a cru-cial factor in successful development.[51] As proof, Sen reminds skeptics that "no substantial famine has ever occurred in any independent country with a democratic form of government and a relatively free press."[52] But how to apply this formula to a global environment in the absence of global gov-ernance? Democracy must come first—justice and the realizations of rights follow; but ultimately only global democracy will suffice. Likewise, infantilization will yield only to democracy, but can be overcome as a global cultural ethos only by a global democracy that can trump frontiers as well as consumers.

Long ago, Jean-Jacques Rousseau observed that "what makes us miserable as human beings is the contradiction between our situation and our desires, our duties and our inclinations, our nature and social institutions between man and the citizen; make man one, and you will render him as happy as he can be. Give him entirely to the state or leave him entirely to himself; but if you divide his heart, you tear him to pieces."[53] Today, however, people can belong exclusively neither to the parochial state nor to the local market because the arena that defines their activity is global. Happiness, like wholeness, looks to a more expansive identity than is afforded by either nations or brands. The infantilist ethos fragment us—consumers versus citizens, this nation against that nation—while the real context in which identity must be worked out is a global marketplace without guiding democratic or integrative norms.

With wealth and the commonwealth in planetary tension, economic prosperity and market entrepreneurship have been unable to serve social diversity or human ends. Culture jammers make fine rebels but cannot be citizens, so that the only semblance of power once associated with meaningful sovereignty goes not to the state but to whoever wins the struggle within the marketplace for dominion: not the Russian people but Gaspol; not the British people but Rupert Murdoch's News Corporation; not the Indian people but Infosys Technologies Ltd.; not the American people but Mobil, Microsoft, and ABC/Disney. Rousseau proposed that we see ourselves entirely as natural individuals or citizens, one or the other. But in truth, not even recluses like Robinson Crusoe or Rousseau himself could live alone in the already complex, interdependent social world that was eighteenth-century reality, let alone in our interdependent modern world today; citizenship can be no refuge for identity where a planetary civic community is required that does not yet exist.

To be sure, brand identities rooted in consumerism girdle the globe, making consumers—above all, kid consumers—the first and only global itinerants: solitary anarchists free to shop everywhere. Yet they are able to root themselves civically nowhere at all. Nikes walk the world and dominate the Olympics; Germans and Finns and Russians and Japanese "win" medals that prove only their atavistic insulation from the global realities that inhere in the Nike swoosh that nowadays adorns almost all athletes.[54]

Religious identity also looms large, transgressing boundaries between nations even as it breaks up nations into warring theological tribes. Religion is too big and too small to hold together Iraq, trumping civil religion and civic identity at every turn.

Yet where market identity is cosmopolitan, and religious identities aspire to global expansiveness, civic identity remains small and parochial. There is a deep incommensurability between citizenship—even when it is allowed to resume its sovereign power over private markets—and these realities of globalization. So the challenge to democrats today is to find a way to globalize democracy not within but among nations; which means to democratize globalization—the ultimate challenge.

The prospects are less than promising. The institutions currently available, whether NGOs or international bodies such as the IMF, the WTO, and the United Nations system, while of potential use, are in the first instance creatures of the sovereign nation-state system rather than genuine transnational bodies, or of elites pursuing interests that are less than civic and democratic.[55] Global civil society is widely and enthusiastically discussed, but generally defined in terms of relatively weak "non-violent, legally sanctioned power-sharing arrangements among many different and interconnected forms of socio-economic life that are *distinct from governmental institutions*."[56] But this separation from power guarantees that global civil society will be incapable either of employing legitimate violence to contain illegitimate violence (say in genocidal wars like the current one in the Sudan) or bring the weight of some form of pooled, global sovereignty to bear on anarchic markets. Global governance involving pooled sovereignty and genuine transnational legal and political power, on the other hand, continues to be seen as, at best, a romantic ideal of naïve, tree-hugging, one-worlders (as Rush Limbaugh might put it) and at worst as a radical conspiracy of treasonous cosmopolitans trying to subvert America's (or Iran's or China's or France's) proud national sovereignty.

The office of the Secretary-General at the United Nations may aspire to autonomous global influence, but the Secretary-General reports to a United Nations that was founded as and continues to be a body constituted by sovereign states. Its ruling body, the General Assembly, is a congress of nations, not a world legislature, while its Security Council only reenforces and enhances the power of the extant superpowers. Likewise, institutions that are part of the international financial infrastructure such as the IMF and the WTO also represent nations rather than a global common good. Indeed, they disproportionately represent powerful nations with market economies, and thus sometimes seem to amplify rather than mute the influence of private market firms over governments. Corporations and banks effectively double dip: they use their influence *inside* states where privatization has secured their hold over politics, in order to defang democratic oversight; *and* they use their role *globally*, as the only international players on the world scene able to exploit global financial capital investment exclusively to their own interest. Globally, they can work through international financial institutions such as the IMF and the WTO (which they control through the G-8 governments they influence) to divert other poorer nations desperate for investment from focusing on their own welfare. Investment capital offered in the name of development is made "conditional" on recipient governments cutting back on spending and social investment. The market economy reinforces the governance of private capital geared toward endless consumerism at home and abroad.

What is missing is a transnational citizenry that might counteract the tendencies of the global market. What is missing are genuinely transnational civic entities on which to found such a citizenry. This deficiency is made more daunting by the paradox of solidarity that faces anyone wishing to construct democratic civic institutions. Religious and cultural identities are already "thicker" than local civic identity, providing more affect, kinship, and solidarity, even if sometimes at the expense of greater exclusiveness. When citizenship is made global, it is obviously thinned down, and its contribution to identity becomes still leaner. Compare a would-be "global citizen" with a zealous Wahabi Jihadic warrior: Whose attachments are likely to be more compelling? Can a Common Cause supporter match the ardor of a Northern Ireland Protestant? When civic identity is local, and embedded in a long civic tradition and the patriotic trappings of a civil religion (e.g., the Declaration of Independence, the Constitution, the Gettysburg Address, the Emancipation Proclamation,

Martin Luther King's "I Have a Dream" speech), it can at least begin to provide an approximation of a kind of social glue that holds a citizenry together. Can it do the same in a watered-down global form? Some social philosophers and global civic practitioners try to promote the idea of a civic calling with global reach: a perspective that yields something more than mere enlightened interest, but what philosopher Virginia Held calls a global ethics of care.[57] Global media coverage opens us to global sympathy, and it is easier today than ever before to extend civic compassion across national frontiers to victims of genocide in Darfur or to abused child-soldiers in Liberia or casualties of a tsunami in Indonesia.

While the kind of social capital that arises out of cultural identity and traditional patriotism is usually (using Robert Putnam's distinction) *bonding* capital that holds people together by excluding others, the kind of social capital that is generated by common civic work and voluntary civic activity across national borders and that is associated with the civic calling is *bridging* capital—capital that links people together.[58] Bridging capital is easier to create with global telecommunications and an emerging global ethics of care. But to be effective, global citizenship needs to mimic what Anthony Appiah has appealingly called "partial cosmopolitanism," an attachment to the human community rooted in "the partialities of kinfolk and community."[59] In civic shorthand, many have used the neologism "*glocal* citizenship," an identity that begins in the neighborhood but spirals out to encompass ever expanding circles of civic diversity and cultural difference that eventually bridge nation-states as well. Glocal citizenship insists on the priority of civic over other identities precisely because civic identity encourages and safeguards other identities, while other thicker identities discourage diversity and repress competing identities.

As I have argued above, it turns out that democratic public authority— the public's right to a monopoly over coercion—is actually what permits a multivalent and pluralistic market order to be established and enforced. Public monopoly is thus the condition needed for private pluralism to flourish. Private authority of the kind supposedly found in free and competitive markets, though definitive of diversity in theory, tends to constrict actual diversity in practice. The American "civic religion" offers a singular civic identity rooted in a singular civic calling and allows America to be home to many different peoples, cultures, nations, and religions. A monocultural (monoreligious or monoethnic) world on the other hand brooks no significant cultural, religious, or ethnic differences.

This is perhaps one reason why American multiculturalism, under the umbrella of an American civic religion, has been so successful, while French or Dutch or German forms of multiculturalism, despite good faith but in the absence of a compelling civil religion that draws immigrants and native born into a single civic calling, have been so problematic. The irony is that the "free market" (free from democratic control) strangles civic freedom and downplays citizenship and the civic calling in ways that undermine democracy and freedom overall, permitting natural monopolies—both business and ethnoreligious—as well as unregulated trusts to dominate; whereas the public monopoly of the sovereign democratic state over power is freedom's and diversity's real guarantor. This is why John Stuart Mill used as the frontispiece to his peerless essay "On Liberty" Wilhelm von Humboldt's impassioned declaration that "the grand, leading principle, towards which every argument unfolded in these pages directly converges, is the absolute and essential importance of human development in its richest diversity."[60] As Mill understood, liberalism concerns a kind of freedom that is not about endless trivial choices but about the pluralism of the human condition and the openness of human development. This is the freedom for which democracy is the condition—and the infantilist ethos the obstacle.

At this moment, however, when markets are global but democracy still national, democratic forces within national societies have a hard time cooperating across national frontiers. Liberal diversity remains invisible in the global setting because neither public liberty nor civic pluralism exist at all. Citizens may wish in theory to collaborate but find themselves constrained by the parochialism of their institutional constituencies. Global producers and global consumers are friends and allies, children of Davos deeply invested in free trade, unrestricted access, the free flow of capital, and the right to impose their standards on nations where they invest through so-called conditionality. Investors, producers, marketers, and shoppers share a commitment to privatization and branding as well as to the ethos of infantilization that allow them to cooperate across national frontiers.

Citizens, on the other hand, face each other across those same frontiers as rivals and enemies, representing competing national economies that share neither a private marketplace nor a global commonweal. They still imagine walls might protect them from the malevolent forces of interdependence and the predatory effects of unregulated markets. Just fifteen years after the Berlin Wall came down, bringing the Iron Curtain down with it, many of the democratic peoples who celebrated its fall are busy constructing new barriers, bulwarks meant to impede the progress of global anarchy and market injustice and to protect sovereignty, but that will be equally futile in the long term. Not just actual walls to fence out illegal immigrants or insurgent terrorists, but government-subsidized trade barriers and media-driven walls of prejudice. Across these protectionist barriers, French farmer faces Nigerian farmer as an adversary, French agricultural subsidies undermining the capacity of Nigerian agriculture to compete, even inside its own borders, with foreign products. Across these walls, Americans seized by fear of terrorism stare down the immigrant labor to which American industry silently beckons. Across these hardened frontiers, German steelworkers face Indian steelworkers as enemies—any market victory for the one, a market defeat for the other—Turkish guest workers caught in the middle. Across these walls, fearful Israelis face desperate Palestinians in a standoff that can bring neither long-term security.

Yet the alternatives are uncertain in a world of persistent sovereignties. Peoples distrust one another's global instincts. Goods advanced as "common" by developed nations, such as global safety standards or child labor restrictions or environmental protection, turn out in application to favor the interests of the developed (where standards are already in place). They are defended in ways that prejudice the interests of the developing, who cannot "afford" new standards without losing their competitive edge over the developed countries. The West hypocritically demands that they forgo the self-indulgent, environment-bashing, children-negligent policies by which the now developed once achieved their own rapid development. As if today's developing nations should pay the full price of the developed world's earlier bad habits. There can be no facile commonweal among these distrustful forces, no common ground for parochial democracies without common global interests who fear one another as much as they fear the free markets that make their workers and farmers so vulnerable.[61]

Democratizing globalization can make the circle whole. In overcoming civic schizophrenia, it revitalizes capitalism and restores the balance between citizens and consumers. It puts the trump card back into the hands of the public, now stretching across the world, and reempowers the voice of grown-ups in remonstrating with cultural infantilization's international influence. In John Updike's novel *The Coup* an African character named Ellellou observes, "I perceived that a man, in America, is a failed boy." Consumers are everywhere failed men, rendered juvenile and grasping by a culture of infantilism that refuses to let them grow up. The civic calling coaxes boys and girls into maturation and then into citizenship. It resonates with the culture of enlightenment which, in Immanuel Kant's conception, was defined by "man's emergence from his self-incurred immaturity." It points to collaborative norms and an "ethics of care" in which "relationships between persons, rather than either individual rights or individual preferences, are a primary focus," suggesting that such relationships can both extend and put a limit on markets and inform and strengthen global civil society.[62] The idea of the civic calling relies on innovative forms of the traditional commons, including a new information commons rooted in new technologies. The new commons, mirroring some of the very technologies that contribute to infantilization, might include democratic versions of *"software commons, licensing commons, open access scholarly journals, digital repositories, institutional commons, and subject matter commons* in areas ranging from knitting to music, agriculture to Supreme Court arguments"—although building such a commons "is neither easy nor costless."[63]

It has been my argument here that the cultivation of the commons is the work of adults. The immaturity about which Kant wrote two hundred years ago is today more than just self-incurred, however. It is abetted and reinforced by external cultural forces that impede maturation and stand in the way of the commonweal. Resistance to these forces can arise out of a renewal of the civic calling. The civic calling invokes a society able to respond generously to children's "irreducible needs" around the world without turning adults into children or seducing children into consumerism in the name of a hollow empowerment. The civic calling takes Wendy's part in the age-old struggle that recurs in each generation between Wendy and Peter Pan. It acknowledges the true delights of childhood, and helps children be children again by preserving them from the burdens of an exploitative and violent adult world. It refuses to "empower them" by taking away their dollies and blocks and toy wagons in which to haul them and replacing them with cell-phones and video games and credit cards with which to pay for them. It refuses to "free" them from parents and other gatekeepers in order to turn them over to market-mad pied pipers who lead them over a commercial precipice down into the mall. Children should play not pay, act not watch, learn not shop. Where capitalism can, it should help protect the boundaries of childhood and preserve the guardianship of parents and citizens; otherwise it should get out of the way. Not everything needs to earn a profit, not everyone needs to be a shopper—not all the time.

WE UNDOUBTEDLY LIVE in an age of capitalism triumphant, but for democracy and variety to survive, capitalism will have to moderate its triumph and citizens renew their calling, globally as well as nationally. We need democratic sovereignty to moderate market anarchy and market monopoly. But sovereignty is no longer viable within nations alone. Paradoxically, as its most enthusiastic advocates acknowledge, capitalism itself requires such moderation for its own flourishing. Yet given the realities of the cultural ethos portrayed here, moderating capitalism and renewing the civic calling are formidable tasks, the more so because that will have to be achieved globally as well as domestically. Formidable but doable. Democracy is always aspirational rather than a done deal, more of a continuing journey than a found destination. Citizenship must have also seemed an improbable destiny for the subjects of monarchical rule in England in 1650 or for the victims of totalitarian Europe in 1940. Yet by 1689, parliamentary rule was secured in England and by the 1950s rival European nations at war for three hundred years had learned to pool their sovereignty and create the beginnings of a European citizenship.

Today, under the hyperconsumerist conditions we have examined here, the civic calling will feel to many people like a vacant phrase, global citizenship like a utopian dream. I do not have a formula for their realization. Yet the brute realities of interdependence make them both necessary and in the long term (if we have a long term) inevitable. The only question is whether we discover or invent and then embrace new forms of global civic governance which the costs of the infantilist ethos cry out for, and which the crises of consumer capitalism mandate; or whether we first pay a terrible price in puerility, market chaos, and unrewarding private freedom. That price is already being paid, but paid by those who can least afford it, the very children we think to emulate and empower with our foolish addiction to the culture of infantilism. This is the critical point to which the history of capitalism and of its ingenious and ever-changing justifying ethos has brought us. Yet as always, it is a history we have made for ourselves. So that as always, even under the harsh but seductive dominion of capitalism triumphant, the fate of citizens remains in our own hands.

NOTES

1 Capitalism Triumphant and the Infantilist Ethos

1. *Webster's New American Dictionary* offered *adultescent* as its "word of the year" in 2004.

2. David Ansen, "Cliffhanger Classic," *Newsweek*, June 15, 1981.

3. Quoted by Maureen Dowd, "Leave It to Hollywood," *New York Times*, August 16, 1997.

4. Philip Hensher, "Harry Potter—Give Me a Break," *Independent*, January 25, 2000.

5. Robert J. Samuelson, "Adventures in Agelessness," *Newsweek*, November 3, 2003.

6. Joseph Epstein, "The Perpetual Adolescent," *Weekly Standard*, March 15, 2003.

7. George F. Will, "Validation by Defeat," *Newsweek*, December 15, 2004. Setting the scene for what will surely be criticism of this book, Will argues that "belief in the infantilism of the American public has been an expanding facet of some 'progressive' thinking for 50 years—since the explosive growth of advertising."

8. Lev Grossman, "They Just Won't Grow Up," *Time*, January 24, 2005; Adam Sternbergh, "Forever Youngish: Why Nobody Wants to Be an Adult Anymore," *New York Magazine*, April 3, 2006. Sternbergh's essay opens this way: "He owns eleven pairs of sneakers, hasn't worn anything but jeans in a year, and won't shut up about the latest Death Cab for Cutie CD. But he is no kid. He is among the ascendant breed of grown-up who has redefined adulthood as we once knew it and killed off the generation gap" (p. 24).

9. "Police at Harrisburg International Airport in Pennsylvania have been sweetening the inspections by passing out lollipops to targeted drivers. 'It's so we don't intimidate,' said Alfred Testa Jr., the airport's aviation director. The policemen are very polite. They will have a smile on their face.'" "The Infantilization of America," posted on February 19, 2004, on the website AFFBRAINWASH.com, citing Eugene Volokh.

10. William Norwich, "The Children's Department," *New York Times Magazine*, July 28, 2002,

p. 41. This remarkable essay, in America's newspaper of record, was designed as a fashion layout under the subtitle "Babes in Coutureland."

11. In 2002 Americans spent $7.7 billion on 6.9 million cosmetic procedures according to the American Society for Aesthetic Plastic Surgery. This included 1.7 million Botox injections, 495,000 chemical peels, 125,000 face lifts, and 83,000 tummy tucks—88 percent of these on women (Samuelson, "Adventures in Agelessness").

12. Among the most popular video games in the world, Civilization (now in four editions from Firaxis) offers players a chance to "rule the world" via sixteen classic cultures, from 4000 BC to AD 2050.

13. Susan Linn, *Consuming Kids: The Hostile Takeover of Childhood* (New York: New Press, 2004), p. 8.

14. Ibid.

15. The $169 billion figure comes from "TRU Projects Teens Will Spend $169 Billion in 2004," Teenage Research Unlimited, December 1, 2004. Retrieved March 30, 2005, at www .teenresearch.com/PRview.cfm?edit_id=287. A Harris Interactive study offers even more compelling statistics: 54 million people in the age eight to twenty-one category, spending about $172 billion, and with an "income" of $211 billion (see link: www.harrisinteractive.com/news/ allnewsbydate.asp?NewsID=667). According to another Harris Interactive study, college students "tote $122 billion in spending power" (see link: www.harrisinteractive.com/news/ allnewsbydate.asp?NewsID=835).

16. "The Kids Are All Right," *The Economist*, December 21, 2000.

17. John Tierney, "Adultescent," *New York Times*, December 26, 2004.

18. Manohla Dargis, "One Word for What's Happening to Actor's Faces Today: Plastics," *New York Times*, January 23, 2005.

19. "More British men holding on to parental nest," *Times of India*, February 22, 2006, available at http://timesofindia.indiatimes.com/articleshow/1423683.cms.

20. "The Top Trends of 2004," *New York Times*, December 23, 2004. The same trend is visible in India, where it is seen as a boon for consumerism since young adults living at home have large disposable incomes.

21. "The Kids Are All Right," *The Economist*, December 21, 2000. These figures would be even older for the United States, but for the role of immigration which lowers mean age across the board.

22. T. Berry Brazelton and Stanley I. Greenspan, *The Irreducible Needs of Children: What Every Child Must Have to Grow, Learn, and Flourish* (Cambridge, Mass.: Perseus, 2000).

23. Figures are from Worldwatch Institute's fact sheet summary of its *State of the World 2004* report, Table 1–1, "Consumer Spending and Population, by Region, 2000," January 7, 2004. Retrieved April 6, 2005, at www.worldwatch.org/press/news/2004/01/07/.

24. Advertising expenditures projection from Robert Coen, Universal McCann's Insider's Report on Advertising Expenditures, December 2000. While the gross aid figure puts the United States on top, when calculated as a percentage of GNP its foreign aid ranks dead last out of 22 Western countries and (at about 0.14 percent of GNP) leaves it well below the European average of over 0.2 percent and far below the United Nations Millennium Development Goal of 0.7 percent of GNP for developed nations. By 2005 it had improved slightly to 0.22 percent.

25. Guy Debord, *The Society of the Spectacle* (1967; reprint, New York: Zone Books, 1994), p. 33. Translation by Donald Nicholson-Smith.

26. Brazelton and Greenspan's list of seven irreducible needs depends to some degree indirectly on economic factors (starving parents are unlikely to be capable of protecting or even loving their children), but except for physical protection and safety, is relational rather than commodity based. See Brazelton and Greenspan, *The Irreducible Needs of Children*.

27. Victoria de Grazia, *Irresistable Empire: America's Advance through Twentieth-Century Europe* (Cambridge, Mass.: Belknap Press, 2005), p. 131.

28. Gene Del Vecchio, *Creating Ever-Cool: A Marketer's Guide to a Kid's Heart* (Gretna, La.: Pelican Publishing, 1997), p. 19.

29. Norma Odom Pecora, *The Business of Children's Entertainment* (New York: Guilford Press, 1988), p. 154.

30. Del Vecchio, *Creating Ever-Cool*, pp. 19, 24.

31. From the Center for a New American Dream website (www.newdream.org), citing reports from the advertising company McCann-Erikson and estimates from "Just the Facts about Advertising and Marketing to Children." Gross advertising expenditure estimates vary widely; depending on the source, they range from $174 billion to $264 billion per annum. What is clear is that they are rising rapidly both in the United States and around the world.

32. World advertising figures from Tobi Elkin, "Just an Online Minute . . . Look East," *MediaPost*, December 6, 2004.

33. Andy Zhang, "Kids' Buying Power in China," Eguo China Retail Group, September 8, 2003. Retrieved April 6, 2005, at www.eguo.com/chinaretail/research_more.asp.

34. Juliet B. Schor, *Born to Buy: The Commercialized Child and the New Consumer Culture* (New York: Scribner, 2004), p. 9. Among the far more extensive list of uncritical celebrations of kids' marketing are David L. Siegel, Timothy J. Coffey, and Gregory Livingston, *The Great Tween Buying Machine: Capturing Your Share of the Multi-Billion-Dollar Tween Market* (Chicago: Dearborn Trade Publishing, 2004), and David A. Morrison, *Marketing to the Campus Crowd: Everything You Need to Know to Capture the $200 Billion College Market* (Chicago: Dearborn Trade Publishing, 2004).

35. See Jenn Shreve, "Let the Games Begin," subtitled "Video games, once confiscated in class, are now a key teaching tool," *Edutopia*, April 2005. Shreve reports that in 2004 educational video game titles accounted for $140 million, or 2 percent of the $7.3-billion-a-year video-game American market.

36. Ibid., sidebar, "Shut It Off" (Shreve cites Prensky and then finishes the thought).

37. Channel One Network, originally founded by Chris Whittle (bought by 3M Corporation and owned today [2006] by Primedia), leases telecommunications equipment to more than 12,000 high schools throughout the United States. In return, it gains the right to show its soft news programming (nine minutes of teen-slanted soft "educational" news with three minutes of hard advertising) with students obliged to watch during regular class time hours. See www.channelone.com.

38. Thorstein Veblen, *The Higher Learning in America* (1918; reprint, with a new introduction by Ivar Berg, New Brunswick, N.J.: Transaction Books, 1993); Clark Kerr, *The Uses of the University* (Cambridge, Mass.: Harvard University Press, 1963); Allan Bloom, *The Closing of the American Mind: How Higher Education Has Failed Democracy and Impoverished the Souls of Today's Students* (New York: Simon & Schuster, 1987); Stanley Aronowitz, *The Knowledge Factory: Dismantling the Corporate University and Creating True Higher Learning* (Boston: Beacon Press, 2000). Commercialization has become so prevalent that nowadays it is less often assailed (in such books as *University, Inc.: The Corporate Corruption of American Higher Education* by Jennifer Washburn [New York: Basic Books, 2005]) than it is rationalized—in the name of job training and market competition among nations. Few actually celebrate a corporative university, but many welcome corporate education and what amounts to a vocationalization of higher education as job training. See, for example, Jeanne Meister, "Ten Steps to Creating a Corporate University," *T&D Magazine*, vol. 52, no. 11 (1998), pp. 38–43. Similar titles include Meister's *Corporate Universities: Lessons in Building a World-Class Work Force* (New York: McGraw-Hill, 1998); Mark Allen, editor, *The Corporate University Handbook: Designing, Managing, and Growing a Successful Program* (New York: AMACOM, 2002); and Kevin Wheeler in collaboration with Eileen Clegg, *The Corporate University Workbook: Launching the 21st Century Learning Organization* (San Francisco: John Wiley & Sons, 2005).

39. Morrison, *Marketing to the Campus Crowd*, p. 225. Morrison cites figures from *American*

Demographics that put campus sales in the early 2000s at $9 billion on telecommunications, $8.5 billion on textbooks, $5 billion on travel, $5 billion on dorm furnishings, $4.4 billion on bottled water and soft drinks, and $2.7 billion on CDs (p. xvii).

40. Richard B. Woodward, "Have Yourself a Merry Little Festivus," *New York Times Book Review*, December 26, 2004, p. 23. The book to which Woodward's essay refers is Maud Lavin, ed., *The Business of Holidays* (New York: Monacelli Press, 2004).

41. Morrison, *Marketing to the Campus Crowd*, p. 225.

42. In his *Civilization and Its Discontents*, Freud associates religion with "the figure of an enormously exalted father" and suggests that "the whole thing is so patently infantile, so foreign to reality, that to anyone with a friendly attitude to humanity it is painful to think that the great majority of mortals will never be able to rise above this view of life" (edited and translated by J. Strachey; New York: W. W. Norton, 1961, p. 21). The view is further developed in Freud's *The Future of an Illusion*. Freud's instrumentalization of religion is itself simplistic; I have argued elsewhere that it is only fundamentalism rather than "normal religion" that has regressive, infantilizing tendencies.

43. Epstein, "The Perpetual Adolescent."

44. Schor, *Born to Buy*, p. 13.

45. Pecora, *The Business of Children's Entertainment*, p. 154.

46. Samuelson, "Adventures in Agelessness."

47. The Cryonics Institute of Clinton Township, Michigan, "offers cryonic suspension services and information. As soon as possible after legal death, a member patient is prepared and cooled to a temperature where physical decay essentially stops, and is then maintained indefinitely in cryostasis. When and if future medical technology allows, our member patients hope to be healed and revived, and awaken to extended life in youthful good health" (from the website www.cryonics.org).

48. Chip Walker, "Can TV Save the Planet?" *American Demographics*, May 1996, cited in Naomi Klein, *No Logo: Taking Aim at the Brand Bullies* (New York: Picador, 2000), p. 119.

49. Klein, *No Logo*, p. 115.

50. A blurb from Helen Boehm, the vice president of Fox Children's Network, on the back cover of McNeal's *Kids as Consumers: A Handbook of Marketing to Children* (New York: Simon & Schuster, 1992).

51. McNeal, *Kids as Consumers*, p. 250.

52. "To put it crudely, capital is being invested in new factories to make more things when the market is already struggling with a mounting shortage of buyers" (William Greider, *One World, Ready or Not: The Manic Logic of Global Capitalism* [New York: Simon & Schuster, 1997], p. 49).

53. Pecora, *The Business of Children's Entertainment*, p. 7.

54. Arundhati Parmar, "Global Youth United: Homogenous Group Prime Target for U.S. Marketers," *Marketing News*, October 28, 2002.

55. David Jones and Doris Klein, *Man-Child: A Study of the Infantilization of Man* (New York: McGraw Hill, 1970), p. 341. The authors believed even in 1970 that "we seem to see an exponential increase in the momentum of the process of infantilization in recent times" (p. 343).

56. Thomas Frank has written brilliantly about the ways in which the advertising and men's apparel industries helped the hippies forge a rhetoric of rebellion and innovation that was a veritable "conquest of cool." See Frank, *The Conquest of Cool: Business Culture, Counterculture, and the Rise of Hip Consumerism* (Chicago: University of Chicago Press, 1997).

57. Del Vecchio, *Creating Ever-Cool*, p. 24. "Cool" remains the most potent word in the youth marketer's vocabulary, cooler even than rivals such as "hot" and "edgy" and "passionate"— conjoint terms also meant to capture what teens are supposed to be and have that adults don't and can't.

58. Mike Davis, "Fortress Los Angeles: The Militarization of Urban Space," in Michael Sorkin,

ed., *Variations on a Theme Park: The New American City and the End of Public Space* (New York: Hill and Wang, 1992), pp. 169, 176.

59. McNeal, *Kids as Consumers*, p. 249.

60. Ginia Bellafante, "Dressing Up: The Power of Adult Clothes in a Youth-Obsessed Culture," *New York Times*, March 28, 2004. Bellafante points out that "From the counterculture movements of the 1960's to the mass embrace of the casual workplace in the 1990's, Americans of a certain age have consistently shown a taste for dressing as if they had yet to be conscripted by adulthood. Not since the late 1950's, in fact, have grown-ups had an identifying look distinctly different from the boys and girls in their charge."

61. Louis Menand portraying Peter Biskind's perspective, in Menand's "Gross Points: Is the blockbuster the end of cinema?" *The New Yorker*, February 7, 2005, p. 83. Maureen Dowd is blunter still: the likes of "Spielberg, Lucas, 'The Flintstones,' Brady Bunches unto the generations, Kevin Costner fairy tales, Stallone and Schwarzenegger: PG 13, NC 17 or whatever," she exclaims, "treat their audiences like children" (Dowd, "Leave It to Hollywood").

62. As reported in the *New York Times*, Sharon Waxman, "Big Films," December 20, 2004, p. E1. Figures from Exhibitor Relations Cò.: Box Office Mojo, through December 19, 2004. Films with an asterisk were still playing at the time of the report, so figures for the year were not complete.

63. Figures from Nielsen Entertainment, cited in Lorne Manley, "Doing the Hollywood Math: What Slump?" *New York Times*, December 11, 2005.

64. There is still some adventure left in the theater in writers-directors-designers such as Robert Wilson, Peter Brook, Simon McBirney, and Josh Fox, among others, but theirs is not the way of convention. See Barber, "The Price of Irony," *Salmagundi*, Fall 2005.

65. Lynn Hirschberg, "Us & Them: What Is an American Movie Now?" *New York Times*, November 14, 2004. An anonymous Hollywood executive told Hirschberg, "Our movies no longer reflect our culture. They have become gross, distorted exaggerations. And I think America is growing into those exaggerated images." It is interesting that Michael Moore's *Fahrenheit 9/11* won the Festival grand prize—primarily for political reasons but perhaps also as encouragement to America's independent producers trying to make serious films.

66. Menand, "Gross Points," p. 85. Menand notes that in the first *Terminator* film, Arnold Schwarzenegger had exactly seventeen lines. This can hardly be a surprise, writes Menand, since global blockbusters generally feature "wizards; slinky women of few words; men of few words who can expertly drive anything, spectacularly wreck anything, and leap safely from the top of anything; characters from comic books, sixth-grade world-history textbooks, or 'Bulfinch's Mythology'; explosions; phenomena unknown to science; a computer whiz with attitude; a brand-name soft drink, running shoe, or candy bar [concessions yield 35 percent of theater revenue and theaters can keep it!]; an incarnation of pure evil; more explosions; and the voice of Robin Williams."

67. Jones and Klein, *Man-Child*, p. 177. Jones and Klein wrote an odd book combining a neo-Freudian analysis of infantilization with a rationalization of the regressive as useful to intelligence and to civilization. Although they saw thirty-five years ago many of the trends toward infantilization I discuss here—"we seem to see an exponential increase in the momentum of the process of infantilization in recent (and especially in our own) times," they wrote—for the most part they regard it benignly or even as positive. This perhaps speaks in part to the dialectical take on childhood I advocate below.

68. Ibid., p. 340.

69. George Lakoff, *Don't Think of an Elephant! Know Your Values and Frame the Debate* (White River Junction, Vt.: Chelsea Green Publishing, 2004).

70. This and subsequent quotes are from Lisa Belkin, "Your Kids Are Their Problem," *New York Times Magazine*, June 23, 2000. See the book by Elinor Burkett called *The Baby Boon: How Family-Friendly America Cheats the Childless* (New York: Free Press, 2000).

71. For examples of the self-described ranting that typifies this "adult" group (which in fact

sounds like a junior-high clique berating the school principal), see Belkin's "Your Kids Are Their Problem."

72. As Dan Cook has observed, "*children's* culture has become virtually indistinguishable from *consumer* culture over the course of the last century" (Dan Cook, "Lunchbox Hegemony? Kids and the Marketplace, Then and Now," August 20, 2001, www.lipmagazine.org).

73. Pecora, *The Business of Children's Entertainment*, p. 20.

74. Cited from Media Awareness Network, "How Marketers Target Kids," January 24, 2005, at www.media-awareness.ca.

75. McNeal, *Kids As Consumers*, p. 18.

76. Ibid., p. 20. It is hardly a surprise then that a world survey of marketing to children in 2001 would boast that "advertising has become pervasive in daily life and continues to expand into new realms." Increasingly, advertisers are marketing to children to shape consumption preference early and to take advantage of the growing amount of money that people are spending on children, which hit $405 billion globally in 2000 ("Marketing to Children: A World Survey, 2001," Euromonitor International, cited in the Worldwatch Institute's *Vital Signs 2003* [New York: W. W. Norton, 2003]).

77. Peter Zollo, *Wise Up to Teens: Insights into Marketing and Advertising to Teenagers* (Ithaca, N.Y.: New Strategist Publications, 2d ed., 1999), pp. 24, 336.

78. Dan S. Acuff, Ph.D., *What Kids Buy and Why: The Psychology of Marketing to Kids* (New York: Free Press, 1997), p. 17.

79. One marketing group offered both a Youth Power 2005 conference aimed at marketing to youngsters fifteen to twenty-four and a Kid Power 2006 conference aimed at kids aged two to twelve, the latter held at the Disney Yacht and Beach Club in Lake Buena Vista, Florida.

80. Alessandra Stanley, "'American Idol' Dresses Up for Its Big Season Finale," *New York Times*, May 24, 2006.

81. Pecora, *The Business of Children's Entertainment*, p. 20.

82. Acuff, *What Kids Buy and Why*. Capitalism's search for consumers is hardly new, and marketing to the young has a history (see, for example, the 1938 book *Reaching Juvenile Markets* by E. E. Grumbine [New York: McGraw-Hill]) nicely depicted by Norma Pecora in her *The Business of Children's Entertainment*.

83. Cited by Dave Itzkoff, who offers the comment on the guidebook in "TV Moves a Step Closer to the Womb," *New York Times*, May 21, 2006.

84. "New Study Finds Children Age Zero to Six Spend as Much Time with TV, Computers and Video Games as Playing Outside," Kaiser Family Foundation, October 28, 2003, retrieved March 30, 2005, at www.kff.org/entmedia/entmedia102803nr.cfm. The Kaiser report is described in Michel Marriott, "Weaned on Video Games," *New York Times*, October 28, 2004, as well as in Benedict Carey, "Babes in a Grown-up Toyland," *New York Times*, November 28, 2004.

85. See Steven Johnson, *Everything Bad Is Good for You: How Today's Popular Culture Is Actually Making Us Smarter* (New York: Riverhead Books, 2005). I deal with Johnson directly in chapter 7.

86. Acuff, *What Kids Buy and Why*, pp. 18–19.

87. Freud, *Civilization and Its Discontents*, p. 91. Freud never got to embark on that journey. I am doing so here.

88. J. M. Barrie, *Peter Pan* (New York: HarperCollins, 2000), pp. 216–217.

89. Freud, *Civilization and Its Discontents*, pp. 13–14.

90. That the juvenile is less responsible as well as less free has been widely recognized not only in psychology but in law. Marketers know full well that they are exploiting rather than empowering the young when they play on their youthfulness or seek to encourage regression in adults. The marketer looks to the juvenile as the ideal consumer precisely because the merchandizing industry shares the understanding of the juvenile favored by the U.S. Supreme Court majority in its 2005 decision outlawing the death penalty for juveniles. In *Roper v. Simmons* (March 2005), a 5–4 majority ruled that juveniles should not be subject to the death penalty

because a "lack of maturity and an underdeveloped sense of responsibility are found in youth more often than in adults and are more understandable among the young." If, as the court ruled, such "qualities often result in impetuous and ill-considered actions and decisions," and if this diminishes juvenile culpability in capital crime cases, then surely it diminishes juvenile responsibility and liberty in consumer decision making. The ruling also noted that "juveniles are more vulnerable or susceptible to negative influence and outside pressures, including peer pressure," and that "the character of a juvenile is not as well formed as that of an adult. The personality traits of juveniles are more transitory, less fixed." (A summary of the case can be found at www.oyez.org/oyez/resource/case/1724.)

The court knows children when it sees them. Market capitalism pretends not to. The infantilist ethos insists they are not children. If we spare juveniles the death penalty when they commit capital crimes, should we not refrain from insisting they are liberated and empowered when we play on their "lack of maturity" and "underdeveloped sense of responsibility" to get them to buy things they don't need, and exploit their tendencies to be "impetuous" and to engage in "ill-considered actions and decisions" in order to condition them to the obligatory shopping consumer capitalism needs to survive?

91. Marketers themselves divide the population into such consumer-targeted categories and develop merchandizing strategies accordingly. A marketing firm called Claritas thus managed to segment America into dozens of neighborhood consumer sectors defined by actual consumables such as "Pools and Patios," "Shotguns and Pickups," "Bohemia Mix," and "Urban Gold."

2 From Protestantism to Puerility

1. Max Weber, *The Protestant Ethic and the Spirit of Capitalism*, with an introduction by Anthony Giddens, translated by Talcott Parsons (London: Routledge, 1992; first published in German in 1904–1905), p. 68.

2. Ibid., p. 27. Weber published other studies in later years examining the economic ethos of other religions.

3. Ibid., p. 172.

4. Elizabeth Kolbert cites this phrase in an essay on Max Weber in which she observes that "in the century since then, there is hardly a claim made in 'The Protestant Ethic,' either about the history of religion or about the history of economics, that hasn't been challenged" (Elizabeth Kolbert, "Why Work: A Hundred Years of 'The Protestant Ethic,'" *The New Yorker*, November 29, 2004).

5. See Max Weber's essay "The Social Psychology of the World Religions" in H. H. Gerth and C. Wright Mills, eds., *From Max Weber: Essays in Sociology* (New York: A Galaxy Book, Oxford University Press, 1946), taken from Weber's "Die Wirtschaftsethik der Weltreligionen" of 1922–1923. Weber writes here of an "economic ethic" that "points to the practical impulse for action which [is] founded in the psychological and pragmatic contexts of religions" (Gerth and Mills, p. 267). He looks at Confucian, Hindu, Buddhist, Christian, Islamic, and Judaic religious ethics. These somewhat scholastic points are important because they indicate that Weber did not regard the Protestant ethos that informed capitalism as a special case, but as one important instance of an interaction between religion and economics that could be found in every society.

6. Daniel Bell, *The Cultural Contradictions of Capitalism* (1976; 20th anniversary ed., New York: Basic Books, 1996), p. 71.

7. Thomas L. Friedman, *The World Is Flat: A Brief History of the Twenty-first Century* (New York: Farrar, Straus and Giroux, 2005), p. 252.

8. Bell, *The Cultural Contradiction of Capitalism*, p. 71.

9. Andrew Carnegie, *The Gospel of Wealth* (Bedford, Mass.: Applewood Books, 1998), p. 10. Originally published in *North American Review*, June 1889.

10. David Brooks, *On Paradise Drive: How We Live Now (and Alway Have) in the Future Tense*

(New York: Simon & Schuster, 2004), p. 196. A former writer for the conservative *Weekly Standard*, Brooks has become a *New York Times* op-ed-page regular.

11. Thomas Frank, *What's the Matter with Kansas? How Conservatives Won the Heart of America* (New York: Henry Holt, 2005), pp. 248–249. I will return to this theme and Thomas Frank's take on it in chapter 7.

12. George Gilder, *Wealth and Poverty* (New York: Basic Books, 1981), p. x.

13. Ibid., p. 266.

14. Ibid., p. 6.

15. John Locke proposed that the division of the classes in its original form grew out of a natural division between the "the industrious and rational" to whom God gave the abundant natural world for their use, and "the quarrelsome and contentious" who preferred theft to hard work; see book 2, chapter 5 (p. 309 of Laslett edition) of *The Second Treatise of Civil Government* (Cambridge: Cambridge University Press, 1960). For Locke's influence on the New England pastors, see Steven Dworetz, *The Unvarnished Doctrine: Locke, Liberalism, and the American Revolution* (Durham, N.C.: Duke University Press, 1990).

16. Gilder, *Wealth and Poverty*, p. 245.

17. *Vancouver Sun*, Monday, December 26, 2005. The editorial argued that it was in the interest of humanity that we spend money. Available at www.canada.com/vancouversun/news/editorial/story.html?id=de5fb8bc-f0a6-4f20-965e-08d0e93a2013.

18. "Religious Rejections of the World and Their Directions," in Gerth and Mills, *From Max Weber*, p. 332.

19. William Greider, *One World, Ready or Not: The Manic Logic of Global Capitalism* (New York: Simon & Schuster, 1997).

20. The quote here is from the concluding pages of Weber's final chapter, "Asceticism and the Spirit of Capitalism," in *The Protestant Ethic and the Spirit of Capitalism*, pp. 181–182. Weber seems almost to be describing Gilder's affecting nostalgia for a Puritan-grounded capitalist ethos when he speaks of the "idea of duty in one's calling" as one that "prowls about in our lives like the ghost of dead religious beliefs" (p. 182). Though his impulse is Weberian, Gilder perhaps knew how far he had strayed from the master since Weber does not appear in *Wealth and Poverty* or its index.

21. Ibid., p. 181. In the first clause, ending "thrown aside at any minute," Weber is citing Richard Baxter. The rest is Weber's own.

22. Ibid., p. 182.

23. Ibid., p. 182.

24. Ayn Rand, *The Fountainhead* (New York: New American Library, 1943), p. 686.

25. *Greed Is Good: The Capitalist Pig Guide to Investing* (New York: Harper Business, 1999), p. 2.

26. Ibid., pp. xvii–xviii.

27. Suze Orman, *The Courage to Be Rich: Creating a Life of Material and Spiritual Abundance* (New York: Riverhead Books, 1999), p. 4.

28. Ibid., p. 361. Or perhaps it is Franklin who sounds like Orman: "Wealth is not his that has it," he famously opined, "but his that enjoys it," so that "if you know how to spend less than you get, you have the philosopher's stone."

29. Ibid., p. 361.

30. Friedrich Engels and Karl Marx, *The Communist Manifesto* (originally published in 1848, translated in 1888 by Samuel Moore; New York: Penguin, 1967), p. 222. Although he discerns the same religious connections as Weber, Marx finds it hard to take them seriously. Thus, in the full paragraph from which the citation in the text is taken, Engels and Marx write, "The bourgeoisie, wherever it has got the upper hand, has put an end to all feudal, patriarchal, idyllic relations. It has pitilessly torn asunder the motley feudal ties that bound man to his 'natural superiors,' and has left no other nexus between people than naked self-interest, than callous 'cash payment.' It has drowned out the most heavenly ecstasies of religious fervor, of chivalrous enthusiasm, of

philistine sentimentalism, in the icy water of egotistical calculation. It has resolved personal worth into exchange value, and in place of the numberless indefeasible chartered freedoms, has set up that single, unconscionable freedom—Free Trade. In one word, for exploitation, veiled by religious and political illusions, it has substituted naked, shameless, direct, brutal exploitation."

31. New York State's DestiNY Mall, comprising an "800-acre waterfront resort featuring the world's largest enclosed and integrated structure," and anticipating up to 20 million visitors a year, was offered a $100 million development grant by Congress—see the *Ithaca Journal*, October 12, 2004, as well as the mall's website at www.destinyusa.com/mainsite.html. As of this writing, however, the project remains stalled, mired in legal disputes.

32. These figures and examples are from John de Graaf, David Wann, and Thomas H. Naylor, *Affluenza: The All-Consuming Epidemic* (San Francisco: Berrett-Koehler Publishers, 2001), pp. 14–15, a popular book based on the television documentaries of the same name.

33. See Nick Burns, "Shaving with Five Blades When Maybe Two Will Do," *New York Times*, January 19, 2006. Thirty years ago, the television comedy show *Saturday Night Live* mocked a triple-track three-bladed razor with the slogan "Because you'll believe anything."

34. Weber, *The Protestant Ethic and the Spirit of Capitalism*, p. 182.

35. Wilhelm Röpke, *A Humane Economy: The Social Framework of the Free Market* (Indianapolis, Ind.: Liberty Fund, 1971), p. 113.

36. Irving Kristol, *Two Cheers for Capitalism* (New York: Basic Books, 1978), pp. 259 and 254. Kristol's curious but very successful book signaled the completion of his journey from the left to the right but still manifested a deep ambivalence about the counterculture whose youthful iconoclasts he disliked but whose complaints about capitalism's sins he partially shared, or perhaps even inspired.

37. Worldwatch Institute, *State of the World 2004: The Consumer Society* (New York: W. W. Norton, 2004). Also see Alex Kirby, "Richer, Stouter, and No Happier," *BBC News*, January 9, 2004.

38. Robert E. Lane, *The Loss of Happiness in Market Democracies* (New Haven, Conn.: Yale University Press, 2000), p. 3.

39. Karl Marx, *The Economic and Philosophical Manuscripts of 1844*, edited by Erich Fromm in Fromm's collection titled *Marx's Concept of Man* (New York: Frederick Unger, 1961), p. 53.

40. Christopher Lasch, *The Culture of Narcissism: American Life in an Age of Diminishing Expectations* (New York: Warner Books, 1979), p. 12.

41. See Rob Walker, "The Hidden (in Plain Sight) Persuaders," *New York Times Magazine*, December 5, 2004, describing, for example, how "Sony Ericsson in 2002 hired 60 actors in 10 cities to accost strangers" asking them to take their picture with—of course!—a Sony Ericsson cameraphone. "Word-of-mouth" marketing conferences are increasingly common: see, for example, the 2005 Chicago-based conference advertised as "The First Annual Buzz Conference for Buzz, Viral, Blog, and World of Mouth Marketers" organized by the Word of Mouth Marketing Association (see www.womma.com). I deal extensively with buzz marketing in chapter 5.

42. Historical determinism entails the idea that history unfolds independently of human will and wholly immune to creative intervention. My argument here assumes rather that the social systems described are the consequence of social philosophies and individual actions in a dialectic that leaves ample room both for a logic of capitalist development *and* for the workings of human will. What varies over time may be how social systems accommodate themselves to collective liberty: whether they are more or less vulnerable to resistance and change.

43. Weber, *The Protestant Ethic and the Spirit of Capitalism*, p. 69.

44. There are some notable and exotic exceptions on the model of America's frontier entrepreneurs like Molly Brown, immortalized in the popular vernacular in Meredith Willson's Broadway musical *The Unsinkable Molly Brown*.

45. Michael Oakeshott, *On Human Conduct* (Oxford: Clarendon Press, 1975), p. 239.

46. Walt Whitman, "Song of Myself," stanza 24, in *The Portable Walt Whitman*, edited by Mark Van Doren (New York: Penguin Books, 1977), p. 56.

47. Walt Whitman, "Song of the Open Road," stanza 5, in *The Portable Walt Whitman*, p. 159.

48. Charles Higham's *Howard Hughes: The Secret Life* (New York: G. P. Putnam's, 1993) offers a limpid if melodramatic portrait which, aptly, became the basis for the 2004 prize-winning Martin Scorsese film, *The Aviator*, in which Leonardo Di Caprio played Hughes.

49. Ron Chernow, *Titan: The Life of John D. Rockefeller, Sr.* (New York: Random House, 1998), p. 97.

50. Ibid., p. 11.

51. Ibid., p. 86, citing historian Allan Nevins.

52. Ibid., p. 81, citing Weber, *The Protestant Ethic and the Spirit of Capitalism*, p. 69.

53. As rendered by Jacob Streider, *Jacob Fugger the Rich, Merchant and Banker of Augsburg, 1459–1525* (original German edition, Adelphia, 1931; translated by M. L. Hartsough, edited by N. S. B. Gras, Hamden, Conn.: Archon Books, 1966), p. 176. See also Mark Häberlein, *"Die Fugger" Geschichte einer Augsburger Familie (1367–1650)* (Kohlhammer, 2006).

54. Streider, *Jacob Fugger the Rich*, p. 171.

55. Ibid., p. 181.

56. Martin Kluger, *The Wealthy Fuggers: Pomp and Power of the German Medici in Golden Augsburg of the Renaissance* (Regio Augsburg Tourismus GmbH, n.d.), p. 26. Aside from the power that came from their worldwide financial and trading empire, according to historian Franz Herre, the family at its zenith owned "half of Swabia . . . a large portion of Bavaria, a portion of Switzerland, the larger part of Alsace and various parts of Tyrol, Hungary, Poland, Bohemia and Saxony" (Franz Herre, *Die Fugger in Ihrer Zeit* [1985], cited in Kluger, p. 29). Ownership of land is of course distinctly feudal and does not qualify the Fuggers as capitalist, but their real power lay in their control of financial capital and trade, land ownership being a product rather than a cause of their worldly dominion. A Fugger private bank continues to operate today.

57. Streider, *Jacob Fugger the Rich*, p. 172. Streider notes that the leadership not only concurred in the importance of monopoly to the German economy, but took the lead in guaranteeing it through statute and policy (p. 173).

58. Luther the German nationalist is said to have felt some pride in the fact that the greatest merchant of the epoch was from Augsburg (Streider, *Jacob Fugger the Rich*, p. 157).

59. Kluger, *The Wealthy Fuggers*, p. 8.

60. Frederic Morton, *The Rothschilds: A Family Portrait* (London: Secker & Warburg, 1963), p. 48. Drawing the line between "mere" financial and banking hegemony, and investment capitalism is of course not easy. Some would insist the Fuggers were finally only financiers (which might also be said of the Rockefellers, particularly in the latter generations), while others might argue the Rothschilds were as crucial to the emergence of full-blown industrial capitalism in nineteenth-century Europe as the Fuggers were to the genesis of seventeenth- and eighteenth-century capitalism in Italy and Austria and beyond.

61. Chernow, *Titan*, p. 49.

62. Ibid., p. 76.

63. Ibid., p. 153.

64. Congregationalism, Methodism, and Northern Baptism described different journeys, but mid–nineteenth century they shared a common devotion to service and social action. As a biographer of the Rockefeller women has pointed out, "In the 1840s, the Baptist witness incorporated many social causes, including the control of alcohol, antislavery and education. . . . Given this involvement of their church in social causes, the Rockefeller children learned that Christian service extended beyond the church walls, into the community at large" (Clarice Stasz, *The Rockefeller Women: Dynasty of Piety, Privacy, and Service* [New York: St. Martin's Press, 1995], pp. 14–15).

65. Gertrude Himmelfarb, *The Roads to Modernity: The British, French, and American Enlightenments* (New York: Alfred A. Knopf, 2004), p. 121.

66. Chernow, *Titan*, p. 76.

67. Wesley cited in Himmelfarb, *The Roads to Modernity*, p. 122. Cotton Mather had warned still earlier, in *Magnalia Christi Americana*, that "religion begot prosperity, and the daughters devoured the mother."

68. Chernow, *Titan*, p. 84.

69. Ibid., p. 133.

70. Ibid., p. 136.

71. Jean-Jacques Rousseau, "A Discourse on the Arts and Sciences," in *The Social Contract and the Discourses* (New York: Random House, 1993; first included in Everyman's Library, 1931).

72. Chernow, *Titan*, p. 145.

73. "The guild united members of the same occupation; hence it united competitors. It did so in order to limit competition as well as the rational striving for profit which operated through competition" (Max Weber, "The Protestant Sects and the Spirit of Capitalism," in Gerth and Mills, *From Max Weber*, p. 321).

74. My research assistant Rene Paddags did extensive research and also helped order the arguments in this section.

75. David Bank, *Breaking Windows: How Bill Gates Fumbled the Future of Microsoft* (New York: Free Press, 2001), p. 17; Stephen Manes and Paul Andrews, *Gates: How Microsoft's Mogul Reinvented an Industry and Made Himself the Richest Man in America* (New York: Doubleday, 1993), p. 167; Michael A. Cusumano and Richard W. Selby, *Microsoft Secrets: How the World's Most Powerful Software Company Creates Technology, Shapes Markets, and Manages People* (New York: Simon & Schuster, 1998), chapter 3.

76. Manes and Andrews, *Gates*, p. 162.

77. *U.S.A. v. Microsoft* (2001). Full ruling available at www.dcd.uscourts.gov/ms-conclusions.html.

78. Ibid.

79. Bill Gates, with Nathan Myhrvold and Peter Rinearson, *The Road Ahead* (New York: Penguin Books, 1996), p. 50.

80. Friedman, *The World Is Flat*, chapter 2. Netscape is one of the ten critical "flatteners" to which Friedman ascribes the new and leveled global playing field that makes the world "flat."

81. Manes and Andrews, *Gates*, p. 202.

82. Bank, *Breaking Windows*, p. 38.

83. Ibid., p. 45.

84. Chernow, *Titan*, p. 149.

85. Ibid., p. 130.

86. Chernow's biography offers a compelling, engaging, and fair portrait of Rockefeller, to which I am much indebted. But on the way to redressing the imbalance of attack biographies, Chernow is perhaps at times just a little too fair. When he writes that the real object of Rockefeller's affinity for monopoly was "replacing competition with cooperation," he gives credence to hypocrisy. And he seems a little carried away when he writes: "At times, when he railed against cutthroat competition and the vagaries of the business cycle, Rockefeller sounded more like Karl Marx than our classical image of the capitalist. Like the Marxists, he believed that the competitive free-for-all eventually gave way to monopoly and that large industrial-planning units were the most sensible way to manage an economy" (pp. 150–151). Rockefeller no doubt saw himself as the "Moses who delivered" the refiners from chaos (p. 153), but collusion is more than cooperation, and monopoly is more than collusion. The great figures of capitalist development from the Fuggers through the Rockefellers and the Gateses might have like Marx condemned cutthroat competition and might like Moses have brought order to chaos. But that is, as Chernow obviously recognizes, not because they sought justice but because they sought and seek total domination—an aim that not only jeopardizes justice and liberty, but puts the capitalist system itself at risk.

87. Chernow, *Titan*, p. 153.

88. Ibid., pp. 154–155.

89. From www.gatesfoundation.org.

90. Cited in Sarah Bosely, "Dream of eradicating disease that drives the world's richest man," *Guardian,* January 25, 2005. Gates has given $750 million to fight deadly childhood diseases and $51 million to high schools in New York City and elsewhere.

91. *Time,* December 26, 2005, pp. 44–45.

3 Infantilizing Consumers: The Coming of Kidults

1. Dan Cook, "Lunchbox Hegemony? Kids and the Marketplace, Then and Now," August 20, 2001, www.lipmagazine.org.

2. Philippe Ariès's *Centuries of Childhood: A Social History of Family Life* (New York: Vintage Books, 1962) was perhaps the first modern study to give childhood not merely a history but a starting point. Neil Postman develops the idea that "the modern idea of adulthood is largely a product of the printing press" (*The Disappearance of Childhood* [first published in 1982; New York: Vintage Books, 1994], p. 99).

3. Postman, *The Disappearance of Childhood,* pp. 98–99.

4. Care must be taken to avoid playing a kids versus grown-ups parlor game, as seen by the grown-ups. Both common sense and experience teach us that the developmental psychology of real life is less reductive and dualistic than these pairs. Such oppositions conceal a complex world of morals, psychology, and metaphysics.

5. Erik H. Erikson, *Childhood and Society* (New York: W. W. Norton, 1963), pp. 404–405. Erikson worries both about fortifying the "adult's defense against his latent infantile anxiety" (p. 413) and about assuring that the uses of childhood play not be lost to the adult.

6. Ibid., p. 222.

7. A more recent version of the Epicurean mandate is philosopher Walter Pater's declaration: "The service of philosophy, of speculative culture, towards the human spirit is to rouse, to startle it to a life of sharp and eager observation. . . . The poetic passion, the desire of beauty, the love of art for its own sake, has most; for art comes to you professing frankly to give nothing but the highest quality to your moments as they pass" (cited in Andrew Solomon, "The Closing of the American Book," *New York Times,* July 10, 2004). John Stuart Mill's classic essay *On Utilitarianism* (1861) is in fact a critique of Bentham's reductionist version. His attack on his erstwhile mentor is even more evident in his essay on Bentham.

8. Slavoj Žižek, "Passion: Regular or Decaf?" *In These Times,* February 27, 2004, www .inthesetimes.com/comments.php?id=632_0_4_0_c.

9. Quoted in David Sheinin, "Baseball Has a Day of Reckoning in Congress," *Washington Post,* March 18, 2005, p. A01. Palmeiro was first suspended and then released by the Baltimore Orioles.

10. From the Center for Academic Integrity, www.academicintegrity.org/cai_research.asp.

11. These companies, many of which carry the "no plagiarism" pledge, include Master-Papers, Paper Masters, Paper Store, and Essay Town (which promises papers on "any topics, any deadline" with "exact specifications guaranteed, no plagiarism." It also promises "custom written dissertations."

12. Philosophers and communitarians such as William Galston and Amitai Etzioni have written intelligently and favorably about the covenant marriage approach, but its most ardent supporters have tended to be devout Christian communitarians. See Gary Chapman, *Covenant Marriage: Building Communication & Intimacy* (Nashville, Tenn.: Broadman & Holman, 2003); Dave Brown and Phil Waugh, *Covenant vs. Contract* (Forest, Va.: Franklin, Son Publishing); and sermons available on-line by Bishop Wellington Boone, Dr. Gary Chapman, Dr. Tim Clinton, Rev. H. B. London, Dr. Fred Lowery, Dr. Greg Smalley, and Rev. Phil Waugh. Marriage certificates and covenant affirmation ceremonies are also available on-line. Author's disclosure: I have

been divorced once, and although I have been happily married since, it was too easy, too fast, too simple the first time both to get married and to get divorced. My own story corroborates the argument made here.

13. Intellectuals who can avoid black and white (Adlai Stevenson? John Kerry?) are sometimes criticized as indecisive, while bold decision-makers who defy nuance (George W. Bush?) are often criticized as simplistic in their judgments.

14. Steal and save the starving kids, or stay honest but watch them die, says Kohlberg in a typical dualism. Explain to the grocer what the problem is (my kids are starving but I can't afford food right now) and find a solution that works for both sides says Gilligan (lend me food, I'll pay you later when I can). See "Kohlberg's Stages of Moral Development" in William C. Crane, *Theories of Development* (New Jersey: Prentice Hall), pp. 118–36. Gilligan, *In a Different Voice: Psychological Theory and Women's Development* (Cambridge, Mass.: Harvard University Press, 1993). See also my cover review essay "Gilligan's Island" in *The New Republic*, December 7, 1982.

15. M. Mitchell Waldrop, *Complexity: The Emerging Science at the Edge of Order and Chaos* (New York: Simon & Schuster, 1992), p. 12. The dialectics of complexity are evident in Waldrop's account as well as in the work of George Cowan and others at the Santa Fe Institute, which focuses on efforts to "uncover the mechanisms that underlie the deep simplicity present in our complex world" (see www.santafe.edu).

16. Rebecca Mead, "A Man-child in Lotusland," *The New Yorker*, May 20, 2002.

17. When he played for them, the Lakers used Superman as Shaq's alter ego, playing the Superman theme when he made his entrance; Shaq himself has framed comic books and pinball machines and Superman on his car headlights.

18. Mead, "A Man-child in Lotusland."

19. Nash, the 2005 and 2006 back-to-back NBA Most Valuable Player, was given plenty of credit for the success of his low-profile, high-scoring NBA team, the Phoenix Suns, which had the best record through the 2004–2005 season before being eliminated from the playoffs in the conference finals by the San Antonio Spurs. Nash, who reads Marx, Dickens, and Kant and is a model of adulthood, is usually singled out as the exception that proves the rule in the otherwise infantilized NBA (see, for example, Liz Robbins, "Nash Displays Polished Look: On the Court, of Course," *New York Times*, January 19, 2005.

20. *Desperate Housewives*, the popular and tawdry television series, ripples through society. The 2005 White House reporters' dinner featured a spoof by Laura Bush, otherwise a putative standard-bearer of strict morals, which had journalists wildly applauding the naughty routine including a puerile joke about her husband trying to milk a horse.

21. Hence, when Antonio Davis, a respected basketball player for the New York Knicks who was a National Basketball Players Association representative, broke the rule by going briefly into the stands to intervene in an altercation involving his wife in January 2006, he was noisily fined and penalized five games.

22. William Berlind, "The Season That Wasn't," *New York Times Magazine*, August 11, 2002, p. 45.

23. Michael Sokolove, "The Thoroughly Designed American Childhood: Constructing a Teen Phenom," *New York Times Magazine*, November 28, 2004. Sokolove reports on IMG Academies in Bradenton, Florida, where families can pay up to $40,000 tuition to enroll in courses designed to enhance a student's skills in a single sport. Another firm, Velocity Sports Performance, charges up to $2,500 a year for making kids faster runners, with forty franchises in twenty-two states. The industry has been estimated by the *Boston Globe* to generate revenues of up to $4 billion a year.

24. Quoted in Sokolove, "The Thoroughly Designed American Childhood."

25. Michael Massing, "The End of News?" *New York Review of Books*, December 1, 2005.

26. Ibid.

27. In the second of his articles for the *New York Review of Books*, Massing comments that

"this summer, Nancy Cleeland, after more than six years as the lone labor reporter at the *Los Angeles Times*, left her beat. She made the move 'out of frustration,' she told me." The *Los Angeles Times* editors were contending with a radical cutback in reporters—six of forty-eight in the business section having been let go (Michael Massing, "The Press: The Enemy Within," *New York Review of Books*, December 15, 2005).

28. CNN's *Crossfire*, October 15, 2004. Jon Stewart is the host of Comedy Central's *The Daily Show*, a favorite of cynical young viewers who generally read newspapers and watch television news less than their elders, and seem content to get the bulk of their news from a wry sceptic's send-ups and put-downs.

29. Center for Media Education (Kathryn Montgomery and Shelley Pasnik), *Children Enter Cyberspace*, 1996.

30. Milan Kundera, in his novel *Slowness* (New York: HarperCollins, 1995), pp. 2–3. Kundera captures the acceleration of culture under conditions of modern speed by suggesting that "the way contemporary history is told is like a huge concert where they present all of Beethoven's one hundred thirty-eight opuses one after the other, but actually play just the first eight bars of each." Ten years later, the concert would include "only the first note of each piece" to constitute "one hundred and thirty-eight notes for the whole concert, present as one continuous melody." Another ten years, and the entirety of Beethoven's music would be "summed up in a single very long buzzing sound" (pp. 92–93).

31. James Gleick speaking with Bruce Weber for Weber's essay "Sing, Goddess, of the Stopwatch," *New York Times*, August 8, 2004. Gleick concludes that "we're getting better and better as athletes. More and more of us—them, I should say—are approaching the limit of human perfectibility. So the differences among them are really small. One of the weird consequences of that is that stuff like Teflon-coated swim trunks and shaving your body hair can become really important. I don't think it's what the Greeks had in mind." See also Gleick's *Faster: The Acceleration of Just About Everything* (New York: Random House, 1999).

32. Gleick, *Faster*, p. 11.

33. Ibid., p. 13.

34. Malcolm Gladwell, *Blink: The Power of Thinking Without Thinking* (New York: Little, Brown & Co., 2005).

35. Mara Reinstein and Joey Bartolomeo, *Brad & Jen: The Rise and Fall of Hollywood's Golden Couple* (New York: Wenner Books, 2006).

36. Sheldon Solomon, Jeffrey L. Greenberg, and Thomas A. Pyszczynski, cited in Len Costa, "Psychology of Shopping: How Much Is That Death Denial in the Window," *New York Times*, December 7, 2003.

37. Steven Johnson, *Everything Bad Is Good for You: How Today's Popular Culture Is Actually Making Us Smarter* (New York: Riverhead Books, 2005), p. 26.

38. Jack Rosenthal, "What to Do When News Grows Old Before Its Time," *New York Times*, August 8, 2004. Rosenthal observes that obsession with the latest news puts a premium on going after tomorrow's big story rather than carefully following up yesterday's big story. Almost as soon as they appear, new stories disappear. Where is the Abu Ghraib prison scandal now, he asks? What's become of that anthrax scare from a couple of years ago? How about the celebrity murder cases, once the trials are over? Slow-moving stories (environmental degradation, the slow spread of nuclear weapons) do not lend themselves to news coverage unless there is a topical hook. How can a people be informed when the news forever trumps the olds?

39. For a full report on the state of the American media, see "The State of the News Media" (www.stateofthemedia.org/2006/index.asp) issued annually by the Project for Excellence in Journalism.

40. Martha Marino, cited by Denny Fleenor, "Meals Together Improve Family Nutrition," October 6, 2003, in a news bulletin published by the Nutrition Education Network (College of Agricultural, Human, and Natural Resource Sciences at Washington State University), available at http://cahenews.wsu.edu/RELEASES/2003/03047.htm.

41. Cited in Renwick McLean, "Spaniards Dare to Question the Way the Day Is Ordered," *New York Times*, January 12, 2005.

42. Postman, *The Disappearance of Childhood*, pp. 128–129. No one knows how old a number of today's stars really are (El Duque of the New York Mets, Pedro Martinez, the former Boston Red Sox phenom who is now a Met, and Rey Ordóñez, also of the Mets, are all probably older than they admit), but everyone knows the prospects are getting younger and younger, that more and more high-school athletes are skipping college altogether, and rushing into professional baseball or basketball or soccer.

43. There is the story of Danny Almonte, the brilliant kid from the Dominican Republic who pitched a perfect baseball game (no hits, no walks, no runs) in the 2001 Little League World Series. Except that he wasn't really twelve, he was fourteen; he wasn't enrolled in school at all; and he was carrying a birth certificate falsified by a Dad hoping to win the kids sweepstakes. As sports columnist George Vecsey wrote with dismay at the time, "The age for exploitation gets younger and younger here in the El Dorado of American sports, where the streets are paved with long-term contracts" (George Vecsey, "Keeping Son from School Was Worse," *New York Times*, August 31, 2001.

44. Vecsey, "Keeping Son from School Was Worse."

45. National Basketball Association Commissioner David Stern called not so long ago for a minimum age of twenty for professional players, but in a field where high-school-freshmen ball players can land on the pages of *Sports Illustrated* and on cable television, Stern's rhetorical gesture resulted only in moving the age from eighteen to nineteen (as per the NBA collective bargaining agreement, available at nbpa.com). Again, it is not just pushy parents or ambitious coaches, but corporate players who underwrite the trend, sponsoring summer preprofessional basketball camps (as Nike and Reebok do) and providing gear for high schools around the nation, as many shoe and apparel companies do. Chris Rivers, a sports shoe company executive, complains that he's "got seventh-grade parents calling me asking if I can help get their kid on a traveling team. One parent whose son is in the third grade wants me to come watch his son play now" (Chris Broussard, "Still in High School, Certified Celebrities Look Toward N.B.A.," *New York Times*, December 11, 2003). There are dozens of basketball players in the NBA who have come directly from high school, including Kevin Garnett, Tracy McGrady, and Sebastian Telfair. Many professionally ambitious players on basketball, football, or baseball teams leave college well before they receive a degree to try out for professional teams or enter the draft. And of course many others, who never make the pros, fail to finish school and are fated to dismal lives in dead-end service jobs afterward.

Note too that where once only senior-high-school teams traveled to encounter competitors around the country, today traveling teams can be found that accept seventh graders.

46. Cited in Ian Fisher, "German Cardinal Is Chosen as Pope," *New York Times*, April 20, 2005.

47. Herbert Marcuse, *Eros and Civilization: A Philosophical Inquiry into Freud* (Boston: Beacon Press, 1955; New York: Vintage Books, 1962), p. 12.

48. Ibid., p. 13. See Freud, *Civilization and Its Discontents* (edited and translated by J. Strachey; New York: W. W. Norton, 1961). Freud yearns for a condition where survival can be made consistent with the pleasure principle but concedes the need, short of this, for repression and taboo to play a role not merely in civilization but in human survival.

49. This is Milton Friedman, citing A. V. Dicey's indictment of democracy's dangers in Dicey's *Law and Public Opinion in England* (2d ed., London: MacMillan, 1914; pp. 257–258), in Friedman, *Capitalism and Freedom* (Chicago: University of Chicago Press, 1962; new ed., 1982), p. 201.

4 Privatizing Citizens: The Making of Civic Schizophrenia

1. Alan Wolfe, "The Revolution That Never Was," *The New Republic*, June 7, 1999.

2. Hannah Arendt, *The Human Condition* (Chicago: University of Chicago Press, 1958;

Anchor Books ed., 1959), p. 27. Ever sensitive to nuance, Arendt adds that this does not mean that "only the necessary, the futile and the shameful have their proper place in the private realm."

3. Thomas L. Friedman, *The World Is Flat: A Brief History of the Twenty-first Century* (New York: Farrar, Straus and Giroux, 2005), p. 252. Friedman notes that outsourcing is not only about lower wages: "When [CEOs] send jobs abroad, they not only save 75 percent on wages, they get a 100 percent increase in productivity" (p. 260).

4. Benjamin R. Barber, *Fear's Empire: War, Terrorism, and Democracy* (New York: W. W. Norton, 2003), p. 216.

5. David B. Truman, *The Governmental Process: Political Interests and Public Opinion* (New York: Knopf, 1951), p. 51.

6. Thatcher's notorious quote, from an interview published in October 1987 in *Woman's Own* magazine, is referenced in Alan Ryan, "Waiting for Gordon Brown," *New York Review of Books*, June 23, 2005, p. 35.

7. This concise formulation belongs to Charles E. Lindblom who, however, in his balanced presentation of the market system, also notes that "it is a harsh and often cruel coordinator . . . both an ally and enemy of personal freedom." While it "destroys many mammoth historical inequalities," it "then introduces inequalities of its own," and while "historically, it has supported democracy . . . it has sabotaged important democratized features of ostensibly democratic states" (*The Market System: What It Is, How It Works, and What to Make of It* [New Haven, Conn.: Yale University Press, 2001], p. 14).

8. Milton Friedman, *Capitalism and Freedom* (Chicago: University of Chicago Press, 1962; new ed., 1982), p. 33.

9. Hannah Arendt, *On Revolution* (New York: Viking, 1963), p. 221.

10. Jedediah Purdy, *For Common Things: Irony, Trust, and Commitment in America Today* (New York: Alfred A. Knopf, 1999), p. 125.

11. In his *Two Concepts of Liberty: An Inaugural Lecture Delivered Before the University of Oxford, on 31 October 1958* (Oxford: Clarendon Press, 1958), written in the same period that Milton Friedman was resurrecting market thinking, the philosopher Isaiah Berlin offered a foundation for the renewal of nineteenth-century liberalism by arguing that liberty necessarily carried a negative meaning, and that attempts to treat it as positive could only have authoritarian and totalitarian consequences. I have criticized this view at length in my *Strong Democracy: Participatory Politics for a New Age* (Berkeley: University of California Press, 1984; 20th anniversary ed., 2004).

12. Walter Lippmann, *The Public Philosophy* (New York: Mentor, 1955); John Dewey, *The Public and Its Problems* (New York: Henry Holt and Company, 1927; reprint, Athens, Ohio: Swallow Press, 1991).

13. Maxine Greene, *The Dialectic of Freedom* (New York: Teachers College Press, 1988), p. 20.

14. John Dewey, *The Public and Its Problems*, p. 138. In keeping with my argument here, Dewey attributes the eclipse of the public in part to the diversions from political and public life made possible by "the movie, radio, cheap reading matter and motor car" and "all they stand for" (p. 139).

15. Friedman, *Capitalism and Freedom*, pp. 196–197.

16. David Harvey, *A Brief History of NeoLiberalism* (Oxford: Oxford University Press, 2005), p. 2. Harvey views neoliberalism as "a *political* project to reestablish the condition for capital accumulation and to restore the power of economic elites" (p. 19). This may well be, but it is also important to understand that neoliberalism provides the conditions for an unregulated consumerism and hence nurtures the endless buying by children as well as adults necessary to capitalism's survival.

17. Robert Westbrook, "Consuming Citizens," in *The Responsive Community*, vol. 13, no. 4 (2003), p. 72.

18. William Greider, *One World, Ready or Not: The Manic Logic of Global Capitalism* (New York: Simon & Schuster, 1997), p. 26.

19. Alexis de Tocqueville, *Democracy in America*, vol. 1 (New York: Vintage Books, 1990), p. 264.

20. Postwar Harvard political theorist Louis Hartz dismissed the Tocquevillian obsession with the tyranny of the majority by noting that the much maligned American majority "has been an amiable shepherd dog kept forever on a lion's leash" (Louis Hartz, *The Liberal Tradition in America: An Interpretation of American Political Thought Since the Revolution* [New York: Harcourt, Brace, & Company, 1955], p. 129).

21. Lizabeth Cohen, *A Consumers' Republic: The Politics of Mass Consumption in Postwar America* (New York: Alfred A. Knopf, 2003).

22. James Surowiecki, *The Wisdom of Crowds: Why the Many Are Smarter Than the Few and How Collective Wisdom Shapes Business, Economies, Societies, and Nations* (New York: Doubleday, 2004), p. xix.

23. Sigmund Freud, *Civilization and Its Discontents* (edited and translated by J. Strachey; New York: W. W. Norton, 1961), pp. 55, 59. Freud's grand schematic no longer has much creditability in the fields of psychology and psychotherapy, but it remains useful as a cultural metaphor for the impact of repression, guilt, regression, and infantilization in political culture; that is to say, it offers what Freud calls "a pathology of cultural communities" that illuminates what I here am calling the infantilist ethos.

24. Ibid., p. 88.

25. For a popular and polemical discussion of the impact of privatization on education, prisons, water, and other public goods, see Si Kahn and Elizabeth Minnich, *The Fox in the Henhouse: How Privatization Threatens Democracy* (San Francisco: Berrett-Koehler Publishers, 2005).

26. Robert B. Reich, "Don't Blame Wal-Mart," *New York Times*, February 28, 2005. That such policies are not indispensable to economic survival is evident from the fact that one of Wal-Mart's most successful competitors is Costco, a company that has combined lower price tags with better health insurance and wage policies for its workers.

27. In his *Democracy's Discontent: America in Search of a Public Philosophy* (Cambridge, Mass.: Harvard University Press, 1996), Michael Sandel looked at the same logic as it played out in the early days of catalog retailers such as Montgomery Ward and Sears, Roebuck & Company which on the way to offering more goods at cheaper prices began the consumer movement that would first undermine local retailers and downtown shopping areas as well as the communities they served.

28. Thomas L. Friedman, *The World Is Flat*, pp. 214, 216. For a more political discussion, see Liza Featherstone, *Selling Women Short: The Landmark Battle for Workers' Rights at Wal-Mart* (New York: Basic Books, 2005).

29. Thus, for example, Thomas de Zengotita entitles chapter 2 "The Cult of the Child" in his *Mediated: How the Media Shapes Your World and the Way You Live in It* (New York: Bloomsbury, 2005).

30. Thus, Keith A. Scarborough, vice president for State Government Relations of the Association of National Advertisers, testified to the Health and Human Services Committee in Montgomery County, Maryland, that while advertisers recognize there is a "problem" with childhood obesity, the advertising industry's self-regulatory system protects children (no need for government regulation); moreover, while "much of the criticism of food advertising to children rests on a fundamentally flawed premise that demonizes certain food products," advertisers tend to "reject this type of governmental paternalism" and "the good food/bad food argument." Instead, they call for "moderation as part of a well-balanced diet"—something for which, however, no food advertiser for children has ever spent a penny (Association of National Advertisers, November 28, 2005, www.ana.net). For the complete testimony, see www.ftc.gov/os/Comments/FoodMarketingtoKids/516960-00009.pdf.

31. Steven Johnson, *Everything Bad Is Good for You: How Today's Popular Culture Is Actually Making Us Smarter* (New York: Riverhead Books, 2005). For a detailed discussion see chapter 7.

32. Harry G. Frankfurt, "Freedom of the Will and the Concept of a Person," *Journal of Phi-*

losophy, vol. 68, no. 1 (1971), pp. 5–20. Frankfurt (the author of a delightful book published in 2005 called *On Bullshit*) suggests that it is not our first-order desires that render us either free or human (all animals have desires that dictate "choices") but our second-order desires *about* our first-order desires that do so.

33. John Stuart Mill, *On Liberty* (Norton Critical Edition, edited by David Spitz; New York: W. W. Norton, 1975), p. 57. Economist David George elucidates the connection between Mill's definition of character and first- and second-order desires in his *Preference Pollution: How Markets Create the Desires We Dislike* (Ann Arbor: University of Michigan Press, 2001), p. 12.

34. This is no mere rhetorical flourish. According to MediaPost's TV Watch, "Nickelodeon has seemingly found the secret for kids' marketers: Don't target children, just the people who influence them" (Wayne Friedman, November 23, 2005, http://blogs.mediapost.com/tv_watch/?p=321).

35. Data from Tamara Draut and Javier Silva, "Generation Broke: The Growth of Debt Among Young Americans," Demos, October 13, 2004 (www.demos.org/pub295.cfm). The report notes that "aggressive marketing to college students" using "free t-shirts, mugs, pizza, and other incentives" has succeeded in reaching nearly all college students, 96 percent of whom now have cards (p. 7). "Between 1990 and 1995, one survey found credit debt had shot up 134 percent, from $900 to $2,100. In 2001, college seniors graduated with an average of $3,262 in credit card debt" (p. 9).

36. Caroline E. Mayer, "Offers Too Good to Refuse," *Washington Post National Weekly*, April 25–May 1, 2005, p. 19. Greedy banks are protected because under bankruptcy laws in the United States "new debt" cannot be forgiven for six years after a bankruptcy is declared.

37. Edmund L. Andrews, "U.S. Offers Details of Plan for Open Markets in China," *New York Times*, October 16, 2005. Though consumer spending in China has grown by about 10 percent a year recently, and home consumer credit is growing, the pace is far too slow for a White House that wants Beijing to "get people to spend more."

38. Amy Waldman, "Mile by Mile, India Paves a Smoother Road to Its Future," *New York Times*, December 4, 2005. Waldman points out that India's highway modernization goes hand in hand with privatization: traditional two-lane roads "have been public spaces, home to the logical chaos that governs so much of life [in India]. . . . The redone highway has challenged that, trying to impose borders and linearity."

39. Kevin Roberts, *Lovemarks: The Future Beyond Brands* (New York: powerHouse Books, 2004), p. 33.

40. Barry Schwartz, *The Paradox of Choice: Why More Is Less* (New York: HarperCollins, 2004), p. 6.

41. Gregg Easterbrook, *The Progress Paradox: How Life Gets Better While People Feel Worse* (New York: Random House, 2003), cited by Robert J. Samuelson, "The Afflictions of Affluence," *Newsweek*, March 22, 2004. Samuelson reports that Americans are consuming more food than ever, but still feeling more alone than before (in 1957, 3 percent of Americans reported feeling alone, while today the number is 14 percent). Meanwhile, 400,000 deaths a year are attributed to obesity. See also Schwartz, *The Paradox of Choice*.

42. Quoted in Eduardo Porter, "Choice Is Good: Yes, No or Maybe?" *New York Times*, March 27, 2005.

43. Schwartz, *The Paradox of Choice*, p. 224.

44. Porter, "Choice Is Good: Yes, No or Maybe?"

45. Ibid.

46. "Under mandated choice, as much as 75% of the U.S. adult population would become committed potential organ donors" (Aron Spital, "Mandated Choice for Organ Donation: Time to Give It a Try," *Annals of Internal Medicine*, vol. 125 [July 1996], pp. 66–69).

"We surveyed members of the International Society for Heart and Lung Transplantation (ISHLT) in conjunction with the Foundation for the Advancement of Cardiac Therapies

(FACT). METHODS/RESULTS: We asked for opinions about how to improve organ donation. Of 739 respondents, 75% supported presumed consent" (M. C. Oz et al., "How to improve organ donation: results of the ISHLT/FACT poll," *Heart Lung Transplant*, vol. 22, no. 4 [April 2003], pp. 389–410).

47. Rousseau used this phrase in his 1762 *Social Contract*, and it has led many liberals focused on private liberty alone to conclude that Rousseau was either incoherent or a dangerous proto-totalitarian thinker of the kind George Orwell would eventually skewer. Yet once we distinguish between private choosing (I need some dope) and public choosing (using dope diminishes my overall capacity to be free), it becomes apparent that constraining the private choice can enhance our real liberty and hence help "force us to be free."

48. The response to the Hurricane Katrina disaster in New Orleans is examined later in the chapter. On space exploration: Richard Branson's company Virgin Galactic has already sold more than $10 million worth of space rides on private flights that will take off from a New Mexico spaceport. Branson has sold $200,000 tickets to celebrities such as the actress Victoria Principal and Hollywood director Bryan Singer, and is purchasing five spacecraft to undertake the flights. The lesson, for pundit John Tierney, is that while "NASA still doesn't have the money to go back to the Moon, much less head to Mars . . . [s]omeone else is on the job." Let people like designer Burt Rutan and his backer, Microsoft billionaire Paul Allen, privatize space flight—employing the reusable spacecraft with which they won the 2004 Ansari X Prize to do the work NASA can no longer afford to do (John Tierney, "Go West, Young Astronaut," *New York Times*, December 6, 2005).

49. Timothy Williams, "In Bryant Park's Rebirth, Some Chafe at Growing Corporate Presence," *New York Times*, December 5, 2005. Williams quotes Assemblyman Richard N. Gottfried of Manhattan as stating: "Parks have never in this city's history been thought of as entities that would fund themselves, and I think that's a dangerous concept. This takes us way down the road to a public park becoming a theme park."

50. Tamar Lewin, "In Public Schools, The Name Game As a Donor Lure," *New York Times*, January 6, 2006.

51. Statistics and citation from Sam Dillon, "At Public Universities, Warnings of Privatization," *New York Times*, October 16, 2005. Dillon notes that Michigan now funds "about 18 percent of Ann Arbor's revenues," while "the taxpayer share of revenues at the University of Virginia is about 8 percent."

52. See for example, Jennifer Washburn, *University, Inc.: The Corporate Corruption of American Higher Education* (New York: Basic Books, 2005), whose cover is decorated with a mortar board affixed with a "sold" label; Derek Bok, *Universities in the Marketplace: The Commercialization of Higher Education* (Princeton, N.J.: Princeton University Press, 2003); and Stanley Aronowitz, *The Knowledge Factory: Dismantling the Corporate University and Creating True Higher Learning* (Boston: Beacon Press, 2000). Aronowitz worries that universities have become education factories for vocational training and McJobs rather than places of critical learning.

53. Andrew Hacker, "The Truth About the Colleges," *New York Review of Books*, November 3, 3005. If evidence for the corporatization of the university is needed, Hacker observes that "employees who are not teachers make up 71 percent of Stanford's total payroll . . . and 83 percent at Harvard."

54. For more on this project, sponsored by the Exxon Educational Foundation, see the November 20, 2002, news release at www2.exxonmobil.com/Corporate/Newsroom/Newsreleases/xom_nr_201102.asp.

55. See both reports at www.redefiningprogress.org.

56. Mara Faccio, Ronald W. Masulis, and John J. McConnell show that "politically-connected (but publicly-traded) firms," in a sample of 450 such firms in 35 countries from 1997 to 2002, ". . . are significantly more likely to be bailed out than similar non-connected firms," even though they "exhibit significantly worse financial performance than their non-connected peers

at the time of the bailout and over the following two years" (Mara Faccio, Ronald W. Masulis, and John J. McConnell, "Political Connections and Corporate Bailouts," AFA 2006 Boston Meetings Paper, available at http://ssrn.com/abstract=676905).

57. Margaret Kohn, *Brave New Neighborhoods: The Privatization of Public Space* (New York: Routledge, 2004), p. 19.

58. For a discussion see my "Dreamers Without Borders," *The American Prospect*, vol. 16, no. 8 (August 2005). Fear of immigration as well as of a corporatized Europe also played a large role.

59. P. W. Singer, *Corporate Warriors: The Rise of the Privatized Military Industry* (Ithaca, N.Y.: Cornell University Press, 2003), p. 7.

60. "Halliburton, the company formerly headed by Vice President Cheney, has won contracts worth more than $1.7 billion under Operation Iraqi Freedom and stands to make hundreds of millions more dollars under a no-bid contract awarded by the U.S. Army Corps of Engineers," wrote Michael Dobbs a few months after the Iraqi invasion ("Halliburton's Deals Greater Than Thought," *The Washington Post*, August 28, 2003, p. A01). As Dobbs notes, such outsourcing "has been spurred by cutbacks in the military budget and a string of wars since the end of the Cold War that have placed enormous demand on the armed forces." Most of Halliburton's work is support and reconstruction, but there are also many corporations directly engaged in security in Iraq and Afghanistan and elsewhere. The brutal execution of four private security contract workers hired by Blackwater USA in Falluja in 2004 was treated by many American media outlets as synonymous with the execution of American soldiers in the field.

61. Jeremy Scahill, "Blackwater Down," *The Nation*, October 10, 2005.

62. Senator Durbin on National Public Radio, cited in Pratap Chatterjee, "Big, Easy Iraqi-Style Contracts Flood New Orleans," posted September 20, 2005, by CorpWatch and available at www.corpwatch.org/article.php?id=12647. The article details private construction contracts in New Orleans after the flood.

63. Singer, *Corporate Warriors*, p. 189.

64. Editorial, "Privatizing Warfare," *New York Times*, April 21, 2004.

65. Joel Brinkley and James Glanz, "Contractors in Sensitive Roles, Unchecked," *New York Times*, May 7, 2004.

66. Singer, *Corporate Warriors*, p. 181.

67. Ibid. Singer notes that Smith eventually went to jail for two years for violating U.S. gun laws, but many other small rogue firms go undetected and unpunished in their bottom-line activities. Since their only motive is profit, little else can be expected, even from large reputable firms which, as Singer notes, may have interests at variance with those of their own national governments.

68. James Glanz, "Modern Mercenaries on the Iraqi Frontier," *New York Times*, Week in Review, April 4, 2004.

69. Barry Yeoman, citing Myles Frechette in "Need an Army? Just Pick Up the Phone," *New York Times*, April 2, 2004.

70. Singer, *Corporate Warriors*, p. 226. Singer is citing an "analyst" quoted in Jack Kelly, "Safety at a Price: Military Expertise for Sale or Rent," *Pittsburgh Post-Gazette*, February 15, 2000.

71. Ironically, it was the former far left MP Ken "the Red" Livingston who, as mayor of London, introduced these anything but socialist innovations, which parade as an innovative form of taxation but in fact, like the toll-paying fast lanes on highways across Europe, privilege the wealthy.

72. Sasha Abramsky, "One Nation, Under Siege," *The American Prospect*, April 1, 2005.

73. James Fishkin has run an impressive experiment in deliberative polling in conjunction with public television demonstrating that citizens can and do change their positions on key issues once they are allowed to consider those issues deliberatively. Yet such methods are marginalized by professional pollsters who see their job as fixing private prejudice rather than helping deliberative public judgments emerge. See James S. Fishkin, *Democracy and Deliberation: New Directions for Democratic Reform* (New Haven, Conn.: Yale University Press, 1991).

74. See, for example, George Lakoff, *Don't Think of an Elephant: Know Your Values and Frame the Debate* (White River Junction, Vt.: Chelsea Green Publishing, 2004) and *Moral Politics: How Liberals and Conservatives Think* (Chicago: University of Chicago Press, 2002); and Jim Wallis, *God's Politics: Why the Right Gets It Wrong and the Left Doesn't Get It* (San Francisco: Harper San Francisco, 2005).

75. Stephen Goldsmith and William D. Eggers, "Government for Hire," *New York Times*, February 21, 2005.

76. Martha Minow, *Partners, Not Rivals: Privatization and the Public Good* (Boston: Beacon, 2002), p. 2.

77. The role of money in politics, and its corrupting impact on democracy, is a crucial subject, but not one that can be explored in depth here. It is the connection to infantilization that is of interest: citizens in a consumer society seek not only "daddy-" and "mommy-politicians" but "sugar-daddy politicians" who remove the burden of publically financed campaigns from the public and take all the responsibility (and power) unto their own shoulders. In defeating Fernando Ferrer for a second term as mayor of New York City, Michael Bloomberg spent around $74 million, outspending his rival ten to one (Gigi E. Georges and Howard L. Wolfson, "Singing the Blues in a Blue City," *New York Times*, November 13, 2005). George Bush "took in a record $360 million for the 2004 election, easily exceeding the $193 million he raised four years earlier"; Senator Kerry was able to raise more than $317 million—and both candidates declined public matching funds during the primary, to free them from the $45 million spending cap on publicly funded primaries (Center for Responsive Politics, www.opensecrets.org/bush/index.asp).

78. See, for example, P. W. Singer, *Children at War* (New York: Pantheon, 2005). Karen Houppert writes about the recruitment of teens for the undermanned American armed forces in her essay "Who's Next?" in *The Nation*, September 12, 2005.

5 Branding Identities: The Loss of Meaning

1. Otto Riewoldt, editor, *Brandscaping: Worlds of Experience in Retail Design* (Basel: Birkhaeuser-Publishers for Architecture, 2002), p. 10.

2. Billy Idol's first punk band of the 1970s carried the name Generation X, but the term was codified by Douglas Coupland in his 1991 book *Generation X: Tales for an Accelerated Culture* (New York: St. Martin's Press, 1991), his title seized on by marketers desperate to identify their new target generation without a name. Paul Fussell addressed the X generation in the final chapter of his earlier book *Class: A Guide through the American Status System* (New York: Summit Books, 1983). Generation X has been estimated at circa 45 million.

3. Kevin Roberts, *Lovemarks: The Future Beyond Brands* (New York: powerHouse Books, 2004), p. 150.

4. Ibid., p. 125.

5. As described in the Indian magazine *Outlook*, and turned into a model of the new entrepreneurship by Thomas L. Friedman in *The World Is Flat: A Brief History of the Twenty-first Century* (New York: Farrar, Straus and Giroux, 2005), p. 184.

6. It is again Friedman who portrays and uncritically celebrates this consumerist paradigm; *The World Is Flat*, pp. 184–186.

7. Cited in Michelle Cottle, "The Gray Lady Wears Prada," *The New Republic*, April 17, 2006.

8. Daryl Travis, *Emotional Branding: How Successful Brands Gain the Irrational Edge* (Roseville, Calif.: Prima Venture, 2000), p. 54.

9. Marc Gobé, *Emotional Branding: The New Paradigm for Connecting Brands to People* (New York: Allworth Press, 2001), p. xiv.

10. Naomi Klein, *No Logo: Taking Aim at the Brand Bullies* (New York: Picador, 2000), p. 120.

11. Shawn Carkonen, Amazon editorial review of David Brooks, *Bobos in Paradise: The New Upper Class and How They Got There* (New York: Simon & Schuster, 2000), posted at www.amazon.com. Brooks sums up the bobo category, an offspring of the Information Age, by argu-

ing that "dumb good-looking people with great parents have been displaced by smart, ambi- tious, educated, and antiestablishment people with scuffed shoes" (*Bobos in Paradise*, p. 39).

12. Product placement of commercial goods in films is today the preferred method of adver- tising, allowing products to be inserted into and identified with the "real life" of Hollywood's reality cinema. Some worry that product placement may come to drive story line, with Red Lob- ster restaurant or Oreo cookies becoming part of the dramatic narrative. See David Bauder, "Integrated ads: Producers concerned about product placement," *Berkshire Eagle*, May 29, 2006.

13. Cited by William Safire, "Brand," *New York Times Magazine*, April 10, 2005. Safire explains that the etymology of *branding* can be traced from the branding irons used to identify animals and then casks of wine and ale to the brand-marks that preceded trademarks in identifying the goods of particular companies.

14. Quoted in Kenneth Hein, "Brand Loyalty 2004," *Brandweek*, October 25, 2004, at www .brandweek.com/bw/research/article_display.jsp?vnu_content_id=1000683707.

15. Ibid.

16. A former client of Saatchi & Saatchi, described in Roberts, *Lovemarks*, p. 152.

17. Melanie Warner and Stuart Elliott, "Frothier Than Ever: The Tall Cold One Bows to the Stylish One," *New York Times*, August 15, 2005.

18. William Leach, *Land of Desire: Merchants, Power, and the Rise of a New American Culture* (New York: Vintage Books, 1994), p. 16.

19. Ibid.

20. Cited in Leach, *Land of Desire*, p. 18. Original Veblen quotes cited by Leach appear in Joseph Dorfman, *Thorstein Veblen and His America* (Cambridge, Mass.: Harvard University Press, 1934), pp. 326, 160.

21. Leach, *Land of Desire*, p. xv.

22. Jackson Lears, *Fables of Abundance* (New York: Basic Books, 1994).

23. Leach, *Land of Desire*, p. 37.

24. Ibid.

25. Gary S. Cross, *An All-Consuming Century: Why Commercialism Won in Modern America* (New York: Columbia University Press, 2000), p. 17.

26. Scott Bedbury, Starbucks's former vice president of marketing, quoted in Klein, *No Logo*, p. 20.

27. Howard Schultz, quoted in Klein, *No Logo*, p. 21.

28. This is once again Scott Bedbury, who Klein reports went from Nike to Starbucks marketing—without, we might add, having to change one word of his justifying philosophy.

29. Geraldine E. Willigan, "High Performance Marketing: An Interview with Nike's Phil Knight," *Harvard Business Review*, July 1992, p. 92, cited in *No Logo*, p. 22.

30. Klein, *No Logo*, p. 22.

31. Roberts, *Lovemarks*, p. 25.

32. Jagdeep Kapoor, "Innovative Marketing to Woo Consumers," *Deccan Herald* (India), November 7, 2005. Kapoor notes that "branded tiles are one of the largest advertised categories which appeal to the minds and hearts of the Indian household. Each and every branded tile is trying to position itself distinctively and through communication, is trying to attract consumers towards its brands."

33. Gobé, *Emotional Branding*, p. 53.

34. Roberts, *Lovemarks*, pp. 197–198.

35. Douglas Atkin, *The Culting of Brands: When Customers Become True Believers* (New York: Portfolio, 2004), p. xi. Atkin writes that "today's most successful brands don't just provide marks of distinction (identity) for products. Cult brands are beliefs. They have morals—embody val- ues. Cult brands stand up for things. They work hard; fight what is right. Cult brands supply our modern metaphysics, imbuing the world with significance. We wear their meaning when we buy Benetton. We eat their meaning when we spoon Ben & Jerry's into our mouths. . . . Brands

function as complete meaning systems. They are venues for the consumer (and employee) to publicly enact a distinctive set of beliefs and values" (p. 97).

36. Atkin, *The Culting of Brands*, p. 202.

37. Ibid., p. 201.

38. Atkin writes, *"Few stronger emotions exist than the need to belong and make meaning.* And brands exploit that need" (*The Culting of Brands*, p. 199, emphasis in original).

39. Ken Auletta, "The Dawn Patrol: The curious rise of morning television, and the future of network news," *The New Yorker*, August 8 and 15, 2005, p. 69. What was at first seen as a special feature of morning news programs has now become the standard by which network news programs are measured in general. The passing from the scene of journalist anchors like Dan Rather, Tom Brokaw, and the late Peter Jennings and the success of cable news and talk radio make branded stars from Rush Limbaugh to Howard Stern the point, and news, talk, and commentary merely a useful package in which to wrap them.

40. Otto Riewoldt defines brandscaping as "staging brand experiences through architecture and interior design" (*Brandscaping*, p. 7).

41. Auletta, "The Dawn Patrol," p. 73.

42. Klein, *No Logo*, p. 24.

43. William Safire, "Brand," *New York Times*, April 10, 2005, cites Evan Morris, author of *From Altoids to Zima*, who writes that "Calvin Klein and Ralph Lauren both strike me as innovators in the reassertion of the personal name as a *brand* with a well-known 'general character' that gives consumers some idea of what tone their product . . . is likely to project (hyper-WASP, in both cases)."

44. Michal Jordan's star has faded, although not until after Nike earned $2.6 billion selling Air Jordans on the basis of a $2.5-million, five-year contract Jordan signed with Nike in 1984. His successor, though not yet iconic, may be LeBron James, drafted by the Cleveland Cavaliers straight out of high school. James signed a seven-year endorsement contract worth $90 million in 2003, not quite twenty years after Jordan signed his contract. Nike ads feature LeBron as "King James," in the hope that he will take a lion's share of the $8-billion American athletic shoe market ("Nike Pins Hopes on LeBron," CNN/Sports Illustrated, May 22, 2003, available at http://sportsillustrated.cnn.com/basketball/news/2003/05/22/nike_sider_ap/). The value of the market is evident in the acquisition of Reebok by Adidas for $3.8 billion in August 2005, in the hope that the merger might challenge Nike (and LeBron James) for a larger market share.

45. Naomi Klein quotes ad executives Sam Hill, Jack McGrath, and Sandeep Dayal as arguing that their research proves "You can indeed brand not only sand, but also wheat, beef, brick, metals, concrete, chemical, corn grits and an endless variety of commodities traditionally considered immune to the process" (*No Logo*, p. 25).

46. As reported on CNN Headline News, August 12, 2005.

47. Rob Walker, "Consumed: Dog Chic," *New York Times Magazine*, August 7, 2005. Walker reports that the kiddie-cartoon SpongeBob franchise brings in $1.5 billion a year in licensed product sales and that Louis Vuitton and Harley-Davidson are moving into the pet market as well.

48. "Standing Above the Crowd, Authors Guild Symposium," *Authors Guild Bulletin*, Summer 2005, p. 21.

49. Roberts, *Lovemarks*, pp. 42, 43, 45–46.

50. Ibid., p. 21.

51. Travis, *Emotional Branding*, pp. 39–40.

52. Marc Gobé, *Citizen Brand: 10 Commandments for Transforming Brands in a Consumer Democracy* (New York: Allworth Press, 2002), p. xxi.

53. Ibid. Gobé is typical of modern marketing in how he "humanizes" brands, arguing that firms must extend "the entire corporate program to become one of insight, personality, and humanity. . . . Corporate identities of the future will need to evolve to become more expressive

and deliver strong personalities in a humanistic way" (p. 127). Gobé concludes that "a brand with personality has a life of its own that is about imagination, beauty, and fun" (p. 144).

54. Roberts, *Lovemarks*, pp. 171–172.

55. Other schools have tried to rebrand by renaming: Beaver College near Philadelphia recently became Arcadia University, the State University of New York at Albany has become the University at Albany, and Western Maryland College has redubbed itself McDaniel College. Many schools have consulted firms like Lipman Hearne, marketing companies that specialize in colleges and nonprofits. See Alan Finder, "To Woo Students, Colleges Choose Names That Sell," *New York Times*, August 11, 2005.

56. Griff Witte, "Branded for Life: What if a Familiar Name Becomes a Different Animal?" *Washington Post*, January 23, 2005.

57. "Corporate Brand Reputation Outranks Financial Performance as Most Important Measure of Success," press release by World Economic Forum, January 22, 2004, available at www.weforum.org.

58. Caroline E. Mayer, "Nurturing Brand Loyalty: With Preschool Supplies, Firms Woo Future Customers—and Current Parents," *Washington Post*, October 12, 2003.

59. Ellen Tien, "Living in the Lap of Labels," *New York Times*, February 15, 2004. The items being touted include a see-through plastic diaper bag by Jimmy Choo for $880 and a Silver Cross pram for $2500, along with "brightly covered trash cans" that hold diapers, for $168 from Garnet Hill. "Babies can now romp around in the same labels as their parents do," writes the enthusiastic *Times* "reporter."

60. Holly Peterson, "What the Well-Dressed Child Will Borrow," *Newsweek*, February 2, 2004.

61. See www.americangirlplace.com.

62. Julia Moskin, *New York Times*, May 16, 2004.

63. Maria Papanthymou, "Branding for Russian Youth," posted at BizCommunity.com, November 3, 2004, available at www.biz-community.com/Article/196/19/5066.html. Also see Paul Temporal, *Branding in Asia: The Creation, Development and Management of Asian Brands for the Global Market* (New York: Wiley, 2001).

64. Roberts, *Lovemarks*, p. 55.

65. Benjamin Barber, "A Dissenting Opinion of Sell-ebration: Living Inside the Book of Disney," FORUM, Summer 1997. Also see Barber, "From Disney World to Disney's World," *New York Times*, August 1, 1995.

66. Mike Budd, Steve Craig, and Clay Steinman offer a stimulating critique of these phenomena in their *Consuming Environments: Television and Commercial Culture* (New Brunswick, N.J.: Rutgers University Press, 1999), p. 126.

67. Jerry Mander, *Four Arguments for the Elimination of Television* (1978; reprint, New York: Perennial, 2002), p. 13 (page citation refers to reprint edition).

68. Neil Gabler, *Life: The Movie: How Entertainment Conquered Reality* (New York: Knopf, 1998), p. 11.

69. Clay Calvert, *Voyeur Nation: Media, Privacy, and Peering in Modern Culture* (Boulder, Colo.: Westview Press, 2000), pp. 2–3. Calvert sees clearly how parasitic mediated voyeurism is. Citing the "circularity" of celebrity makeover shows, he observes how *"Extreme Makeover* neatly combines the double gesture of transforming members of the audience into real television celebrities while rebuilding them to fit the conventional image of celebrity beauty.

70. www.iconoclaststv.com. On August 5, 2005, ABC's *20/20* ran a piece on six young people, four of whom said Grey Goose was their favorite, engaged in a blind taste test of premium vodkas. None actually chose their favorite brand. Vodka, like bricks, is a generic, and the companies that market it know that consumer loyalty derives from image not taste. Thus, Grey Goose's clever "Iconoclasts" campaign.

71. Jesse Lichtenstein, "The Wired World: The Real Orkut," *The New Yorker*, March 29, 2004. Similar websites include Friendster and MySpace as well as Microsoft's new Wallop, all virtual

spaces where young people congregate to instant message and interact. Orkut sells an unearned intimacy and trustworthiness by making its site "by invitation only" and suggesting because you have a passing acquaintance with at least one other member, the site is what Kevin Roberts would deem a trustmark.

72. Yahoo! also stakes an actor dressed in armor outside the theater wearing an ad for Yahoo! Mail Spamguard. Hilton Hotels recently sponsored *Chitty Chitty Bang Bang* (playing at the Hilton Theater) in New York. Turtle Wax sponsored (the failed show) *Good Vibrations*, while Visa sponsored the national tour of *Movin' Out*. See Stuart Elliott, "On Broadway, Ads Now Get to Play Cameo Roles," *New York Times*, April 22, 2005.

73. Peter T. Kilborn, "The Five-Bedroom, Six-Figure Rootless Life," *New York Times*, June 1, 2005.

74. Ibid.

75. These themes are explored in William Safire, "Goodbye to Privacy," *New York Times Book Review*, April 10, 2005, a review of Robert O'Harrow Jr.'s *No Place to Hide*.

76. Adam Gopnik, "Times Regained: How the Old Times Square was made new," *The New Yorker*, March 22, 2004.

77. Alissa Quart, *Branded: The Buying and Selling of Teenagers* (New York: Basic Books, 2004), pp. 126–127. "In only one year, from 2000 to 2001, the number of cosmetic surgeries on teens eighteen and under has jumped 21.8 percent, from 65,231 to 79,501. Almost 306,000 of the 7.4 million plastic surgeries performed in 2000 in the United States were alterations of teens and children. In 2000, according to the American Society of Plastic Surgeons (ASPS), breast augmentation was the third most popular surgery for people eighteen and under, when 3,682 girls underwent the surgery. The same year, 29,700 teen noses were reshaped, 23,000 teen ears were done, 95,097 teens were chemically peeled, another 74,154 young faces were microdermabraded, and 45,264 kids had hair removed by laser" (p. 114).

78. Roberts, *Lovemarks*, p. 68.

79. See www.dga.com.

80. Roberts, *Lovemarks*, p. 87.

81. Harry Frankfurt argues in his short book *On Bullshit* (Princeton, N.J.: Princeton University Press, 2005) that bullshit is worse than lies in that lies at least acknowledge truth in their departure from it, while bullshit just doesn't care about the truth. It is in this sense that brand advertising distorts reality.

82. Roberts, *Lovemarks*, p. 57.

83. How fitting that this painting, long since borrowed as a "brand" item, was actually itself stolen from the Munch Museum in Oslo, Norway.

84. Marc Peyser, "Absolutely the Pitts," *Newsweek*, April 12, 2004. Kate Winslet allowed her February 2003 *GQ* cover photo to be airbrushed and then, in a later interview, berated women for trying to live up to an unrealistic ideal of sexiness. See Hugh Davies, "The Secret of Slimline Kate," *London Telegraph*, October 1, 2003, available at www.telegraph.co.uk/news/main.jhtml?xml=/news/2003/01/10/nkate10.xml.

85. Don Kaplan, "Make a 'Face': The ugly side of getting movie-star looks," *New York Post*, April 18, 2005.

86. Martha Minow, *Partners, Not Rivals: Privatization and the Public Good* (Boston: Beacon, 2002), p. 15. As Minow writes, "stand back and watch the boundaries [between education and commerce] blur" (p. 21).

87. Daniel Kraker, "Private Names, Public Spaces," posted by PopPolitics.com, August 30, 2002, available at www.poppolitics.com/articles/printerfriendly/2002-08-30-namingrights.shtml.

88. Ibid.

89. Fred Gehrung, "Hey, Sports Fans, Guess What We've Named Your Stadium," *New York Times*, July 10, 2005.

90. Kraker, "Private Names, Public Spaces."

91. Gehrung, "Hey, Sports Fans."

92. Kraker, "Private Names, Public Spaces."

93. Murray Chass, "Advertising Casting Its Web Over Young Fans at the Park," *New York Times*, May 6, 2004.

94. Kraker, "Private Names, Public Spaces."

95. Katie Zezima, "A Bill to Sell Park Names," *New York Times*, May 10, 2003.

96. Strawberry Saroyan, "Christianity, the Brand," *New York Times Magazine*, April 16, 2006.

97. Roger Cohen argues that selling democracy as a brand has a long history, dating back to the selling of the Marshall Plan in a series of films made after World War II. See his "Democracy as a Brand: Wooing Hearts, European or Muslim," *New York Times*, October 16, 2004. Cohen thinks we have much to learn from the film series called "Selling Democracy: Films of the Marshall Plan, 1948–53" shown in New York in 2004.

98. Cited by William Safire in "Brand," *New York Times Magazine*, April 10, 2005.

99. Cited in John Cassidy, "The Ringleader," *The New Yorker*, August 1, 2005, p. 47.

100. Cited in "Rebranding America," *The Weekly Standard*, March 1, 2004.

101. John M. McNeel, "America, spare Arabs the spin," *International Herald Tribune*, June 9, 2005. Actually, the Business for Diplomatic Action/McNeel spin is more or less the same as America's spin, and has had little impact. See also Naomi Klein, "Can Democracy Survive Bush's Embrace?" *The Nation*, March 28, 2005.

102. Gobé, *Citizen Brand*, p. 230. Gobé cites as examples Verizon's post-9/11 free minutes for Northeastern customers initiative, to "help them find comfort in the support of friends and family in this difficult time," and Merck's free medication for the elderly campaign.

103. Vanessa O'Connell, "Veteran Beers Helps U.S. Craft Its Message," *Wall Street Journal*, October 15, 2001.

104. Christopher Marquis, "Promoter of U.S. Image Quits for Wall St. Job," *New York Times*, April 30, 2004.

105. In a September 2005 tour of the Middle East, Hughes introduced herself repeatedly to Muslim women as "a working Mom" who understood the needs of women—as if America too were a working Mom looking out for women in the Middle East. The women were not buying the story, however, insisting on talking about American cultural hubris (in her Riyadh stop) and the Iraqi war (in Turkey).

106. Cited in Brian Knowlton, "Humility has its uses, new U.S. envoy signals," *International Herald Tribune*, August 15, 2005.

107. See Steven R. Weisman, "Bush Confidante Begins Task of Repairing American Image Abroad," *New York Times*, August 21, 2005. The *Newsweek* story became a cause célèbre, not because it was disproved but because it had not been fully documented. There can be little doubt that while this may have caused *Newsweek* some embarrassment, it did little to compensate the far greater embarrassment that the well-documented truths about both Guantanamo Bay and Abu Ghraib prison have caused Americans to feel.

108. Cited in Brian Knowlton, "Humility has its uses, new U.S. envoy signals."

109. George Lakoff, *Don't Think of an Elephant: Know Your Values and Frame the Debate* (White River Junction, Vt.: Chelsea Green Publishing, 2004). Lakoff's slim volume carries a foreword by Democratic National Committee Chairman Howard Dean.

110. Coca-Cola's global brand power already accommodates a score of different formulas to suit the tastes of the many different cultures where the company does business. In the 1930s it sold Coke in Nazi Germany by altering its bottle caps and to some degree dissociating itself from its "American" branding.

111. See Clay Risen, "Remaindered: The Decline of Brand America," *The New Republic*, April 11, 2005. For background, consult Simon Anholt and Jeremy Hildreth, *Brand America* (London: Cyan Communications, 2005).

112. Risen, "Remaindered."

113. Cited in Murray Campbell, "Asterix Promoting McBurgers in France," *Globe & Mail* (Toronto), January 24, 2002. My account here tracks Campbell's excellent reportage.

6 Totalizing Society: The End of Diversity

1. I have offered the epigraph in a slight variation of the original version, which reads: "The arts, literature, and the sciences, less despotic though perhaps more powerful, fling garlands of flowers over the chains which weigh them down. They stifle in men's breasts that sense of original liberty, for which they seem to have been born; cause them to love their own slavery, and so make of them what is called a civilized people" (Jean-Jacques Rousseau, "A Discourse on the Arts and Sciences," in *The Social Contract and the Discourses* [New York: Random House, 1993; first included in Everyman's Library, 1931], p. 5).

2. Alexis de Tocqueville, *De la démocratie en Amérique*, vol. 2 (Paris, 1864), p. 151, quoted by Max Horkheimer and Theodor Adorno, *Dialectic of Enlightenment* (first published in German in 1944; New York: Continuum, 1993), p. 133.

3. Michel Foucault, *Discipline and Punish: The Birth of the Prison* (New York: Vintage Books, 1995; originally published in London, 1977), p. 177. Foucault argues that power can no longer be depicted in negative terms in the sense that it excludes, represses, censors; rather it "produces reality; it produces domains of objects and rituals of truth" (p. 194).

4. Ibid., p. 201. Foucault used the same metaphor favored by Max Weber, calling the panopticon a "cruel, ingenious cage," akin to my own metaphor of the African monkey trap.

5. Horkheimer and Adorno, *Dialectic of Enlightenment*, p. 121.

6. Herbert Marcuse, *One-Dimensional Man: Studies in the Ideology of Advanced Industrial Society* (Boston: Beacon Press, 1964), p. xv.

7. Ibid., p. 3.

8. Ibid., p. xv. Marcuse was a subtle thinker, and had qualified his use of the term *false consciousness*. He spoke only of "false needs" which were "most of the prevailing needs to relax, to have fun, to behave and consume in accordance with the advertisements, to love and hate what others love and hate" (p. 5). Still, Marcuse fell into oxymorons—consciousness that was somehow not really conscious, and a form of totalitarianism that "may well be compatible with a 'pluralism' of parties, newspapers, 'countervailing powers'" (even though pluralism and totalitarianism were antonyms) (p. 3).

9. In a provocative essay called "Repressive Tolerance," Marcuse had even argued that "universal toleration becomes questionable when its rationale no longer prevails, when tolerance is administered to manipulated and indoctrinated individuals who parrot, as their own, the opinion of their masters, for whom heteronomy has become autonomy" (Marcuse, "Repressive Tolerance," in R. P. Wolff, Barrington Moore, Jr., and Herbert Marcuse, *A Critique of Pure Tolerance* [Boston: Beacon Press, 1965], p. 90).

10. Paul Berman, *Power and the Idealists; Or, The Passion of Joschka Fischer and Its Aftermath* (Brooklyn, N.Y.: Soft Skull Press, 2005), p. 39. This sort of rhetoric was especially popular in France where E. Ionesco was quoted as saying in 1960 that "the world of the concentration camps . . . was not an exceptionally monstrous society. What we saw there was the image, and in a sense the quintessence, of the infernal society into which we are plunged today" (cited approvingly in Marcuse, *One-Dimensional Man*, p. 80).

11. Eric Hoffer, *The True Believer: Thoughts on the Nature of Mass Movements* (New York: Perennial Classics, 2002; originally published by Harper & Row, 1951).

12. Douglas Atkin, *The Culting of Brands: When Customers Become True Believers* (New York: Portfolio, 2004), p. 202.

13. Matthew W. Ragas and Bolivar J. Bueno, *The Power of Cult Branding: How 9 Magnetic*

Brands Turned Customers into Loyal Followers (and Yours Can, Too!) (Roseville, Calif.: Prima Publishing, 2002); Douglas B. Holt, *How Brands Become Icons: The Principle of Cultural Branding* (Boston: Harvard Business School Press, 2004).

14. Marc Gobé, *Citizen Brand: 10 Commandments for Transforming Brands in a Consumer Democracy* (New York: Allworth Press, 2002), p. 230.

15. David George, *Preference Pollution: How Markets Create the Desires We Dislike* (Ann Arbor: University of Michigan Press, 2001), p. 13.

16. Juliet Schor, *The Overspent American: Why We Want What We Don't Need* (New York: Harper Perennial, 1999).

17. Harry G. Frankfurt, "Freedom of the Will and the Concept of a Person," *Journal of Philosophy*, vol. 68, no. 1 (1971), pp. 5–20.

18. Michael Walzer, *Spheres of Justice: A Defense of Pluralism and Equality* (New York: Basic Books, 1983), pp. xiv–xv.

19. Ibid., p. 8.

20. Kathryn Harrison, " 'On Desire': I Am, Therefore I Want," review of *On Desire: Why We Want What We Want* by William B. Irvine (New York: Oxford University Press, 2005), *New York Times Book Review*, November 6, 2006.

21. David Carr, "I Want My Ubiquitous Conglomerate," *New York Times*, November 7, 2005.

22. Johnnie L. Roberts, "Small TV, Big War," *Newsweek*, October 24, 2005, commenting on the Apple-Disney deal that allows iPods to carry Disney/ABC content such as *Desperate Housewives* and *Lost*.

23. Alan Riding, "Unesco Adopts New Plan Against Cultural Invasion," *New York Times*, October 21, 2005.

24. One clever youngster has attracted marketing attention by coining the term "Bumvertising" to sell an ass-frontward version of the branded forehead; he has specialized in enlisting the homeless ("bums") to give up begging in order to shill other people's wares: pandering in place of panhandling as a new form of buzz (down) marketing. See Claudia Rowe, " 'Bumvertising' stirs debate," *Seattle Post-Intelligencer*, September 13, 2005.

25. Margaret Webb Pressler, "Coming to One's Senses," *Washington Post National Weekly Edition*, February 27–March 5, 2006. Pressler reports "AriZona Beverage Co. is at the forefront of a new wave of high-tech-packaging [the aroma is in the bottle cap!] in consumer products. As people increasingly ignore commercials and spread their attention across many types of media, traditional television, radio and print advertising is losing effectiveness, and marketers are looking for new ways to get noticed. One promising way appears to be targeting as many of the five senses as possible via packaging itself."

26. Campbell Robertson, "It Had to Happen (or Did It?); Ads at the Theater," *New York Times*, May 24, 2006.

27. Doreen Carvajal, "Advertisers Count on Sheep to Pull Eyes Over the Wool," *New York Times*, April 24, 2006.

28. See George Gilder, *Telecosm: The World After Bandwidth Abundance* (New York: Touchstone, 2002). Gilder's "Technology Reports" continue to follow these trends.

29. Quoted in Seth Schiesel, "For Online Star Wars Game, It's Revenge of the Fans," *New York Times*, December 10, 2005. Even as it tests the porousness of the boundaries between virtual reality and everyday life explored earlier in chapter 4, this example points to how time itself has been altered to accommodate virtuality as a surrogate for reality.

30. Adam L. Penenberg, "The Fight Over Wireless: Will we get Internet access from big government or big business?" *Slate* magazine (www.slate.com), October 24, 2005. Most of the attention inspired by municipal wireless has been on the battle between cable carriers like Verizon, Sprint, and AT&T and the broadband operators who would displace them. The social impact of universal wireless has been relatively ignored, other than as it affects obvious needs such as police and rescue services and information providers.

31. Robert Kuttner, *Everything for Sale: The Virtues and Limits of Markets* (New York: Alfred A. Knopf, 1997), p. 3.

32. Ibid.

33. The issue was widely discussed in the media, and criticized by the American Society of Magazine Editors. Target, founded in Minnesota in 1962, had from the start situated itself as a tasteful, middlebrow discounter. It associated itself with couture designers like Isaac Mizrahi and postmodern architect Michael Graves, and made its peppermint bull's-eye logo a synonym for middle-class discount shopping. Before its *New Yorker* experiment, it had purchased a whole issue of *People* magazine. See Bryan Curtis, "Target: Discount retailer goes to *The New Yorker*," *Slate* magazine (www.slate.com), August 17, 2005.

34. There was a campaign in New York City to paste stickers throughout the MTA subway system to advertise Microsoft's latest version of MSN, MSN 8. The city ordered the decals removed. For details, see Margaret Kane, "Microsoft decals don't stick in NYC," CNET News.com, October 25, 2002, available at http://news.com.com/2100-1023-963330.html.

35. Michael Barbaro, reporting on a 12:05 A.M. opening at CompUSA in Manhattan on the day after Thanksgiving: "Dawn Rush Hints at Strong Start to Holiday Sales," *New York Times*, November 26, 2005. A companion essay in the Business section notes that competitive early-bird shopping has become a holiday norm (Melanie Warner, "The Doorbusters," *New York Times*, November 26, 2005).

36. Cited by Nathan Dungan in "Media Habits May Lead to Over-Spending," October 25, 2005, available at www.foxreno.com/money/5171041/detail.html.

37. Ibid.

38. Kelly Kahl, quoted in Marc Peyser, "TV: Changing Their Tune," *Newsweek*, October 17, 2005.

39. Gavin O'Malley, "Yahoo!, OMD: Global Youth Get Music Fix on Web," Online Media Daily, September 27, 2005, available at http://publications.mediapost.com/index.cfm?fuseaction=Articles.showArticleHomePage&art_aid=34498. The study surveyed 13- to 24-year-olds in eleven countries and was released in September 2005. Another study, by Mediamark Research, found that "nearly 60 percent of children between the ages of 6 and 11 go online at least once a month, and . . . about one in 12 goes online daily." It also reported that 42.6 percent of young-sters play online games at least once a month" and that 84.2 percent of respondents play video games each month, with one fifth reporting they play every day—30 percent of boys and 11.1 percent of girls (Shankar Gupta, "One in 12 Kids Visits Web Daily," November 22, 2005, Online Media Daily, November 22, 2005, available at http://publications.mediapost.com/index.cfm?fuseaction=Articles.san&s=36586&Nid=16742&p=335276).

40. Nat Ives, "No Skipping: Children Still Watch TV Ads," www.MediaWorks.com, November 21, 2005.

41. Peyser, "TV: Changing Their Tune."

42. Dungan, "Media Habits May Lead to Over-Spending."

43. Jodi Kantor, "The Extra-Large, Ultra-Small Medium," *New York Times*, October 30, 2005. Content providers have already reacted to these new realities by offering canned and abridged versions of regular programming, four-minute editions of *Desperate Housewives* and *Alias*, along with new original series called "mobisodes" that "deliver a few minutes of action at a time" on original series geared to tiny, portable screens on the move.

44. Warren Buckleitner, editor of *Children's Technology Review*, commenting on the new baby game V.Smile, quoted in Tamar Lewin, "See Baby Touch a Screen, But Does Baby Get It?" *New York Times*, December 15, 2005.

45. See Lewin, "See Baby Touch a Screen." Lewin cites experts who agree, despite the "vast uncontrolled experiment on our infants and toddlers growing up in homes saturated with electronic media," that "there's not an educator alive who would disagree with the notion that concrete and real are always better." But always less profitable.

46. Michael Barbaro, "Mommy, Help Me Download 'Farmer in the Dell' to My MP3 Player," *New York Times*, February 11, 2006.

47. Quotes and figures are from Derrick Z. Jackson, "Why Obesity Is Winning," *Berkshire Eagle*, August 24, 2005.

48. Ibid. The Center for Science in the Public Interest is filing a lawsuit against the beverage industry seeking a ban on school soda machines that sell drinks like Coke and Pepsi and contribute to youth obesity across the nation. But half of America's public schools (including 70 percent of high schools) have exclusive contracts with beverage companies from which they derive significant revenue.

49. Marian Burros, "Federal Advisory Group Calls for Change in Food Marketing to Children," *New York Times*, December 7, 2005. The federal advisory group, The Institute of Medicine of the National Academies, offered Congress "compelling evidence linking food advertising on television and the increase in childhood obesity."

50. Jeffrey Gettleman, "As Young Adults Drink to Win, Marketers Join In," *New York Times*, October 16, 2005.

51. Ibid. The homepage at www.collegedrunkfest.com announces that "this website contains nudity, violence, explicit language and everything else that your mother would never let you see." Among the porn advertisements and special alcoholic drink promotions ("Extreme Absinthe" from the Czech Republic with 70 percent alcohol by volume) can be found the rules for hundreds of drinking games.

52. April Lane Benson, ed., *I Shop, Therefore I Am* (Northvale, N.J.: Jason Aronson, 2000).

53. Gregory Karp, "Shopping addiction no laughing matter," *Chicago Tribune*, online edition, March 13, 2005.

54. Schor's *The Overspent American* is the most thoughtful and serious. Others, mostly directed at women, include Karen O'Connor, *Addicted to Shopping . . . and Other Issues Women Have With Money* (Eugene, Oreg.: Harvest House Publishers, 2005); Benson, ed., *I Shop, Therefore I Am*; Carolyn Wesson, *Women Who Shop Too Much: Overcoming the Urge to Splurge* (New York: St. Martin's Press, 1990), and Olivia Mellan, *Overcoming Overspending: A Winning Plan for Spenders and Their Partners* (New York: Walker & Co., 1995). William Gibson's *Pattern Recognition* (New York: G. P. Putnam's Sons, 2003) and Max Barry's *Jennifer Government: A Novel* (New York: Doubleday, 2003) offer two provocative fictional accounts of shopping addiction in a totalizing commercial society.

55. See www.proctor.org and www.addictionrecov.org/index2.htm.

56. Look for addiction under Yahoo! Health.

57. Robert D. Manning, *Credit Card Nation: The Consequences of America's Addiction to Credit* (New York: Basic Books, 2000). How this "addiction" impacts the young is graphically portrayed in Tamara Draut, *Strapped: Why America's 20- and 30-Somethings Can't Get Ahead* (New York: Doubleday, 2006).

58. Sarah Kershaw, "Hooked on the Web: Help Is on the Way," *New York Times*, December 1, 2005.

59. Ibid. Internet/Computer Addiction Services offers fifteen "symptoms" or danger signs of addiction, including an inability to tell how much time is spent on the computer, having a sense of euphoria while online, craving more computer time, neglecting family and friends, and feeling restless and irritable when not on the computer (see www.icaservices.com).

60. According to www.addictions.co.uk, "the shopping habits survey by the market analyst Mintel asked more than 1,000 people which category they fell into: addicted, happy, purposeful, reluctant or obstinate. It found the number of shopoholics has soared. Twenty-two per cent of people questioned admitted their addiction, against just 18 per cent in 1993. But while only 15 per cent of men said they were addicted, 29 per cent of women owned up." While these numbers in what is clearly less than a scientific survey appear suspect, they indicate how seriously the problem is viewed in Britain. The survey, now well out of date, is at www.mintel.co.uk.

61. From www.addictions.co.uk/statistics.asp#30.

62. "Addiction to shopping becomes a serious mental disorder," *Pravda*, September 23, 2005, available at http://english.pravda.ru/society/family/23-09-2005/8951-shopping-0. Most of the data in this domain cannot be verified, and are at best journalistically suggestive, certainly not to be taken as definitive. This popular article from Russia attributes the shopping problem primarily to psychological factors such as a "shortage of human care and tenderness" in childhood. But it does acknowledge that while "addiction to shopping is a psychological disease of the future," it is also linked to "the purchasing capacity" of new market societies which "is growing along with the number of services. It is an open secret that shopping addiction is common in the countries with stable economies. One may infer that stable economies generate more shoppers."

63. Kershaw, "Hooked on the Web."

64. Quoted in Schiesel, "For Online Star Wars Game, Its Revenge of the Fans."

65. Kershaw, "Hooked on the Web."

66. Materials here are also from Kershaw, "Hooked on the Web."

67. David Barboza, "Ogre to Slay? Outsource It to Chinese," *New York Times*, December 9, 2005. Such figures often include repeat log-ons, and may represent what according to an AP story are 20 million regular gamesters playing what are called MMORPGs, or Massively Multiplayer Online Role-Playing Games (Peter Svensson, "Telecommuting to a brave new world: The rise of virtual jobs," an AP story in *Metro*, November 7, 2005).

68. Kershaw, "Hooked on the Web."

69. See Debtors Anonymous General Service Board, Inc., *A Currency of Hope* (Needham, Mass.: Debtors Anonymous, 1999).

70. Heather Hatfield, "Shopping Spree, or Addiction?" WebMD.com, November 23, 2004, available at www.webmd.com/content/article/97/104241.htm.

71. Mellan, *Overcoming Overspending: A Winning Plan for Spenders and Their Partners.*

72. In my book *Jihad vs. McWorld* (rev. ed., New York: Random House, 2001), I related the Coca-Cola Company's efforts, described in its 1992 annual corporate report, to dominate the India beverage market by making "war" on Indian tea culture.

73. James Ridgeway, *It's All for Sale: The Control of Global Resources* (Durham, N.C.: Duke University Press, 2004), p. xvii.

74. Ibid.

75. Marcuse, *One-Dimensional Man*, p. 57.

76. Buzz marketing is typically representative of consumerism's penchant for replication. As we have already seen, it uses what is often covert peer-to-peer marketing to sell young people fresh, new, and uncommon fashions which, when marketed in this way, become common fashions. The result is less variety rather than more.

77. A Canadian department store advertising slogan, cited by Naomi Klein, *No Logo: Taking Aim at the Brand Bullies* (New York: Picador, 2000), p. 119.

78. Horkheimer and Adorno, *Dialectic of Enlightenment*, p. 121.

79. The title of a pop-psychology best-seller first published in 1969 by Dr. Thomas A. Harris.

80. Marcuse, *One-Dimensional Man*, p. 75.

81. Ibid., p. 57.

82. See Tom Wolfe's classic portrait of radical chic in his essays *Radical Chic & Mau-Mauing the Flak Catchers* (New York: Farrar, Straus and Giroux, 1970).

83. Horkheimer and Adorno, *Dialectic of Enlightenment*, p. 121.

84. Neil Postman, *Amusing Ourselves to Death: Public Discourse in the Age of Show Business* (New York: Penguin Books, 1986), p. vii.

85. Ibid.

7 Resisting Consumerism: Can Capitalism Cure Itself?

1. Jackson Lears, *Fables of Abundance: A Cultural History of Advertising in America* (New York: Basic Books, 1994), p. 9.

2. With the simple wisdom of the ascetic, Rousseau wrote "what makes us miserable as human beings is the contradiction between our situation and our desires, our duties and our inclinations, our nature and social institutions between man and the citizen; make man one, and you will render him as happy as he can be. Give him entirely to the state or leave him entirely to himself; but if you divide his heart, you tear him to pieces" (*Fragments politiques* [Paris: Gallimard, 1964], vol. 2, p. 510.

3. In *Jihad vs. McWorld* (rev. ed., New York: Random House, 2001), I noted the demoralizing irony of the fact that poverty was the only sure way for a society to save itself from McWorld and its totalizing consumerism.

4. Cited in John Burns, "Al Qaeda Ally Declares All-Out War on Iraqi Elections," *New York Times*, January 23, 2005.

5. In Damon Linker's review of Neuhaus entitled "Without a Doubt: A Catholic priest, a pious president, and the Christianizing of America," in *The New Republic*, April 3, 2006. The book Linker reviewed is Richard John Neuhaus, *Catholic Matters: Confusion, Controversy, and the Splendor of Truth* (New York: Basic Books, 2005). Neuhaus's controversial *First Things* Symposium included contributions by Robert H. Bork, Charles W. Colson (who calls for "some kind of direct, extra-political confrontation"), and Robert P. George.

6. In *Jihad vs. McWorld*.

7. See Paul M. Kennedy, *The Rise and Fall of the Great Powers: Economic Change and Military Conflict from 1500 to 2000* (New York: Vintage Books, 1989). The limits of the creolization argument, discussed below, are evident in the fact that Kennedy's assessment of Japanese domination proved to be exaggerated, while the United States turned out to be a more difficult leader to overtake than he had suggested.

8. David Howes, ed., *Cross-Cultural Consumption: Global Markets, Local Realities* (London: Routledge, 1996), p. 7.

9. Constance Classen and David Howes, "Epilogue: The Dynamics and Ethics of Cross-Cultural Consumption," in Howes, ed., *Cross-Cultural Consumption*, p. 182. Also see Ulf Hannerz, *Cultural Complexity: Studies in the Social Organization of Meaning* (New York: Columbia University Press, 1992).

10. Tyler Cowen, *Creative Destruction: How Globalization Is Changing the World's Cultures* (Princeton, N.J.: Princeton University Press, 2002), p. 22. Cowen's title is drawn from classical economist Joseph Schumpeter's description of the dialectic in which capitalism "creatively" destroys the stages it traverses as it evolves. For a detailed critique of Cowen, see my review "Brave New McWorld," *Los Angeles Times Book Review*, February 2, 2003.

11. Cowen, *Creative Destruction*, p. 44.

12. Constance Classen, "Sugar Cane, Coca-Cola and Hypermarkets: Consumption and Surrealism in the Argentine Northwest," in Howes, ed., *Cross-Cultural Consumption*, p. 39. Classen notes that in rural Argentina, locals assume that Coca-Cola is a local product, suggesting that despite universal commercial culture, Latin America "is far from being de-Latinized" due to the capacity "to selectively incorporate the products and technologies of the global market while sustaining a strong and distinct local identity" (p. 53). As I will argue below, this seems overstated, but nonetheless at least partially true.

13. Scott Wilson, "Israeli Pop Singer Rocks Ultra-Orthodox Community," *Miami Herald International Edition*, January 2, 2006. Since 700,000 of Israel's population of seven million are ultra-orthodox and Elbaz has sold over 80,000 copies of his best-selling album *Meanings*, his influence would seem to be real.

14. Ibid.

15. From www.visualcliff.net.

16. The song was "Who Can Bwogo Me" by the rap duo GidiGidi MajiMaji. See Marc Lacey, "To the Beat of a Hit Song, the New Kenya Sends Spirits off the Charts," *New York Times*, February 16, 2003. The song opens "I am unbwogable / I am unbeatable / I am unuseable / So if you like my song / Take it from me / Who can bwogo me / I am unbwogable."

17. Klaus Farin, ed., *Die Skins: Mythos und Realität* (Berlin: Ch. Links, 1997). Cited in Timothy Scott Brown, "Subcultures, Pop Music and Politics: Skinheads and 'Nazi Rock' in England and Germany," *Journal of Social History*, vol. 38, no. 1 (2004), pp. 157–178. Labels such as Rock-O-Rama and the White Noise Club promoted this music starting in the 1970s. The right-wing protester Stuart Donaldson played a key role in joining the English skinhead movement to the more political German ultranationalist neo-Nazi right.

18. Cited in Brown, "Subcultures, Pop Music and Politics." For more see Devin Burghart, ed., *Soundtracks to the White Revolution: White Supremacist Assaults on Youth Music Subcultures* (Chicago: Center for New Community, 1999). The American connection is explored in "White-Power Rock 'n' Roll: A Growing Industry," in Jeffrey Kaplan and Tore Bjørgo, eds., *Nation and Race: The Developing Euro-American Racist Subculture* (Boston: Northeastern University Press, 1998).

19. Mecca Cola was introduced in France in 2002 by Tawfiq Mathlouthi, whose advertising campaign consisted of real news film footage (one ad showed the dramatic footage of the Palestinian father trying to protect his son right before he is killed in a cross fire) and a contribution of 10 percent of profits to Palestine relief. Saudi Arabia ordered five million bottles, with other orders coming from the Middle East, Pakistan, China, Russia, and even the United States. See Gretel C. Kovach, "Cola: 'Pepsi' for Palestine," *Newsweek*, December 16, 2002.

20. Deborah Sontag, "The Ambassador," *New York Times*, January 29, 2006. As many Korean stars do, Rain performs in television soap operas.

21. See the discussion in my *Jihad vs. McWorld*.

22. This is according to Brotin Banerjee, vice president of marketing for Barista. Banerjee adds: "With the liberalization of the economy, there are a large number of young Indians with good jobs and attractive incomes. Many still live with their parents. So their income is largely disposable and they need to spend it on something. Why not on gourmet coffee?" (Parija Bhatnagar, "Starbucks: A passage to India," *CNN/Money*, November 1, 2004, available at http://money.cnn.com/2004/10/28/news/fortune500/starbucks_india.

23. See Jamie James, "Battle of Borobudur," *Time Asia*, January 27, 2003.

24. Farish A. Noor, "Youth culture & Islamic intelligentsia: Ignoring the popular cultural discourse," *Musilmedia*, April–August 1996. Noor concludes with this plea: "Let it not be said that one day in the future the eminent Ulama and Doctors of the Islamic universities and think-tanks would wake up and realise that their grand ideological projects were foiled by something as (seemingly) innocuous as the smiling Barbie Doll."

25. "Bible Studies at *The Moorings*: Three Crises in Growing Up," from the Christian website www.themoorings.org/life/family/crises/ycult.html. Fundamentalist hyperbole aside, the site gets it right in insisting that "the driving force . . . behind youth culture is greed," with "an entertainment industry lusting after money" because it has figured out that "sin is profitable."

26. For those wishing an introduction to Mikhail Bakhtin's perspective on carnivals, see Lauren Langman and Katie Cangemi, "Transgression as Identity," available on-line at www.angelfire.com/or3/tss2/transid.html.

27. M. M. Bakhtin, *Rabelais and His World*, trans. Hélène Iswolsky (Bloomington: Indiana University Press, 1984), p. 10.

28. Lears, *Fables of Abundance*, p. 9.

29. For this reason, while George Gilder celebrates modern capitalism, he does so by confounding its Protestant virtues, which he admires, with its recent virtues, which are altogether different. See his *Wealth and Poverty* (New York: Basic Books, 1981).

30. John Fiske, *Reading the Popular* (Boston: Unwin Hyman, 1989), pp. 17–19 passim. See Thomas Frank's discussion of Fiske, *The Conquest of Cool: Business Culture, Counterculture, and the Rise of Hip Consumerism* (Chicago: University of Chicago Press, 1997), pp. 17–18.

31. In his *A Contemporary Guide to Economics, Peace, and Laughter* (1971), cited in James B. Twitchell, *Lead Us Into Temptation: The Triumph of American Materialism* (New York: Columbia University Press, 1999), p. 58.

32. Twitchell, *Lead Us Into Temptation*, p. 286.

33. Ibid., p. 286.

34. Ibid., p. 58. As a personal testimony, Twitchell cites his affection for his own Miata sports car (p. 274), the same car whose advertisement is cited in chapter 6 as defining modern branded identity.

35. Frank, *The Conquest of Cool*, p. 9.

36. William Leach, *Land of Desire: Merchants, Power and the Rise of a New American Culture* (New York: Vintage Books, 1994), p. 5. The phrase belonged originally to merchant and department-store pioneer John Wanamaker.

37. Rem Koolhaas et al., *Mutations*, Koolhaas, "Project on the City," Bordeaux, France, ACTAR, arc en reve, centre d'architecture, no date, p. 125. See also Michael Sorkin, "See You in Disneyland," in Michael Sorkin, ed., *Variations on a Theme Park: The New American City and the End of Public Space* (New York: Hill and Wang, 1992).

38. Koolhass et al., *Mutations*, pp. 125–126.

39. Gary S. Cross, *An All-Consuming Century: Why Commercialism Won in Modern America* (New York: Columbia University Press, 2000), p. 215.

40. The phrase is from Mike Davis, *City of Quartz: Excavating the Future in Los Angeles* (New York: Verso, 1990), p. 47.

41. Mike Davis depicts Marcuse as "able to make the organic connection to [California's] indigenous radicalism that had eluded a majority of his exile comrades in the 1940s" (*City of Quartz*, p. 54). Davis offers the Baudrillard insight based on an anonymous interview he cites.

42. Langman and Cangemi, "Transgression as Identity."

43. Ibid.

44. Twitchell, *Lead Us Into Temptation*, pp. 14–15.

45. Ibid., p. 38. Citing Oscar Wilde's quip "the only way to get rid of a temptation is to yield to it," Twitchell adds "for better or worse, in the last century, we pretty much have. Tallyho" (p. 15).

46. Cross, *An All-Consuming Century*, p. 248.

47. Ibid., p. 236.

48. Ibid., p. 175. Cross is an ambivalent critic, and wants to understand why consumerism has been so firmly embraced. "For many American intellectuals of the early twentieth century, consumerism in all its forms reflected the poverty of desire, the substitution of titillation, conformity, and display for true joy, social solidarity, and individual fulfillment." Yet, Cross writes, and here enters the carnivalesque, "consumerism was also a response to desire, providing not only instant but multiple gratifications that religion, politics, and learning separately had not been able to deliver. . . . Consumer culture was and is, as James Twitchell notes, the 'return to the puerile, the raw and uncontrolled,' a rebellion against the 'civilizing process' imposed by church, classroom, and the etiquette of the dinner table and a release into fashion, amusement, and junk food" (p. 64).

49. Ibid., p. 31.

50. Lears contrasts "the deceptions of confidence men" (very much like the Wild Bill Rockefeller I depicted in chapter 2) "and the plain speech of the self-made man" (very much like Wild Bill's son, John D. Rockefeller), that is, between "spontaneous force of consumer desire and the managerial drive for predictability and control" (*Fables of Abundance*, p. 9).

51. Lears, *Fables of Abundance*, p. 10.

52. Ibid., p. 51.

53. Ibid., p. 43. This is in a chapter aptly called "The Lyric of Plenty."

54. Ibid., p. 39. Lears's historical account describes a "modernization of magic" and "stabilization of sorcery" aimed at "the containment of Carnival." Hence, in his view, "after 1900 the sheer amount of flesh on display decreased; the grotesque body of Carnival virtually disappeared" (p. 117).

55. These quotes are all from the preface in Steven Johnson, *Everything Bad Is Good for You:*

How Today's Popular Culture Is Actually Making Us Smarter (New York: Riverhead Books, 2005). Johnson's focus is on video games and their impact on intelligence, but his claims are far more expansive. Tyler Cowen offers a similarly straightforward celebration of consumerism, especially in its putative capacity to sustain serious culture, in the book that preceded his *Creative Destruction* discussed earlier, a book appropriately titled *In Praise of Commercial Culture* (Cambridge, Mass.: Harvard University Press, 1998).

56. Johnson, *Everything Bad Is Good for You*, pp. 198–199. For a debate on dumbing down, see Katharine Washburn and John F. Thornton, eds., *Dumbing Down: Essays on the Strip Mining of American Culture* (New York: W. W. Norton, 1996).

57. I have written about the mall and the vanishing of public space in the suburbs in my "Malled, Mauled, and Overhauled: Arresting Suburban Sprawl by Transforming Suburban Malls into Usable Civic Space," in Marcel Hénaff and Tracy B. Strong, eds., *Public Space and Democracy* (Minneapolis: University of Minnesota Press, 2001).

58. Sorkin, "See You in Disneyland," p. 208.

59. James C. Scott, *Domination and the Arts of Resistance: Hidden Transcripts* (New Haven, Conn.: Yale University Press, 1990), p. 176. Indeed in many carnival rituals "a figure representing the spirit of carnival is ritually killed by a figure representing Lent, almost as if to say, 'Now that you've had your fun we shall return to the sober pious life,' " (p. 177).

60. In the regular video-game column in the sports section of the *Times*, Seth Schiesel wrote about World of Warcraft, a new multiplayer interactive video game with over 5.5 million subscribers worldwide. The game, Schiesel enthuses, involves "epic challenges, like conquering Blackwing Lair and its master, the black dragon Nefarian" (Seth Schiesel, "Kill the Big, Bad Dragon [Teamwork Required]," *New York Times*, January 28, 2006). Elsewhere, Charles Herold reviewed the game with childish glee: "Monkeys scatter as you throw your opponent down to a low roof on which they are resting. On a gaudy, neon-lighted version of the Las Vegas strip, pedestrians watch bemusedly as your street fight is interrupted every time you are tossed into the air from the impact of a speeding car. You can even fight in a dinosaur sanctuary and throw your opponent onto an annoyed velociraptor" (Charles Herold, "Mayhem With a Beautiful View," *New York Times*, January 21, 2006). See also Jonathan Dee, "Joystick Nation: How and why video games conquered music, TV and the movies to become America's *popular* pop culture," *New York Times Magazine*, December 21, 2003.

61. An Abbie Hoffman yippie title on which, despite the joke, he earned more than a few dollars, and which is still available in a paperback reprint.

62. Guy Debord, *The Society of the Spectacle* (1967; New York: Zone Books, 1995), p. 146.

63. Kalle Lasn, *Culture Jam: The Uncooling of America* (New York: Harper Collins [Quill], 1999), p. xi.

64. Ibid., p. 111.

65. Ibid., pp. 111, 113.

66. Ibid., pp. 113, xvi.

67. Ibid., pp. 135, 113.

68. Carlo Petrini, ed., *Slow Food: Collected Thoughts on Taste, Tradition, and the Honest Pleasures of Food* (White River Junction, Vt.: Chelsea Green Publishers, 2001); Carl Honoré, *In Praise of Slow: How a Worldwide Movement Is Challenging the Cult of Speed* (Toronto: A. A. Knopf Canada, 2004). *Adbusters'* website, www.adbusters.org, also markets Peter C. Whybrow's *American Mania: When More Is Not Enough* (New York: W. W. Norton, 2005).

69. A recent *Adbusters* magazine posted ratings for the number one, two, and three "terrorist" slots in the modern world. Russia's Putin got the number-one rating, followed by Ariel Sharon (before his stroke) at number two and President Bush at number three. On its face, such silliness seems unhelpful in combating consumerism, which is not by any means solely a leftist preoccupation.

70. Typical of the jammers' ironic approach is a widely circulated Adbusters' postcard, the

376 NOTES FOR PAGES 286-291

front side showing a gray smoke smudge with the legend "rethink the cool," and the back carrying a message reading "Dear [Nike CEO] Phil, Nice shoes. Too bad about the sweatshops. I'm helping build the Blackspot anti-brand and we're going to unswoosh your swoosh. Regards . . . " and then a space for you to sign your name and forward the card to Nike World Headquarters in Beaverton, Oregon (addressed and ready to post!).

71. Charles C. Mann, "How Click Fraud Could Swallow the Internet," *Wired*, January 2006. Mann is more worried about the kinds of fraud perpetrated by rivals who repeatedly click on competitors' sites (at up to $10 a click) to drive them off the web, but used by hundreds of thousands of jammers, the jammers could really "swallow the internet."

72. To a request for information about the commercial success of its shoes, a Blackspot marketing manager refused to release financial statements and declined to comment. Apparently it is not possible to run such a company transparently, which will confirm the fears of critics that when a countercultural company goes for-profit it is likely to take on the vices of the culture it affects to critique.

73. Rob Walker, "What's Wrong With Adbusters' New Anti-Nike Campaign?" at www .adbusters.org. Finally, writes Walker, the Blackspot campaign seems merely to "broadcast a facile message about how anticorporate (and therefore cool) you are. . . . [I]sn't that precisely as vacuous as the ideology of the swoosh, which assumes that there is no better way to express ourselves than through the logos we choose (or reject)?"

74. Naomi Klein, quoted in William MacDougall, "Just Screw It!: Adbusters takes on the might of Nike," *Seven Oaks* magazine, March 29, 2004.

75. Lasn, *Culture Jam*, p. 119. One recalls the Paris 1968 slogan "Reforms = Chloroform."

76. Frank, *The Conquest of Cool*, p. 7.

77. Thomas Frank, *What's the Matter with Kansas?: How Conservatives Won the Heart of America* (New York: Henry Holt, 2005), pp. 248–249.

78. The irony of "flouting 'the Man'" is the subject of a recent Cingular television ad, in which a self-mocking corporate executive comes to work one day ready to flout "the Man." "But you are the man," his obsequious assistant protests. "Yep," replies the unflustered, super-hip corporate self-mocker. Bingo! Buy that cool phone!

79. Michael McCarthy, "Fond Memories of Past Nike Ads," *USA Today*, June 16, 2003. The same *White Album* from which "Revolution" came, with its song "Helter Skelter," was supposedly an animating motive in Charles Manson's murder spree. Meaning cannot be controlled. Even the Beatles were ambivalent: the lyrics to "Revolution" read: "You say you want a revolution / Well, you know / We all want to change the world / You tell me that it's evolution / Well, you know / We all want to change the world / But when you talk about destruction / Don't you know that you can count me out." Except that on the actual song track "out" is followed by "in," allowing Paul McCartney to have his revolution and stay politically correct at the same time.

80. Quoted in John Bickerton, "You Say You Want a Sneaker Revolution," *Underscore*, vol. 1, no. 3 (August 2004), available at www.uniquetracks.com/issues/August2004.html#say.

81. Virginia Heffernan, "Earnestly Pursuing the Gentle Art of Nastiness Behind a Radio Microphone," *New York Times*, January 12, 2006. I single out the *Times* because it is not *Rolling Stone* or some alternative countercultural tabloid but the nation's leading family newspaper and journal of record.

8 Overcoming Civic Schizophrenia: Restoring Citizenship in a World of Interdependence

1. Immanuel Kant, "What Is Enlightenment?" in *Kant's Political Writings*, ed. with an introduction and notes by Hans Reiss, trans. H. B. Nisbet (Cambridge: Cambridge University Press, 1970), p. 54.

2. The frontispiece of Mill's "On Liberty" (1859) is taken from Karl Wilhelm von Humboldt's *The Sphere and Duties of Government*, translated into English in 1854 (London: John Chapman).

3. The National Advertiser ad from a 1926 *Life* magazine, reprinted in Jackson Lears, *Fables of Abundance: A Cultural History of Advertising in America* (New York: Basic Books, 1994), p. 228.

4. Lears, *Fables of Abundance*, p. 229.

5. Lizabeth Cohen, *A Consumers' Republic: The Politics of Mass Consumption in Postwar America* (New York: Alfred A. Knopf, 2003), p. 411. Cohen deems critics to be unrealistic and suggests that "rather than fantasize jettisoning this Janus-faced citizen consumer who still stands guard at our gates, we might be wiser to identify a usable legacy that maximize its benefits and minimizes its costs" (p. 412).

6. Cohen, *A Consumers' Republic*, p. 32, quoting a 1939 *Harvard Business Review* article.

7. For details, see Cohen, *A Consumers' Republic*, pp. 347–349.

8. Key bills included the Air Pollution Control Act of 1962, the Water Quality Act of 1965, the National Traffic and Motor Vehicle Safety Act of 1966, the Child Protection Act of 1966, the Consumer Credit Protection Act of 1968, the National Environmental Policy Act of 1969, the Equal Credit Opportunity Act of 1974, and the Toxic Substances Control Act of 1976. For a complete list, see Cohen, *A Consumers' Republic*, p. 360.

9. The boycott was organized by the National Association of Teachers in Further and Higher Education (NATFHE) union in Manchester and attracted as many as 700 international supporters. It quickly succumbed to popular outrage and the intervention of Prime Minister Blair. See Francis Elliott and Catherine Milner, "Blair vows to end dons' boycott of Israeli scholars," *London Telegraph*, November 17, 2002. Another boycott was proposed a year later by NATFHE, reigniting the controversy. For a justification of such boycotts see www.academicsforjustice.org. Even democracies may opt for boycotts that seem unjust or unfair, but at least they have met the minimal conditions of legitimacy, and represent a "public" decision rather than a private one.

10. Federal Trade Commission, "Marketing Violent Entertainment to Children," September 2000. Despite nearly universal compliance with the call for ratings, there was "little change in the practices of all three industries with regard to advertising violent R-rated movies, M-rated games and explicit-content labeled recording in media popular with teens." The report and an FTC follow-up of June 2002 have shown that half of the nation's movie theaters regularly admit children under 18 to R-rated films, while music and video-game producers often explicitly target those who are underage by their own labeling codes as the principal audience for their products in their marketing plans. For a critical discussion, see Joe Gross, "Senators Equate Hazards of Music, Film, Video Games with Tobacco," *Addicted to Noise*, June 17, 1999.

11. For a succinct and fair capsule history of the earlier debate, see Michael Scott, "The Tuna-Dolphin Controversy," *Whalewatcher Magazine*, vol. 30, no. 1, August 1988.

12. See www.rugmark.org.

13. Cohen, *A Consumers' Republic*, p. 405.

14. Ibid., p. 406.

15. An irony of the ban on boycotts is that they are directed at "national boycotts" by international trade bureaucrats who apparently cannot imagine a consumer boycott that is not sponsored by a state.

16. From a Calvert Investments advertisement in *Kiplinger's*, March 2006.

17. In his *An Empire of Their Own: How the Jews Invented Hollywood* (New York: Crown, 1988), Neal Gabler tells the story of Hollywood's creation of the American mythology by which we once lived. Ironically, this Hollywood mythology is now seen as imperiled by . . . Hollywood!

18. David Ansen, "Cliffhanger Classic," *Newsweek*, June 15, 1981.

19. Leon Wieseltier, quoted by Maureen Dowd, "Leave It to Hollywood," *New York Times*, August 16, 1997.

20. Maureen Dowd, writing on the then new *Leave It to Beaver* film in "Leave It to Hollywood," *New York Times*, August 16, 1997. Dowd concludes that "Spielberg, Lucas, 'The Flintstones,' Brady Bunches unto the generations, Kevin Costner fairy tales, Stallone and Schwarzenegger: PG 13, NC 17 or whatever, they treat their audiences like children."

21. The "inmates" description came from Metro Pictures studio head Richard A. Rowland. Recently, Sony and Comcast bought United Artists (along with its parent company MGM). For a clear picture of ownership patterns in Hollywood, see the *Columbia Journalism Review*'s useful and up-to-date "Who Owns What" essays, available at www.cjr.org/tools/owners/.

22. So startling was this display of good (even transgressive) taste by the Academy of Motion Picture Arts and Sciences that America's leading newspaper of record ran an editorial at the beginning of 2006 expressing bewilderment and asking sardonically whether Hollywood could "just send an e-mail message" explaining why it had nominated for best picture "mostly independent films with low budgets and serious subjects." More earnestly, the editorial proposed that the nominations might "be the academy's response to the grievous condition our world is in" ("Oh, Oscar!" *New York Times*, February 2, 2006).

23. Full disclosure: Weitz actually cited my book *Jihad vs. McWorld* in discussing the philosophy behind his film *In Good Company* that assails the ethics of corporate hierarchy in America, and the book appears in the hands of the character playing President Staton in Weitz's controversial terrorist comedy *American Dreamz*.

24. Tina Rosenberg, "Editorial Observer: What Lara Croft Would Look Like if She Carried Rice Bags," *New York Times*, December 30, 2005. The game cost only $350,000 to develop (against $7 million for the Army's game) and attracted the National Football League as a partner. Since in the real world one person dies every five seconds of hunger and most of these are children, and since scores of peacekeepers have actually died in the field, this is a rare case where the game is probably much tamer than the reality. See www.food-force.com.

25. Chris Suellentrop, "The Evildoers Do Super Mario Bros.: The War on Terror's least-frightening video games," *Slate* magazine (www.slate.com), August 12, 2005. Suellentrop tests and writes about Islamicist games which he has actually played in an interesting essay that minimizes both their ingenuity and their impact.

26. Benjamin R. Barber, *Strong Democracy: Participatory Politics for a New Age*, Twentieth-Anniversary Edition (Berkeley: University of California Press, 2003), p. 274. (The original edition appeared in 1984.)

27. Neal Gabler, "When You Wish Upon a Merger," op-ed, *New York Times*, February 2, 2006. Gabler's *Walt Disney: The Triumph of the American Imagination* (New York: Knopf, 2006) makes a case along the lines of Thomas Frank's argument introduced above treating certain archetypical business figures in the 1960s advertising industry as innovators and rebels against traditional business culture. Capitalism here seems to work at curing itself of its maladies through that creative destruction about which Joseph Schumpeter writes.

28. In the case of Howard Dean's campaign, however, it did attempt to explore and exploit citizen-to-citizen communication in which elites and leaders were less central than was civic community-building. This turned out, in political terms, to be something other than a virtue, as Dean found out in the Iowa caucuses. There, it seemed to some critics that Dr. Dean's "Dean-iacs" brought together by the web were more interested in the communities they were creating than in political outcomes. A number of loyal web partisans failed to turn out to canvass, caucus, or vote. For an account by Governor Dean's web-minded campaign manager, see Joe Trippi, *The Revolution Will Not Be Televised: Democracy, the Internet, and the Overthrow of Everything* (New York: Regan Books, 2004).

29. Hypocrisy abounds in such matters. Google insists such censorship is simply good business practice, no more than respecting the rules and regulations of its hosts. Except that it apparently refuses to cooperate with its local hosts in the United States of America, where Google has been uncooperative with the government's attempt to block child porn and track down users. In China, it is about the right of local hosts; in the United States, it is about rights of privacy and liberty. One would like to credit principle, but the only consistency evident here is for the bottom line: cooperating with China but resisting the U.S. government's intrusions helps business on both sides of the Pacific. For background, see Arshad Mohammed, "Google Refuses Demand for Search Information," *Washington Post*, January 20, 2006.

30. Lee Drutman and Charlie Cray, *The People's Business: Controlling Corporations and Restoring Democracy* (San Francisco: Berrett-Koehler, 2004).

31. Harold Bloom, *The American Religion: The Emergence of the Post-Christian Nation* (New York: Simon & Schuster, 1992), p. 22.

32. Robert N. Bellah, Richard Madsen, William M. Sullivan, Ann Swidler, and Steven M. Tipton, *Habits of the Heart: Individualism and Commitment in American Life* (Berkeley: University of California Press, 1985), p. 219.

33. See Jeff Faux, *The Global Class War: How America's Bipartisan Elite Lost Our Future—and What It Will Take to Win It Back* (Hoboken, N.J.: John Wiley & Sons, 2006). Faux was the founding president of the left-leaning Economic Policy Institute. Harvard economist Jeffry A. Frieden, a more centrist analyst, writes in his history of global capitalism that success is anything but inevitable, and depends in part on the leadership of powerful nations, like England in the nineteenth century and the United States in the twentieth. See Jeffry A. Frieden, *Global Capitalism: Its Fall and Rise in the Twentieth Century* (New York: W. W. Norton, 2006).

34. Jeffrey Sachs, *The End of Poverty: Economic Possibilities for Our Time* (New York: Penguin Press, 2005).

35. Michael Wines, "Hope for Hungry Children, Arriving in a Foil Packet," *New York Times*, August 8, 2005.

36. See Sachs, *The End of Poverty*.

37. On PBS's *Charlie Rose* television show, June 26, 2006. Buffett, the second richest person on earth following Bill Gates, offered the greater part of his $30 billion fortune to the Gates Foundation.

38. Abraham Maslow's hierarchy of needs include self-actualization, the aesthetic, the cognitive, esteem, love and belongingness, safety, and the physiological (material). Brazelton's and Greenspan's include "ongoing Nurturing Relationships; Physical Protection, Safety and Regulation; Experiences Tailored to Individual Differences; Need for Developmentally Appropriate Experiences; Need for Limit Setting, Structure, and Expectation; Need for Stable, Supportive Communities and Cultural Continuity; protecting the Future" (*The Irreducible Needs of Children: What Every Child Must Have to Grow, Learn, and Flourish* [Cambridge, Mass.: Perseus, 2000]).

39. Brazelton and Greenspan, *The Irreducible Needs of Children*, p. x.

40. According to the Organisation for Economic Co-operation and Development, in 2004 the United States contribution to foreign aid was about 0.17 percent of GNP, second lowest after Italy which was 0.15 percent of GNP. Only a handful of countries met the 0.7 percent benchmark set by the Millennium Development Goals. From the OECD list of twenty-two countries, only Luxembourg, the Netherlands, Norway, and Sweden exceeded 0.7 percent, while fourteen of them fell below 0.4 percent. See the OECD website www.oecd.org/dataoecd/40/3/353879786.pdf. Complete data are available at the Sustainable Development website: www.globalissues.org/TradeRelated/Debt/UsAid.asp.

41. C. K. Prahalad, *The Fortune at the Bottom of the Pyramid: Eradicating Poverty Through Profits* (Upper Saddle River, N.J.: Wharton School Publishing, 2004), pp. xi–xii. The publication of two articles, "The Fortune at the Bottom of the Pyramid" in *Strategy + Business* (January 2002), with Stuart L. Hart, and "Serve the World's Poor, Profitably" in the *Harvard Business Review* (September 2002) with Allen Hammond, signaled Prahalad's success in breaking through into the business community with his ideas.

42. For background, see David Bornstein, *The Price of a Dream: The Story of the Grameen Bank and the Idea That Is Helping the Poor to Change Their Lives* (Chicago: University of Chicago Press, 1997).

43. Indeed, one of the problems of microcredit has been that those institutions like the Grameen Bank that offer the first-round loans are edged out later on by big banks unwilling to take the initial risk, but who want to cash in later on second- and third-round loans where the lendee has already proven her creditworthiness.

44. Hence, Yunus argued, "In fixing the interest rate, market interest rate is taken as the ref-

erence rate, rather than the moneylenders' rate. Reaching the poor is its non-negotiable mission. Reaching sustainability is a directional goal. It must reach sustainability as soon as possible, so that it can expand its outreach without fund constraints." Yunus also gives a high priority to building social capital, which helps sustain individuals in their new endeavors. Muhammad Yunus, "What Is Microcredit?" January 2003, available on-line at www.grameen-info.org/mcredit/.

45. Alan Budd, "A Mystery Solved," *Times Literary Supplement*, December 15, 2000.

46. Hernando de Soto, *The Mystery of Capital: Why Capitalism Triumphs in the West and Fails Everywhere Else* (New York: Basic Books, 2000), p. 49.

47. Allen D. Kanner, "Globalization and the Commercialization of Childhood," *Tikkun*, vol. 20, no. 5 (2005), p. 49.

48. See Peter W. Singer, *Children at War* (New York: Pantheon, 2005). Child soldiers used to be a rarity, but now, as Singer shows, they are commonplace in Africa and parts of Southeast Asia. Even the U.S. military campaigns to draw youngsters fresh out of high school into the military, in effect promising them that if they do military service they will in time have careers and incomes that will allow them to be consumers.

49. At the beginning of the new millennium, India had only one kids' television channel, the Cartoon Network. Today it has nine or ten, with global corporations like Nickelodeon, Disney, Sony, and Turner pushing for larger market share. World brands such as McDonald's spread worldwide not only via their franchises but through links with bands such as Destiny's Child, whose 2005 world tour sponsored by McDonald's visited not just the U.K., France, Germany, and Spain but Japan, Australia, and Brazil.

50. Amartya Sen, *Development as Freedom* (New York: Alfred A. Knopf, 1999), p. 147.

51. Ibid., p. 151.

52. Ibid., p. 152.

53. Jean-Jacques Rousseau, *Fragments politiques* (Paris: Gallimard, 1964), vol. 2, p. 510.

54. Nike is only one of many intrusive Olympic sponsors: "There were just 2,500 athletes here [in the 2006 Turin Winter Olympics]," writes Sally Jenkins, "compared to 10,000 guests of the 11 top Olympic sponsors—including Visa, Coca-Cola and McDonald's—which pay about $50 million each for sponsorship rights" (Sally Jenkins, "A Fiat Caveat: Don't Urbanize the Olympics," *Washington Post*, February 27, 2006).

55. David Chandler approaches what he calls the "imagined concept" of global civil society critically, arguing that it is more attuned to state power and elite economic interests than to the normative interests of international governance about which Mary Kaldor, David Held, and other ardent advocates of global civil society write. See David Chandler, *Constructing Global Civil Society: Morality and Power in International Relations* (Basingstoke, U.K.: Palgrave Macmillan, 2004). For those wishing to follow the academic debate on these matters, the new journal *Globalizations* headquartered at Newcastle upon Tyne in England is extremely useful.

56. Emphasis added. This is the definition of political scientist Anne-Marie Slaughter in her *A New World Order* (Princeton, N.J.: Princeton University Press, 2004), p. 18. See also the enthusiastic account of John Keane in his *Global Civil Society?* (Cambridge: Cambridge University Press, 2003).

57. "The ethics of care builds concern and mutual responsiveness to need on both the personal and the wider social level," and can be linked to feminist concerns that soften the patriarchal Hobbesian view of the social world that dominates thinking about the global marketplace (Virginia Held, *The Ethics of Care: Personal, Political, and Global* [Oxford: Oxford University Press, 2006], p. 28).

58. See Robert D. Putnam, *Bowling Alone: The Collapse and Revival of American Community* (New York: Simon & Schuster, 2000), chapter 20.

59. Kwame Anthony Appiah, *Cosmopolitanism: Ethics in a World of Strangers* (New York: W. W. Norton, 2006), p. xviii.

60. The frontispiece of Mill's "On Liberty" is taken from Karl Wilhelm von Humboldt's *The Sphere and Duties of Government*, translated into English in 1854.

61. For an elaboration of this argument in the context of the defeat of the European Constitution in 2005 and transatlantic relations among progressives, see Benjamin Barber, "Dreamers Without Borders," *The American Prospect*, August 2005, pp. 39–42. My new organization under CivWorld, called The Paradigm Project, is designed to facilitate global thinking among internationalists looking for ways to encourage collaboration across borders. See www.civworld.org.

62. Held, *The Ethics of Care*, p. 119.

63. Nancy Kranich, "The Information Commons: A Public Policy Report," Free Expression Policy Project, Brennan Center for Justice at NYU School of Law, 2004, p. 1, available on-line at www.fepproject.org (italics as in original). Also see John Willinsky, *The Access Principle: The Case for Open Access to Research and Scholarship* (Cambridge, Mass.: MIT Press, 2006).

INDEX